slightly rounded edges, but are easily distinguishable. As the bandwidth is decreased the transitions from one bit to another occur more slowly. At the lower bandwidths you will note that the signal has not reached the maximum value for the current bit when that bit ends and the next bit begins. Hence, the receiver has more difficulty in determining which bit was actually sent.

Noisy Data Detection Simulation: A data receiver accepts the incoming signal (noisy and bandlimited) and processes it to determine the original transmitted string of zeros and ones. Sometimes the receiver makes errors in this determination. The receiver processing can be quite complex, but for each bit this processing ends with a comparison of the processed result to a number called the threshold. If the result is less than the threshold, then the receiver assumes that a zero was sent. If the result is greater than the threshold, then the receiver assumes that a one was sent. In this applet you have the ability to choose the transmitted bit string, the signal to noise ratio, and the threshold for the data decisions. For a given SNR (such as -10 dB) try various thresholds and observe the errors (indicated by red boxes in the output data in the applet). Can you determine what level is best for the threshold, i.e., the threshold that minimizes the errors?

Image Coding and Compression

This series of applets demonstrates the means by which images are processed and reproduced by computer, and the visual effects of some types of processing and data compression.

Basic Image Manipulation: With this applet you can display several different images, and see the dramatic effects of removing one of the three primary colors that are used for color image representation. You may also observe the effects of changing image size. Note that when the image size is doubled, no new information is added. Hence, while the picture is larger, it also appears less sharp. Each picture element is larger in size, leading to stair-step effects.

Image Color Encoding: The values of red, green, and blue intensity at any point of a displayed image may be seen by simply moving the cursor over the desired point.

Run Length Lossless Image Compression: The results of run-length compression with five different input images can be demonstrated here. The results make clear that the effectiveness of this simple compression algorithm is quite dependent on the input image content.

Predictive and Run Length Image Compression: Another type of image coding takes advantage of the fact that adjacent picture elements tend to be similar in intensity. This property can be exploited by calculating the difference in values between successive picture elements, and then either transmitting these differences directly or run-length encoding them. The effectiveness of image difference coding is quite dependent on the qualities of the image being coded, as is demonstrated by this applet, which makes use of the same images as the previous applet. Note the differences in results.

A Lossy Image Compression Algorithm: The previous compression methods introduce no degradation in the images, but they generally produce rather modest compression ratios. Greater compression may be achieved at the cost of some reduction in quality of the image. The design goal in lossy compression algorithms is to maximize the amount of compression while minimizing the loss in image quality. This first algorithm is quite simple, and is described in the applet. Unfortunately, this simplicity results in a small amount of compression.

Image Difference Compression: Substantial compression of image sequences that represent motion can be achieved by comparing successive images and only storing the changes from one image to the next. This is illustrated in this applet.

Median Filtering of Images: A particular type of lossy compression called median filtering is demonstrated in this applet. The user may select a filter parameter and control the amount of compression and the corresponding loss in image quality.

Spatial Resolution: The visual appearance of varying image resolutions (numbers of picture elements in the horizontal and vertical directions) is illustrated in this applet, which allows the user to select from among four images, and to adjust the resolution.

Color resolution: "Color resolution" refers to the number of different color and intensity values that can be displayed at each picture element. The effect of varying this number can be demonstrated with this applet. The reduced color resolution effect is quite apparent with the bicycle image (particularly in the shadows on the concrete) at 4096 colors and below.

Error Correcting Codes: Hamming Code Example: Hamming Codes represent a popular set of codes that enable data errors to be both detected and corrected. The code that is implemented here enables a single error in each 4-bit group to be both detected and corrected. With this applet the user may enter some text, see the encoded result, change some of the coded bits to represent errors, and observe the effect of the decoding.

Information Technology
Inside and Outside

Information Technology
Inside and Outside

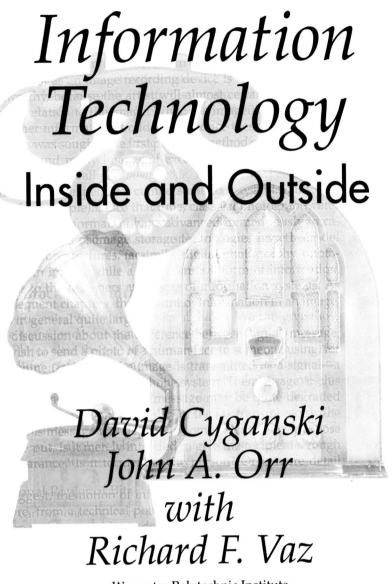

David Cyganski
John A. Orr
with
Richard F. Vaz

Worcester Polytechnic Institute

Sponsored by a grant from the National Science Foundation,
and based on a course developed in the Electrical and Computer
Engineering Department at Worcester Polytechnic Institute.

Prentice
Hall

Prentice Hall
Upper Saddle River, New Jersey 07458

Library of Congress Cataloging-in-Publication Data

Cyganski, David.
    Information technology : inside and outside / David Cyganski, John A. Orr, Richard F. Vaz.
      p. cm.
    ISBN 0-13-011496-0
    1. Information technology.   I. Orr, John A.   II. Vaz, Richard F.   III. Title.
    T58.5. C95   2000
    621.39—dc21

                                                        00-033645

Vice president and editorial director, ECS: **MARCIA HORTON**
Publisher: **TOM ROBBINS**
Associate editor: **ALICE DWORKIN**
Assistant vice president of production and manufacturing: **DAVID W. RICCARDI**
Executive managing editor: **VINCE O'BRIEN**
Managing editor: **DAVID A. GEORGE**
Production editor: **LAKSHMI BALASUBRAMANIAN**
Art editor: **XIAOHONG ZHU**
Art director: **JONATHAN BOYLAN**
Manufacturing buyer: **PAT BROWN**
Editorial assistant: **JESSICA POWER**
Marketing manager: **DANNY HOYT**
Composition: **INTEGRE TECHNICAL PUBLISHING CO., INC.**

Prentice Hall

© 2001 by Prentice-Hall, Inc.
Upper Saddle River, New Jersey 07458

"Graceland" and "The Boy in the Bubble," from *Graceland*, used by permission
of the publisher, Paul Simon Music. Copyright © 1986 Paul Simon.

The author and publisher of this book have used their best efforts in
preparing this book. These efforts include the development, research,
and testing of the theories and programs to determine their effectiveness.
Printed in the United States of America

10 9 8 7 6 5 4 3 2 1

ISBN 0-13-011496-0

Prentice-Hall International (UK) Limited, *London*
Prentice-Hall of Australia Pty. Limited, *Sydney*
Prentice-Hall of Canada Inc., *Toronto*
Prentice-Hall Hispanoamericana, S.A., *Mexico*
Prentice-Hall of India Private Limited, *New Delhi*
Prentice-Hall of Japan, Inc., *Tokyo*
Pearson Education Asia Pte. Ltd., *Singapore*
Editora Prentice-Hall do Brasil, Ltda., *Rio de Janeiro*

To Janet, our parents, and Nicholas
To Margery, Heidi, Robert G., Mary C., and Robert H.
To my parents and students

Preface

Information Technology: Inside and Outside has been written as the basis for a one-semester course introducing the engineering behind a modern information infrastructure. This infrastructure is the foundation for the revolution in economic and social systems that we are currently experiencing. The topics covered are suitable for use in a wide range of educational environments, from which educators may select appropriate materials given the preparation of students and the nature of the curricular context. This book may be used to offer courses to students in business, management, law, the arts, the humanities, the social sciences, geography, and other degree programs, but also includes supplementary and deeper treatments that are suitable for students of mathematics, physics, and engineering. We have been careful not to introduce concepts requiring previous exposure to topics unique to preparation in electrical and computer engineering or other technical fields.

The book provides the foundation for a course accessible to students from many different disciplines. Such a course can prepare students to take advantage of new information technologies during the remainder of their education, as well as throughout their careers. The goal of such a course in information engineering is to teach *leadership skills* rather than just *survival skills*. Students will be in a position (after further study) to make changes in their particular profession based on the continuing emergence of new information technologies and associated capabilities.

Audience

To prepare students from many disciplines to interact with the engineers and service providers of the information infrastructure, we seek in this book to provide knowledge regarding such concepts as the nature of information, bandwidth, types of transmission and storage media, and the fundamental principles governing information technology. We endeavor to give students a systems-level appreciation of information systems, including computer network organization, specification, and economics, so that they will have the context in which to perceive opportunities for these technologies in their professions. Exposure to general networking concepts, in addition to hands-on experience with related hardware and software tools for information capture, conversion, display, and management, will provide students with the knowledge needed to bring the appropriate information-related technologies to bear on their disciplines.

Goals

Because of the wide audience that we seek to engage, the exercises in this book likewise address a wide range of backgrounds. This course is intended for first- or second-year students who are not majoring in electrical or computer engineering; thus, the formal prerequisites are intentionally kept to a minimum. Many of the exercises will be within the skill set of first-year students with no special preparation beyond knowledge of college entrance-level algebra. The exercises for these students are aimed in particular at developing skills in key areas.

Prerequisites

vii

- *Communications skills:* It is widely recognized that development of written, oral, and visual communications skills is a vital part of education, and that students are frequently deficient in these areas compared to their teachers' expectations. In the context of modern communications media, this course will provide opportunities for students to practice and enhance their abilities in the "old-fashioned" communications principles, including clarity of thought, organization of presentation, and a focus on the goal of the communication.

- *Web skills:* Use of the World Wide Web as a tool across the course will ensure that students become familiar with this means for the accessing and archiving of information. Furthermore, an appended HTML version of the book has been included on an enclosed CD in a Web format to enable rapid searches for information and direct linking to virtual laboratory programs that provide every student with a hands-on experience with information technology.

While the formal prerequisites are few, it is very much the intention of this course to build upon students' backgrounds and experience, including precollege experience and preparation. Three broad areas are emphasized for development through the exercises.

- *Mathematics:* Concepts of mathematics will be used to quantify important principles such as information content (of an image, a sound, a document, etc.), and to demonstrate the interrelations among disparate concepts such as auditory and visual acuity, bandwidth, information content, and transmission media limitations.

- *Computer skills:* Most students today have some degree of familiarity with computers, but the range of skill levels and understanding varies widely. Some exercises are directed at allowing students with these skills to derive further understanding of information technology by providing a path toward implementation of these technologies with a minimal programming effort.

- *Science skills:* By definition, the "physical sciences" deal with the physical world, while the mathematical sciences deal with abstract concepts. In secondary as well as postsecondary education, these branches of science are often kept quite separate. Further, too often students do not achieve an understanding of how their physical world relates to the physical and mathematical sciences. Engineering is the primary discipline that brings these worlds together by the application of science and mathematics to meet human needs. Some exercises in this book bring science to bear on the engineering of systems for humans; this connection can be quite thrilling to novice science majors who may not yet have had the opportunity to experience the power of applying the tools they have been acquiring in a human context.

HTML Version

The version of the book on the CD contains links to a set of Java-based virtual laboratory experiments that are also found on the CD. The integration of Java and Java Script-based applets with the textbook greatly enhances the presentation of the course material by allowing students to experience the underlying components of information technology in action, rather than merely by description. Further, the use of Java provides a great degree of computer system independence for the exercises. Following is a summary of the types of applets that are included:

- Applets related to the concepts of digital audio;
- Applets illustrating the basics of digital imaging;
- Applets illustrating various approaches to image data compression;

- Applets illustrating the elements of the computer representation of numbers;
- Demonstrations of digital data transmission;
- Demonstrations of error detection and correction coding.

Most of these applets are not simple demonstrations; they enable the student to vary one or more parameters, and observe the results. It is clearly advantageous that students with access to PCs will be able to immediately use these applets as they read the text, rather than having to go to a specific lab where the software must be installed. For details regarding the applets, see the inside front cover.

A review of the list of topics in this book will show many examples of the relationships between the physical and the abstract. These concepts include physical realizations such as images, sounds, and pages of text, related to abstract concepts such as information, bandwidth, and the number systems. Hence, students from all disciplines will have the opportunity to understand the interdependence among many branches of knowledge and, by extension, the value of a broad education in helping people achieve their goals.

Acknowledgments

Several persons and organizations deserve thanks for their valuable contributions to this book. The National Science Foundation provided financial support to begin the project, and WPI, particularly president Ed Parrish and provost Jack Carney, have encouraged and supported us. Several groups of Lucent Technologies employees made use of a preprint version of this text, and two groups of WPI students enrolled in experimental offerings of a course based on the initial notes. A large number of students contributed substantially to the creation and refinement of the graphics, software, and content of the book: Joe Alba, Mike Andrews, Deb Fraser, Brian Hazzard, Carleton Jillson, Mike Roberts, Joshua Resnick, Pedro Soria-Rodriguez, and Ryan Tomasetti. The contributions of reviewers Bob Strum, James McClellan, Gordon Couturier, and Jeff Farah are appreciated. Finally, we would like to thank everyone at Prentice-Hall with whom we worked, including David George, Lakshmi Balasubramanian, and our editor, Tom Robbins.

Foreword

In 1999 the College of Engineering at the University of South Carolina changed its name to the College of Engineering and Information Technology. The process for change involved much discussion of what the new name really meant. What did adding the words "information technology" imply? What would be different? The term information technology means different things to different people. The financial community uses the term information technology to describe not only the technical aspects of how we deal with information, but also the broader context of those technical aspects.

Information technology allows those who provide, interpret, manage, and otherwise use information to make fundamental changes in what they do and how they do it. These changes have created a need for a broad understanding of information technology and the ways in which it can be applied.

The authors speak to this audience by using a language that does not require an understanding of advanced mathematics or advanced electrical engineering. Arithmetic, algebra and, perhaps, a little geometry are the mathematics needed to read the book. They describe and then use bits, bytes, data, bandwidth, information theory, networks, and other terms in the information technology lexicon as they offer a broad exploration of the information technology landscape.

Understanding today's information technology is the basis for learning tomorrow's information technology. Those who have played a sport—whether it is golf, soccer, or tennis—enjoy being a spectator more than those who have not played; and those who play a musical instrument enjoy a concert or other musical performance more than those without the experience as a participant. So, also, those who have the benefit of a broad understanding of information technology will be better users of information technology than those for whom information technology remains vague and a bit of a mystery.

One of the recommendations offered by engineering education leaders during the past decade has been for engineering colleges to become more pro-active in providing the education for technological literacy needed by so many baccalaureate graduates. In a workshop sponsored by the ASEE Engineering Deans Council and the ASEE Corporate Roundtable (1994) one of the action items stated, *"Engineering Deans should take responsibility for helping more non-engineering majors on their campuses better understand the importance and relevance of technology in their lives, and seek to better equip those students to progress in an increasingly technological world..."* A course offering a broad understanding of information technology is an excellent response to this recommendation. This text makes it easier to offer that course.

Information and its uses have always been with us. Very early uses focused on storage and retrieval of information in pictographs and hieroglyphics. Retrieval was accomplished by simply reading these images. Choosing the particular images to represent the information (the ideas) is a coding process, just as reading the images becomes a decoding process. As language developed further, the coding/decoding process became more ordered and writing (storing) the images as manuscripts allowed the information to be shared more readily. Fast-forward to the fifteenth century to Gutenberg and his printing press with movable type. One finds another great change in the way information may be stored. The images stored on paper could be more readily copied and communicated to others. Today's information storage and retrieval uses bits and bytes on electronic, magnetic, and optical media communicated from place to place by electrical and optical systems over both short and long distances, but always at the speed of light. Today's information communication systems include satellites, wired and wireless (terrestrial) electronic signals, optical fibers, and over the air optical signals at very wide band widths.

The information technology revolution was enabled by the semiconductor device (transistor) revolution. Early (about 1950) semiconductor devices were small and power- efficient only by comparison with the vacuum tubes they made obsolete. Today's very-large-scale-integrated (VLSI) circuit places millions of transistors on a single silicon chip to perform many information processing functions. These chips are energy efficient, reliable, nearly error free, low cost, and small. They not only control the flow of information and perform the coding/decoding functions but also the storage and retrieval processes. Without these chips today's world would be very different: no personal computers, no World Wide Web, no affordable cell phone system, and automobiles of far less efficiency and greater cost, to name a few important items that are completely dependent on modern semiconductor chips.

Two explosions in the information technology firmament have come in the latter half of the twentieth century: the digital computer and the Internet or World Wide Web. The electronic computer had its origins during World War II but owes its ubiquitous place in the information revolution to the semiconductor revolution mentioned above. The semiconductor revolution moved us quickly from room-filling mainframe computers to minicomputers to microcomputers and microprocessors to the personal computer (PC), the personal digital assistant (PDA), and the digital cell phone. This rapid evolution saw the random access memory (RAM) move from 64kB to 128MB (or larger), processor speed from tens of kilohertz to hundreds of megahertz, hard disk storage from ten megabytes to 50 gigabytes (or larger), removable storage from 160 kilobytes to over 600 megabytes. As speed and capacity grew, the cost of computers actually decreased! The ability to buy more computing power for less money rapidly expanded the market for the PC. This expanding market further reduced costs due to mass production, fueling the positive spiral of performance and ubiquity.

The ability of PCs to communicate with each other transformed the PC from a computing device to a communications device. The revolution in communications centered on the Internet and the World Wide Web, making access to information available to everyone. This universal information access is an equalizer and will continue to expand the base of interlinked information users and providers. The greatest significance of information technology is that this technology is an enabler. As processes improve, so does quality, productivity, functionality, and flexibility. Information technology is becoming the key to industrial competitiveness.

As noted previously, information technology describes the technical content (engineering, science, and math related) and the context of how we deal with information. This could readily lead to the conclusion that this book is solely for students in these technical programs. For those in electrical engineering, computer engineering, and computer science this book provides a broad overview of much they will study about information technology. By helping these students to see this broad overview as first-year students, this text can enhance their deeper study of computers, communications and information systems.

But the contents of this book are even more needed by other groups. Those studying other engineering, science, and mathematics disciplines need to understand information technology as it will continue to increase its impact on their disciplines. The authors recognize the broadest audience for the book—the information users and information providers linked by information technology to the information so critical to their work. They have presented the broad concepts so necessary for understanding information technology, for realizing how information technology can and will change what they do and how they do it.

Edward W. Ernst
University of South Carolina
College of Engineering and Information Technology

Introduction

This book is intended to serve as a text for several types of introductory courses across the breadth of the emerging area of Information Technology. Courses based on this book may choose one of several possible focuses: general literacy in the underlying principles and vocabulary of IT; a more focused background in the major details and ongoing changes (such as data networking and wireless communications) underlying the IT revolution, a solid background in the information and communications principles that underlie specific disciplines (such as virtual reality, image analysis and synthesis, business information systems), or preparation for further study by students in the computer science, electrical and computer engineering, or MIS areas.

The contents of the book are organized into sections and subsections to facilitate the selection of appropriate topics for specific course objectives. Several examples of possible choices of material for different course objectives are presented below. For all courses, it is recommended that Chapter 22 be included. This chapter addresses the important topic of the rapid convergence of computation and communication as it draws on material of the previous chapters and demonstrates the interrelations among the topics of this book.

For a course emphasizing networking, communications, and business applications, either as an introduction for further study, or as general background, it is suggested that Chapters 1–4 and Chapters 14–22 form the basis of the course, with supplementary material from Chapters 5–13.

Particularly for students in electrical and computer engineering, it may be desired to emphasize audio and video, in which case it is suggested that Chapters 1–14 be studied in detail, together with Chapter 22, with additional material selected from the introductory sections of Chapters 14–21.

If it is desired to provide an overview of IT, without going into mathematical details, it is suggested that the course begin with Chapters 1–4, then focus on the introductory sections of Chapters 5–7, 10, 13–16, and 19–21, and conclude with Chapter 22.

Each chapter concludes with a selection of exercises of varying types, with expected responses ranging from the purely qualitative to the moderately quantitative. The instructor may make a selection of exercises appropriate to the course objectives and to the student backgrounds.

Contents

Part II
Fundamentals of Binary Representation

3 *Representing Information in Bits*   38

4 *The Need and Basis for Data Protocols*   61

Part III
Graphics and Visual Information

5 *From the Real World to Images and Video*   76

Part IV
Data Compression

Part V
Bandwidth and Information Theory

Part VI
Transmission and Storage Technology

19 *The Local Area Network   258*

20 *Organization of the Internet   268*

21 *Electronic Commerce and Information Security   277*

Information Technology
Inside and Outside

Introduction

These are the days of miracle and wonder. . .

Paul Simon, "The Boy in the Bubble," Graceland

This book will show you the world's growing information infrastructure from the inside and from the outside. It will take you inside communications networks and systems to show you how they work, and in particular how communications, computation, and information can be integrated in powerful new ways. It will also show you the view from outside this infrastructure that supports new ways of doing business, new forms of recreation, enhanced access to friends and family, and new ways of just living life that the information revolution introduced during the last years of the 20th century. The authors believe that to become conversant in the potentials and limitations of the applications of information technology it is necessary to become familiar with the internal workings of the systems and concepts that are behind the creation, transmission, storage and presentation of information. However, these concepts alone would be fallow ground if not for the creative ways in which they have been put to use by the many pioneers of the information age. So, throughout this book we also talk about the problems, the solutions, things coming, things gone; that is, the outside. Thus the two chapters that make up the first part of this book are a small introduction to the inside and outside of information systems.

Now, here's a shocker: The information revolution has only just begun. The changes we've seen during the past ten years are hardly the beginning. We are headed toward an unprecedented change in every aspect of how we communicate, educate, track information, solve medical problems, and manage every aspect of life. We have chosen one particular change that is just around the corner as a target for this book. The last chapter of the book is about the complete redefinition of the telephone system as a part of the World Wide Web.

As you read this first part of the book, try the exercise of writing a list of the changes that would have to be made to make the Web a viable replacement for the telephone system and a list of the reasons to do it and not to do it. Keep that list with you as you read the later parts and note the technological problems that might arise and your thoughts about the solutions.

By the way, TV, radio, shopping, banking and the rest will also soon collapse into the Web. So whatever your career may be, you won't be left out, and we have addressed the relevant technologies in the book, too. You might keep another list of similar thoughts about your own area of expertise.

1

What Is the Information in the Information Revolution?

Objectives

Over the past few years, the word *information* has become both very common and very fashionable, often paired with another word in phrases such as "information economy," "information technology," or "information age." In this first chapter you will learn:

▲ the precise definition and explanation of what information is, and the important distinctions among the terms "information," "message," and "signal";

▲ the names and functions of components that make up information systems, including the transducer, transmitter, channel, storage, and receiver;

▲ the arrangement of these components in common information systems such as the telephone system;

▲ the distinctions between analog and digital information; and

▲ the reasons why digital information systems are quickly replacing analog systems.

1.1 Introduction

As the world has become increasingly interconnected by modern telecommunication and computer technologies, the concept of *information* has taken on new meaning and importance. Accordingly, new fields related to designing, using, and managing systems that handle information have emerged.

Even though we all use modern information technology, we may not necessarily concern ourselves with the details of how these new technologies operate. These details are primarily the concern of professionals in technical areas, which we will refer to as the field of *information engineering*. Traditionally, the profession of engineering has been organized by the physical things that we can build. Civil engineers build bridges, mechanical engineers build jet engines, electrical engineers build computers and electric generators. However, another way to organize the profession would be with respect to what we want to accomplish. Then we would have titles such as transportation engineer, energy engineer, and information engineer.

An information engineer must understand first what information *is* and how to make it useful to people—for example, by transforming it, storing it, or transmitting it. The purpose of this book is to give an introduction to this broad field. However, the book is not intended only for persons who will be engineers by profession. Rather, it is aimed at all users of information and modern information technology. This includes virtually all professions; essentially everything we might do involves information and could potentially benefit from the appropriate use of technology.

Why is this book needed now? The answer is simply that the area of modern information technology has become so rich, and full of potential and options, that some organization is needed. Otherwise an information user will not be able to make informed decisions about information. As a simple example, if a few years ago we had a photograph that someone across the country needed, we had almost no options. The choice was surface mail or air mail special delivery, which might get it there in a few days rather than a week. Now we can choose among many options, including not only regular mail, priority mail, and next-day express mail, but also fax transmission and computer file transmission. How we make the decision is based on the information in the photograph, how important it is, and when and how it might be used by the recipient. These factors determine how we might choose among the different options, each of which has implications regarding the fidelity of the received image, the cost of the transmission, and the need for technology on both ends of the transaction.

In this chapter, we will discuss what information is and its importance in everyday life. Using familiar examples, we will illustrate how we are constantly surrounded by systems that (often without our worrying about it) must represent, store, manipulate, and transmit this information. We will then discuss some of the different forms that information can take—forms that are of as much interest to artists, musicians, historians, architects, salespersons, managers, and public officials as they are to the scientists and engineers usually associated with information technology.

By the end of this chapter, you should have a qualitative understanding of what information is, and should be able to identify ways in which it comes into play in your personal and professional life. This will set the stage for the rest of the book, in which we will examine some of the ways in which modern information technology works, with the goal of helping you make informed choices about using information in your daily life.

1.2 Information, Messages, and Signals

Let's begin with a dictionary definition of *information*: "Knowledge communicated or received concerning some fact or circumstance; news." The world is full of facts, some discovered, some remaining to be discovered. These become information when they are used in some way. This is the fundamental connection between information and communication: a fact only becomes useful as information when it is communicated. This communication is often to a person, but that is not necessary! For example, information on the temperature in a room is communicated to the furnace via a thermostat, with no human involvement.

In addition to the term *information*, we will be discussing two different, but related concepts: *signal* and *message*. A *signal* is the actual entity (electrical, optical, mechanical, etc.) that is transmitted from sender to receiver. For example, birds send out mating signals, which are specific sound patterns they create. Similarly, human vocal cords send out audible signals such as speech. A *message*, on the other hand, is the knowledge that is transmitted. For example, in the case of the birds, the message might be "It's mating season and I'm available." Whereas the signal is a specific sequence of sound waves, the message is the meaning conveyed by that sequence. *Message* and *information* are quite closely related, and in some (not all) situations may be used interchangeably; the subtle difference between them will be discussed later in this chapter. The concept of a signal is quite distinct from both, however; a signal need not convey any knowledge or information.

In the following section we will discuss some common examples of information systems to illustrate the differences between information, messages, and signals. We will also use these examples to begin explaining the differences between analog and digital forms of information, and take a first look at how information might be measured or quantified.

1.3 Examples of Information Systems

When we use a modern information system, we are usually quite unconcerned with how it operates; we just turn it on and use it. This is becoming ever more true as systems become increasingly complex. In this section, several examples of information systems will be presented to provide some insight into both their technical operation and the relation between form and function.

1.3.1 The Phonograph

The human voice is an example of what we might call a "natural signal"; that is, a type of signal that occurs as part of our human existence, and that typically carries information of great interest. Many other types of sounds also fit this description. Because sound in general, and voices in particular, are so central to human interaction, and so personal to each individual, there has long been a strong desire to store and transmit sounds and voices. The physics of acoustics lends itself to simple storage devices, and the first practical storage device, the phonograph, was invented by Thomas Edison in 1877. Sound is essentially mechanical vibrations, transmitted in air, and capable of stimulating vibrations in materials on which the vibrating air impinges. This is the principle behind how a basic phonograph records sounds: a diaphragm, which vibrates when sound waves impinge on it, is connected to a stylus which can cut or emboss grooves in a solid material. As the stylus is moved over the recording material (originally tinfoil, then wax cylinders, and eventually vinyl), the vibration induced into it from the diaphragm (which in turn is responding to the vibrating air) produces a groove whose depth or displacement is proportional to the instantaneous sound intensity. In this way, a physical, permanent record of the sound is etched into the recording medium.

The same mechanism that records the sounds can be used to play them back. If a playback stylus is allowed to travel across the grooves in the recording, it vibrates according to the groove pattern. This, in turn, vibrates the diaphragm, which creates sound waves that can be heard. Some amplification may be necessary for the sound waves to be acceptably loud, but aside from that, the recording and playback processes are quite symmetrical.

This system is simple and elegant; its operation is made obvious by looking at it. There are a few basic design parameters: a recording medium soft enough to be embossed by the stylus, a source of motion for the recording medium that is steady and of the proper speed so that each oscillation of the acoustic wavefront is faithfully recorded, and a mechanical linkage that interfaces the moving air to the stylus. Certainly, there is no high technology at work here. But in fact, this simple phonograph, as seen in Figure 1.1, contains all the components of any *communications system*:

- an *input transducer* (the device that converts a physical signal from a source, in this case sound, to an electrical, electromagnetic, or mechanical signal more

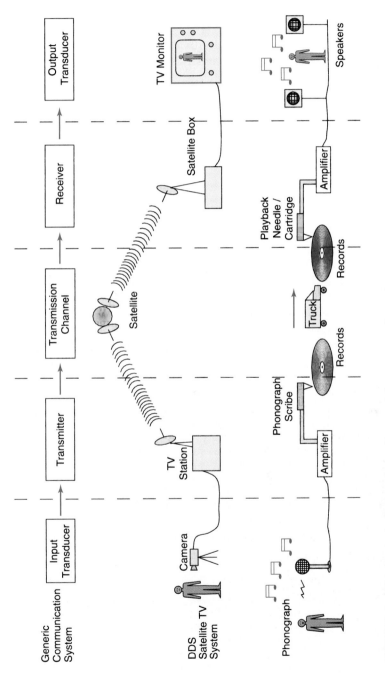

FIGURE 1.1 All communication systems share certain common elements.

suitable for communicating): in this case, the vibrating diaphragm during recording;

- a *transmitter* (the device that sends the transduced signal): in this case, the recording stylus;

- a *transmission channel* (the physical medium on which the signal is carried): in this case, the wax cylinder or other recording medium;

- a *receiver* (the device that recovers the transmitted signal from the channel): in this case, the playback stylus; and

- an *output transducer* (the device that converts the received signal back into a useful physical quantity): in this case, the vibrating diaphragm during playback.

You can see the arrangement of these basic elements at the top of Figure 1.1. This type of abstract representation is known as a *block diagram*, and it is a very useful tool for representing complex systems. Each block represents a *subsystem*, which performs some function; the specific function determines the relationship between the signal entering the block and the signal leaving the block. The signals themselves are represented by arrows. Notice that the block diagram allows us to represent subsystems conceptually, without the need to worry about the actual physical components that make up each subsystem. This particular block diagram provides a *model* for many different communications systems; we have shown how it can be used to represent a phonograph and a satellite TV system.

Note that in many of the communication systems with which you are familiar (telephone, radio, television), the transmission channel conveys the signal to the receiver immediately. However, systems such as this in which signals are stored for future use are also considered communication systems, because they can be used to convey information from some source to a destination. Whether the source and destination are separated by space, time, or both, the system still conveys communication between these two parties.

Within this system, we can also see examples of the quantities that we discussed earlier:

- *Signals:* the original sound waves, the mechanical vibration of the recording stylus, the pattern on the wax cylinder, the mechanical vibration of the playback stylus, and the recreated sound waves are all signals.

- *Message:* the content of the recording is the message, whether a song, a speech, or some other recorded sound.

- *Information:* whatever the content of the recording conveys to the listener constitutes the information.

FIGURE 1.2 Zenith, 1951 vintage, combination Phonograph and Radio (from the collection of John C. Pelham).

This gives us a chance to discuss when message and information may be different. Information, in the context of this book, refers to conveyed knowledge that is in some way useful and not known previously. A message may contain a great deal of information (for example, a new song from your favorite recording artist), or it may contain very little (for example, a single note played over and over again).

Although the basic phonograph (see Figure 1.2) constituted a breakthrough in the communication of information, it contained some significant limitations. If you have ever listened to a vintage recording on an old phonograph, you have heard evidence of these shortcomings. Desire for the reduction of these limitations has led us to the compact disc (CD) as the common commercial sound storage and playback medium today. In later chapters, we will not only discuss how CD tech-

📖 **CD**

nology works, but will provide explanations for *why* it does a better job of reproducing sound than did the basic phonograph.

1.3.2 The Telephone

The phonograph provided capabilities for sound storage, and thus a form of long distance transmission of sound, because recordings could be physically carried or sent from place to place. The value of this type of communication should not be minimized; although "real-time" sound transmission (via the telephone) was developed at about the same time as the phonograph, it is only quite recently that it has been possible to think about instantaneous transmission of essentially all types of information around the globe. For example, live global television dates back only to the 1970s, having been made possible by the advent of communications satellites, and later facilitated by fiber optic cable. Prior to that time film or videotape was regularly flown from country to country, using the same communication system concept as did the phonograph.

Real-time long distance sound transmission was first made possible by Alexander Graham Bell, who patented the telephone in 1876. As users we see only the user interface devices (like the telephone set), but to make information systems function, there must be many other components. Let's examine the current telephone system in some detail.

Figure 1.3 depicts the transmission system of a complete telephone system. The five fundamental components of a telephone connection are:

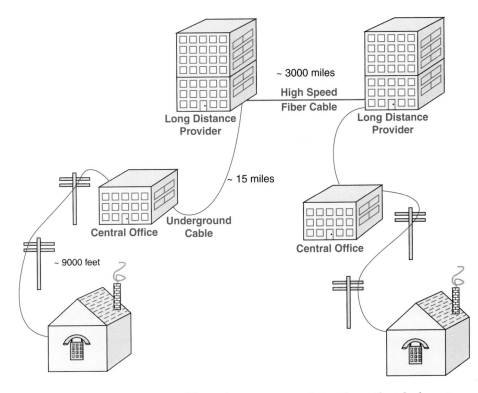

FIGURE 1.3 Pictorial description of the major components that make up the telephone transmission system.

- The transmitter, which responds to the input sound and converts it to electrical energy.
- The transmission medium, which conveys the electrical energy from one end to the other. This may be as simple as a wire.
- The receiver, which accepts the electrical energy and converts it back to audible sound.
- The switching system, which connects one particular transmitter to a particular receiver (and also the corresponding reverse direction for two-way communication).
- A signaling system, which tells the switches what connections to make.

Referring to Figure 1.3 again, the transmitter and receiver are located on the telephone set in each house. Several types of transmission systems are shown: wires strung on poles from the local telephone central office to the houses, wire cables laid underground between some central offices, and high-speed fiber optic cable connecting major telephone switching centers. The telephone offices also contain the switching systems that make the correct connections for each telephone call.

The telephone transmitter responds to air pressure variations (which we interpret as sound) to produce a corresponding variation in an electrical signal. This signal may easily be carried distances on the order of a few miles by a pair of wires. If the distance is large, then this the transmission system becomes somewhat more complicated, and devices called amplifiers are needed to boost the electrical signal level. At the receiver the signal creates a corresponding magnetic field in a coil of wire (an electromagnet). If an iron disk is placed near the electromagnet it will vibrate in synchronism with the transmitted signal, which in turn is in synchronism with the original sound waves. Hence the sound is reproduced at the far end.

The switching system could be as simple as a light switch, or could be an old-fashioned telephone switchboard system in which the operator connects the wires from transmitter to receiver manually. Modern switching systems, on the other hand, are in fact specialized computers. The signaling system (telephone jargon for the part of the telephone system that establishes and controls connections; that is, the part that handles dialing) was originally the sound itself: the switchboard operator said "number, please" and then made the correct connection based on what the caller said. This system was replaced with the original "dial pulse" system, which used pulses of electric current to transmit the number to the switch automatically. This in turn has mostly been replaced with the "touch-tone" systems that use different audio tones to transmit the numbers.

📖 **Analog**

📖 **Digital**

The above describes a system that has been unchanged in basic form for 100 years. It is fundamentally an "analog" system, although more and more components are being converted to "digital" operation. Within a few more years the system will become completely digital, except for the transmitter and receiver, which are needed to interface with the users. We will be describing the exact meaning of *analog* and *digital* in the following sections. For now it will suffice to say that the telephone system is transitioning from radio-like electronics to computer-like electronics.

1.3.3 The Camera and Other Image Recording Devices

Like sound, visual images are central to human existence, and the recording and communication of images have stirred similar interest through the ages. The contrast in technology between the two is striking: for sounds, a whole new technology was required for their storage; for images, a talented artist could create a representation of a natural scene with simple drawing tools. Hence, we have some excellent examples of images from the beginning of recorded history, but none of sounds!

Of course, the human artist as an image recording device is quite limited, and to some extent untrustworthy, because the artist will almost certainly add some element of personal interpretation to the image. When the image is drawn, some information is lost and other information is added. To reduce these limitations, a device for recording images was sought. The first practical method of photography was demonstrated in 1839, and many images of excellent quality are available today from the mid 1800s.

Of course, early cameras were expensive, cumbersome to use, and limited (to black and white images, for example). Since that time, classical photography and other forms of capturing image information have advanced tremendously in capabilities, and several other types of image storage technologies have been developed, including video, motion pictures, facsimile, digital photography, photocopying, and file storage. An image, while a very common form of information, can pose many challenges to the designers and users of information systems. As will be discussed in subsequent chapters, the amount of information in an image, while very subjective, is in general quite large.

Consider the earlier discussion about the difference between signal, message, and information. If we wish to send a photo of a human face to someone using, for example, a facsimile machine (fax), then the image is transmitted as a signal—a pattern of electrical impulses sent over the telephone system. The message, in this case, is the image itself (note how the received message may be quite degraded from the original message, depending on the quality of the fax transmission). The information contained in this message will depend to some extent on the purpose to which the image will be put. Is it merely intended to give the recipient a rough idea of the person's appearance? Is it to identify the person? Or is more detail needed?

As these questions suggest, the notion of information has some philosophical implications. Furthermore, from a technical point of view, we wish to be able to quantify both information and our capacity to deal with it, so there are mathematical implications as well. In the next section, we will discuss means for representing information; this discussion will introduce some of the concepts that connect these philosophical and mathematical issues.

1.4 Representing and Quantifying Information

Let's revisit the examples we've discussed from two other perspectives: the "fidelity" and "information content" of the signals involved. There are mathematical definitions of these terms, but we will begin with less formal concepts. *Fidelity* is a measure of the difference between the original and reproduced forms of the information. In the case of a telephone conversation, for example, does the received voice sound the same as it would if the person were standing in the room? Probably not. Is the person easily recognizable? Quite possibly. Yet answering these questions may be quite different from determining the information content of the message.

Consider, for example, the message "You have won $1,000,000." Most of the information content is contained in the distinction between "won" and "not won." As long as you have received that correctly, you don't really care whether the message was high fidelity or not. On the other hand, with music reproduction, the fidelity is central to the information content. Much of the value of music is lost if the reproduction is not accurate.

So, how do we determine what is "information" and what is not? And how do we measure the amount of information? The first question is easier to answer (at least informally) than the second. The dictionary definition of information was given earlier: "knowledge communicated or received." Now you might reasonably ask, "What is knowledge?" As was seen above, this discussion could become more philosophical than engineering-based. Indeed, the mathematical definition of information that technical professionals use is based on the likelihood or improbability of the message, and so it is impossible to completely avoid issues of philosophy in this discussion. A reasonable operational definition of knowledge is "everything that your brain is capable of dealing with, interpreting, using, and that you may have some desire to remember." One useful informal definition of the information content of some signal is whether it has "told us what we want to know and did not know in advance."

Some examples of information common to our everyday lives are the date, the temperature, and the address of your residence. These examples are obviously knowledge. But, music is a type of knowledge also. Random noise ("static") such as you hear between stations on a radio is a very limited kind of knowledge. To most people at least, it just means "there is nothing here." Note the difference between music and random noise: listening to 1 minute of music is fundamentally different than listening to 10 seconds. But with random noise, this is not the case; more is not better! This explanation is quite qualitative and imprecise, but hopefully it conveys some idea of what information is.

There is a formal mathematical definition of information, one that also tells us how much information we have. In fact, there is an entire specialty in electrical engineering called "information theory," which deals with information measurement and analysis. We will only give the most basic introduction here, as we will devote several chapters to this topic later in this book. As you might already know, the unit of information is the "bit" or *binary digit*. In the binary number system there are only two digits: zero and one. The formal definition of information allows us to determine (in bits) exactly how much information is in a given sample of data. That is, the bit is used as a measure of information.

A simple example can be given by the random noise mentioned above. For all of its complexity at the detailed level, it contains only one bit of information to most listeners. That is, it provides the answer to a single "yes or no" question: Is a radio station present? The single bit of information contained in the answer to this question can be represented by using either of two different symbols. If we choose to use numbers, for example, we could use a "one" (radio station present) or "zero" (radio station not present) to answer the question. On the other hand, if a station is present, the answer to the question "what is playing on the station?" is much more complex; the radio station's signal contains many bits of information. Indeed, because it is continually sending information, we speak of its signal as having a rate of information flow, in "bits per second."

However, there is a further distinction to be made. To be precise, we need to think of the radio signal as two different signals, each with its own bit rate: the "data rate" and the "information rate." The data rate is an electrical specification telling us the rate at which the message is being transmitted; for example, just as a computer modem might provide a data rate of 28,800 bits per second, the radio signal could be represented by some number of bits per second. The information rate, on the other hand, relates back to you as a person, and the knowledge conveyed to you by the message the signal carries. If you listen to a three-hour broadcast of a football game but are only interested in whether the New England Patriots won or lost, then for you there is only one bit of information (won or lost) in those three hours (ignoring the possibility of a tie, and including the halftime show). This is true even though the data rate may have been something like 28,800 bits per second for that entire period. If, on the other hand, you are intently listening to the entire game and interested in each play, comment, and commercial, then every one of those data bits (which are converted in the receiver into the broadcast of the game) potentially contained real information. The information content for those three hours would then apparently be (28,800 bits/second × 60 seconds/minute × 180 minutes) = 311,040,000, or over 311 million bits. This simple calculation, however, assumes that every aspect of the broadcast conveyed useful information to you; the actual amount of information would be less than this total.

If this discussion has left you somewhat confused about the distinction between message, signal, and information, do not be alarmed. These are subtle points that we will seek to clarify in subsequent chapters of this book. As you will see, it is the difference between these concepts that has allowed so many recent advances in information engineering. The key to taking advantage of these differences has been the advent of *digital* information technology; this is the subject of the next two sections.

1.5 Analog and Digital Information

The basic telephone, phonograph, and camera are examples of "analog" information storage and receiving systems. The word "analog" comes from the word "analogy," referring to the relation that one thing has to another. For example, the undulating groove in the phonograph recording is an analog of the original sound vibrations in the air. In engineering terms, we use *analog* to refer to the natural world, where time is continuous, and most parameters (like light and sound intensity, temperature, position, etc.) can vary smoothly and continuously over some range, taking on an infinite number of possible values. Conversely, there are some parameters that change only in discrete steps. Examples include the days of the month, games won or lost, and the squares on a checkerboard. Engineers use the term *digital* to refer to information representations for which both time and the value being measured move in discrete steps—that is, when there are a finite number of possible values. For example, the stock market close is reported on a daily basis (discrete in time) and in sixteenths of a point in rise or fall (discrete in value). As humans, we naturally experience both analog and digital phenomena. As we look at an outdoor scene, the color and light vary continuously, but each tree or building is either present or absent!

Very often we move back and forth between the analog and digital worlds without giving the details much thought. Consider Figure 1.4. The temperature at a given location versus time is an analog quantity, with an infinite number of possible values at each instant of time. On the other hand, temperature is reported by the Weather Service once per hour, to the nearest degree. Hence, a quantity that is fundamentally continuous in both amplitude and time is made discrete in both amplitude and time.

Most modern communications and storage systems are built around the digital computer, and the computer exists, at least in theory, purely in the digital world, even though we, and much of the information we care most about, live in an ana-

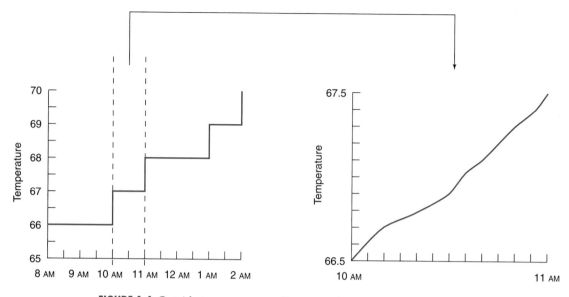

FIGURE 1.4 Outside temperature; a discrete and continuous view.

log world. Fortunately, it is possible to convert back and forth between these two quite different worlds. At least for human consumption, this conversion takes advantage of the fact that humans have limited sensory acuity; that is, we cannot resolve small differences. Hence, if a continuous value is made digital (discrete), but with very many small steps, the human observer will be unable to distinguish it from the original (analog) signal. If, on the other hand, the steps are not sufficiently small, the observer will be able to discern the difference. As an example, television systems operate by forming an image with individual horizontal lines (525 lines in US systems). This is enough lines to form a reasonably good image, but is not enough to "fool" the viewer into thinking that he or she is viewing a perfect image; the lines are quite apparent upon close inspection. Future developments (such as High Definition Television) will improve the image quality by adding more lines to the display. We will see in later chapters why this seemingly simple step is just now becoming a reality.

1.6 The Move Toward Digital Information Technology

The previous sections have described some classical information transmission and storage systems, such as the phonograph and the telephone. These systems developed over periods of decades or even longer. In contrast, some new information systems have sprung up and achieved widespread usage almost overnight. For example, the phonograph was invented by Thomas Edison in 1877, and remained unchanged in principle until the CD was introduced in 1983. Within a period of 10 years, phonograph records, which had been the sound recording norm for 100 years, essentially disappeared. How did this happen? Such fundamental changes happen as a result of two conditions: (1) the new system either enables some totally new capability or is much better than the one it replaces; and (2) the cost of the new system is reasonably low compared to people's willingness to pay.

The CD meets both criteria. While the capability (music reproduction) is not fundamentally new, the quality of the reproduction (as well as convenience of use) is substantially better than with the phonograph; also, the cost of CD playback systems from the beginning was competitive with phonograph systems. Why was the CD player cost so low? The system is technologically much more complex than the phonograph system; it uses a laser and control system to follow the very narrow optical (rather than enscribed as on the record) track on the CD. But even though these devices are sophisticated, they are very cheap to manufacture in large quantities. At their heart are several forms of solid state devices, particularly digital integrated circuits. Most integrated circuits cost only a few cents to manufacture, and they are very reliable and amenable to mass production. The phonograph, in contrast, requires large, precise moving parts, and simple but expensive electronics.

Why were the phonograph's electronics expensive? The answer to this lies at the heart of the information revolution: the phonograph is an analog device, and analog electronics are expensive; conversely, digital electronics are cheap! We will not go into detail in explaining why this is the case right now, but as you read further you will learn some of the reasons. Another factor with the phonograph is that it is a large mechanical device. The CD player also contains mechanical components, but they are smaller and integrated with the electronics in a way that makes them inexpensive to build in large quantities.

Similarly, telephone systems, cameras, and virtually all other types of information systems in use have converted to, or are in the process of converting to, digital versions. Digital information systems, almost without exception, have proven to be more reliable and less expensive than the analog systems they have replaced. This combination of better performance and lower cost devices, further facilitated by the seemingly unending development of faster, smaller, and cheaper digital electronics, has revolutionized the way in which we communicate and manage information. At the heart of this revolution is the fundamental connection between what information is and how digital systems operate.

Summary

In this chapter, we've used some familiar examples to illustrate what is meant by information, and have described how some systems convey information by sending and receiving messages in the form of signals. We've discussed differences between analog and digital information, and have provided some examples of how the technologies we use have evolved. Although we live in an analog world, most information processing can now be carried out in a digital world where the processing, storage, and transmission components are reliable and inexpensive. This recent development has provided the basis for the current information revolution. It has also motivated the need for anyone who uses information to understand some of the basics about digital information and digital information processing. The rest of this book will be dedicated to providing that information.

Try These Exercises

1. List as many different forms of information relevant to your intended major area of study or profession as you can. If you are undecided concerning your profession, then choose something that you are considering.
2. In Section 1.3.1, the phonograph was analyzed as a communication system by identifying the following five components: the input transducer, the

transmitter, the transmission channel, the receiver, and the output transmitter. Identify the same five components for each of the following communication systems. If you are not sure how something works, you might want to do some research in a library or on the Web.

(a) Broadcast radio

(b) A doorbell

(c) Cable TV

3. For each of the three communication systems listed in Exercise 2, identify the following as best you can

(a) Any signals used in the system

(b) The message

(c) The information contained in the message

4. List two examples (other than those used in the text) of commonly encountered information that are analog. Then, list two examples that are digital. Finally, list two examples that are *hybrids* (i.e., contain both discrete and continuous aspects). For these, indicate which aspect is continuous, and which is discrete.

5. List as many information systems as you can (at least four) that are found in your home or residence, and identify, as best you can, whether these systems are analog, digital, or both. Briefly explain the analog and/or digital aspects.

6. Identify one new type of information system which has either been proposed, or is just appearing for sale or use. Describe this system in terms of the aspects discussed in this chapter (i.e., is it analog or digital, what is the bandwidth or data rate, etc.). Describe the new aspects of this system, compared to any previously existing systems which are similar.

2 The World Wide Web: A Unique Product of the Information Age

Objectives

The World Wide Web is such an important component of the modern information age that it is the subject of Chapter 2. Here you will learn:

▲ the ways in which the Web is a fundamentally new and different information medium, with major advantages over all other such systems;

▲ the fundamentals of the underlying operations and facilities that make the Web possible and make it work;

▲ principles of Web browsers and Web servers;

▲ the significance and basic operation of a hypertext markup language (HTML); and

▲ the significance of the Java programming language, and its relation to the Web.

2.1 Introduction

You are probably familiar with the World Wide Web, which has become a basic tool for research, recreation, commerce, and communication. In this chapter, we will go beneath the surface of the Web to explain how it works, and why the ideas behind it were so important and revolutionary.

2.2 Why Introduce the Web This Early in the Book?

We are introducing the World Wide Web (also called the WWW, or simply the Web) at this point for two reasons:

• It is an excellent example of a modern, general-purpose communications system, and it will be used in several places in this text to illustrate important concepts.

• Many of the homework assignments in this book are based upon use of the Web and/or use of material found on the Web. In fact, this book is packed in Web-compatible format on the accompanying CD, and the *Virtual Laboratory* on the CD is executed through the application of a Web browser program.

In this chapter, we will introduce the World Wide Web from the perspective of how it operates. This will not involve a description of the specific tools that one uses such as specific Web browsers, plug-ins, and HTML editors; you can find this information in many introductory books about the Web. Nor will it have the

📖 HTML

technical detail of those books that address the needs of network administrators, Web masters, programmers, and Web page authors. Our intention here will be to describe the *mechanisms and machines* that form the foundation of the Web, as well as the *innovations* that it has introduced, resulting in its rapid adoption throughout the world.

2.3 What Is the Web, and Why Was It Created?

To understand the World Wide Web, it's useful to take a look at how and why it was developed. The answer to the question "What exactly is the World Wide Web?" is not as straightforward as is a similar question about the telephone or some other more traditional communications system. We will begin by describing its origin as the solution to a particular problem. This will be followed by a description of its components and operation at a fairly nontechnical level. It is the implementation of these components that will be addressed in many of the following chapters.

The Web was developed originally to solve a very specific problem; fortunately, it turned out to be useful for many other problems and needs as well. It was created to facilitate communications among nuclear physicists located throughout the world. These physicists make use of data gathered at specialized facilities, such as CERN (European Particle Physics Laboratory) in Geneva, Switzerland, and LANL (Los Alamos National Labs) in the United States, to name two. The work of physics takes an effort that interweaves highly mathematical theories and measurements that either confirm these theories or provoke the need for new theoretical work to generate explanations for the observations.

Thus, physicists need to communicate with each other so that they can share analyses and hypotheses and to transfer experimental data to their own locations for analysis. Of course, these transactions should be rapid, and they should be able to convey information containing a mixture of text, graphics, images, and mathematics. Similar needs exist among many other geographically distributed groups, but it was these nuclear physicists for whom the first implementation of the Web solution was developed. The first new communication tool to benefit these physicists in their work was *e-mail*. Originally, e-mail only provided for the sending of what is often called *raw text* between correspondents. Later in this book we will discuss the details of what makes some text *raw* and other forms more sophisticated; for now, consider raw text be anything that you could represent by the characters on the keys of a computer keyboard in a single font style, with one size, no emphasis, and no adornments. While this raw text capability addresses the needs of many kinds of communication, it certainly falls short in the depiction of the concepts of both art and science. One of the first problems associated with e-mail was the very limited capability of rendering even so much as rich textual content, let alone nontextual media components such as images. E-mail evolved during the first twenty years of the operation of the Internet to address the needs of those who wished to send copies of material different than raw text. In 1991, a system known as MIME (Multipurpose Internet Mail Extensions) was introduced to allow e-mail users to make *attachments* of additional documents to an e-mail. These additional documents were not read and displayed by the e-mail program directly; instead, they were included as separate files sent along with the text message. Upon receiving a message with a MIME-based document, the recipient could detach the document and display it with a program that understood the format of the attached document. The e-mail sender could even provide additional information for the e-mail system to use so that the appropriate viewer application could be launched automatically at the receiving end. This so-called *association* between document types and viewer programs was handled through special conventions for the naming of documents, and through a list of associations created by the user that assigned viewing programs to specific file types.

Using the MIME system, it became possible to send e-mail that contained documents with special characters (Greek, mathematical symbols, etc.), images, sound, spreadsheets, and software. In fact, most e-mail systems of most Web browsing software applications still employ the MIME system at some level to connect document types with display software.

The existence of this extension of Internet mail raises two questions that we will answer in what follows.

1. *Why was the MIME system needed; couldn't the mail-reader software application just be extended to read and display all the documents?*
2. *Why wasn't the MIME solution alone good enough to address the needs that we have been considering?*

There were two main problems with extending the original e-mail system directly to read all possible document types:

- There are too many people simultaneously inventing too many things during this information age for any single e-mail system to supply means to handle all the possible variations of document types and related displayers. Document types, image types, multimedia content, and so forth, are all products of human invention and human convention. Thus, there is almost no end to the variations of content type and variations of ways to package and transmit that content (using the technologies that we will consider in the following chapters).
- For every document type display system, there may be dozens of displayers that have been created, each expressing some personal preference, and a group of followers who want access to the displayer that suits their preference.

Thus, the MIME e-mail extension technology was developed. To understand why the existence of this technology still did not satisfy the general needs of most people and organizations, we need to consider how it would be used in a common situation.

Suppose that you are part of a fairly large organization; this could be a formal organization such as the physicists at CERN, or an informal one such as a group of English-speaking cat lovers throughout the world who share experiences, pictures, and so forth. For the sake of this discussion we will concentrate on the former. Further suppose that you have an observation you would like to share with members of your scientific group that includes some images and data. So, you write an e-mail that explains your observations, attach a set of pictures and graphs to the e-mail, and then send it.

Several of your recipients, who don't really share your intense interest, simply delete the material and send e-mail to you indicating that they should be left off your future e-mail list because it took several minutes of precious time for your large, image-laden e-mail file to download over their slow telephone connection to the Web.

Other recipients read your e-mail, but they suffer the need to display the various components of the package and try to figure out which images you are referring to, because the images and the text are not directly connected in any way. Some readers, in fact, completely misunderstand the observation you are making because of this confusion and attack your theory.

Still other recipients tell friends and colleagues about your observations. This news spreads by word of mouth, and nearly every day for a month you get an e-mail from someone asking you to assemble and send the same e-mail package to them. Furthermore, others write their own e-mails about what your e-mail led them to try in their own laboratories. Soon, a slew of e-mail is flying across the Internet with cross references that would take a monumental effort to unwind back to your seminal message.

Finally, when new people join the group, they are completely unaware of your work. They may go on to replicate your work, or lose time by asking around until they encounter a rumor about your observations, eventually leading to yet another request for that e-mail you composed several years ago.

The problem we have outlined in this example is connected with the need for *asynchronous access* (at any time, from any place) to stored and *indexed* (organized in some logical way) information that can include a wide variety of content types with some clear association between the various content components. In the following discussion we will see how the World Wide Web answers these needs when we revisit the above example.

The original implementation of the Web was aimed at allowing a group of physicists scattered around the world to access a wide variety of data easily and quickly, and to easily add to that collection of data so that fellow scientists could have immediate access to the new results. No previous existing communications system provided anything like these capabilities. What made it an immediate success for them, and what made it catch on for so many Internet users, was that it provided a new means for communications based on immediate access, instantaneous unwinding of cross references, and searchability.

2.4 The Origin of the Web

The highest award that the community of computer users can bestow upon a piece of software is to add it to the very short list of programs generally recognized as *killer apps*. Killer apps are software applications that have taken on importance due to broad acceptance and wide applicability. These applications have been so successful in solving the problems of computer users (commercial and individual) that they have been purchased in large quantities, and in some cases have been so emulated as to have spawned whole new industries. Furthermore, killer apps can cause existing industries to change via computerization; for example, accountants quickly saw the value of spreadsheets in their work, and in a short period of time, the way accountants work was changed in a fundamental way. Typically the killer app list includes the Visicalc spreadsheet (Software Arts, May 1979), the WordStar word processor (MicroPro, June 1979), and the dBase (Aston-Tate, 1980) database system for personal computers.

The phenomenon of the killer app is usually recognized as having been born with the introduction of the Visicalc Spreadsheet by the Software Arts company in May 1979. A lone programmer, Dan Bricklin, envisioned and wrote this first spreadsheet program while he was still a student at Harvard University. While the spreadsheet began humbly as an Apple II program written in the BASIC programming language, it ultimately resulted, indirectly, in the success of the Apple II computer platform, spawning several generations of successful businesses based upon spreadsheets. Furthermore, it forever changed the way in which business people plan, review, and present their work.

The story of the World Wide Web is similar in that its success has certainly qualified it to be called one of the killer apps of the 1990s. The WWW was the brainchild of Tim Berners-Lee, an Oxford University graduate working at the CERN facility, who is now Director of the World Wide Web Consortium (W3C). Berners-Lee undertook the task of finding a simple, extendible, and distributed approach to solving the communication problems of the particle physicists described above. He described information flow within CERN in his seminal document[1] in a way that applies to all organizations and essentially any human endeavor involving more than a few individuals:

> The actual observed working structure of the organization is a multiply connected "web" whose interconnections evolve with time. In this environment, a new person arriving, or someone taking on a new task, is normally given a few hints as to who would be useful people to talk to. Information about what facilities exist and how to find out about them travels in the corridor gossip and occasional newsletters, and the details about what is required to be done spread in a similar way. All things considered, the result is remarkably successful, despite occasional misunderstandings and duplicated effort.

To address the problem of facilitating and enhancing communication within this type of structure, in 1992 the CERN team introduced the first version of a Web browser, along with the required Web server software. An Internet *Web server* is a software application that executes on a computer connected to the Internet and offers a service to other computers on the Internet. The purpose of a Web server is to receive requests for information from Web browsers, and to send, via the Internet, the requested documents (a term we will use to refer to any content type).

The *Web browser* is an application that presents a user interface for requesting and viewing these documents. Chances are that you are familiar with one or more browsers, which include Netscape Navigator, Netscape Communicator, and Microsoft Internet Explorer. The original browser developed at CERN was simple but complete in implementing the solution to the access problems that we discussed above. Berners-Lee leveraged the especially flexible programming environment that was provided on a specialized workstation (the NeXT computer) to create a simple graphical interface that strongly foreshadowed the look and feel of all current Web browser software (Plate 1).

In the early 1990s, the programmers at the National Center for Supercomputing Applications (NCSA) at the University of Illinois at Urbana-Champaign (funded by the National Science Foundation) saw the utility of this communication technology and undertook writing their own improved Web browser. However, they developed it on a more generic software base, so that it would be transportable to the much larger number of Unix operating system based workstations in use by scientific users. The Mosaic Web browser introduced extensive graphical rendering and text font and format flexibility. Mosaic 1.0 for the UNIX Xwindows was introduced in April of 1993, and it ignited the interest of computer users throughout the world. By late 1993, Version 2.0 had been released, and versions for the PC and Apple McIntosh were introduced.

---

[1] *Information Management: A Proposal.* Tim Berners-Lee, CERN, March 1989, May 1990. http://www.w3.org/History/1989/proposal.html

The lead programmer in the effort to create Mosaic, Marc Andreessen, soon left NCSA along with several others from the team to form the company Netscape Communications. Here they developed the Netscape Navigator Web browser that was to catapult the Web to fame. Since then, the Web has become an essential tool on computers in homes, businesses, and schools.

2.5 How the Web Solves Our Document Distribution Problem

Let's examine the fashion in which the Web distributes documents by continuing the example that we began earlier. Working in your physics laboratory, you make what you believe to be an important observation. You compose a note that describes it, but this time you create the document using a *Hyper-Text Markup Language (HTML) editor*. This process may be done using a specialized editing program, or may be provided by a special format conversion system in a word processor. In either case, you are able to insert pictures and graphs within the textual flow of the document; there is now no longer any doubt regarding the association of the various content types.

When you complete the document, you "publish" the document by delivering it to a computer that runs a Web server program. This process involves freedom on your part to assign a name that will be associated with this new document; this name is called the document's *Universal Resource Locator (URL)* address. Later in this chapter we will discuss the nature and origin of the URL; in the meantime, let's just say that the URL identifies your document uniquely among all other documents in the world.

Now, let's explore the first of two options you have with respect to informing your colleagues about the existence of this new document. You could send an e-mail to all colleagues whom you think might have an interest in the observations you have made. Unlike before, you need only send a one-line e-mail:

New observations of neutrino mass oscillations:

http://www.nlab.org/masstrans/Dec99/exp23anal.html

In this case, there ought not to be many complaints about wasted download time, and those who have an interest can simply enter (by cutting and pasting with a mouse pointer) the stated URL into a Web browser to see the full information in context. If one of your colleagues thinks that some of her friends ought to look at it, she merely sends a similar e-mail and includes your URL. In this way, your involvement is no longer required for others to have future access to the information. The real versatility of this approach is revealed when some of your readers decide that this information is closely connected to their own work. Not only can they add this URL to their own Web documents, but they can do so in a special way that makes it very easy for future readers to track the connections between the documents and the underlying work. They can use their HTML editor to create a *hypertext link* (or what some people like to call a *hot button*) in their document. Readers of this document can simply click their mouse pointers on the hypertext link and their browsers will immediately read and display your original document. Through the use of these hypertext links, we can emulate the Web-like connections between many pieces of related thought and work.

The other option we may exercise to advertise the availability of our new information is to simply place a hypertext link that connects to our new document in an existing document that is known to many colleagues as a *home* for many such links related to this field of endeavor. We expect that those who have an interest in such work will make a habit of scanning this and other related *home pages* for new additions. In this way, the Web allows us to *browse* for new information rather than having to wait to be actively contacted by someone.

Furthermore, another opportunity is created by the Web's structure: we can take an active role in discovering new documents even when we have no knowledge of established home pages for the information we seek. This new approach is made possible by the existence of special pieces of software, called *search engines*, which we can access at special URLs (*Web sites*). These search engines become known to us through advertising in magazines, books, and other Web sites, and they give us access to large, indexed sets of data that have been gathered and are continuously being updated by the operators of the search service providers. The data is gathered by software that automatically scans every existing Web site and catalogs key words that appear in the associated Web documents.

So, continuing our example, people looking for information about observations of "neutrino oscillation" might ask the search engine to generate a list of all Web sites that contain that phrase. This list will certainly include our document's location, and, by noting the recent *document update date* that can be listed with each URL by some Web search engines, the users will recognize it as new information and be inclined to look at it.

2.6 How the Web Was Won

The World Wide Web represents a sophisticated system for information capture and delivery, and its creation required that many technical hurdles be cleared. In this section, we will review and discuss several of the innovations that were introduced by the World Wide Web concept and its associated software applications.

2.6.1 The Universal Resource Locator (URL)

As we saw in the example above, there is great value in being able to denote a document uniquely. The URL provides a value similar to that of the ISBN number assigned to all published books. However, the URL goes well beyond the ISBN when it comes to locating a copy of the document. If you have an ISBN you could discover the publisher of the book, author, title, and so forth, but you would still not know where you could get a copy of the book. On the other hand, the URL is not only a unique name for the document, it is a set of directions for obtaining a copy of that document!

    URL

A key idea behind the Web is that the URL is a single, universal address mechanism that denotes an information service or document type, the location of the hosting server within the Internet, and the location of that information within the host, and may also actually include information to be forwarded to that server for processing. The URL address was immediately embraced by the entire industry as a standard for referencing services as well as data.

An example of using a URL to access a *service* was seen in our previous example, when we used a search engine service located at one URL to locate data at other URLs. In general, we can attach software to a URL that does specific jobs for us, as if the URL were a document. The key idea behind this is that any service, in the end, simply generates a document for us to see, and hence can be handled like an ordinary document by the browser program. The information we supply for processing by the software (such as a search phrase in the case of the search engine) in many cases is simply tacked onto the URL. That is, the URL locates the software, and then the software looks back at the URL you used and clips off the information that it needs to do its work.

2.6.2 Virtual Path Addressing

If you were using an ordinary word processing system, you could specify your document simply by the *file name* that you choose to assign to it. Part of the Web document publication process, however, requires that you also provide a *path name* for your document. The path name serves two roles:

1. It constitutes an *address*; that is, it provides instructions that allow the Web server software to find your document within whatever permanent storage space it occupies. In simpler terms, if your Web server has all documents stored on several hard disk drives, the path name serves to describe on which disk, and in which directory on that disk, the document is located.
2. It provides means for creators of many documents to collect them in related groups and to impose a *hierarchical*, or tree-like (in the sense of a family tree), structure to groups of such collections. That is, it provides a system similar to that of the directory structure used with most computer folder and file systems.

When publishing a new Web document, we can attach it to an imaginary hierarchical tree of documents. This structure begins with the root of the tree. While we can give our new document any name we please, it inherits a larger path name connected to the location at which we placed it in our Web server's directories (and actually related to a number of choices we can make when setting up the Web server). The full path name consists of the names of each branch along the tree leading to your document, and finally the name of the document itself. For example, as illustrated in Figure 2.1, the file "exp23anal.html" obtains the path name: `masstrans/Dec99/exp23anal.html` by inheriting the names of the directories one must enter in following the pathway to it. This pathway begins at what is termed the *root* of the directory tree that our Web server accesses.

Finally, the full URL is generated by appending components that signify the type of server program and technique that will be used to handle the interaction and the location on the Internet of the computer running that server program.

FIGURE 2.1 The Web is a set of document trees with names that are derived from the name of the tree (set by the Web server host computer and Web server) and a path down the branches to a specific document.

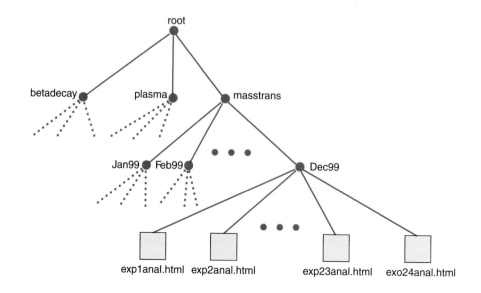

Thus, again in our example, "http:" indicates that a *hyper text transfer protocol* server program will be used and that it is located on a computer to be found at the Internet location designated by "www.nlab.org." The flexibility of the system used actually goes well beyond the level portrayed above. The path addressing scheme which is allowed is actually a *virtual path* scheme. What this means is that there need not really be any hierarchy of directories (or folders) in the computer's permanent storage area corresponding to those portrayed by the path name in the URL. The software administrator who configures the behavior of the Web server has the opportunity to name and rename parts of the path and to assemble a virtual (i.e., in name only) tree from branches spread out all over the actual permanent memory of the computer. This allows Web administrators to present a simple, intuitive, and unchanging form to the information available from their Web servers despite the often messy and/or changing forms that real information tends to have in real organizations.

This is a similar situation to having a post office box; no matter where you move, your mail can still find its way to you via a simple, unchanging address. Virtual path addressing, which is handled by the server, permits flexible movement of content files and directories while keeping the original URL address. In fact, material can change host computers or even be distributed among several host computers while URLs can remain unchanged with appropriate configuration of the server.

2.6.3 The Hypertext Markup Language (HTML)

The first Web server and browser software application also introduced the *hypertext markup language*, HTML, as a universal, simple language for formatting, embedding of graphics, and *hypertextual* linking of documents. With HTML the menu becomes the document and vice versa.

Previous approaches to creating software that would allow users to share and browse information did not have the huge appeal of the Web; this was in part due to the wide variety of document types and the lack of means to associate components such as text, graphics, and images with each other. At first glance one might think: "Then yet another document type, HTML, is just what we didn't need!" But, as you will see, HTML presents a solution, not just another contribution, to the modern version of the curse of Babel. HTML is more than just a word processing file format; it is a *glue language*. That is, we can use language elements (specialized phrases) to build hypertextual links to other documents to loosely "glue" them together. Additional language elements allow us to glue other document types inside the displayed HTML document page. That is, we can refer to images within an HTML document, for example, in such a way that when the Web browser renders the document for display on the computer screen, the image will be displayed as requested within the flow of the text. It is worth noting that the ability to create hypertextual links, or *hyperlinks*, has provided an entirely new medium for the presentation and retrieval of information. Unlike traditional written documents, which are intended to be perused *linearly*, from beginning to end, hypertextual documents allow the reader to freely move around the document, following links to subjects of interest. If the document structure is well designed, this can facilitate users' ability to more directly access desired information, as they can customize the information flow according to their needs. The ability to create hyperlinks has also spawned new forms of literature, such as hyperfiction, in which readers follow hyperlinks to determine the flow of a narrative. Another important notion, that of *markup languages*, was also incorporated in HTML. This was derived from pioneering work that culminated in the creation of SGML (Standard Generalized Markup Language). SGML is a language that can be used to describe other languages that, in turn, describe documents. In fact, HTML is defined by an SGML description. The important notion that HTML inherited from this work is that a document structure can be defined in terms of appearance, without specific reference to the display device characteristics. This went to the heart of problems that had been previously encountered when people who did not share the same computer types, software types, display types, and so forth, tried to share documents.

For example, consider that I may write a document on a computer that presents the text screen in a format of 132 characters per line, with 80 lines per visible page, using 8 different font styles. You, on the other hand, may have a computer and display configured for at most 80 characters per line, 25 lines per page, and 3 font styles. These differences can make my document appear very disorganized and confusing on your computer; my longer lines may be chopped off or continued on the next line, in which case the alignment of tables, for example, is completely upset. In addition, important distinctions that I encoded using special fonts may be lost.

HTML provides a means to describe a document so that text and other document components are "reflowed" in an appropriate way to fit the display area. Furthermore, the user of the Web browser can configure options that connect a set of possible font types with the allowed display capabilities of her computer. Thus, given only two display fonts (as might be found on some older computers) such as normal and bold, we might choose to *map* normal fonts to our normal display font, and map all other fonts to our bold display. Thus, any form of emphasis, such as bold, italic, color, or large sizes would be displayed using the distinctive boldface font. It is this "reflow" capability that we see in action every time we use a Windows-based Web browser and change the size or shape of the window. The fact that the content remains unconfused over large variations of window sizes is due to the intelligent interpretation of the markup information in HTML.

2.6.4 Viewer Extensions

Web browser software incorporates *helper applications* and *plug-ins* that can be associated with particular file content types, so that the types of documents that a browser can display may be extended easily. Again, building upon existing protocols where possible, the Web browser uses the MIME protocol standard to describe file content type for proper interpretation by the browser.

📖 MIME

As was the case using MIME for support of multimedia e-mail, Web browsers may be supplied with a list of special programs, called *helper applications*, to invoke on encountering a given document type. For example, some documents are distributed in a format called *postscript.* Postscript was a language developed by the Adobe corporation to describe exactly how a printer should create a printed copy of that document. Wishing not to waste paper, we sometimes want to see a postscript-described document on our computer screen. Several software applications, called postscript viewers, are available to render a postscript document on our display. If we have such a viewer application on our computer, we can configure our Web browser to automatically call the application when encountering a hypertext link to a postscript-style document. Selecting this link will cause another window, in which the postscript viewer displays the document, to pop up on the screen.

A related capability of newer Web browsers is that of accepting a special kind of viewer known as a *plug-in.* As the name implies, a plug-in has a rather intimate relationship with the Web browser software. In some cases, this may simply mean that the content is displayed or played (in the case of audio and video content) more quickly than if another program had to be started. But in some cases, if a plug-in has been supplied for a particular content type, that content can be displayed as part of the Web page that referred to it. For example, a spreadsheet plug-in would allow us to see a spreadsheet within a text document, alongside the text and graphs that describe the spreadsheet's contents.

2.6.5 A Network of Distributed Servers

Probably the greatest innovation of the World Wide Web concept was that of a *loosely interconnected network* of independent content servers distributed throughout the world's Internet. Anyone with a computer connected to the Internet can run a Web server and thereby become a content distributor. That gives everyone the chance to be not only a writer, but also a publisher, media outlet, and network content provider. The fact that authors can fully control the content and access to their own publishing empire is behind the burgeoning success of the Web. There is great appeal to the idea of being able to publish one's own work and that of like-minded others without yielding editorial control and with virtually no space, content, or time limits.

Distributing the burden of content storage and content distribution across a large network of servers was also responsible for the rapid growth of the Web. Suppose that a government agency created a single system to provide capabilities like those of the Web, in which users must submit all material to the agency for distribution. This agency would then be faced with providing ever-increasing numbers of computers and amounts of disk storage space to cope with the storage and flow of information. Furthermore, network connections to this agency would become a bottleneck for the flow of data to all other parts of the world. In the final analysis, the agency would have to institute limits on personal use, and apply editorial discretion as to what content was actually worthwhile to add to the system.

Instead, with the World Wide Web, every computer can be a server. If we are using a professional Web server service and don't like the content space limits or other rules, we can buy a computer and put up our own Web site. When we run out of space, we can simply buy more disk space. With this system there is no single bottleneck, as the servers are as distributed as are the users. Of course, this freedom comes with certain social implications, as can be seen from the proliferation of objectionable material on the Web. Without debating the relative pros and cons of this type of civil liberty, we will merely summarize by noting that the personal freedom that the Web provides has been instrumental in its quick adoption by a wide audience.

2.7 The Success of the World Wide Web

It is not hyperbole to say that the World Wide Web constituted as much of a revolution in communications as did the telephone. Fundamentally, the Web provided a new capability that was seen as being both *useful* and *widely applicable*. In this portion of the chapter, we will discuss the factors that made the Web a success. As we've already discussed, a major factor is that the Web provided answers to problems associated with distributing varied types of information to largely unknown recipients. We summarize here some of these capabilities provided by the mechanisms of the Web:

1. The ability to access remote information instantly and conveniently;
2. The potential for every user to be a world wide publisher;
3. The ability to incorporate formatted text, images and, later, interactive components, permitting artistic expression. This was important in attracting widespread participation by individuals and by the commercial sector, which found the Web to be a ready-made canvas for high quality advertising;
4. Multimedia communications capability all channeled through a single device, your computer;
5. Hyperlinks that enable the user to pursue desired topics immediately without regard to location of the source material;
6. Powerful search capabilities to locate desired information anywhere on the Web; and
7. Flexibility and upgrade capability—the fact that different computer architectures running different operating systems can simply display the same information and be upgraded via various plug-ins to deal with new data types.

The success of a new concept, however, often requires more than innovation and a good set of capabilities. For example, when Wang Computer introduced the Wang 1200 word processor in 1971, they enjoyed a good measure of commercial success. But this success was soon dwarfed by sales of word processing software for PCs, a market established by the introduction of WordStar in 1979. WordStar introduced the notion of a word processor running on a low-cost, general-purpose PC that could also be used for spreadsheet computing, drawing, filing, and so forth. It was this low price-point (driven by sales to all PC owners rather than to a few specialized word processor owners) and flexibility that caused it to be propelled to killer application status, and eventually led to the commercial demise of Wang's innovative, but less flexible, word processor.

What were the keys to the success of the World Wide Web concept beyond the notion of useful capabilities as summarized above?

- The Web uses open (public and unprotected) specifications, and well-constructed and documented protocol standards; thus, a freely distributed sample implementation allowed rapid emulation, deployment, experimentation, and improvement;
- The Web coopted existing services (e.g., ftp, gopher, and telnet) by supporting their protocols within a new user-friendly context; and
- While it was believed by some industry pundits that the Web would die under the weight of its distributed nature ("no one in charge," "no obvious way to find anything"), the availability of advertising space (on a huge number of Web pages each of which drew the attention of people who had the resources needed to use the Web and hence probably more resources to spend) led to the funding of information search engines that made the Web work regardless of the number of participants.

2.8 The Structure of the Web

If anyone had conceived the Web in full prior to existence of the systems that we are about to describe, the idea would have been instantly shelved. The infrastructure upon which the Web is built is quite large and it involved the work of many researchers and businesses to construct it over a period of several decades.

As is shown in Figure 2.2, the Web is really a *system of systems*. Here is a very short and simplified list of the systems that make it possible.

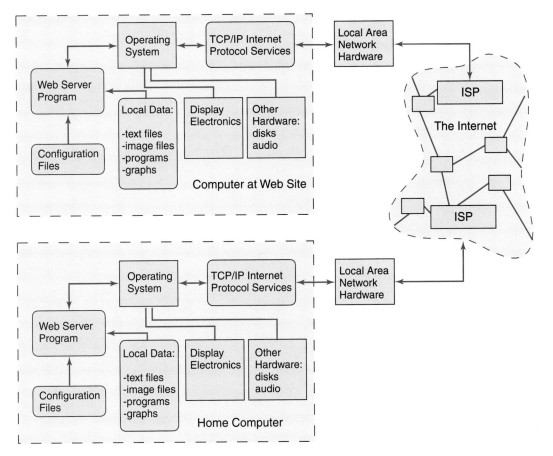

FIGURE 2.2 Some of the systems that make up the World Wide Web.

- Individual computers of many makes, models, generations, capabilities and using different and incompatible software operating systems[2] such as PCs, Macs, workstations, Web-TVs, Network Computers that host the client (Web browser) and server programs.

- Electronic document storage, sometimes just simple text files on disk, may include graphics, audio, video, and executable programs providing services such as databases.

- Means for capture or creation of sounds (such as audio recording equipment or music synthesis software), images (such as electronic cameras, software for drawing and painting), and video (such as digital video cameras, virtual reality modeling, rendering and animation software).

- A computer program called a *Web server*, which accepts requests for linked files and fulfills these requests by delivering the data stream back to the client browser.

---

[2] The personal computer market has so coalesced around the PC and operating system model provided by Microsoft and Intel that some users of computers are unaware that there is no universal computer architecture. But indeed, there are a wide variety of computers and operating systems in use, especially outside the household and business office, that are incapable of using software created for other computers and can only exchange information if special data conversion software is available, which is often not the case.

- A computer program called a *Web browser*, which displays files in the desired format, provides links to other files, and manages details such as indices and print requests.
- Local area networks (LANs) that are used to interconnect many computers within a room or within an entire company. These LANs provide a conduit for information to travel from one computer to the next within the LAN and a means for information to be delivered to and from a connection with an Internet Service Provider (ISP).
- Physical global communications links (based on wire and fiber optic based cables and the equipment that places information signals on one end and retrieves them from the other) supplied by telephone companies or companies specializing in delivery of computer data;
- Equipment and software creating organized collections of computer networks and global connections that allow information to be routed properly between the many ISPs and computers and are known collectively as the Internet;

These components are described rather informally here; the intent is to convey the general scope of this vast system. Explanations of the operation of many of these components will be expanded on later in this book after the essential background material has been discussed. The computer hardware and software that implements many of the above systems would not be possible without well-constructed and well-documented rules for their interactions. The precisely defined instructions for these operations are contained in a list of rules known as *protocols*. The majority of the documents that make up the Web are based on the HTML protocol. HTML is an excellent example of a communications standard; it specifies how to write a Web document, and how to name the files, so that all other Web-enabled computers can make use of the document to provide the features we have described. Examples of these protocols at work in the system of systems we have been discussing include.

- The MIME system of naming and organizing files so that file locations may be uniquely identified (Internet addresses, the domain name system, and URLs);
- The operation of LANs and ISPs, founded upon the availability of software that can execute on the connected computers that implement globally understood protocols for the transmission and reassembly of information (such as TCP/IP and HTTP);

Not all of these components are necessary to produce a functioning Web. For instance, a particular Web document may be accessed from the same computer on which the browser is executing, without any computer network involved at all. In technology-speak we say that the Web is highly *scalable*. That is, we can change the scale of implementation from a single computer being used to view text documents on a CD, to a system of millions of computers being used to exchange multimedia on an as-needed basis. The CD included with this book, for example, contains the text of this book in the form of a Web document that can be read using your own computer, with only the help of Web browser software and none of the other components mentioned above.

In general, the Web is becoming recognized as such a well-conceived format for information presentation that essentially every type of document and communications service has been or is being made Web-compatible through browser application viewers and plug-ins. Already, one can just as easily read e-mail or usenet news, place an Internet telephone call, listen to a radio station, or watch a news clip video via the Web as one can browse hypertext. In fact, the idea of the Web is so attractive as a standardized means for communicating that some see it as the ultimate interface between people and any machine or information system. Microsoft's Windows 98 operating system goes as far as replacing the special purpose human interface that had been evolving for their operating system with one that uses a Web browser as the primary connection between the user and the computer.

2.9 Technologies That Enhance the Power of the Web

The original purpose of the Web, as described above, was to provide easy, remote access to a wide variety of documents. However, success stimulates enhancements, and the Web is growing in capabilities far beyond its original function. Most of these enhancements are moving in the direction of making the Web *dynamic*, *active*, and *interactive*. We will define each of these attributes below and identify some examples of each that you may have already encountered while browsing the Web.

2.9.1 Dynamic, Active, and Interactive Web Pages

A dynamic Web page is distinguished from a static one in that there is no one unchanging document that you and others will obtain when your browser downloads a document from a certain URL. An example of a dynamic Web page would be one that provides a weather map with the most current radar image, temperature, winds, and weather observations for a given location. These dynamic Web pages are made possible through an early extension of the Web concept known as the *server side executable* or sometimes *server side script*. When your Web browser makes a request for the document associated with this URL across the Internet, the Web Server does not simply retrieve a document associated with that URL, but runs a software program that builds the document on the fly from current information and returns this newly constructed page to your browser. These server side programs may be so simple as to generate only a number that displays the total number of visitors to the Web site. Or, they may be so complex as to identify who you are relative to all past users of that Web site through the invisible exchange of small pieces of information (often called *cookies*) with your Web browser so that information tailored to your needs is delivered. An active Web page may take many forms, but the key concept is that it generates new information to be displayed at your computer using your computer's own resources. This is typically done with software known as a *client side executable* or *applet* (which is a word coined to describe a small application which needs the help of the browser to work). Typically, the Web server you contact sends a program to your computer instead of a document. Your Web browser then enlists the aid of your computer to run this program, which generates text, pictures, audio, and so forth, on the fly.

📖 **Applet**

An example of an active Web page is one that allows you to assemble a puzzle from many pieces by moving them about with your computer's pointing device (mouse, trackball, etc.). Because many people might simultaneously access this same Web page, it is obvious that they are not simply being sent the same document—they would be affecting each other's play. Rather, a puzzle program is simply downloaded (invisibly) to each of their computers. Despite the fact that the Web browser seemingly stays *tuned* to the same URL, from this point on, each user is playing with his or her own copy of the game and all computations are being done on their own computer.

The active Web page approach has several virtues:

- You can interact with the displayed information at much greater speeds than you could have if the program were located at the Web Server location. That is because your computer can react to your inputs nearly instantly. As you will see later in this book, it takes time for information to travel a given distance, and, if we are sharing the equipment and wiring of the Internet with millions of other users, this time delay can become quite large.

- If hundreds of users are interested in the same information, the server computer's computational resources are similarly divided. By downloading the program that generates the multimedia to your computer, the remotely located server offloads its responsibility for generating that content for your computer.

Finally, an interactive Web page is one that allows the user of the Web browser to send information back to the server (momentarily reversing their roles), which then acts upon or saves it in some way. The most common example of interactivity is found in Web pages with forms. (This functionality is typically provided by means of a protocol that is known as the Common Gateway Interface, or CGI protocol.) For example, if you have ever purchased an item via a Web page, you will have filled out a form with your name, address, credit card number, and other information vital to your purchase. The information in this form is sent back to the server where it is analyzed by a server side program for completeness, possibly saved in an order database, and an appropriate response is generated and sent to your browser for display.

FIGURE 2.3 Some of the elements that provide the services and data that are delivered by a Web server.

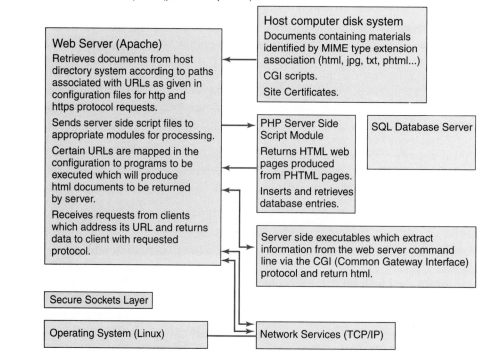

Client Host Computer

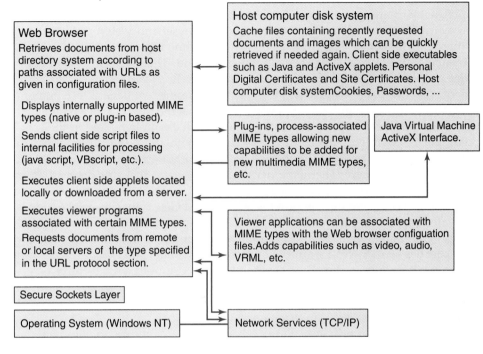

FIGURE 2.4 Some of the elements that provide the services and data that are delivered by a Web browser.

Figures 2.3 and 2.4 outline some of the elements in Web servers and Web clients that provide the static, dynamic, active and interactive Web services. These diagrams illustrate the fact that the client (browser) and server systems, which comprise the end points of the Web, are themselves systems built from smaller independent systems; that is, systems of systems.

2.9.2 Java and the Web

In the previous subsection we discussed advantages of active Web pages that download programs that are then executed on your computer. But earlier in this chapter we remarked on the general incompatibility of computers and operating systems. While it would be possible for a given Web page to provide multiple hyperlinks to follow depending upon your system's software requirements, it is highly unlikely. That is, the effort to create software specifically suited to each possible *computer platform* would be so prohibitive that all but the largest of companies would simply forego the use of active pages.

A great boon to the concept of the active page was the development of a computer language and computer platform technology known as Java. Java was announced by Sun Microsystems at the SunWorld '95 conference in May 1995. The initial idea that had grown into Java with Sun Microsystems was that a new kind of programming language and system technology was needed if the many pieces of electronics in a home or business were to be someday interconnected for the purposes of sharing information and central control. That is, if we ever expected to be able to call our VCR on the phone and program it with our cellular telephone's keypad, these devices would have to have an entire infrastructure and design philosophy in common. Java technology was intended to provide just such a framework and related system construction tools.

Over the course of the development of the Java-related technologies it was realized that Java also provided means to make active Web documents easy to build and distribute. Thus, Netscape, the largest Web browser and Web server provider at that time, announced their adoption of Java technology into their systems on the same day its availability was announced by Sun. The usual process of computer programming involves someone (or more likely a team) writing a description of what the computer is to do in some programming language. These human-readable computer languages are constructed so that the programmer is shielded from knowing the details of how many actions will be implemented in the computer, but is provided sufficient expressive power to allow the programmer to get the machine to do exactly what he or she wants. The resulting description is known as *source code*. The name derives from the fact that this description is the ultimate source of the instructions (code) that the computer will follow, but is not the actual code that the computer will be shown. Generally, this source code is translated by another program, constructed for this purpose and aimed at a particular programming language and a particular computer architecture, into *machine code*, which is actually read by the computer (the machine) and *executed*. If a given program needs to be executed on several different computer architectures (say a PC using the Windows 98 operating system and an iMac from Apple Computer) then the same source code would have to undergo translation (this step is called compilation) into two different machine codes.

Java was meant to provide, among other attributes, a means to eliminate the need to know the ultimate destination of our program. That is, the intention was to translate the source code into a form that could be transported to any computer and be executed. Java revived an old notion, connected with a programming language and compilation system known as UCSD Pascal and the P-code system developed in the late 1970s by Kenneth Bowles. The idea is not to compile source code to target a specific computer, but to compile it for use with no real computer! A program written with the Java language is generally converted into executable software for the *Java Virtual Machine* (JVM), a *simulated* computer that can be simulated on any other computer platform. How can JVM programs be executed on diverse machines? As the name implies, the Java Virtual Machine is a software implementation of an entire and different computing platform than any one of the other popular computers. Java programs utilize the *virtual* hardware and its own operating system to conduct their business. The execution of the programs is handled by a JVM interpreter, a program now built into most Web browsers. The JVM interpreter simulates this new computer platform inside your own. Hence, the original author of the software needs to know nothing about your computer.

What does this mean to the user? From the user's perspective, Java permits a vast expansion of Web capabilities, changing the Web from an information retrieval mechanism to a complete computational environment. For example, rather than buying and installing a computer application such as a word processor (or game) on your home computer, with Java you can with a few clicks (and perhaps some payment to the provider) run the latest version on your machine.

Downloadable programs that run within the context of your Web browser are referred to as "Java Applets." This textbook's CD has an assortment of Java Applets that can be executed with a Web browser that provide a virtual laboratory experience to illustrate certain key concepts in this book. Thanks to Java technology, it does not matter whether you are using a Microsoft/Intel platform computer, an Apple iMac or a Linux-based workstation.

Summary

Perhaps the best way to summarize the significant aspects of the World Wide Web is to list its major characteristics and the problems that it solves:

- The Web provides information access in ways that were not previously possible, or were very inconvenient. This includes access to various forms of pictorial and other nontext information, information that changes rapidly, and information from a variety of sources.
- The Web combines the best attributes of a library (large store of indexed information) with immediate access, with multi-user access to the same information at the same time (try that with a book!).
- The Web does *not* require any new or dedicated facilities. Rather, it simply needs the appropriate computer programs (servers and browsers) to access the existing information and transmit it over the existing data communications facilities.
- While the Web was conceived primarily as a one-way (information access) medium, it has rapidly evolved into a two-way communications medium.
- The Web is quite user-friendly, hiding most of the complexities behind a pictorial user interface. The only interface most users need is a Web address, which often very easy to remember, something like www.vacation.edu, for example.
- The Web is also author-friendly. With the help of software tools (often as extensions to standard word processing or presentation graphics programs), it is straightforward to publish material on the Web. Commercial organizations (ISPs) are readily available to provide the necessary servers.

Try These Exercises

1. Describe succinctly and in your own words how the World Wide Web originated.
2. The Web is said to be *distributed*; explain what this term means, and what the implications are for users.
3. In what ways is a URL more powerful and flexible than other types of addresses?
4. Go to your favorite location on the Web, and make note of the URL. Then, break the URL down into its individual components, and explain the role or meaning of each part.
5. Explain the difference between a Web client and a Web server. Which basic role does each play? Are there any roles which they both can play?
6. Locate examples of Web pages that feature static, dynamic, active and interactive content. Describe how each such page is an example of one of these content types.
7. Using a Web search engine, find and outline a history of the development of Java.
8. Has any company produced a non-virtual Java machine that directly executes JVM machine code without simulation? If so: from whom is it available and what are the proposed applications of it?
9. The Web is not without its political intrigue: Write a summary of information you locate on the Web that describes the legal action taken by Sun Microsystems against Microsoft, and subsequent rulings, regarding Sun's licensing of

the Java language. What were the provisions of the license that they felt were not being respected and why were these provisions put in place?

10. Describe some of the limitations of basic HTML, and list some useful features which are not provided by it. Explain why it may be difficult to provide these features. Now describe newer or extended versions of HTML and some of the features provided.

11. Explain in your own words why Java code cannot run directly on a computer, but needs the concept of a "virtual machine."

Fundamentals of Binary Representation

This is the long distance call. . .

Paul Simon, "The Boy in the Bubble," Graceland

The only reason that we can use the Internet and the Web as a conduit for text and pictures today, soon telephone conversations, and someday our regular TV viewing, is that we can convert all these forms of information into the same form: binary bits. This part of the book addresses the question: just what are bits and why are they so powerful? The treatment in this part should help you to recognize how we convert voices in a telephone conversation into the same stuff that percolates between computers on the Internet. It is this universality of bits as a medium that will make the total integration of telephone, Web and all other information services possible.

This part should also remove some of the mystery from the word "bit" and the concept of "digital." In fact, you will see that representing something like a fancy font in your word processor is just a matter of human agreement about the implied meanings of the otherwise lifeless marks on paper, or the blips of light we call bits.

3 Representing Information in Bits

Objectives

In Chapter 1 the idea of digital information was introduced briefly. As this is the basis for almost all modern information systems, in this chapter we explain:

▲ the fact that the same information may be represented in many different ways, by a variety of physical or logical elements;

▲ the concept of a "code" for information, with examples such as the Roman alphabet and the Chinese character set;

▲ the binary number system and the means by which all information can be represented by codes containing only zeroes and ones;

▲ specific examples of the representation of numeric and text data with binary digits (bits);

▲ the properties of signals that vary with time, such as sound, and of image signals that require two-dimensional representation; and

▲ the means by which errors in stored or transmitted information may be detected and corrected.

3.1 Introduction

In this chapter we will discuss how information can be represented in binary form—that is, by using a code containing only two distinct symbols, called bits. We will also explain why this binary code is a convenient and appropriate choice for representing information. In particular, we will show how it facilitates the use of inexpensive and reliable equipment for information storage, processing, and transmission. We will also discuss how binary representation of information directly leads to a method for quantifying how much information is present.

We will then present some familiar examples of information—numbers, text, music, and images—and introduce the notion (and some of the details) of representing these in binary form. We'll discuss some simple examples of protocols, which are commonly agreed upon rules for using these binary codes. We'll talk about convenient ways of packaging and referring to large amounts of binary information. Finally, we'll introduce the idea that binary information lends itself directly to systems that can detect and even correct their own errors.

By the end of this chapter, you should have an understanding of how and why we use binary digits (**bin**ary dig**its**) to represent information, regardless of its original form. Through the examples presented, you should learn about the idea of a protocol, and become familiar with the details of a few simple binary protocols.

You'll also become familiar with some of the terminology and quantities used to refer to binary information.

3.2 Information and Its Representation

Since mankind's earliest efforts to record events, there has existed the need for representing information. Human progress in this endeavor can be traced from cave drawings and stone tablets, through scrolls and Gutenberg's revolutionary printing press, and into our current age of electronic information technology. Each age has, in turn, seen the development of new means for representing information in useful ways.

Certainly, we frequently encounter information or data that is meaningful to us; this information may be based on observations or measurements of our surroundings, or it may be something of our own creation. Whatever form it takes, we often wish to store this data for future use, or to manipulate it into a more useful form, or perhaps to transmit it to a distant location for use or storage there.

Before we can do any of these things, we must first capture this information; we must convert it into some representation that will facilitate our tasks. Useful information and interesting data, however, appear to us in many different forms. Some of these are inherently numerical: the amount of money in a checking account, the score of a baseball game, the time at which dinner will be served. Information can also take on other forms, such as voice messages, pieces of music, photographs, and video; these are less obviously quantitative or numerical.

To capture information for such purposes as storage, manipulation, or transmission, we require a process of encoding the information. The result of this encoding will be a pattern, or *code*, representing the original information. We will also require a process of decoding to convert the information back into its original form—music, images, or anything else. This encoding and decoding process should be *unique*; that is, each code must represent one and only one thing, so that information can be represented unambiguously and recreated accurately. We seek some standard means for representing information, so that we might be able to use the same information storage, manipulation, and transmission systems to handle them. Of course, we want these systems to be affordable and reliable. Thus, whatever form we convert our information into must be well suited to the development of inexpensive and reliable equipment for handling it.

In this chapter, we will describe a technique for representing information, keeping in mind the requirements we have just specified:

- the technique must allow us to *uniquely* represent information and to recreate it in its original form;
- the technique must be *standardized* so that it can be used for many different applications: numerical data, text, audio, still and moving images, and more; and
- the technique must be *compatible* with inexpensive and reliable technology for handling the information.

3.3 The Search for an Appropriate Code

In our search for an appropriate code for representing information, we will start by restricting ourselves to codes with a finite number of basic elements, called an *alphabet*. Such codes have a limited number of different symbols that can be used to represent information. This, as we will see, leads to reliable means for storage and transmission of the symbols. But how many different symbols should the code have? We can gain some insight by looking at some familiar codes.

3.3.1 A Look at Written Alphabets

The alphabet used for the written English language is commonly thought to contain about 96 elements (26 lower case characters, 26 upper case characters, 10 numbers, and 32 special characters, such as a space or a dollar sign). We use this code daily to represent information for purposes of storage (in books and other documents) and transmission (in the form of letters and e-mail, for example). How "good" is this code for representing information?

It might appear, at first glance, that we could develop a more useful and powerful code by using more elements than just 96. An example of such an alphabet would be the Mandarin profile of the Chinese. The system was developed over 4,000 years ago. It uses a set of logographs (characters) of several types: pictographs, ideographs, compound ideographs, loan characters, and phonetic compounds. The latter forms over 90 percent of the total set of as many as 40,000 characters.[1] Certainly this is a "powerful" code; one complex character can convey an entire concept to the skilled reader. Because there are many different symbols, each one conveys much information (Figure 3.1). Therefore, fewer characters are needed to communicate a set of ideas than if we were to use the letters of written English.

However, this written form of Chinese is thought of as one of the most "difficult" written languages to use. Because there are so many characters, some quite similar to others, the task of distinguishing one from another is very challenging. On the other hand, it is a relatively simple task to distinguish the comparatively few symbols of the English language from each other. English letters are fewer in number, and therefore each one *conveys less information* than a Chinese character. But this also makes English letters *simpler to distinguish from one another*, and thus, less likely to cause misinterpretation.

3.3.2 The Need for a Robust Scheme

In the design of our code, we must consider the question of which is more important to us: that each symbol of the code convey a lot of information, or that we be able to readily distinguish the symbols from each other. The answer lies in our requirement, discussed earlier, for an information code that is compatible with inexpensive and reliable equipment for handling it.

As we will see, reliable manipulation of information depends upon *tolerance to errors*. Because we must encode, store, manipulate, transmit, and decode information using real equipment, operating in the physical world, we will be subject to the laws of nature. Our equipment will not operate perfectly, and will be subject to unpredictable disturbances (for example, improperly formed characters due to a smear in the printing process). Accordingly, our information code must represent

FIGURE 3.1 Chinese characters and their English translation.

Chinese :

English :   assemble, meet together; meeting   good, excellent, fine; well   learning, knowledge, school

---

[1] Li, C. and S. A. Thompson. 1987. "Chinese." In B. Comrie, ed., *The World's Major Languages*, pp. 811–833. New York: Oxford University Press.

information in a way that is *robust*, or tolerant to errors. Because our purpose is to represent information reliably and to be able to recreate it correctly later, both in an imperfect world, we will place a premium on robustness.

For a code to allow us to represent information in an error-resistant, unambiguous fashion, it would appear that we want as few different symbols as possible. The fewer symbols the code has, the easier it is to distinguish the symbols from each other, and the more robust the code will be. A code with just one symbol, however, would convey no useful information; only one character would be available, and there would be no unique way to encode and decode information using this code.

A code with just two symbols, called a *binary code*, might at first seem to be almost as useless. Certainly, it should be a simple task to distinguish between only two characters. But it would seem as if each symbol would not be able to convey much information. What good is a code that can only convey one of two symbols at any time? The answer to this question will, more or less, extend over the rest of this book!

3.4 Bits as Building Blocks of Information

Consider, then, a code with only two symbols in its alphabet. We can give those symbols any names we want, and represent them in any way we choose. The names we give them will not alter the fact that there are just two symbols; their essence is that they are different from one another. A common way of representing the two different symbols in a binary code is by using the first two integers, "0" and "1." Another common way to represent them is by "T" and "F," short for "true" and "false," respectively. The latter scheme emphasizes that these are the only two choices and that they can be considered opposites of each other. It also reveals that one of these symbols can be used to give the answer to a single, unambiguous, true-or-false question.

3.4.1 The Representational Power of Bits

How much information can we convey with one binary symbol? We can convey the answer to a single true/false question. However, for many reasons (most of them mathematical), it is more common to represent the symbols of a binary code by the digits 0 and 1. Indeed, because these are **bi**nary dig**its** (digits that can only take on one of two values), they are known as *bits*.

📖 Bits

One bit, clearly, has its limitations; but so, for that matter, does one letter from the English alphabet. What happens when we begin to string together collections of these bits into longer structures, or *words*? A two-bit word can be arranged in any of four patterns: 00, 01, 10, or 11. Thus, by using two bits (or equivalently, by answering two true/false questions) we can represent any one of four different things.

We could therefore (by prior agreement between the transmitter and receiver) use a pattern of two bits to represent any one of the four directions:

- 00: North
- 01: South
- 10: East
- 11: West

and we could transmit the bit pattern "10" to represent the direction "East," if we wanted to send someone in that direction. Note that the recipient of this message

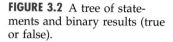

FIGURE 3.2 A tree of statements and binary results (true or false).

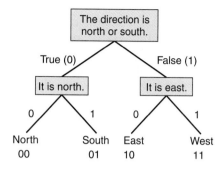

would need to know how we encoded this message so that the message could be decoded into "East." Figure 3.2 illustrates the situation using a *binary tree*. The statements in the boxes result in one of two answers (represented by a bit) and after two such statements, one can conclude which direction was being discussed.

Adding a third bit increases the representational power of our bit string to one of eight patterns: 000, 001, 010, 011, 100, 101, 110, and 111. We could use one of these three-bit words to represent any of Santa's eight reindeer (not including Rudolph). Indeed, every time we add a bit, we double the number of possible combinations, and so we double the number of different things these multibit codes, or *codewords*, could be used to represent. This can be seen from the fact that each existing code-word can be changed into two new codewords by adding another bit—either a 0 or a 1—to the end of it. Because each additional bit doubles our representational power, we can determine the number of possible patterns for a binary codeword of any length. Four bits can be used to represent $2 \times 2 \times 2 \times 2 = 2^4 = 16$ different messages. In general, if we have n bits in the codeword, then there are 2^n different codewords, which can represent one of 2^n different messages. For example, 8 bits can be assembled in $2^8 = 256$ different patterns, and thus can represent any one of 256 different messages.

Another way of looking at this is that if we want to be able to represent any one of 256 different messages by a binary word, we require a wordlength of 8 bits. In general, if we have 2^n messages, we require n bits for representation. This gives us some insight into how much *information* is contained in one of those messages. Each bit can be considered one piece of information, and the number of bits required for the code tells us how much information the message could convey. The reason we say that this is how much information the message *could* convey is that the message will not always live up to this potential; for example, if the message contains a lot of redundancy, then the information content will be less than the number of bits used to transmit it. The field of mathematics known as *information theory* can be used to quantify precisely, in units of bits, how much information is contained in a message. We will not need to go into a mathematical treatment here, except to note that the relationship between the representational power of a string of bits and the length of a string is exponential: n bits can represent any one of 2^n different messages.

3.4.2 Bits in the Physical World

Our primary motivation for using binary digits, or bits, was to create a representation that would be immune to errors. This immunity must extend to every aspect of the system—storage, transmission, and processing—for the entire system to be reliable. A look at some familiar technologies for handling information reveals that a binary code is well suited to practical equipment.

Storage Equipment   One of our goals is *storage* of information. To store binary data, we require only that our storage medium be capable of representing two different states. A common example is a magnetic disk, which has many small areas, called *domains*, each of which can store a single bit of information. Each domain can be magnetized in one of two directions—"up" or "down"—corresponding to whether the bit to be stored is a 0 or a 1. A magnetic device can be used to detect in which of the two directions each domain is magnetized, and thus retrieve the information from the disk.

Another common example is the compact laser disk. Whether it is used to store music or computer data, a CD consists of many tiny domains, each of which stores one bit of information. In each domain, there is either a smooth surface, which will reflect a laser, or a pit, which will not. The pattern of pits and smooth areas is used to encode the desired pattern of bits. A laser is used to "read" the pattern of smooth and pitted domains. Thus, the system operates as a binary information storage and retrieval system.

Now, both of these types of media could conceivably be used to store information using a code with more than two symbols. For example, the magnetic disk domains could be magnetized to different strengths. In this case, each domain could take on more different possible values; thus, each domain would store more information. Similarly, it is conceivable that the surface of a laser disk could be encoded with different levels of reflectivity. But equipment for these schemes would be difficult to design and complex to build, and therefore expensive and/or unreliable to use. Consider, for example, a CD system that uses three symbols, represented by domains of zero, partial, and high reflectivity. A fingerprint would now cause an error more readily, by making a highly reflective domain appear to be a partially reflective domain. To further complicate the situation, this case would be more likely to happen than the same fingerprint causing a partially reflective domain appear to be a zero reflective domain; thus, we would need a more complex decoding and error detection scheme. Because we need only detect one of two symbols using the conventional binary CD system, the system is comparatively simple and reliable. Other storage media are similarly well suited to storage of binary information.

Transmission Equipment: Another of our information-handling tasks is *transmission* of the information. An information transmission system, at its simplest, consists of a *transmitter*, a *channel* over which the information travels, and a *receiver* at the destination. A diagram representing this simple system description is shown in Figure 3.3. Common examples of transmission channels are wires, electrical cables, optical fibers, and even the air in the case of information broad-

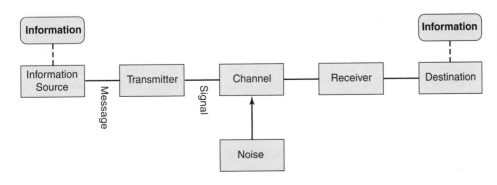

FIGURE 3.3 The generic components of an information transmission system.

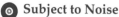
Subject to Noise

cast in the form of radio waves. The goal of this system is for information to be transferred, without loss or modification, from the transmitter to the receiver.

Unfortunately, the channel of an information transmission system typically is subject to *noise*, or unwanted and unpredictable interference from external sources. This may come from other information systems, or from natural sources such as lightning or radiation. We usually have no direct control over the channel environment, but must do the best we can with an imperfect channel. Figure 3.3 shows the effects of noise from the channel; in reality noise can be a problem throughout the whole system.

This noise, which cannot be completely avoided, tends to distort our information. Consider a page of printed text in a book. A reader can retrieve most (or all) or the information from the message conveyed by the printed text. If though, by some mistake in the printing process, another page (different from the first) was printed over the original text, the reader may not be able to (easily) read the entire page. The "noise" in this case is the second printed page, which distorts (or completely destroys) the information contained in the original page.

The physical channel itself is also an imperfect thing. Transmissions sent over long distances become weaker and weaker as they travel far from the source (as do audio transmissions such as the the spoken word over long distances). This is also unavoidable, and is due to the fact that physical wires, cables, and other channels are not perfect media for transmitting information.

Because of all of these problems, the receiver is faced with the difficult task of interpreting a received message that is likely to have been distorted or corrupted during transmission. As anyone who has listened to AM radio knows, the result can be less than satisfactory. This problem, however, is greatly alleviated when the information is in binary form. In a binary system, the receiver must simply interpret each received symbol as a "0" or a "1." That is, it does not matter whether a binary message has been distorted, as long as the receiver can still distinguish the message "0" from the message "1." In this sense, the system is *immune* to moderate amounts of noise or disturbance. We should note that literal "1"s and "0"s are not actually transmitted. Rather, two physical or electrical quantities, one representing a "1" and one representing a "0," are actually transmitted. Later chapters will provide more details on how this is done.

Of course, this would also be the case for any code with a finite number of symbols; the important task is to decide which symbol was sent. But, as we have seen in the comparison of the English language with the Chinese language, it is easier to distinguish symbols from a code with a short alphabet than it is to distinguish symbols from a code with a lengthy alphabet. In many important situations, binary codes, because they have the fewest number of symbols of any useful code, provide the maximum amount of noise immunity of any code. Thus, our information transmission is more reliable when encoded in this fashion. A special case of an information transmission medium is the fiber optic cable. Information is sent down the cable in the form of pulses of light, which reflect off the inside of the cable and propagate along its length from one end to the other. Due to the unpredictable way in which this light's strength will vary along the length of a fiber optic cable, the only practical way to send information with light is in a binary fashion: the light is *either on or off*. The information bits are "encoded" into a pattern of light and darkness, and the optical receiver need only distinguish light from dark.

Processing Equipment   Another important task in many information systems is *processing* of the information. This processing may be intended to modify the actual information content, just as an editor modifies the content of a document. Or, the processing may be intended to "repackage" the information in a form more suitable to transmission or storage. In any event, the most suitable mechanism for processing binary information is electronic circuitry, usually in the form of a computer. The circuits in a computer that process information are comprised of devices which, like the rest of our equipment, can introduce noise and unwanted distortion to the messages they process. However, every component of information in a computer system—from the commands that operate the computer itself to the information which the computer processes—is in binary form, so as to be resilient to noise and distortion.

Computer circuits, however complex, can be broken down into simpler and simpler subcircuits until we reach the fundamental building block from which the entire computer is made. This building block is the electronic switch. The electronic switch is a circuit designed always to be in one of two states: *ON* or *OFF*. These states are similar to the two positions of a physical switch.

When we use a computer to process information, the information is in binary form at every point of the process, from input to output. We can determine how the computer will process the binary information by programming the computer, thereby determining the states of its electronic switches. These switches route and modify the information according to the instructions that have been programmed in—also in binary form!

Computers, of course, are composed of an enormous amount of switches, operating at very high speeds. The complexity of a modern computer processor, and the speed at which it operates, easily can obscure the fact that it is only doing one thing—distinguishing "0" from "1"—at a very rapid speed, and with a complex and carefully designed network of binary switches. Because the basic component of the computer is the simple, reliable, inexpensive, and robust electronic switch, it is possible for complex, high-speed operations. This *high-level* complexity is made possible by the simplicity and reliability of its *low-level* operations.

3.4.3 From Numbers to Bits

Integer Formats   Now that we have established that bits might be used to represent information, we can discuss some of the standard techniques, or *formats*, which are commonly employed to do so. First, we will take a look at integers.

Representation of integers is a fairly straightforward task with binary words. We have seen that the word length of a binary word determines how many different things the word can represent: an n-bit word can represent 2^n different things. So, if we know how many integers we need to represent, we can set an appropriate word length.

Because $2^{16} = 65,536$, we could represent each of the integers from 1 to 65,536 (or 0 to 65,535) by using a different 16-bit word. If, on the other hand, we are interested in representing both positive and negative integers, we see that we could use these same 16 bits to represent the integers between $-32,768$ and 32,767 (including zero). The manner in which we do this depends on the format being used. One type of format uses a single bit (the first or last, usually) to indicate whether the integer is positive or negative, and the rest of the bits to represent the integer's magnitude. Other formats are less direct, but make internal computer arithmetic easier to accomplish.

Once again, we see the role of prior agreement between the communicating parties. In the case of integer formats, both the transmitter and receiver must agree to the number of bits used to represent an integer. Establishing this agreement

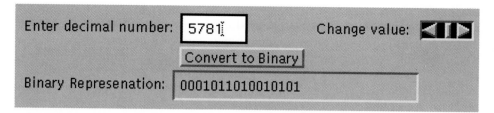

FIGURE 3.4 A decimal integer to binary conversion applet.

FIGURE 3.5 A binary to decimal integer applet.

Binary to Decimal Integer Conversion

is like agreeing upon whether shaking one's head means "yes" or "no" before undertaking a dangerous activity.

Figure 3.4 depicts a screen shot of a decimal integer to binary conversion "applet." Similarly, Figure 3.5 shows a screen shot of a binary to decimal integer conversion applet. These applets can be used to make sure that you understand how the conversions are made. Both applets are included on the CD-ROM included in the distribution of this textbook.

If we are interested in representing much larger integers, we can use binary words to represent the integers using *scientific notation*, just as we might do with paper and pencil. For example, consider the integer 62,000,000,000,000,000; we would require a very long word length (56 bits, as it turns out) to represent this number using the scheme described above. But instead we can use scientific notation to write this number as 62×10^{15}, and then use the two numbers 62 and 15 to represent the large integer. Even though we must store these two numbers separately, together they can be represented by a smaller number of bits than would be required for the method described earlier. For our example, the numbers 62 and 15 could be stored using 6 and 4 bits respectively, for a total of 10 bits. As this simple example shows, use of scientific notation can result in a much more compact form of representation for large integers.

BCD Representation   Of course, use of these formats requires that we know what range of integers we are interested in representing! An alternative representation of integers is simply to represent the individual numerals that comprise them. This approach is consistent with the way in which we represent numbers ourselves. A number, after all, is an abstract concept. When we write the number 749, we are choosing to represent this number as three numerals: 7 (representing 700), 4 (representing 40), and 9 (representing 9). So, we could convert this number to a binary form by converting each of the numerals, one at a time, into a binary code. Such a scheme is referred to as *binary coded decimal* form, or *BCD*. If we wish to represent the 10 Arabic numerals 0, 1, 2, 3, 4, 5, 6, 7, 8, and 9, then we see that 3 bits, which can represent $2^3 = 8$ different things, are not enough. We instead must use 4 bits, even though this is "wasteful" in the sense that we will only be using 10 of the possible 16 patterns. The BCD codes commonly used to represent numerals are:

Numeral	BCD Representation
0	0000
1	0001
2	0010
3	0011
4	0100
5	0101
6	0110
7	0111
8	1000
9	1001

Using this scheme, we can represent any integer by a string of binary digits. For example, we can represent 749 as:

$$0111 \quad 0100 \quad 1001,$$

where spaces have been inserted only for convenience. The actual BCD representation of 749 would consist of only zeros and ones.

3.4.4 Representing Text with Bits

In the above discussion of BCD format, we discussed how binary codes can be used to represent the numerals 0 through 9. A similar approach, called *ASCII*, is commonly employed to represent text.

ASCII, pronounced "ask-key," is an acronym for *American Standard Code for Information Interchange*. ASCII is used to encode text, and in particular is useful for representing information which is entered via a computer keyboard. Therefore, ASCII must be able to represent:

▪ ASCII

- numerals;
- letters in both upper and lower cases;
- special "printing" symbols such as @, $, *, &, and %; and
- commands that are commonly used by computers to represent carriage returns, line feeds, and other text-formatting directives.

Commands in the last category of keyboard input are referred to as *control characters*; these characters can be generated from a keyboard by invoking functions such as "backspace" or "enter," or they can be created by special-purpose keys such as "control," "escape," or numbered "function" keys.

The need for a code to represent all of these components of text motivated the development of ASCII and other similar codes. When ASCII was developed, the decision was made that 128 different characters would suffice for representation of text. Because $2^7 = 128$, this means that each text character or command is represented by a 7-bit word. A complete list of ASCII characters is given in Appendix A. For example, the following piece of text, consisting of four letters, two spaces, an ampersand, and a comma:

You & I,

would be represented in ASCII by the 56-bit sequence:

1011001 1101111 1110101 0100000 0100110 0100000 1001001 0101100,

where again, spaces have been added to the string for convenience, but are not part of the binary stream.

This code contains a pattern of 7 bits for each of the 8 characters (including two spaces and a comma) in the piece of text. We will soon discuss a more convenient form for writing and viewing this ASCII code.

Figure 3.6 shows a screen shot of an alphanumeric string conversion applet. This utility is used to convert a text string to its ASCII equivalent in several different formats (7- and 8-bit binary, decimal, and hexadecimal). The applet is included on the CD-ROM included in the distribution of this textbook.

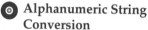

Alphanumeric String Conversion

3.4.5 Binary Representation of More Complex Information

Representing Real Numbers—Precision and Accuracy When we first discussed the need for a convenient form for representing information, we agreed that it would be desirable for any type of information to be represented in this form. We have seen how binary code can be used to represent integers and text, but we have not discussed such types of information as real (noninteger) numbers, functions of time such as music and speech signals, or still and time-varying images. The question now is: Can we use bits to represent more general types of information? The answer to this question, from a practical standpoint, is yes, even though it may not seem so at first.

Real Numbers Consider the problem of trying to record a temperature measurement. The temperature we are measuring can take on any value between, say, 60 and 70 degrees Fahrenheit. There is an infinite number of possible different temperature readings in this range; the temperature, in degrees, is a "real" number and not an integer or other subset. Thus, if we want to use a string of binary digits (a bit word) to perfectly represent this temperature, we need a bit word that can represent an infinite number of different things. Such a word would require an infinite number of bits!

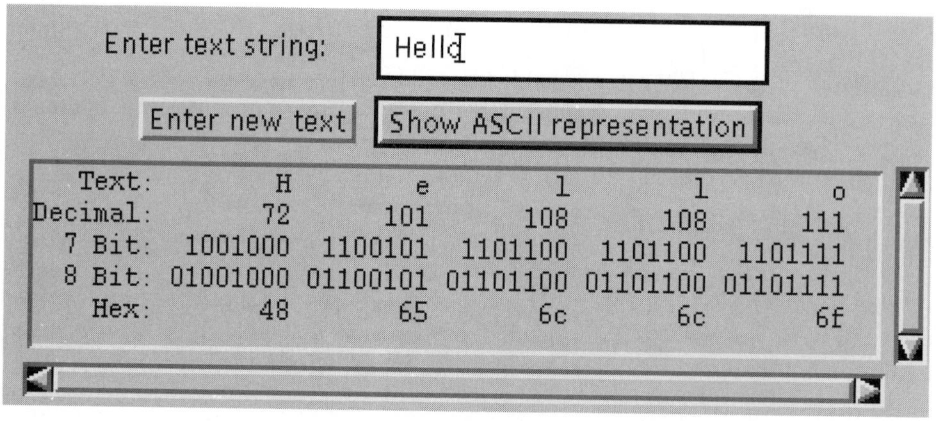

```
    Enter text string:    Helld

         Enter new text   Show ASCII representation

    Text:          H         e         l         l         o
  Decimal:        72       101       108       108       111
   7 Bit:   1001000   1100101   1101100   1101100   1101111
   8 Bit:  01001000  01100101  01101100  01101100  01101111
     Hex:        48        65        6c        6c        6f
```

FIGURE 3.6 An alphanumeric string conversion applet.

We can neither generate, store, nor transmit an infinite bit stream. However, we can use a finite-length stream of bits to provide an approximation to the actual temperature value. Furthermore, we can determine the *precision* with which we will represent the temperature by using the appropriate number of bits. We have already seen that an 8-bit word can take on $2^8 = 256$ different values, and a 16-bit word can take on $2^{16} = 65,536$ different values. So, if we use an 8-bit word to represent this temperature, we can represent 256 different temperatures between 60 and 70 degrees. These temperatures which we can represent are separated by

$$\frac{70 - 60}{256} = 0.039°.$$

Thus, we could use the 8-bit word to encode the following values:

Binary Codeword	Temperature, ° F
0000 0000	60.000
0000 0001	60.039
0000 0010	60.078
0000 0011	60.117
.	.
.	.
.	.
1111 1101	69.883
1111 1110	69.922
1111 1111	69.961

We then would round our temperature measurement to the nearest value on this table, and store the rounded value in the form of its corresponding binary codeword. If this precision is not sufficient for our purposes, then we can use more bits. For example, if we were to use 16 bits, the temperatures represented by the binary codes would differ by

$$\frac{70 - 60}{65,536} = 0.00015°.$$

However, it is important to balance a desire for *precision* with an appreciation of how it differs from our need for *accuracy*. Precision is a measure of *how much data we have*; accuracy is a measure of *how valid or correct that data is*. In the above example, it is unlikely that a typical temperature measurement system can measure temperatures accurately enough to make more than 8 bits necessary for representation. Furthermore, it is also unlikely that we need to know a temperature to the nearest thousandth of a degree Fahrenheit.

From this example, we see that limitations on our ability to acquire information accurately, and limits on our need for accuracy, will typically determine what level of precision is appropriate for a binary representation. Because we can never make a perfectly accurate measurement, we will never need to use infinite precision to represent the measurements! Furthermore, we would have no way of benefiting from such precision in any practical application. Thus, for all applications of practical interest, we can represent any quantity—that is, any real number—with a finite-length binary codeword. The number of bits we use is determined by our need for precision, which is related to the accuracy with which we collect and use the information in the real world. In practice, the form in which real numbers are

Floating-Point Representation

usually stored and processed by digital computers is called *floating-point* representation. This representation is based on the idea of scientific notation presented earlier. It allows the representation of very large and very small numbers in an efficient fashion, and it is also compatible with special-purpose hardware for performing calculations, which makes processing these real numbers more efficient as well.

We will not go into the details of floating-point representation in this textbook, except to make the point that, as with the temperature example above, the result is a system that allows real numbers over some range to be represented to a particular level of precision which is known to the user of the computer. This standardized way of representing real numbers is motivated by the need for efficient storage and processing of real numbers.

Functions of Time   Another type of information we often wish to capture, store, process, or transmit is time-varying information; many information sources vary as a *function of time*. Consider again our previous example of temperature. The temperature in some location changes with time; at every moment in time, we can record the temperature and use some graph to visually represent the changes.

In Figure 3.7, the dotted line in the left-hand graph represents a temperature that is varying continuously between about 65.7° and 70° between the times of 8 AM and 2 PM. However, as we showed, we might want to convert this function of time into sample values, and so we must round off the temperature values so that we can store the temperature information in bits.

The process of rounding off can be thought of as creating a new function of time—one that only takes on certain values. The solid, staircase-like lines in Figure 3.7 represent the new values of temperature at each time *after* the values have been rounded off to the nearest whole degree. Notice that the error we introduce by this rounding off is never more than one-half degree; as explained above, we can make this error as small as we like by using more bits to represent each value. After rounding off, we are left only with the function of time shown on the right side of Figure 3.7. The graphs in this figure are known as *waveforms*, and they will be very useful to us in our attempt to understand different types of informa-

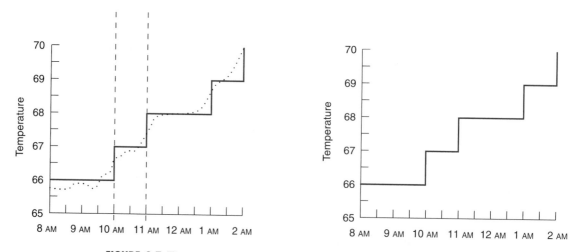

FIGURE 3.7 Time varying *waveforms* that represent the temperature variation in a certain place over time.

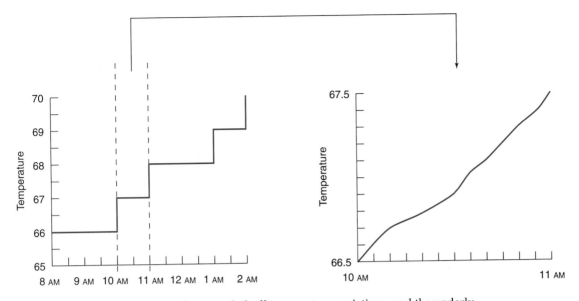

FIGURE 3.8 Waveforms representing rounded-off temperature variations, and the underlying true temperature, as functions of time.

tion. The axis along the bottom shows all moments in time between 8 AM and 2 PM, and the dotted and solid lines specify certain temperatures at each point in time—the dotted line shows the actual temperature, and the solid line shows our approximate, rounded-off temperature, which is ready to be converted into some bit pattern.

Indeed, when we receive temperature information from a weather broadcast, or from a digital thermometer display, the rounding off has already been done for us. The graph on the left side of Figure 3.8 shows us the rounded-off values we might hear on a news broadcast. Let's take a closer look at the 1-hour interval between 10 AM and 11 AM, corresponding to the section of the graph between the dotted lines. In reality, the temperature during this time is always changing. However, because it is always between 66.5° and 67.5°, the temperature is reported to be 67° for this whole hour. However, we should be aware that this report hides from us the true story of the actual temperatures. The function of time on the right side of Figure 3.8 shows how the actual temperature may have been varying during that hour. Notice that this underlying function of time is *continuous*; that is, it does not change "all at once" from one value to another, the way the rounded-off approximation does.

A common example of time-varying information is an *audio signal*, which is a voltage or other physical quantity that varies with time according to some voice pattern, piece of music, or other sound. Later in this book, we will discuss how audio signals are created from sound, and how they are handled by information processing systems. For now, our simpler question is, "Can binary numbers effectively be used to represent time-varying quantities such as audio signals?" Anyone who has listened to a CD recording can tell us that the answer is yes. Although an audio signal varies continuously with time, we are able to represent it by representing only its values at certain instants of time. For a CD, for example, we represent the audio signal's value every 0.0000227 seconds, for a total of 44,100 values every second. Figure 3.9 shows an audio waveform; like the temperature waveform, it specifies a certain value at each point in time, although this time scale

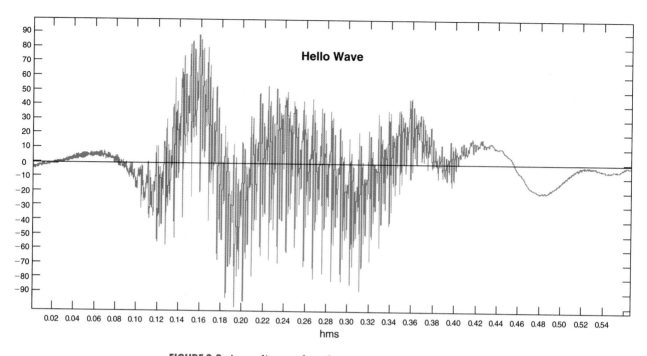

FIGURE 3.9 An audio *waveform* that represents the modulation of air pressure that took place when a person spoke the word "hello."

is much different, covering only one-half second. At each point, the value shown as the height of the function represents the *air pressure* recorded at some point by a microphone. It is these rapid changes in air pressure that we perceive as sound. The microphone converts these changes in air pressure to an electrical signal, and these signal values are used to create the waveform representation shown. Each of these air pressure values is a measurement similar to the temperature measurement in the example above; that is, we can approximately represent each value by some number of bits. The number of bits we choose to represent the value determines the precision of our representation; for a CD, 16 bits are used for each value we represent.

In this way, a music recording or other similar audio signal can be represented by generating 16 binary digits every 0.0000227 seconds, or, by generating 16 bits 44,100 times per second. This is, in fact, what is stored on a CD: 16 bits—ones or zeros—are used to represent the "value" of each channel (here, the word channel corresponds to the audio destined for the left or right speaker) of the music 44,100 times *for every second* of music. In addition to this, extra bits are included for purposes of error recovery, which will be treated later. Therefore, there are more than

$$16 \text{ bits/value} \times 44{,}100 \text{ values} \times 2 \text{ channels} = 1{,}411{,}200 \text{ bits} \qquad (3.1)$$

stored as patterns of shiny areas or pits on a CD for every second of music on the CD. If there is 1 hour's worth of music on the CD, there are over 5 billion bits of information stored on the disc to represent the music. We will not go into exactly what these "values" that can be used to represent an audio signal are until later. At that time, we will also discuss how to determine the amount of information needed to represent each value, how many values per second are used, and why. But for now, we will simply conclude that binary digits can be used to represent audio and other time-varying quantities with any precision we require, as long as we use enough bits. How many bits is enough depends, as it did when we were measuring temperatures, on how accurate our information is, and what the requirements of our application are.

Still and Time-Varying Images   The final type of information we will consider is imagery. A picture, it has been said, is worth ten thousand words. Well, we have learned how to represent ten thousand words with ASCII. Can we use binary digits to represent images as well? The answer, as you probably know, is yes. An image can be broken down into small regions, sometimes called picture elements, or *pixels*, each of which can be represented by one or more values. For a *monochrome* (noncolor, often called black-and-white) image, each pixel can be represented by a number indicating how bright or dark that small region is. And, as we have seen, each of these numbers can be represented using binary information.

Furthermore, time-varying imagery—pictures that change with time—can be represented using the same principle as we used with audio signals. That is, we can represent the imagery at certain closely spaced intervals of time, just as television creates the illusion of smooth motion by displaying 60 "visual fields" every second. The reason that these images do not need to be spaced nearly as closely together in time as do the values of an audio signal has to do with human capacities for vision and hearing. That is, human vision responds much more slowly to changes in stimulus than does human hearing—we'll say more about that in later chapters. The point is that when the information we are storing or transmitting is for human use, there is no necessity to represent it with greater precision than a human can use or appreciate! If we can represent 60 images per second in binary form, the result will be good enough for the purposes of human visual perception, so in this way we can provide a complete binary representation of a video signal. And, with some "tricks," this number can be reduced to 30 images per second, the standard rate used for most video applications.

We will discuss binary representation of images in Chapter 5. For now, however, consider that the display of a computer screen may have more than 1,000,000 pixels, each of which must be represented by three values if you have a color display. Each of these values must be represented by some number of bits, and they must change 60 times every second. Suddenly, you might realize why your favorite graphics-intensive video game or multimedia PC requires a lot of memory!

3.5 Convenient Forms for Binary Codes

The examples we have used so far in this chapter illustrate that binary words—strings of zeroes and ones—are often used to represent numbers, text characters, or other quantities. For these words to be conveniently and efficiently stored and manipulated by computers, they are typically used in sizes of 8, 16, 32, or 64 bits long. That is, the most common word lengths are powers of two—numbers of the form 2^n, where n is some integer. Furthermore, so that we might easily handle large amounts of these binary words, they are commonly grouped into standard sizes for convenient measurement and analysis.

3.5.1 Bits, Bytes, and Beyond

Internal representation of quantities by computers is usually done with binary words of length 8, 16, 32, or 64 bits. Because these are all multiples of 8, a binary word of 8 bits, which is known as a *byte*, is a convenient measure of binary word size in a computer. If a particular computer uses a 32-bit representation for a real

Byte

number, for example, we can say that 4 bytes are used to represent the number. The use of bytes is convenient and commonly used for measuring binary information in large quantities, as well. The amount of memory space—that is, the number of binary digits that the computer can store—is also measured in bytes, each of which in turn represents 8 bits of storage. Because the architecture of computers makes it more practical for memory and other forms of information storage to be in sizes that are powers of 2, it is common to encounter memory sizes such as "64 KB" and "8 MB."

However, the "K" and the "M" do not stand for exactly the same thing as they usually do when used as prefixes for units of measurement. Typically, a "k" stands for "kilo-" (notice that the lowercase prefix indicates "kilo-") and the "M" for "mega-"; these are the standard prefixes to represent thousands (10^3) and millions (10^6), respectively. However, when these prefixes are used to describe quantities of bytes, "K" is used to represent $2^{10} = 1024$, and "M" is used to represent $2^{20} = 1,048,576$, or 1024×1024. This is done so that these prefixes can represent powers of two; as a result, the number of KB (1,024 bits) or MB (1,048,576 bits) is usually a convenient number, easy to remember. Because there is not much difference, for example, between 1 MB and 1 million bytes, the distinction between the use of these prefixes for binary data storage sizes and for the rest of their applications is often ignored. However, when it is necessary to know how exactly much storage is needed for or is available for an application, the distinction can make a big difference.

3.5.2 Octal and Hexadecimal Representation

When we are dealing with collections of bits—for example, binary words representing text characters using the ASCII code—we find it inconvenient to deal with each individual bit. However, sometimes it is necessary to examine particular bit patterns, to determine whether a system is operating properly, for example. For such applications, we find it easier to develop some alternative notations for groups of binary digits. Two such alternative notations are *octal* representation and *hexadecimal*, or *hex* representation. Those familiar with number systems may have already recognized that the representations we used in Section 3.4.3 to represent integers in binary form are the *base 2 representations* of these numbers. That is, we are representing the numbers using a consistent counting system having only two numerals: 0 and 1. This is in contrast to the usual *decimal* (base 10) system, with 10 different numerals, which we deal with every day.

We do not need to go into the details of number systems here, but instead will present two other systems commonly encountered when dealing with binary information. These are the *octal*, or base 8 system, and the *hexadecimal*, or base 16 system. As you might guess, the octal system uses 8 numerals: 0 through 7. And the "hex" system uses 16 numerals—meaning we have to invent 6 new symbols to represent these numerals, because there are only 10 Arabic numerals, 0 through 9.

Octal   The octal system is a counting system that uses just the first eight numerals, starting with zero. So, the first 20 numbers in this system are: 0, 1, 2, 3, 4, 5, 6, 7, 10, 11, 12, 13, 14, 15, 16, 17, 20, 21, 22, 23. Because each numeral can only take on one of 8 values, and because 8 is a power of two, we can use an octal numeral to represent a grouping of bits. Specifically, we can use an octal numeral to represent 3 bits:

Octal Numeral	Bit Pattern
0	000
1	001
2	010
3	011
4	100
5	101
6	110
7	111

Because there are 8 numerals and also 8 patterns that can be formed by three bits, we can use this table to represent groups of three bits by a single octal numeral. Thus, if the following 12-bit pattern is stored in a computer's memory:

$$010110011101_2,$$

we can represent these bits in octal as:

$$2635_8.$$

Note that the subscripts are used to indicate that the first representation is binary (base 2) and the second is octal (base 8).

Hexadecimal   The hex system is a counting system that uses 16 numerals, starting with zero. Because our standard decimal system provides only 10 different symbols, the letters A through F are used to fill out a set of 16 different numerals. So, the first 20 numbers in this system are: 0, 1, 2, 3, 4, 5, 6, 7, 8, 9, A, B, C, D, E, F, 10, 11, 12, 13. Because each numeral can take on one of 16 values, and because 16 is another power of two (2^4), we can use a hex numeral to represent a grouping of four bits. The table below shows all of the possible 4-bit patterns, along with their decimal, octal, and hexadecimal representations:

Decimal	Octal	Hex Numeral	Bit Pattern
0	0	0	0000
1	1	1	0001
2	2	2	0010
3	3	3	0011
4	4	4	0100
5	5	5	0101
6	6	6	0110
7	7	7	0111
8	10	8	1000
9	11	9	1001
10	12	A	1010
11	13	B	1011
12	14	C	1100
13	15	D	1101
14	16	E	1110
15	17	F	1111

Looking at the last two columns of this table, we see that there are 16 hex numerals, and also 16 patterns that can be formed from four bits. Therefore, we can use this table to represent groups of four bits by a single hexadecimal numeral. This is particularly handy when the bits occur in multiples of 4.

A common application for hexadecimal is representing ASCII code. As we have discussed, in ASCII code, text characters are each represented by a pattern of 7 bits. Using hex, we can represent the bits comprising these ASCII codes using just two hex characters per text character: the first hex character represents the first three bits (with a 0 added in front), and the second hex character for the last four bits.

Recall that we converted the piece of text:

You & I,

into its ASCII representation, the 56-bit sequence:

1011001 1101111 1110101 0100000 0100110 0100000 1001001 0101100.

Now, we see that we could more compactly represent this ASCII code using the hex code:

59 6F 75 20 26 20 49 2C.

Note that this representation is more compact and easier to read than the binary representation, but it still retains the binary information, because we can convert any hex character into the corresponding four bits using the table above. This way, we can inspect relatively large amounts of stored binary information, and if we know what we are looking for, determine whether our system is operating as we think it should be.

3.5.3 Introduction to Error Detection and Correction

So far, we have seen that binary codes can be used to represent different forms of information. The information, once in binary form, can be stored, transmitted, and retrieved with a great degree of convenience and reliability. However, in any physical situation, it is inevitable that problems might occur. In particular, when binary information is sent across some physical channel—wires, coaxial cable, optical fiber, or the airwaves—there always exists the possibility that some bits will be received in error due to interference and other unpredictable events. Binary representation of information makes it possible to perform *coding* of information to ensure reliable performance. Coding involves changing the original information (pattern of bits) into a new, *encoded* pattern that is usually longer but in some way more desirable. Of course, this requires us to *decode* the information later, so that the original pattern can be recreated.

One important function of coding is to enable the *detection* (and often *correction*) of errors that can occur in data transmission across a noisy channel. In fact, this ability to detect and correct errors is one of the primary advantages of using digital transmission instead of analog. A fundamental aspect of error control coding is *redundancy*. From an information standpoint, it may appear that we do not want our messages to contain redundant information, because that will result in longer messages and a waste of transmission or storage resources. However, we can benefit greatly from extra bits that are added to the transmitted data that repeat some of the previous information in some particular way. It is this repetition of the data that can allow the receiver to detect errors. If an error is detected, the receiver can either request that the data be retransmitted, or can possibly even correct the data itself. As an example, consider one of the simplest forms of error detection, data

Error Control

Transmitted Character	Transmitted Information	Transmitted Parity	Received Information	Received Parity	Do We Detect an Error?
H	1001000	0	1000000	0	Yes
e	1100101	0	1100101	0	No
l	1101100	0	1101100	0	No
p	1110000	1	1110000	1	No

TABLE 3.1 Even Parity Example

coding using a one-bit *parity code*. Under this coding system, the number of ones in each data block is counted, and a zero or a one is appended to that block to make the total number of ones even (for *even parity*) or odd (for *odd parity*). By appending this additional bit (called a parity bit) we are ensuring that every block (or codeword) leaving the transmitter is known to have an even number of ones if even parity coding is used, or an odd number if odd parity coding is used. Upon receiving a codeword, the receiver counts the number of ones. If the number of ones does not match the parity (for example, when the system is using even parity and a codeword with an odd number of ones is received), then we know that an error has occurred.

Consider the example in Table 3.1, in which a friend tries to send you the message "Help." Because the channel is noisy, one of the bits is misinterpreted by the receiver and, without a parity bit, would be decoded as "@elp" (suggesting, perhaps, that he is at a meeting of the local chapter of Environment Loving People, which you may or may not interpret as a call for help). If the information includes a parity bit, however, the receiver can detect that the message contains an error, and you can request a retransmission (if it is not too late).

Careful thought will reveal that this error detection code can detect only an odd number of bit errors. That is, an even number of bit errors will result in a received word of the correct parity, and be interpreted as a correct bit sequence. Returning to the previous example, we might receive the message "Kelp" and unfortunately believe, even with the parity check code, that our friend is again on his seaweed diet. Note also that while we were able to detect a one-bit error, there was no indication as to which bit was in error. Clearly, this system for error detection has its limitations. Can we do better than this? Certainly; in fact, just about every system that uses digital information employs a coding technique for detecting and correcting errors that is more complex, and performs much better, than the simple parity example above. For example, the information contained on a CD is carefully encoded to allow the CD player to detect and correct errors that can occur during playback due to smudged or scratched discs, or misalignment of the playback mechanism.

As you might suspect, these high-performance methods for error coding are based on more sophisticated approaches involving mathematical theories developed in support of information theory. There are many versions of these coding techniques, but they all rely on the fundamental idea of *adding structured redundancy* to information before it is stored or transmitted. This redundancy results in the need to store and send extra bits, but can greatly improve the reliability of digital information systems by allowing the detection and correction of errors. The more error-resistant we want our system to be, the more redundancy we should add, while keeping in mind that this redundancy reduces the rate at which we are transmitting or storing actual information. The tradeoff between error detection and correction capability and the desire to store or transmit as few bits as possible is one of the key areas of current research in data communication, and must be carefully considered by system designers in light of the requirements of the systems they are designing.

Summary

In this chapter, we have introduced the idea of representing information in binary form. We have explained that binary form is appropriate for representing information for purposes of storage, processing, and transmission, for a variety of important reasons:

- binary representation allows us to *uniquely* represent information and to recreate it in its original form;
- binary representation is *standardized*; it can be used for many different applications: numerical data, text, audio, still and moving images, and more; and, most importantly,
- binary representation is *compatible* with inexpensive and reliable technology for handling the information.

We have presented some basic techniques for representing integers and text in binary form, and also discussed how binary digits, or bits, are used to represent more general types of information, such as audio and still or time-varying imagery. We have discussed some of the units and number systems used for counting and representing binary digits. Finally, we presented a brief introduction into the subject of error detection and correction.

In the following chapters, we will provide more in-depth information regarding specific techniques for representing useful information in binary form. Specifically, we will discuss how one can determine the amount of bits needed to represent some information according to the application of interest. This will lead to an understanding of how this determines the amount of memory storage, rate of data transmission, or time for information processing necessary for a particular application.

Try These Exercises

1. Explain why a *binary code*, with just two symbols, is preferable for purposes of information systems to a code with many symbols.
2. How many bits would you need to represent the letters *a* through *z*? How many would you need to represent the decimal numbers 1 through 1000?
3. Until recently, stock prices were quoted in units of one sixteenth of a dollar. Determine how many bits are needed to represent stock prices to this precision. Note that another piece of information is needed before the answer can be determined. State what this is, make a reasonable assumption, and proceed with the problem.
4. Explain the concepts of redundancy and parity in your own words, indicating similarities and differences in these concepts. Illustrate with examples.
5. Using the Java applet Decimal to Binary Conversion, find the largest and smallest decimal numbers that the applet can convert to binary. Give the decimal and binary representations of each. Consider both positive and negative numbers. Comment on the manner in which negative numbers are

 Decimal to Binary Conversion

represented. Note that you should be able to answer this question without literally converting all possible numbers!

6. Using the applet "Decimal integer to Binary conversion," find the binary representation of each of the following numbers: 0, 1, 2, 3, 4, −1. Briefly explain your result in each case.

Decimal Integer to Binary Conversion

7. Using the applet "Decimal integer to binary conversion," find the binary representations of 2, 4, 8, 16, 32, 64, 128. What is special about these binary numbers? In terms of their simplicity, what decimal numbers do they correspond to?

Decimal Integer to Binary Conversion

8. Using the applet "Binary to decimal integer conversion," find the decimal numbers represented by the following binary numbers: 0, 01, 10, 1111111, 10000000. What can you say about the compactness of representation of numbers in the binary and decimal systems?

Binary to Decimal Integer Conversion

9. Four different number representations are used in this chapter: binary, octal, decimal, and hex. Explain what particular benefits and possible disadvantages each representation has. The advantages and disadvantages may depend on the intended use.

10. Using the applet, "Alphanumeric String Conversion," find the ASCII representation of the letter "t." Give the results in your answer. How many characters does each form of the representation require? Explain why we would want to use a different representation than the letter "t" itself, particularly given that the representations require more characters.

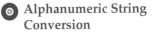
Alphanumeric String Conversion

11. Using the applet, "ASCII code to Character conversion," find the character represented by the binary number 1000001. What character is represented by 1000010? Do you see a pattern?

ASCII Code to Character Conversion

12. Some ASCII codes do not represent printable characters. Why are these codes necessary? As a hint, note that ASCII can be thought of as a code to allow remotely-controlled printed or typewritten output.

13. Similar to the exercise above, use the Java applet "Binary to Decimal Integer conversion" to find the range of decimal numbers represented by the complete range of binary numbers that the applet can accept. List the binary and decimal representations for each end of the range. Comment on the manner in which negative numbers are represented.

Binary to Decimal Integer Conversion

14. Using the text to ASCII applet "Alphanumeric String Conversion," find the ASCII code (in 7-bit binary) for the word "test." Now assume that we want the code for the same word in italics: *test*. Can you determine the code? Explain what is happening here, and what can be done about it.

Alphanumeric String Conversion

15. Assume that you are building a digital system to measure and display the speed of your car. Further assume that the speeds you wish to represent vary from 0 to 120 miles per hour. If you were to use a 4-bit word to represent the speed, how *precisely* could you measure the speed? Do you think this would provide enough precision for normal purposes?

16. Identify a favorite piece of music, and calculate the number of bits required to store it on a CD. You may ignore any extra bits that are used for error recovery.

17. A simple way to provide error detection is with a parity code. Explain the significance of the number of bits that is chosen to associate with the parity bit. Why can this number not be made arbitrarily large?

18. Is there any form of error detection or correction in standard written language? Explain, and if possible, give an example.

19. One form of error correcting code, the Hamming Code, may be investigated with the "Hamming code example" applet. Enter the word "test" and observe

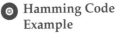
Hamming Code Example

the coded data string. Explain why the coded string is longer than the string of ASCII bits. Try adding errors (by changing ones to zeros or zeros to ones) at various places in the string of coded bits. Observe the results. Note that the number of errors which can be detected or corrected varies as a function of the location of the errors. What is the maximum number of errors which can be corrected if the errors occur at the optimum locations? If the errors are grouped in the worst way, how many bit errors can be corrected?

4   The Need and Basis for Data Protocols

Objectives

Now that we understand that all information may be represented by binary bits (zeroes and ones), it is reasonable to ask how to organize the large number of bits needed to represent complex information. The answer is via *protocols*, which are discussed in this chapter. Here you will learn:

▲ that protocols are an integral part of our everyday life, in the human as well as digital world;

▲ about examples of simple but important protocols, such as the positions of delivery and return addresses on envelopes;

▲ about actual protocols used for information storage on magnetic tape, CD-ROMs, and so on;

▲ the ASCII protocol for transmission of text data; and

▲ protocols used by word processors and the World Wide Web.

4.1 Introduction

So far, we have seen how various forms of information can be converted into bits. This new digital representation allows the information to be stored, transmitted, and processed rapidly, cheaply, and efficiently. However, the same feature of this digital representation that allows us to use information systems to represent a wide variety of information—the fact that everything can be represented by zeroes and ones—presents us with some challenges in handling and interpreting this new form of data. In this chapter, we'll present some examples of how digital information systems organize, manage, and interpret information according to a set of widely accepted standards.

4.2 Using Protocols to Organize Information

Protocols are agreed upon sets of rules that provide order to different systems and situations. For example, the military has developed various protocols that govern behavior and actions, and there is a strict protocol to be followed when one is visiting a monarchy and encounters members of the royal family. These examples show how protocols can be used to bring order to human behavior, which in the absence of rules and standards (or even in their presence) can lead to chaotic situations in which nothing useful can be accomplished. In a similar way, data protocols bring order to information systems, allowing them to share information in a useful way.

Consider a familiar and reliable information system: the book. A book is not just a continuous collection of words; rather, the words are organized within a well-defined structure. Words are grouped into sentences marked by periods, sentences are grouped into paragraphs, and paragraphs into chapters; pages are numbered, chapters are listed in a table of contents, and key words are listed in an index. To provide more structure, the book also carries a title. When many books are gathered together they are indexed in some fashion, both with regard to each book's physical location and the information content. For example one "protocol" for organizing written works is by displaying them in bookshelves, ordered from left to right and then top to bottom, in correspondence with the alphabetical order of the author's name followed by the alphabetical order of the book name. And, this protocol is built upon another one: the protocol that dictates the order of the letters in the alphabet.

These protocols are so common that we don't think about them as protocols. But, there is nothing *natural* or even *mathematical* about these protocols. They are all the result of widely accepted, well documented, widely distributed agreements between participating groups of humans. In another country, even if the same alphabet is used, the accepted order of the letters may be different. For that matter, the protocol for human information exchange itself is apt to be different: they may speak another language altogether. We may even use several different protocols to save and access the same information. For example, the above protocol for books is rarely used in a library. In the United States, the Dewey decimal system (named after Melvil Dewey) is often used; in this system, each library book is given an *address* that is organized according to information about the book's content class, author, and year of publication. For example, the 400 class is assigned to all books about language, and the 420 subclass to books about English. So the Dewey decimal system is sufficient to classify and organize any set of books. However, another address protocol exists that also allows any given publication in the world to be identified: the ISBN number. The ISBN (International Standard Book Number) provides information in its 10-digit code regarding the national language, geographic origin, publisher, title, edition and volume number of the volume. This is an example of using more than one protocol to organize the same set of information. From these examples, we see that a protocol is just a set of organizational rules that provides a basis for communication and interaction. Groups of people must agree upon which protocols will be used, and these *standards* must be widely distributed so that the information can be used. Similarly, electronic information is encoded, stored, and transmitted using agreed-upon protocols. These protocols enable users of a computer or communications system to keep track of important details such as what order the information is in, where it is located, who owns it, to whom it is being sent, and where it starts and ends. For example, data storage on a computer disk storage system requires a protocol to enable storage and retrieval. Just as in a library, the disk system must know what is on the disk and where it is located so that the information can be retrieved.

A postal letter provides an excellent introduction to several important concepts in information protocols: the content is enclosed (in an envelope) so that it is clear where the message starts and ends; this envelope contains the address of the intended recipient, a return address that identifies the sender, and a postmark showing the date it was handled and the post office that handled it.

Now consider the equivalent electronic message; it will consist entirely of ones and zeroes. Thus patterns of ones and zeroes must perform all the functions of the envelope, address, return address, message, and even in some systems the postage. This protocol must be sufficiently well defined such that there is no uncertainty by any entity that handles it as to the division between these various parts of the stream of binary digits, because there are no physically differentiating aspects to the bit stream, as there are in the case of the letter, in which the paper and envelope are clearly distinguishable as conveying different information. The separation of information in the electronic message is much more like the separation of the addresses on the face of an envelope: by protocol-based agreement, we look for the recipient's address in the front and center of the envelope, and the return address in the upper left corner or on the back. A fundamental aspect of decoding any binary string is determining where to begin, that is, identifying the first bit in a protocol. This may occur in the middle of a bit stream, as many messages will be strung together. In some situations there may be some help, analogous to the situation of a person reading a book, who begins on the first (top) page in the upper left corner, at least for reading English. Similarly, some storage media, such as memories or certain types of disks, have physical locations and corresponding bits that can be identified as *the beginning*. However, this is not always the case, as shown in Figure 4.1.

For some information-carrying bit streams, the situation is analogous to coming in on the middle of a conversation; the stream of bits is continuous, and the computer must begin decoding them wherever the first opportunity arises. This situation is encountered in digital data transmissions over telephone systems, to and from satellites, and in the reading of a computer disk. In these situations, nothing marks the true beginning of a bit stream because, for example, communication systems may temporarily fail and yet communications must be quickly restored. In the case of disk-based systems, the data is located on circular *tracks* with no interruptions or physically identifiable points, as will be further discussed later. Again, no beginning of the data stream in this track is physically identifiable. Thus, a protocol often includes means to identify the beginning of the next separable component of the message. Also, it is important to note, again, that the computer *lives* in a purely binary world: everything is either a zero or a one to it. We often assume the existence of a third level of *nothing present* in this binary world. If this were true, the computer could distinguish three states: one, zero, and nothing. In a few specialized situations at the interface of the analog and digital worlds, this may be an appropriate view, but it is not true in general. We will consider a few simple examples to show how information technology deals with this challenge.

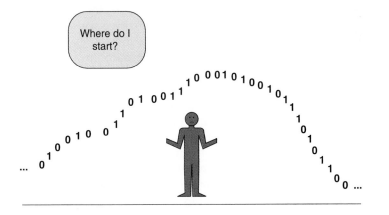

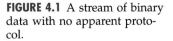

FIGURE 4.1 A stream of binary data with no apparent protocol.

4.2.1 How Numbers Can Be Packaged

The simplest type of data stream to analyze in this context is that generated by the representation of integers. Computers are often categorized by the size of the binary integers (called *word size*) that they can store or manipulate with a single operation. (By an operation we mean the act of storing, retrieving, or changing a set of bits.) The first microprocessor (the brains of a smart machine or computer) manipulated data in 4-bit groups, often called "nibbles." The first commercial personal computers (PCs) were 8-bit machines; that is, they manipulated a word size of one byte with each operation. Later, 16-bit computers, then 32-bit computers, and more recently, 64-bit machines were introduced. Thus, the first PCs stored and processed 1 byte at a time, and we are now using machines that handle 4 or 8 bytes at a time.

📖 **Byte**

📖 **Binary**

As we recall from our introduction to the binary number system, we can convert back and forth between the binary and decimal number systems. However, this conversion process requires that we make some decisions about what the bits represent, because we do not have symbols such as negative signs and decimal points to work with—only zeroes and ones. We will enter this discussion with a simplifying assumption: our protocol will address the storage of only positive integers represented in the usual binary fashion we discussed in the last chapter. On the face, this might appear to eliminate any further need to discuss protocol, but it doesn't. A computer typically stores its 16-bit integers as two 8-bit bytes, as the byte is commonly accepted to be the smallest division of information for storage and manipulation. Now, using the approach for writing binary numbers presented in Chapter 3, what would the following pair of bytes found in computer memory represent: 00000001 1000000?

It all depends! A reasonable assumption might be that we are meant to just concatenate the two bytes—just combine them into one 16-bit binary word—giving the number 0000000110000000, which in decimal is $256 + 128 = 384$. Some computers operate in this mode, but other computers reverse the order of the two bytes before they are concatenated so that we have 1000000000000001, which in decimal is $32768 + 1 = 32769$. This large difference in result is caused by an arbitrary decision on how the particular computer was designed and wired. Can the second approach be considered "wrong" given the reasonableness of the first approach? Consider this argument. The places in computer memory where data is stored are numbered. We call these numbers the *addresses* of the data, because we use these numbers just as you would use postal addresses; that is, to identify uniquely the source and destination of some information.) Now, the first byte we displayed above will have a lower address number, and the second a higher address. Isn't it natural to suppose that the higher-order byte (that is, the one with the bits that we will want to place left-most in the 16 bit number we are constructing) should be in the higher address location in memory? Thus there is also a reasonable argument for using the second approach. The first approach, in which the byte in the lower address location is taken to be the high-order byte, is called the *big-endian* protocol, while the other is called the *little-endian* protocol. The common Pentium processor-based PC is an example of a big-endian computer, while the line of computers sold by Silicon Graphics are examples of little-endian computers. The most important lesson to learn here is simply: *assume nothing; verify everything*. This is but one example of the need for, and importance of, protocols and formats in the storage, transmission, and processing of information.

This description only involved the simplest type of numbers: positive integers. Obviously, other protocols must be established to permit the representation of negative numbers and fractions. There is no one, correct, way to enact this representation, so it is essential that standards be adopted. The simplest (but not most common) way to represent negative numbers is to use the *signed magnitude* format. In this format the most significant (leftmost) bit indicates the sign of the number (0 for positive, 1 for negative). For representation of fractions and large numbers, exponential notation is used, usually according to the IEEE-754 standard (maintained by the Institute of Electrical and Electronics Engineers). The IEEE is an organization that promotes the adoption of, and maintains specifications for, many protocols. This set of standards specifies such details as the number of binary digits to use for the parts of the exponential representation, their arrangement in data bytes, the sign representation, and so forth. The details of these standards are beyond the scope of this book, but their importance should be recognized. For example, they set limits on the largest and smallest numbers that the computer can represent, as well as the fundamental numerical accuracy of the computer. In casual applications a computer may appear to be exactly correct in its calculations, but this is not true. In certain situations a knowledge of the accuracy limits is essential to proper interpretation of computed results.

⊙ **Representation of Fractions and Large Numbers**

4.3 Saving Information: Tapes, Disks, and CDs

Protocols for *data storage* are determined to a large extent by the physical characteristics of the memory medium being used. For example, the conventional computer memory devices called RAM (random access memory) can be thought of as simply a linear string of bytes, numbered consecutively from zero to the last storage location. Those numbers represent the addresses of the data in each location, and are used by the computer to locate and retrieve the data. With RAM, if the address is known, the data may be retrieved directly. This may be compared with three other types of memory—magnetic tape, rotating disks, and CD-ROMs—in which such direct and immediate access is not available.

4.3.1 Magnetic Tape

In the case of magnetic tape, data is written on the tape in a linear fashion, and in that sense tape seems similar to RAM. There is a major difference, however; with RAM it is possible to retrieve data directly from a given memory address, while on tape there is no direct way to access a desired address. Essentially, the tape drive must read the tape sequentially; it cannot instantly jump to a location in the middle of the tape. So, it must determine the current location on the tape, compare that to the desired location, and decide whether to move the tape forward or backward. This is obviously a much slower process.

To avoid having to read (and store) an address with each byte location, the data on the tape is divided into sections called *blocks*, each of which contains hundreds or thousands of bytes. Each block has a distinctive binary code that the tape drive looks for as the tape is moving by. The access of information on tape is thus a two-step process: first the desired block is located, then the data is retrieved. For this reason, tape is called a *sequential access* medium, compared to the *direct access* or *random access* provided by RAM.

4.3.2 Rotating Memory Devices

Another type of sequential access medium is the rotating disk. This description applies to the familiar *floppy disk* as well as to the internal, larger-capacity *hard disk*. The storage means for these disks is magnetic, as it is in the magnetic tape. Each

FIGURE 4.2 A CD-ROM with spiral tracking, and a conventional floppy disk with cylindrical tracking.

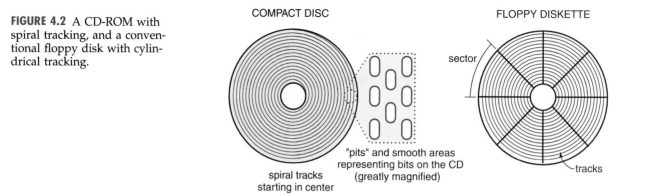

COMPACT DISC

FLOPPY DISKETTE

sector

"pits" and smooth areas representing bits on the CD (greatly magnified)

spiral tracks starting in center

tracks

disk surface is organized into many circular *tracks.* These tracks are concentric circles, arranged from the outside edge toward the center of the disk. The ubiquitous 3 1/2 inch, 1.44 MB floppy disk, for example, has 80 such tracks defined on each of its two sides, for a total of 160 addressable tracks.

In the reading process, the magnetic read/write head is positioned over a track, and the pattern of ones and zeroes is read as the spinning disk brings them under the head sequentially. Obviously, this pattern repeats itself as the disk makes successive revolutions under the head. A distinctive pattern of bits identifies the start of the track, which is then subdivided into *sectors* (Figure 4.2 illustrates this division). The sectors are identifiable from the initial bits in the sector (the sector header), which are defined by the disk format protocol. The 3 1/2 inch floppy divides each track into 18 such sectors; each of these sectors packages 512 bytes. The total number of bytes contained on the disk is therefore $160 \times 18 \times 512 = 1,474,560$ bytes.

The reason that a drive of this capacity is called a 1.44 MB drive is related to another protocol used by many computer engineers, one that we already introduced in Chapter 3. Recall that the number of values that can be represented by binary digits increases as powers of two, and so computer engineers use powers of two to create shorthand methods for referring to large numbers of bytes. It is convenient to express large numbers of bits on the basis of kilobytes (1 Kbyte = 1024 bytes, or 2^{10} bytes), and for even larger numbers, we use megabytes (1 Mbyte = $1024 \times 1024 = 1,048,576$ bytes, or 2^{20} bytes). The storage capacity of this conventional floppy disk is 1,474,560 bytes, which is exactly 1.44 megabytes. As we have discussed earlier, it is useful to remember that these memory size specifications are referred to using the *protocol* of Kbytes and Mbytes, which are slightly different than thousands and millions.

Disks are commonly used to store and transport files of information; they may be moved from one machine to another. Each disk must then contain all the information needed to allow any compatible computer to identify the desired files and read them. This is accomplished by storage on each disk of two more types of information: the *disk directory,* which lists the file names and other information such as file size, and the *file allocation table,* which keeps track of exactly where on the disk the data for each file is located.

How does the computer locate pieces of information on a disk? It does this by knowing the physical location on the disk where the directory and file allocation table tracks are always located. This information must be known in advance, and is one example of the reasons why disks are generally not transferable from one type of computer system to another (such as from PCs to Macs). The extent to which such protocols are a matter of human invention and agreement is illustrated by the state of floppy disk formats at the beginning of the personal computer revolution in the late 1970s. The predecessor of the familiar IBM PC clone machine running some variation of the Microsoft DOS or Windows operating system was a family of computers based on earlier hardware technology and executing the CP/M or CP/M-86 operating system from Digital Research Corporation. Because no single vendor dominated the market, almost every vendor introduced their own unique format for the then common 5 1/4 inch floppy disks. Because the formats were unique, they were incompatible. Eventually, some 140 different formats were in use, which required special software and sometimes special disk controller hardware for reading a disk created by one CP/M based system on another CP/M based systems. The sudden domination of the market by the IBM PC in the early eighties had the positive effect of greatly unifying the floppy disk format protocol.

The CD-ROM retains some of the characteristics of both the magnetic disk and tape. The data storage and reading are sequential, but they are based on an optical interaction rather than a magnetic one. Physically, the CD-ROM looks similar to a magnetic disk, but in terms of data storage organization it is more similar to the tape (see Figure 4.2). This is because data is written in a single track that spirals its way from the inside edge of the disk to the outside. However, through use of the CD-ROM directory and file allocation table, the read head (which contains a laser and photosensitive sensor rather than a magnetic pickup) may be quickly positioned anywhere radially on the disk. Thus it is not necessary to read or even roll past all the previous data to reach the desired data, as it is on a tape.

4.4 Protocols for Sending Data

The final application of protocols that we will introduce is the use of protocols for *data transmission*. Some of the myriad technologies and formats for data transmission will be described later in this book. For now it is sufficient to consider a single example. This example will illustrate some of the many considerations that come into play in establishing a reliable transmission protocol.

Consider that there is some message to be transmitted; it may be destined to travel on the memory bus inside your computer, on the cable to your printer, on a local area network in your office building, or across a transcontinental communications link. First, the message must be encoded into a stream of ones and zeroes. Let us assume that it is simple text; then ASCII (refer to the discussion of ASCII in Chapter 3) can be used. Each ASCII code can be concatenated to form a readable stream of bits; the result is a long string of ones and zeroes, which must be broken up at the receiver into individual seven (or eight) bit numbers that can then be decoded back to characters (see Figure 4.3).

📖 ASCII

If we were to know where the string starts, and if no bits in the string were to be lost during transmission, the decoding of the string back into the original characters at the receiver would be easy: we would simply count off every seven

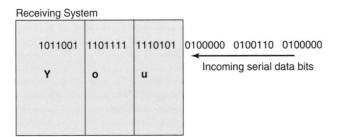

FIGURE 4.3 Decoding of serial ASCII data.

(or eight) bits, identifying each such group as an original ASCII character. Those two assumptions are not trivial to accomplish, however. To establish where the start of the message is, the transmitter must add a unique binary code that means *start-of-message*.

Even if such a start-of-message code is used, we must also consider that a bit may be lost in the transmission. In this case, our *counting off* of every seven bits for decoding would be off by one bit, making each decoded character incorrect. To account for these inevitable errors that can easily occur in long messages, the start-of-message or a similar code is inserted periodically during the message, in between separable message components. Then, if an error occurs, the decoding will be wrong only until the next start code appears, at which point the system is able to resynchronize itself. A commonly used strategy for what are known as *bit-oriented transmission* methods is based on an approach that was popularized by a data transmission protocol known as HDLC (High-level Data Link Control), an international standard that was defined by the ISO (International Standards Organization). In this protocol, each group of data that is to be separably identifiable in a bit stream is called a *frame*. The frame is always transmitted with the following sequence of bits first: `01111110`. This is known as the start-of-frame pattern or *flag byte*, because it "flags" or labels the start of the frame. The receiver of an HDLC transmission could, then, begin at any point in a bit stream and start looking for this pattern on a bit-by-bit basis. That is, it could examine the last eight bits received; if they match the start-of-message pattern, the beginning of a frame has been found. If not, the receiver waits for the next bit to arrive and once again examines the most recently received eight bits (seven old ones and the newest one). Eventually, the receiver should encounter the start-of-message pattern, as long as no errors have occurred.

 ASCII Text

Of course, this scheme would fail if, for example, the above pattern occurred somewhere in the stream of data bits itself. For example, if simple ASCII text were transmitted, then the ˜ character appearing anywhere in our text would confuse a receiver, because the ASCII code for this character matches the flag. Furthermore, because we look for the flag on a bit-by-bit basis, many pairs of characters transmitted in sequence could generate the same pattern. So, how do we prevent this problem?

One approach would be to define a new set of codes to represent characters. But, there is a great deal of benefit in layering new protocols upon old. So, we will not so lightly abandon the use of the ASCII protocol for text representation. The approach that HDLC takes is called *bit stuffing* or *zero bit insertion*. The software or hardware handling the insertion of information into the transmitted data stream looks for any sequence of `ones` that is five in length. On seeing such a sequence, it inserts a `0` into the bit stream. Because the frame flag has six ones in a row, and the bit stuffing prevents the data from ever having six ones in a row, we can never confuse any part of the stream for the flag. The frame flags are added after the bit stuffing procedure.

Has the insertion of the zero in our data stream forever corrupted the data and made it useless to the recipient? Yes, *if* we do not know the protocol that was being used. However, armed with the protocol, the recipient knows that any time five ones appear in a row, the following zero should just be removed and thrown away. The result is a reconstituted version of the original data stream.

You may have noticed that although these methods take into account the possibility that a bit will be "lost" from the data stream, they rely on the correct reception of each bit that arrives at the receiver. That is, they do not allow for any zeroes or ones to be misinterpreted. This is prevented by the addition of yet another layer of protocol, that of error detection and correction. A brief introduction to this topic was presented in Chapter 3; the fundamental idea behind it is that extra bits can be added to the transmission to add the "structured redundancy" necessary to ensure, to the extent needed, error-free transmission.

As complicated as it may seem, the description given above of HDLC is incomplete, and just barely touches on the complexities of formats and protocols. However, it can serve as an example of many of the essential ideas behind data transmission, and the importance of using protocols for data transmission.

4.5 Word Processor and Web Protocols

So far in this chapter, we have introduced the necessity for creating and applying protocols and standards for handling binary data. Without these agreed-upon formats, we would be drowning in a sea of ones and zeroes, with no idea what they represented. In this section, we will show how we can extend these concepts to "higher level" activity in information engineering, such as the operation of word processors and the World Wide Web. Consider a printed document that we desire to produce on the computer and then transmit electronically. To represent the document internally, we could use just the ASCII code that was introduced earlier. This, however, would produce a document that would appear to have come out of a typewriter, with no choices of font or point size, no boldface, no italics, no subscripts, and so forth. Clearly this is unacceptable today (although that is just what early word processors did). We want a way to represent the myriad of possible typefaces. The direct approach would be to assign a binary code to each possible form of every possible character; this is conceivable, but very inefficient. In any one document we would use only a fraction of the possible codes, and the rest would just take up space in the number of bits required per character. Further, the code would be inflexible; how would new typefaces be accommodated?

📖 ASCII

The alternative is to *describe* what we want in the style of a programming language rather than to directly specify each character. For example, we tell the word processor the default settings at the beginning (for instance *10 pt Times Roman font, double spaced*). Then when we want to change the default we instruct the word processor to make a note to that effect in the document (for example *start boldface*). In early word processors the user literally typed a command in the text such as `# boldface` to indicate this. The text was then run through a program that processed these commands, removed them from the output text stream, and sent the appropriate data to the printer. In modern word processors, however, the selections are usually made from menus, and the commands themselves are hidden from the user. HTML is an example of this type of *document markup* language. TEX and LaTeX are other examples (this book is in fact being written with LaTeX). In both cases, special *tags* are used that are expressed in simple human readable character groups that are not not ultimately rendered by the display or printing system. When characters that signify tags (called escape characters) must themselves be displayed, special sequences of characters must be used in their place. That is, if an ampersand (&) is used to signify that a tag sequence of characters is beginning, then a special new sequence must be used in the text if we want to simply indicate that an ampersand was the desired character at this spot.

An HTML document that renders the following sentence:

```
A short text file.
```

in boldface font would contain the following textual description:

```
<HTML>
<BODY>
<b>A short text file.</b>
<\BODY>
<\HTML>
```

while a LaTeX document for the same sentence would read

```
\documentstyle{article}
\begin{document}
{\bf A short text file.}
\end{document}
```

PostScript is a somewhat different type of document description language. It is not designed to be produced directly by humans, as are HTML and LaTeX. Instead, the PostScript description of the document is generated by a computer program such as a word processor; the development of the description is guided by selections that the composer has made.

A *raw* text document consisting of only the following sentence represented in ASCII codes:

```
A short text file.
```

expressed by one printer preparation program for printing with the PostScript protocol produces the following new data stream:

```
%!PS-Adobe-1.0
%%DocumentFonts: Courier
%%Creator: lpscript
%%CreationDate: Sat Jan 17 20:23:58 1998
%%Pages: (atend)
%%EndComments
initmatrix
/a4 [ [300 72 div 0 0 -300 72 div -52 3436 ] 292 3365
60 45 {dup mul exch dup mul add 1.0 exch sub} /setscreen load
{} /settransfer load /initgraphics load /erasepage load ] cvx
statusdict begin bind end readonly def
a4
/stm usertime def
/pgc statusdict begin pagecount end def
clippath pathbbox pop pop exch pop 0 exch translate
clippath pathbbox /pgtop exch def pop pop pop
/ps { print flush } def
/page { copypage erasepage restore save home } def
/home { newpath 0 pgtop moveto } def
/mf { statusdict /manualfeed true put
  usertime 5000 add { dup usertime lt { pop exit } if } loop
  } def
/af { statusdict /manualfeed false put } def
af
/y { currentpoint exch pop } def
/dopage false def
/dpage { dopage { page /dopage false def } if } def
/n
{ spacing 0 3 -1 roll ashow
```

```
   0 y linepitch add moveto
   /dopage true def
   y pgbot lt { dpage } if
} def
/r
{ spacing 0 3 -1 roll ashow
   0 y moveto
   /dopage true def
} def
/Courier findfont [ 10.0 0 0 10.0 0 0 ] makefont setfont
/linepitch -10.0 def
/spacing 0.0 def
/pgtop pgtop linepitch add def
/pgbot currentfont /FontBBox get 1 get neg 1000 div 10.0 mul def
18.0 0 translate

save
home
%%EndProlog
('a:test.txt' ...\n) ps
(A short text file.)n
dpage ( ---\n) ps

%%Trailer
(\ttime (s) = ) ps usertime stm sub 1000 div ==
(\tpages = ) ps statusdict begin pagecount end pgc sub == flush
```

While the above PostScript file certainly appears to represent overkill for the text that it prints, an examination of the file will give some indication of the versatility of the PostScript language, and hence of the number of parameters that must be set.

Sometimes protocols are introduced as bridges between existing protocols that are incompatible with one another. For instance, the RTF (rich-text format) standard was introduced by Microsoft as a method for encoding formatted text for transfer between MS-DOS, Windows, OS/2, and Apple Macintosh word processors and other application software. The idea behind the RTF protocol is to introduce a simple-to-decode language that can "richly" describe the many font, format, and other style variations that modern word processors may use. From the RTF description, another word processor can replicate the original presentation of that document to the greatest extent possible, although the replication may be limited by certain incompatible features.

The document consisting of only the following sentence:

```
A short text file.
```

when entered into the Microsoft WordPad application using the default font and no special settings, produces the following RTF protocol file content:

```
{\rtf1\ansi\deff0\deftab720{\fonttbl{\f0\fswiss MS Sans Serif;}
{\f1\froman\fcharset2 Symbol;}{\f2\fmodern Courier New;}}
{\colortbl\red0\green0\blue0;}
\deflang1033\pard\plain\f2\fs20 A short text file.
\par }
```

Within this protocol, one can see that a variety of default fonts and a default color scheme are defined prior to the occurrence of the user-typed text.

Summary

In this chapter, we have presented a look at the protocols that are used at various levels within some information storage, transmission, and processing systems. At the lowest level, we saw how streams of bits must be formatted so that they can be generated and used in some organized fashion. Then, we discussed some examples of how protocols at "higher levels" can be used to package the information into a form suitable for storage on a variety of familiar devices. Finally, we presented yet a higher level of organization, giving an example of how word processing software organizes information in an efficient, flexible form that is compatible with a wide range of computers.

Try These Exercises

1. Book numbering systems and postal addresses were given as examples of *protocols* encountered regularly. Give two additional examples of protocols in daily life.
2. Determine a protocol for transmission of stock prices while minimizing the number of bits to be transmitted. Assume that there are 100 stocks whose prices are to be transmitted, and that they are transmitted continuously. You may also assume that an initial list of all the stock names and any other relevant information is sent to the receiver in advance. Explain your protocol with examples, and give illustrations of the functions that a protocol is to perform. Assume that the stock prices range between zero and $200, and that a precision of one cent is needed. Given that, and your protocol, determine the needed bit rate so that all of the stock prices are transmitted in one second.
3. List some advantages and disadvantages of each of the following storage media: solid state RAM memory, magnetic tape, magnetic disk, CD-ROM disk. Relate each to the protocol for accessing specific data.
4. A "floppy" disk has the data arranged in concentric tracks (i.e., circles of decreasing diameter from the outer edge of the disk), while a CD arranges the data in a single spiral track. Explain the effect of this difference. Is one better than the other?
5. Why did so many different formats for word processors develop? What could be done to reduce this number? Is it important to reduce the number?
6. Assume that it is desired to represent financial amounts ranging in size from zero to 1 billion dollars, with a precision of one cent. How many decimal digits are needed to handle this requirement? How many binary digits are required? Explain your answer.
7. Given the following received binary data stream: 1101001110111011001101101111. Explain in general what we need to know to make use of this data. As an example, assume the data represents 7-bit ASCII and decode this data. Are any additional assumptions needed in this case?

⊙ Decoding Data

Graphics and Visual Information

The way the camera follows us in slo-mo...

Paul Simon, "The Boy in the Bubble," Graceland

While we are targeting a discussion about telephone/Web integration at the end of this book, we are going to begin our in-depth treatment of the representation of information and matters of bandwidth with a discussion about visual information. The discussion will serve two purposes.

First, it explains why the Internet can be used to transmit images in the fashion that it does. It introduces the idea of the fidelity of the image, too. This is our first introduction in the book to the links among fidelity, information content, time to download, data rates, and bandwidth.

Second, it addresses the fact that most people have a much better intuition about how vision works and how images can be captured, recreated, simplified, and numerically represented than they have about audio. This fact results in a much easier first-time introduction to the ideas of sampling, quantization, and other concepts that used to be of concern only to technologists.

5

From the Real World to Images and Video

Objectives

This chapter describes the world of images. From it you will learn:

▲ the various ways in which an image represents the real world, and the ways in which it is never a perfect representation;

▲ how images are formed, optically, photographically, and electronically;

▲ how the quality of images is measured and expressed;

▲ how images that were never visible in the real world (such as radar, medical ultrasonics imaging, and so forth) may be created by computer;

▲ how images are represented in computers by binary numbers;

▲ how color information is expressed and stored;

▲ how the human eye works, including its color discrimination and stereo vision capability; and

▲ how it is possible to represent continuous motion with still images.

5.1 Introduction

Much of the information we take in from our surroundings comes in visual form. The old adage that maintains that "a picture is worth ten thousand words" recognizes that a visual image conveys a lot of information at once.

The topic of this chapter is images: their formation, storage, and interpretation. This is a topic about which most of us have an abundance of experience, though perhaps we have not given it much thought. For those of us who are not blind, a very large part of the world as we know it is made up of images received through our eyes. In forming and interpreting these images, our eyes and brain are functioning as a very sophisticated imaging and processing system (or, alternatively, cameras and computers approximate, in a primitive way, the functions of our eyes and brain).

In this chapter, you will learn about the many components of imaging systems, and become more familiar with their functions and design. At the beginning, it is important to be clear about the distinction between images and objects. An *image* is a representation (usually two-dimensional) of objects in the real world. If this definition seems vague, please have some patience as you read the chapter; hopefully some examples will make it more clear!

We will discuss the methods by which images of varying types (e.g., color, black and white) may be formed from objects illuminated with light, X-rays, or other types of energy. We will cover some basic physics and physiology to see how a camera (or your eye) forms images. You will learn how these images may be stored, either in traditional (photograph) form, or digitally in a computer. You will learn the various aspects of an image (color, resolution, etc.) that make it a sufficiently accurate representation of the original object. You will learn how images may be stored as strings of binary digits in a computer, transmitted or processed, and then reassembled for viewing. Finally, you will learn how humans perceive motion, and how this perception puts requirements on storage of a series of still images. This chapter contains much basic information related to two of our example information systems: geographic information databases and artwork imaging.

5.2 Images: Information Without Words or Numbers

Images play a fundamental role in the representation, storage, and transmission of important information throughout our professional and personal lives. In many professions, including publishing, art, film making, architecture, and medicine, it is crucial to be able to represent and manipulate information in image form. Furthermore, with the development of multimedia technology and virtual reality, many other professions are beginning to explore the power of representing information in visual form.

In Chapter 3, we introduced the ideas behind *binary representation of information*, and in particular showed how integers and text can be converted into binary form. We also mentioned that other types of information can be represented by bits, and briefly described the process one might use to convert an image into binary digits. We then suggested how this would extend to representation of time-varying imagery, or video.

5.3 Cameras and Image Formation

As mentioned in the introduction to this book, the film-based camera is over 150 years old. Recent advances have provided a variety of alternatives to the use of conventional film, but the basic image formation process has not changed. This process may be familiar to you from experience with basic optics, and is illustrated in Figure 5.1. The essential components of this system are: the *object or scene* to be imaged, the *lens*, and the *image recording medium* (retina of the eye, film, or other device). The image recording medium is usually located in a plane parallel to the lens, known as the *image plane*. Note that the image that is formed is inverted; this

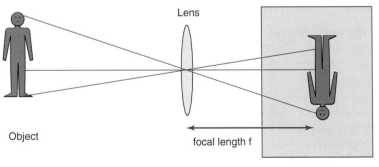

FIGURE 5.1 The operation of an imaging system based upon projection by a lens of a scene onto an imaging plane.

is usually of no consequence because the display device may easily correct this condition. The resulting image represents a *projection* from the three-dimensional object world to the two-dimensional image world. The *focal length* specifies the distance from the lens to the image plane. More useful to us, it also indicates the degree of magnification of the lens. From 35 mm photography, we know that a lens of 50 mm focal length is considered "normal" (in the sense that the resulting photo will contain the same expanse of image that a human would see from the same point as the camera); one of 28 mm focal length is "wide angle," and one of 135 mm focal length is "telephoto." For a different film (image) size, those focal lengths would change, but the principle remains the same.

While we will not delve into the details here, it is important to understand that there is a precise mathematical relationship between the location of each point in the image and the corresponding points in the real world. So for example, if we have an aerial photograph of farmland and we know the altitude of the camera, we can calculate the area of each field or other object in the image. Similarly, if we have X-ray images of the heart as it pumps, we can determine the cross-sectional areas of the ventricles, and hence their pumping efficiencies. In robotics, a video camera may be used to determine precisely the location of a robot arm with respect to the work, and hence provide motion guidance.

This process of reducing the dimensionality of the information (from three dimensions to two in photography) is referred to as projection and is fundamentally a mathematical concept. Inevitably, information is discarded irretrievably when a projection is made, as is reflected in the fact that we are losing a dimension, in this case depth. Also, there are many different types of projections that may be made in each situation. For cameras (including video and film cameras and our eyes), the image formation system is referred to as "perspective projection," the most well-known characteristic of which is that images of objects become smaller as the objects become farther from the camera. This is the effect that causes railroad tracks to appear to converge as they become farther from the camera. From geography, you may be familiar with the "Mercator projection" for transforming the three-dimensional earth onto a two-dimensional map, and the resulting distortions. Each of our eyes can be thought of as a camera that records a two-dimensional view of the three-dimensional world in front of us. Because our two eyes are some distance apart, the views from each eye are slightly different. Our brains take these two images and merge them to recreate three-dimensional images in our brain. (Try closing one eye and see how the world seems to flatten!) Similarly, two different camera-acquired images of the same scene can be used to reconstruct the third dimension, which would be lost if only one image were used.

5.4 Human Visual Discrimination and Acuity

What are the limitations of the human eye's ability to discern gray levels and spatial resolution? Such limitations have long been the subject of multidisciplinary studies by physicists, physiologists, and psychologists. It has been determined experimentally that the minimum discernible difference in gray level, called contrast sensitivity, is about 2% of full brightness.[1] Hence, a gray scale image need only have about 50 levels of gray (approximately what you saw in the 6-bit gray scale images above) to meet the needs of apparently continuous gray scale representation. However, if a small section of that image were to be cut out and brightly

---

[1]   Warren J. Smith, *Modern Optical Engineering*, McGraw Hill, 1990, page 126.

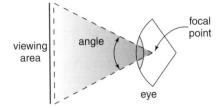

FIGURE 5.2 Depiction of the geometry of the viewing angle of the eye.

illuminated, we might again see edges between the pixels because the definition of full scale for the new image has been changed by removing a portion of the image.

In describing the ability of the eye to resolve fine detail, we generally speak in terms of "lines per degree of visual arc." This complex statement simply refers to the fact that as an image is brought closer to our eye, we can resolve more detail, until it becomes too close for our eye to focus clearly. In bright illumination, the adult, visually unimpaired human can resolve approximately 60 lines per degree of visual arc.[2] By visual arc, we mean the angle covered by the area being viewed at the apparent focal point of the eye, as shown in Figure 5.2.

Thus, if more than 60 lines are crowded side-by-side (with white space between them with the same width as the lines) into a single subtended degree of viewed space, they will appear to merge into a single gray mass to the human viewer. This is a good point at which to clarify a potential confusion in the use of the terms "lines" and "pixels." Note that to form a line out of pixels, we need to arrange a string of black pixels parallel to a string of white pixels. The eye will discern this black-white transition as a line. Hence, one line requires two strings of pixels. Therefore it is equivalent to say that the human eye can individually discern 120 pixels per subtended degree of visual arc, or 60 lines per degree. This spatial resolution limit of human visual acuity derives from the fact that the color-sensing *cone cells* that are concentrated at the center of your retina are packed approximately 120 across a distance of 290 micrometers of your retina. Also, one degree of a scene is displayed across 290 micrometers of the retina by the eye's lens. Hence, human visual acuity is a determined by the digitization of the analog image on your cornea!

Pixels

To make this more concrete, consider the act of holding a common 8.5 by 11 inch piece of paper one foot in front of your face with the longer dimension held horizontally (this is often called "landscape orientation"). We can apply some geometry and determine the subtended angle in both directions. These results in the horizontal and vertical directions are the specific values for the arc marked "angle" in Figure 5.2. The horizontal angle turns out to be 49.25 degrees, and the vertical angle is 39 degrees. Thus, if the paper were crowded with $39 \times 60 = 2340$ horizontal lines, a person with normal (20-20) vision would just be able to discern the individual lines on the paper. Similarly, if the paper were crowded with $49.25 \times 60 = 2955$ vertical lines, they would be just discernible. Recalling that two pixels are required to make the black-white transition of a line, these resolutions correspond to 4680×5910 or 27,658,800 pixels per page. This number of pixels would be sufficient to represent any image on the 8.5×11 inch page with no visible degradation compared to a perfect (unpixelized) image at a distance of one foot.

When dealing with printers we often quote the resolution in terms of dots per inch, which in our example would correspond to pixels per inch. Using the num-

---

[2] R.A. Weale, *Focus on Vision*, Harvard University Press, 1982, page 15.

bers above, we have seen that 550 dots per inch would be sufficient to fool any eye into thinking a picture was rendered without pixelization if the paper were held at distances of a foot or greater. This explains the long-term popularity of 600 dots per inch (dpi) laser and ink jet printers. Of course, by holding the paper closer, we can get greater perception of resolution; this explains the utility of printers with even higher resolutions than 600 dpi. How close we will hold a picture for viewing is, of course, a consideration in judgments about sufficient resolution. We call the shortest distance at which a person can focus on an object that person's *accommodation distance*. This distance typically varies with age from about 7 cm (2.75 inches) at age 10 to about 200 cm (78 inches) at age 65. At age 47, the accommodation is approximately the 12 inches used in the above example, and anything better than about 600 dpi resolution is wasted on the unaided eye. The student at 17 years of age with an accommodation of 9 cm (3.5 inches), on the other hand, feels cheated with anything less than a printer capable of 1200 dpi, motivating the use of 1200 dpi and greater printing resolutions in the magazine industry.

5.5 Other Types of Image Formation

Lens-based cameras are not the only means by which images may be formed from the real world. Several other examples of image formation systems include radar, sonar, X-rays, and tomography ("CAT scans"). These systems differ from traditional cameras in two ways: (1) the type of energy used to form the image (instead of visible light, radio, sound waves, X-rays, or radio emissions of nuclei under the influence of a magnetic field are used); and (2) the geometry of the system that relates the locations of the objects in the real world (three-dimensional) to the image world (two-dimensional). A type of image that we are all at least somewhat familiar with (from TV weather forecasts) is the *radar* image. "Radar" stands for "Radio Detection and Ranging," and is an excellent example of an imaging system that is fundamentally different in several ways from normal photography. These differences include:

- The type of energy used to form the image (radio waves vs. light waves);
- The fact that the illumination must be supplied by the imaging system, rather than the surrounding ambient conditions. That is, cameras and human eyes operate with visible light; radar, however, must supply its own "illumination" using radio waves;
- The geometry of the image (based on polar coordinates rather than rectangular coordinates). The image is formed by rays emanating from the center of the image, corresponding to the radar location; and
- The fact that the radar site (camera) is located in the image plane rather than perpendicular to the image plane and some distance away. This is convenient because it means, for example, that to get a radar image of several hundred square miles of the earth's surface, we don't have to take a camera an equivalent distance above the earth; we just position the radar on the surface at the center of the area.

Radar operates by sending a narrow beam of radio waves in a particular direction (like a searchlight) and waiting for reception of some reflected energy (from rain in the weather radar example). This is illustrated in Figure 5.3. Based on the speed of light, the distance to the reflector can be calculated by measuring how long it takes for the energy to bounce off of the imaged object and return to the sensor. The other dimension is the known angle of transmission. This gives us the

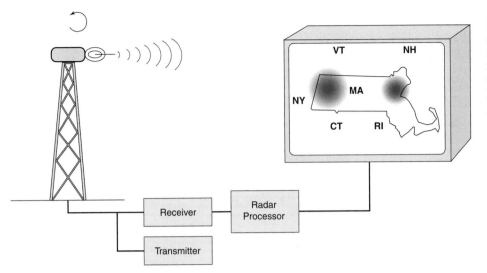

FIGURE 5.3 Diagram of a radar system. The antenna is like a rotating searchlight, sending rays of radio energy at successive angles around the compass. Wherever the searchlight beam strikes an object, energy bounces back to the radar, and is plotted on the image at the appropriate angle and distance from the antenna. The antenna is located at the center of the radar image.

two dimensions of a polar coordinate system (each point can be associated with a particular distance and set of angles). A dot is placed on the radar image at the point corresponding to that distance and angle from the radar site. The intensity of the dot corresponds to the intensity of the received reflection (the intensity of the rain in our example). Medical ultrasound systems operate very similarly to radar, but they use sound waves rather than radio waves.

One more type of imaging system that will be mentioned briefly is *holography*. This system is fundamentally unique in that it captures three-dimensional information from the original scene. It requires illumination from a special (laser) source, and a rather complex optical setup. The viewing requirements for a single holographic image are modest; recently advances in viewing technologies allow video holograms, color holograms, and presentation of holograms to groups of people.

📖 **Laser**

5.6 Converting Images to Bits

We live in an analog world, but almost all image processing is now performed digitally. Hence, we need to understand the methods for converting images to digital format, and back again. We also need to understand the implications of the various ways in which these conversions may be done, which inevitably involve approximations. To develop a binary representation of an image, we will want to determine what approximations we will be making. This depends on the nature of the image we are starting with, on our capability for converting, storing, and transmitting the image, and on the use for which the image is intended. Consideration of these issues requires making decisions, or *tradeoffs*, based on our desire for precision, our need to stay within the limitations of our equipment or budget, and the practical matter of how precisely we need to represent the image. First, we will discuss the general issue of digitization of information, and then we'll specifically consider the digitization of images of different kinds.

5.6.1 From Continuous Information to a Discrete Representation

In Chapter 3, we discussed how different types of information could be represented by binary digits. The process of representing information in binary form is sometimes known as *digitization*. In its most general form, this means the process by which anything and everything in our analog world can be converted into numbers for computer processing and storage. By *continuous* information, we mean a quantity that can take on the infinite number of possible values that belong to a continuum. *Discrete* information, on the other hand, implies that the quantity can assume only a finite number of values (at finite instances in time or finite locations in space). Much of what we measure in the world is continuous, whether or not our measurements are capable of representing continuous information. By definition, binary digits are discrete, because they can take on only two values. Furthermore, *only discrete information can be perfectly represented using binary digits*. This means that whenever we use bits to represent some continuous quantity, we are making an approximation and introducing some error by "throwing away" information. We must convert information from continuous form to discrete form as the first step in digitizing the information. Such a conversion, also known as an *analog to digital conversion*, necessarily requires some loss of information and precision.

Examples of continuous information include measurements of temperature, distance, voltage, pressure, speed, volume, and other quantities that take on a continuum of values, or an infinite number of possible values within some finite range. As we have discussed, we would require an infinite number of bits to perfectly represent any such quantity, because representation of the precise value would require infinite precision. In practice, however, we can satisfy our need for any level of precision by using enough bits to provide a sufficiently precise approximation of the continuous quantity. As we have mentioned, real-world applications do not require infinite precision; in practice, we have no use for it. Another example of continuous information would be an image of a scene. For an example, let us consider a so-called *black-and-white* photograph of a scene, which we wish to digitize and store. (Note that by a black-and-white photograph, we usually mean a photo with more than just black and white in it, and are really referring to the fact that shades of gray from black to white appear.) This example is actually continuous in two senses: the brightness may take on an infinite range of values at each point in the image, and the image contains an infinite (continuous) number of points. By *brightness*, we refer to the fact that at every point in the photo, there is some value that could describe the shade of gray at that point. These shades of gray, known as gray levels, range from black to white and are continuous—there are an infinite number of them. The actual value that we could associate with each gray level would be a measurement of how much light that shade reflects. Further, this photo is also *continuous in space*, because there is a different gray level at each point and, assuming a perfect camera, an infinite number of such distinguishable points distributed in the photo. So, we have an infinite number of locations, each of which can take on one of an infinite number of gray levels. How can we develop a binary representation of such a photo? The answer is that we must perform two processes, each of which provides an approximation to transform a continuous quantity into a discrete quantity. First, we must reduce the spatial resolution of the image from a continuous area representation into a finite number of small picture elements, or *pixels*, each representing small areas rather than infinitesimal points within a spatial continuum. Then, we must convert the brightness level corresponding to each pixel into a code representing the approximate gray level.

5.6.2 Pixels: A Matter of Spatial Resolution

Each pixel in an image corresponds to a small area (usually, but not always, square) of that image. Each pixel represents a single intensity (brightness) level. Ideally, we would choose this pixel area to be small enough so that when these pixels are put next to each other on a display, they present a pleasing representation of the original analog image to the viewer. This process of breaking a continuous image into a grid of pixels is sometimes called *pixelization, sampling, scanning,* or *spatial quantization.* Plate 2 shows a pixelized image and an inset that allows us to see the pixels.

The definition of "pleasing" is driven by the use to which the picture will be put. For an artist or an intelligence analyst, the sampled picture would have to have lost no content so far as the human eye with its limitations can detect. To the Internet user, the idea of pleasing often centers around the idea of conveying the content with a minimum of download time; hence, requiring as few pixels as make the picture recognizable. From the point of view of this book, the key is to determine the desired information that the digitized image is to convey, and then to choose the appropriate digitization procedure.

Pixels are usually arranged in a rectangular grid, as shown in Figure 5.4. In this figure we have artificially introduced a black border around the pixels so the individual pixels stand out. This picture consists of 169 pixels arranged in a 13 × 13 grid. Other spatial arrangements and shapes of pixels are sometimes used as well, such as concentric circles of truncated wedge-shaped pixels in radar imaging, but this grid arrangement of square pixels is by far the most common.

One way to create a pixelized image is to photograph a scene with a digitizing camera. There are many different types of these cameras; most of them have an array of light-sensitive devices, each of which is responsible for measuring the brightness at a single pixel's location. Another way to create a pixelized image is to put an image through a digitizing device, such as a scanner.

Let's return now to our example of the black-and-white photograph we wish to digitize for storage. How do we determine the number of pixels to use? Given an image of fixed size, the spatial resolution of the image—which affects our perception of the *quality* or *fidelity* of the image—is dependent on the number of pixels in the image. If we use too few pixels, then the image appears "coarse" or "blocky," and the effects of pixelization are apparent. Plates 3 through 6 show the same image for four different pixelization resolutions. The image in Plate 3 uses a 256 × 256 grid of pixels, for a total of 65,536 pixels. Plates 4, 5, and 6 show the same image with resolutions of 128 × 128 grid of pixels (6384 pixels), 64 × 64 (4096 pixels), and 16 × 16 (256 pixels), respectively.

⊚ **Different Pixelization Resolutions**

Each image in this sequence uses significantly *fewer pixels* than the previous version. This, of course, directly determines how much data storage or transmission will be required for the digitized versions of these images. If we know our capac-

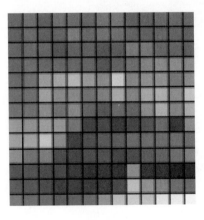

FIGURE 5.4 A 13 × 13 rectangular grid of pixels with black borders clearly delineating pixel boundaries.

ity for storage and have decided what degree of image quality we wish to retain, it would seem that we might be ready to make a decision on how to digitize and store the photo. But the amount of retained information is also dependent on how the brightness level at each pixel is digitized into a gray level value.

5.6.3 Shades of Gray

Let us continue with our example. Each pixel must be converted into binary data. To do this, we first determine the number of brightness levels that we wish to represent. For example, if we wish to use 8 bits to represent the brightness at each pixel, we would have 256 brightness levels (recall that a binary number with 8 bit positions may take on 256 different values, or equivalently that 2 raised to the power 8 equals 256), which we generally evenly distribute between pure black and brightest white. Then, each pixel would be associated with an 8-bit number corresponding to whichever of the 256 brightness levels is closest to the actual analog image brightness at that location in the image. This process is known as *quantization*; in fact, any time a continuous quantity is "rounded off" for purposes of digitization, the term quantization can be used to describe the process. Then, we can use binary digits to represent the quantized gray levels, and store each pixel as a collection of bits. As usual, we will want to have a number of gray levels that is a *power of two*, so that a given bit word length can be used to represent as many different gray levels as possible. Recall the images in Plates 3 through 6. Although you were not told this, each of the pixels in these images had gray levels represented by a *6-bit word*. This means that a total of $2^6 = 64$ possible gray levels were used to generate all four images. Each pixel was quantized and stored as six binary digits of memory, using codes ranging from black (000000) to white (111111). In Figure 5.5, the 256 × 256 version of this photograph is shown, again using a 6-bit gray-scale resolution. In Figures 5.5 through 5.7, the same photo is shown *at the same spatial resolution*, but with 6 bits (for 64 gray levels), 3 bits (8 gray levels), and 1 bit (2 gray levels) used to represent and store each pixel. You

FIGURE 5.5 A 6-bit (64 gray levels) image.

FIGURE 5.6 A 3-bit (8 gray levels) image.

FIGURE 5.7 A 1-bit (black and white only) image.

can see that the effect of differing gray-scale resolutions on image quality is clearly discernible, *but is of a different nature than the effect of differing spatial resolutions.*

Therefore, to determine how much storage will be required for our photo, we must choose both a spatial resolution, which sets the number of pixels, and a brightness resolution, which sets the number of bits used to represent each pixel.

The total number of bits required to store this image (directly) is just the product of the total number of pixels and the number of bits used per pixel. For our example, if we choose to represent the photo by an array of 64 × 64 pixels, and decide that 32 gray levels (5 bits) is enough, then our image can be stored using 64 × 64 × 5 = 20, 480 bits, or 2560 bytes, or 2.5 kB.

Note, however, that depending on how the storage system we use represents integers, we may wind up using a full byte, or even two bytes, for each pixel, even if we are only using 5 or fewer bits per pixel. This is due to the *standard formats for data representation* as described in Chapter 4. In later chapters, we will discuss the implications of this for different applications, and present some techniques for reducing the amount of storage required without adversely affecting the image quality.

It is important to note again that the resolution appropriate for a digitized image depends on the use for which it is intended. Images that are meant to be viewed by human beings do not require more resolution than the limits of human visual acuity can appreciate. Or, in some cases, the means of reproducing the image sets the underlying limit of picture fidelity. We encounter such reproduction limitations, for example, in the presentation of an image on a television or by printing on paper using a given laser printer.

For example, the image in Plate 3, with 256 × 256 pixels, and six bits per pixel for a total of 64 gray levels, was determined to be *good enough* for an image of this size in an application such as this textbook. A higher-quality representation might require more storage, yet would appear no different to an observer. On the other hand, if this image were to be stored for use by a computerized image analysis routine, there might be advantages to using more pixels, more bits per pixel, or both.

5.6.4 Color Representation

So far, we have considered only black-and-white images. How can we represent *color images* in binary form? Students of art may recall that any color can be created by adding the right proportions of red, green, and blue light. These should not be confused with the "subtractive primary colors"—magenta, yellow and cyan—that are used when combining pigments. While other colors may be used, red, green, and blue are the standard colors which are mixed to form other colors of light. Each color can be created by these colors in the appropriate combination; thus, *we can represent a color with three numbers indicating the amounts of red, green, and blue light* that combine to produce that color. This system for specifying colors is known as the RGB system. For example, 10 units of red, green, and blue will form white of a certain intensity. If we increase this to 20 units of red, green, and blue, we will still have a white light, but it will be more intense. Why does the eye perceive combinations of red, green, and blue as a full spectrum of colors? The unimpaired human (that is, someone who possesses "trichromatic vision" and does not suffer from a variety of color blindness ailments such as monochromatism or dichromatism) has three kinds of cells in the eye that are sensitive to different ranges of wavelengths of light and are used to distinguish color. The three values for red, green, and blue content in an RGB can produce a response by the eye like that of any other color because our eyes can only interpret a color from the three responses or the respective cells.

Standard color televisions use tight clusters of red, green, and blue color sources to create the illusion of other colors. Because these sources are small and closely spaced, the human eye cannot discern the individual components, and we just see the color combination as a single shade. However, standard color television systems do not use a completely digitized version of the image; each row of the display, or *raster*, is transmitted as continuous information for each of the color components.

When we wish to digitize a color image, we must first spatially quantize the image into pixels, as we did for black-and-white imagery. Then, we must determine the RGB representation for each pixel. That is, we must determine the amount of red, green, and blue needed to represent the color at the pixel's location. Finally, we must digitize these three numbers, to represent each value by a binary number of a predefined length. Consider digitizing a particular pixel. Note that because we are representing these color components in binary form, we must approximate their contributions by a finite number of bits. If, for example, we use 3 bits for each color value, we would be able to represent $2^3 = 8$ different intensity levels of red, of green, and of blue. This representation would require a total storage of *9 bits* per pixel—three bits for each of the three colors. This would give us $8 \times 8 \times 8 = 512$ different possible color combinations. In more mathematical terms, because we are using 9 bits, we should be able to represent 2^9, or 512 different colors. Another system used to represent color imagery is called HLS (hue, luminance, and saturation). This system does not represent colors by combinations of other colors, but it still uses three numerical values. The *hue* of a pixel represents where its pure color component falls on a scale that extends across the visible light spectrum, from red to violet. The *luminance* of a pixel represents how bright or dark the pixel is. The *saturation* represents how "pure" the color is; that is, how much it is or is not diluted by the addition of white, with 100% indicating no dilution with white. Thus, for example, pastel colors have saturation levels well below 100%. This set of three numbers, like RGB, is sufficient to represent any color. So, in an HLS system, the color of each pixel is again represented by three binary words, each of which represents a digitized value. The effects of variations in hue and saturation are depicted in Plate 7.

◉ **RGB Representation**

Yet one more approach needs to be described to convey the way in which colors in pictures are coded in real systems. Suppose that only a few bits were going to be used to represent our images; we might choose to only use a small number of bits so as to speed transmission over a network, or to allow more images to be stored on a computer disk of a given size. If we decided to use nine bits as in our example above, we would be allowed a total of 512 colors. But, using exactly the scheme described above, this would be 512 specific colors that may not well represent the range of colors in our picture.

For example, if our picture happened to be a reproduction of a "black and white" photograph, we might be quite disappointed with the result: the above scheme has a total of eight shades of gray available among its 512 colors. Thus our picture would have a very coarse representation of the shades in our photograph. The representation of our photograph would, of course, be greatly enhanced if we had 512 shades of gray available to us. This kind of optimization of the use of the colors used to represent an image is actually used. Prior to representing an image in discrete colors, a software procedure can be used to scan the entire image and determine the *most useful set* of colors to have if we are limited to a specific number. Then, carrying our example forward for the 9-bit case, the total picture representation will consist of a list of 512 colors, each specified in perhaps 24 bits, 8 for each RGB color component. Then, the picture will be represented with each pixel given a 9-bit number, which is simply an index that may be used to look up the 24 bits of color information from the complete table. We call this a *palette color representation*, because the table describes a palette of colors from which the final picture is rendered.

5.6.5 Color Discrimination

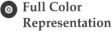

Full Color Representation

Studies such as those described above for human spatial and luminance discrimination have also been conducted for color discrimination. The average person can discern about 100 saturated (that is, pure) colors from each other. When both luminance and hue are varied, one can discern about 6,000 variations of color intensity. Finally, about another 60 levels of saturation are discernible, for a grand total of approximately 360,000 recognizable colors. With appropriate encoding, we would expect to need 19 bits per pixel for full color representation, with the same caveats as before of the effects of examining cutouts of such an image in isolation. In practice, though, 8 bits per color or 24 bits per pixel are general used for full color representation, for the sake of convenience.

In Plates 8–10, we see a sequence in which the number of colors used to represent the image is decreased progressively from 24 bits down to 4 bits. For many natural scenes in which we have a good intuitive feel for the true appearance and abundance of color variations, the first reduction from 24 to 16 bits is noticeable in a comparison. As we drop to 8 bits, even without a comparison it is easy to discern the fact that the picture is no longer true in the sense of an accurately rendered scene.

In Plate 11 we see the application of yet another means to better represent a picture with a limited number of colors. Here a process known as *dithering* has been applied. As is done with the color images in a newspaper, color dots from the available palette have been arranged in clusters to approximate a new color when the result is viewed from a sufficient distance. The dithering process produces a rather coarse-looking picture when viewed too closely, but the results are quite appealing from the appropriate distance. In particular, compare this picture at a good distance with the previous one, which used the same number of colors.

5.7 Binocular Vision and 3D displays

As humans, most of us see the world through two eyes. This binocular (or stereo, or 3D) vision provides us with additional visual information referred to as *depth perception*. It is in fact a misnomer to refer to this type of vision as 3D, because only very limited information in the third dimension is available. This limited information is sufficient to do two things: it makes the scene look more "real" to the viewer, and it provides some specific information as to the location of objects in the front-to-back direction.

Figure 5.8 illustrates the two images forming a binocular vision pair. Of course, in normal vision your eyes see not two separate images, but the fused image with the depth dimension added. We are used to having this additional dimension in our vision, and two-dimensional displays eliminate this additional information. Hence, development of three-dimensional displays has been an active research area for many years.

The principle behind stereo vision displays is simple: different images must be presented to each eye, corresponding to the two images that the eyes would form from their disparate positions in the human head. This is easy to accomplish for one viewer with still images, as illustrated by the old-fashioned stereoscope in which one photograph was simply held in place in front of each eye. For multiple viewers and moving images, the situation becomes more complicated.

FIGURE 5.8 Example of images produced by binocular (stereo) vision with camera separation equivalent to the spacing of the human eyes. Some people can cross their eyes in such a way as to fuse these two pictures in their minds into a single stereoscopic scene. The role of stereo displays is to produce this without effort, talent, or eye strain.

The original 3D movies that were shown in theaters made use of color to isolate the images. The images that one eye was meant to see were presented in blue, while those for the other eye were presented in red. The audience wore plastic glasses that placed a blue filter over one eye and a red filter over the other. While a true sensation of 3D images was produced, the color of these images was something like black-and-white with disturbing tinges of blue and red at the edges. That is, all color realism was abandoned to achieve depth realism. New systems for 3D display make use of optical *polarization* to separate the images. Polarization is a property of light that may go unnoticed in your day-to-day experience. Briefly, in addition to being being able to break up white light into colors, we can also break light up into two components known as polarizations. There are actually two ways to do that, but we will dwell upon the easier to explain: linear polarization components. Special filters can be used to produce light that has only a vertical component, and other filters can produce light with only a horizontal component. Each of these streams of light would then pass again through a filter of the same type or be totally blocked by a filter of the opposite type. Because any color of light has these two possible components, we can use such filters to selectively pass or block entire color images. Thus, if we project the two stereo images in color, but, with each projected by a different polarization of light, then the audience wearing polarized glasses (opposite filter types over each of their eyes) would perceive a 3D display.

Yet another approach makes use of what are known as *shutter glasses* such as those shown in Plate 12. In this case, the two images that we wish to present to the viewer's eyes are presented alternately. The viewer wears a pair of glasses that have electronic shutters in front of each eye that allow each image in the sequence to be seen only by the appropriate eye. The states of the shutters in the glasses are of course synchronized with the presentation sequence; this is usually done via an additional signal from the display or a wired connection to the display electronics. The mechanism behind the operation of the electronic shutters is typically the same liquid crystal technology that is used to draw numbers on the face of a calculator display.

5.8 From Images to Video

Most people have seen old films of live or animated sequences, in which the choppy motion makes clear that the viewer is actually looking at a sequence of still images. Indeed, everything which we call "video," including television, movies, and computer graphics, consists of a series of still images that are displayed so as to appear in continuous motion to the human eye. The only difference between your latest laser disk movie and "The Birth of a Nation" is how well the eye is fooled into thinking it is viewing actual continuous motion.

5.8.1 Human Visual Persistence

If you look at a well-lit scene and then close your eyes, you will notice that the image can still be sensed for some time after the eyes close. This is due to the amount of time that the retina retains some of the information with which it has been stimulated. This phenomenon, which places limits on how fast our visual system can react to changes, is known as *visual persistence* or *visual latency*. Simply put, our visual system has a slow response to change in stimulus. We can take advantage of this to develop techniques for digital video systems. Although an image on the retina decays gradually, rather than lasting a specific amount of time, there is a critical period during which the stimulus changes so little that the visual system cannot take in any new information even if the eyes are open. This period, on average, is about 50 milliseconds, or one twentieth of a second. Thus, the average human visual system can only take in about 20 different images per second before they begin to blur together. If these images are sufficiently similar, then the blurring which takes place appears to the eye to resemble motion, in the same way we discern it when an object moves smoothly in the real world.

Another way to measure visual persistence is to determine the number of flashes of light per second that would appear to be a continuous, flicker-free illumination. Studies show that this varies as a function of the intensity of the flashes, but that almost no flashing is evident at above 50 flashes per second, and perception even for the brightest of lights disappears for rates above 80 flashes per second.[3]

In fact, if your eyes had a faster response than this, you might find it quite annoying, since the 60 Hz electrical system used in the United States causes electric lights to flicker at a rate of 120 times per second. Because of human visual latency, we only see continuous light. In Europe, the power fluctuates at 50 Hz and hence illumination pulses at 100 flashes per second; they are living closer to the edge of perception there.

The above phenomenon has been used since the beginning of the 20th century to produce "moving pictures," or movies. Thomas Edison, the inventor of the motion picture camera, needed to balance the needs of human perception with the desire to minimize the amount (hence cost) of film that needed to be taken. He determined experimentally that 10 frames per second sufficed to provide the illusion of continuous motion (just barely). He also determined that viewers were quite annoyed by 10 flashes per second caused by the shutter opening and closing to accommodate motion of the film between looks. This phenomenon was addressed simply by having the shutter open and close three times for each single motion of the film, producing a 60-flashes-per-second presentation. This higher flash rate was tolerated nicely by humans. Soon after, the frame rate was increased by the motion picture industry to provide a more pleasing 24 frames per second

---

[3] Tom N. Cornsweet, *Visual Perception*, Academic Press, 1970, page 389.

to provide an improved illusion of continuous motion. Again the phenomenon was addressed by having the shutter open and close, this time twice for each single motion of the film, producing a 48-flashes-per-second presentation. This rate is still used for motion pictures. Television, interestingly enough, displays 30 new images per second, but suffers from the same flash phenomenon if simply presented. This phenomenon is also addressed by presenting the images twice per frame, in a sense. The way this is accomplished is that 60 times per second, *every other line or raster is changed*. Each new image is *painted* onto the screen in a two-step process—first the odd rows, then the even ones—so that at every point on the screen, things are locally changing at a rate of 60 times per second. In this way we do not discern the choppiness we would see if the image were refreshed all at once 30 times per second. This same phenomenon can be used to create *digitized video*—a video signal stored in binary form. We have already discussed how individual images are digitized; digital video simply consists of *a sequence of digitized still images*, displayed at a rate sufficiently high to appear as continuous motion to the human visual system. The individual images are obtained by a digital camera that acquires a new image at a fast enough rate (say, 60 times per second), to create a *time-sampled* version of the scene in motion. Because of human visual latency, these samples at certain instants in time are sufficient to capture all of the information that we are capable of taking in! When we discuss digitization of audio signals, we'll go into more depth about the idea of sampling a quantity at different times.

5.8.2 Adding Up the Bits

In Chapter 3, we calculated that one hour's worth of music stored on a compact disc would require storage of over 5 billion bits (608 MB) of information. How does this compare to one hour's worth of digital video?

Let's make some simple assumptions to get a rough idea: let's assume a screen that is 512×512 pixels—about the same resolution you can get on a good TV set. Of course we want color—let's say we'll use 3 bits per color per pixel, for a total of 9 bits per pixel; that seems pretty modest. Now, let's say we want the scene to change 60 times per second, so that we don't see any flicker or choppiness. This means we will need (512×512) pixels $\times 9$ bits per pixel $\times 60$ frames per second $\times 3600$ seconds = 500 billion bits per hour—just for the video. Francis Ford Coppola's *The Godfather*, at over 3 hours, would require nearly 191 GB—over 191 billion bytes—of memory using this approach. This almost sounds like an offer we can refuse. But, do films actually require this much storage? Fortunately, the answer is no. The reason we can represent video with significantly fewer bits than in this example is due to *compression* techniques, which take advantage of certain predictabilities and redundancies in video information to reduce the amount of information to be stored. In the following chapters, we'll discuss some of these techniques and the data storage requirements for video that they help us achieve.

Summary

So, *is* a picture worth ten thousand words? That depends on the picture and the words, of course! But 10,000 words, at an average of 6 characters per word, and 8 bits per character for the ASCII representation, would require 480,000 bits—approximately 60 KB—of storage. And an image which is 256×256 pixels, with 8 bits used for the gray level of each pixel, is also 524,288 bits, or approximately 64 KB. So, it seems as if the writers of those old adages might have had more insight into information representation than one might first suspect.

In this chapter, we have discussed how images—still and moving—can be represented in binary form for purposes of storage, processing, or transmission. We've talked about the two processes required to form a binary representation of an image—pixelization and quantization—and described how these processes affect both image quality and storage size. We've discussed a few ways of representing color information, and talked about how video standards are based on the performance of the human visual system.

In the next chapter, we will go into some specifics regarding how digital imagery is typically acquired, represented, stored, and transmitted. We'll talk about standard formats for common image-rendering devices, such as fax machines, printers, and PC monitors. And, we'll discuss some more implications of the large amounts of storage needed for video, which will lead to the need for schemes to reduce the storage without compromising the information.

Try These Exercises

1. Locate three images: one of a natural scene (containing such objects as buildings, trees, or people); one related to your major academic interest (e.g., artwork, architectural drawing, or piece of equipment); and one containing text. Describe the information content in each scene. Determine appropriate spatial, intensity, and color (if appropriate) resolution for each scene. Calculate the number of bits needed to store each scene. If possible, digitize each scene to the stated resolutions.

2. In the process of image formation, a 3D scene is reduced to a 2D image. Describe a specific 3D scene and then describe what information is present and what is lost when pictures are taken from various angles. Use specific examples. How many pictures must be taken to represent all of the information in the original scene?

3. List three different projections that might be used to portray the 3D earth in two dimensions. Sketch the effect of each of these. Explain the advantages and disadvantages of each, and where each might be most useful.

4. Download a "NEXRAD" weather radar image from the Web; get one that displays some interesting weather. You may use any NEXRAD site nationwide. Locate the radar site, and explain the geometry of the image formation with respect to the radar site. Explain (and illustrate if possible) artifacts such as shadowing and beam elevation effects.

5. Draw a 6 × 6 rectangular grid on your paper. On that grid print or write a single alphanumeric character. Generate the transmitted bit string for the binary encoding of that character, assuming black–white encoding, and a left-to-right, top-to-bottom scan.

6. Draw a replica of the 6 × 6 grid and decode the binary data stream from the previous problem, being sure to use only information contained in the data stream. Comment on the legibility of the reconstructed character.

7. Comment on the characteristics of the encoding procedure used in the previous problem. How many unique characters is it theoretically capable of encoding? Use "characters" in the broadest sense here. Now consider the set of English alphanumeric characters (the ASCII character set, to be specific). Comment on the "universal" and "unique" nature of this encoding procedure with respect to this set of characters. How does the way in which a character is written impact the situation?

8. Use the "Image color encoding" applet to examine the individual pixels in the stained glass and fire hydrant images. From your observations, what is the apparent number of possible values of each of the primary colors? From this result, in total how many different colors can be represented at each pixel? How many bits are required to represent this data for each pixel?

⊙ Image Color Encoding

9. Use the "Image color encoding" applet to examine the pixel values for the professor.gif image. Explain your observation.

10. Use the "Basic Image Manipulation" applet to examine the fire hydrant image. In succession, remove the red, green, and blue from the image. Comment on each resulting image. Why is there relatively little change when the blue component is removed? Why is the hydrant no longer yellow when either the red or green is removed?

11. A wall-mounted image display is being designed. It will be seen from a minimum distance of 5 meters. The display measures 3 meters by 2 meters. For the image to appear essentially perfect to observers, determine the number of picture elements needed horizontally and vertically.

12. Conventional TV will soon be supplemented by a high-definition television system (HDTV). The standards will be (approximately): 1,000 display lines vertically, and a width-to-height ratio of 3:2, 60 images per second. Aspect ratio is the ratio of screen width to height. For standard TV the width-to-height ratio is 4:3, which is rather narrow compared to the eye's field of view. Given this data, determine the approximate number of picture elements along each line, the time required to scan each line, and the approximate digital data rate (assuming no coding techniques are used to reduce the data rate, which is unrealistic).

13. Scoreboards at sports stadiums typically are now capable of displaying full-motion images. Determine (using reasonable approximations) the overall size of the screen, resolution, and actual size of each pixel, for such a screen. Assume the apparent resolution to spectators will be approximately equal to standard television.

14. Conventional television, and even HDTV, is quite limited in the images which can be presented. Determine an approximation of the data rate required to transmit true, high-definition three-dimensional images with motion. Explain your assumptions. Comment on the result. Are there any obvious ways to reduce the data rate?

📖 HDTV

15. A mirror appears to reverse the "left" and "right" orientation, but not "up" and "down." Explain this phenomenon. Compare this to image formation by a lens.

16. Consider a radar system that can display images at ranges from 1 mile to 50 miles from the radar site, with each pixel on the radar screen representing an area on the ground that is no more than one mile in length or width. What range of time delays must this radar system measure? If the "real world" pixel size at the 50 mile range is approximately 1 mile in width, what is the pixel size at the one mile range? Discuss the considerations in determining the speed at which the radar antenna should rotate. To complete this problem, you may wish to make use of additional information on radar systems beyond that which is contained in this text.

6 Computer Graphics and Virtual Reality

Objectives

Now that we understand what images are, and how they represent the real world, we can extend those principles to the virtual world, creating images that appear real but are formed synthetically. These concepts include:

▲ two fundamentally different ways to store image information (bit maps or scene descriptions);

▲ the means of rendering stored image information into a visible image;

▲ types of display devices, their features and limitations;

▲ fundamentals of the Virtual Reality Modeling Language (VRML); and

▲ basic means of making the artificial appear real (lighting, texture mapping, etc.).

6.1 Synthesizing Images

The previous chapter dealt with the formation of images from the real world. Of course, it is also possible to form images that do not come from existing objects in the physical world. An obvious example is a sketch that a person might draw on a piece of paper, perhaps representing a mechanical part that has not yet been manufactured. To be precise, we might refer to that as a "diagram" or "sketch," but it is common to use the term "image" rather loosely. In the recent past, it would have been easy for a person to tell whether a given image came from the real world or not; with today's high-quality computer graphics, this may be nearly impossible. It is still important to keep the distinction in mind, however! In synthesizing images, it is only necessary to have the information describing those aspects of the object that we wish to see in the image. One such approach, called *vector graphics*, allows images such as mechanical drawings to be produced. This concept can be extended to describe many more features of the desired objects, such as surface color and texture, to permit so-called *virtual reality* images. Beyond realistic-looking images, a vital component of virtual reality imagery is the ability for the image to change in response to inputs from the viewer. The Virtual Reality Modeling Language (VRML) provides a set of capabilities to permit the construction, via a set of computer instructions, of a synthetic world through which the viewer may move. Given that we have the information describing the desired image, we will also need some information on the capabilities and operation of the display device on which the image will be produced or *rendered*. This information includes such aspects as resolution in dots per inch, and color capabilities. It is easy to think of many examples of synthetic images. The familiar weather radar image is synthetic, in that it in no way represents anything like what the human eye would see from any vantage point. Also, a data set in a geographic information database is not an image; it is a collection of numbers that may represent elevations, roads, and so forth. As humans, we could not make sense of these thousands of numbers if we looked at them directly. However, if these numbers are converted into an image (for example by using different colors to represent different surface features, and placing those colors on a two-dimensional surface), the eye and brain may quickly understand their meaning.

6.2 Two Ways to Store Images

A computer can represent an image in one of two fundamentally different ways:

- By *storing* the light intensity (and possibly the color) of each point in the image, or
- By *describing* the image content.

The latter method is called the *vector graphics* approach, and it is commonly used for Computer-Aided Design (CAD) software. Using this approach, a circle might be represented by its center, its radius, its color, and the width of the line used to draw the circle. This is a very powerful approach that fundamentally involves storage of more than just a single image. It involves storage of a description of the objects themselves, from which one or more images may be "rendered." Vector graphics began with computerization of hand-drawn mechanical drawings, and has broadened in scope to become a central part of what is referred to as Virtual Reality. One might argue that this is a contradiction in terms, because virtual means "unreal." In this usage, "reality" refers to the fact that a description of some part of the world, real or synthetic, is stored. The term "virtual" indicates that this world may not physically exist, and is not stored literally, in image form, in the computer. The former example of stored imagery—-direct point-by-point storage, also known as literal imagery—is what we usually think of as a digital picture, and is the digital equivalent of a photograph or painting, which does the same thing in an analog fashion. In the digital photograph approach (known as *bit-mapped graphics*), the image is quantized spatially and with respect to the number of colors (or grey levels). The amount of storage required is determined by the number of pixels and the number of different colors (and/or light intensities) that we wish to be able to represent. As an example, consider storing an image of a black circle. Using the vector graphics (Figure 6.1) approach, we might only have to store the parameters used to describe the circle: center at (0,0), radius of 20 mm, line width of 1 mm, and color black. With bit-mapped graphics (Figure 6.2), we must store the intensity (black or white in this case) at each point in the image. If the image area is 50 mm × 50 mm and each pixel is 1 mm in each direction, this requires the storage of 2,500 intensities.

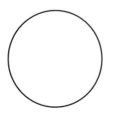

FIGURE 6.1 Representation of a circle using vector graphics.

FIGURE 6.2 Representation of a circle using bit-mapped graphics.

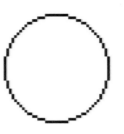

Notice that the vector graphic image can be reproduced as perfectly as the output device (printer or display monitor) will allow. The bit-mapped graphic, on the other hand, has fixed resolution and may appear different on different output devices (as evident from Figures 6.1 and 6.2).

The above example demonstrates two advantages of vector graphics, but there is one very large disadvantage: many images (most natural images) cannot be represented in this way. In most cases, only images that we generate synthetically are amenable to this representation, although when we discuss image data compression we will discuss the possibility of applying it to natural images.

6.3 Displaying the Bit-Mapped Image

Any digital image contains two fundamental aspects: (1) the digital representation of the image stored in computer memory; and (2) the image that the user actually sees, which is referred to as the *rendering*. This is analogous to the performance of music, for which the score contains the basic information, but the performer generates (renders) the actual sound. Clearly, in the music example the rendering will vary greatly as a function of the instrument and ability of the musician. Similarly, a digital image will appear very different as a function of the graphics processing and physical display characteristics.

The stored bit-mapped image information determines the ultimate limits on displayed quality and characteristics. Following are these basic characteristics for bit-mapped graphics:

- Numbers of pixels in the horizontal and vertical directions, or equivalently, size and spatial resolution;
- Presence or absence of color information;
- Resolution in the intensity domain (number of gray levels, number of bits); and
- Resolution in the color domain (expressed in RGB, HLS, or other coordinates).

The above represent the parameters that determine maximum image quality for bit-mapped images in standard formats. In the future some additional parameters will become important:

- Multiple views of the scene for stereo vision or alternative viewpoints, or a complete 3D data map from which any view or set of views may be generated;
- Multiple-resolution information so that image resolution may be matched to display resolution; and
- Additional information pertaining to each pixel, such as type of entity represented (object, foreground, background, etc.).

The fundamental limitation in rendering the image is imposed by the display device, which may be a CRT display, LCD display, projection system, laser printer, and so forth. Some combination of hardware and software processes the digital image information and presents it to the output device. In the case of hardcopy output devices, a variety of software standards and complete languages exist to facilitate this processing, such as PostScript and HP-PCL (Hewlett Packard Printer Command Language).

6.4 Display Device Formats

Many standard formats for the display of bit-mapped image information have been devised, and several are presented in the following sections. These examples illustrate only a few of the more common formats.

6.4.1 Visual Display Devices

In the PC world, various versions of the so-called VGA (Video Graphics Array) standard are most common. These variations on the VGA standard are identified principally by the image and color resolution. Standard VGA began with a resolution of 640 × 400 pixels (horizontal and vertical resolutions), with only 16 possible color values for each pixel. Note that in reference to graphics displays, the term "colors" refers to the full range of luminance, hue, and saturation (i.e., to both brightness and hue). This soon evolved into what is called "super VGA," with a resolution of 640 × 480 and 256 colors, which has also become obsolete. Higher resolutions and more colors have become the norm today. Computer displays are of two fundamental types: CRTs and LCDs. CRT stands for cathode ray tube; the name describes the essence of this device. It is a glass tube which uses beams (rays) of electrons emitted from a device called a cathode to cause fluorescent chemicals (phosphors) to light up on its face. This device has been the basis of television since its origin more than 50 years ago. While still common, these CRT displays are gradually being supplanted by flat-panel devices called LCD displays. LCD stands for liquid crystal display; in this device, chemicals (liquid crystals) are made to become transparent or opaque at each pixel location, thereby blocking or transmitting light from a source mounted behind the liquid crystal. By controlling the pattern of transparent and opaque areas in the display, a desired image can be formed.

CRT displays are fundamentally dynamic devices, in which the image must be continually *refreshed*, or recreated, regardless of whether or not any changes are occurring in the image. In other words, for the super VGA standard referred to above, all 307,200 pixels must be refreshed often enough so that they appear continuous to the eye. This implies a refresh rate of at least 50 times per second to satisfy the human eye. For 256 colors, this implies 1 byte per pixel, or 15,360,000 bytes to be read every second. This is a high data rate, and this data must be converted to analog form to drive conventional CRT monitors.

LCD displays do not require this constant refreshing; each pixel remains in the state to which it was last set until the state is changed. This accounts for the fact that LCD displays do not have the flicker sometimes noticeable on CRT displays.

In either case, data storage, data retrieval, and monitor interface issues are usually performed by a dedicated piece of hardware called a *video interface board* (or card). It would be difficult to acquire data at the needed rate from standard computer memory, and doing so would slow the computer (perhaps severely) in its performance of other functions. How much video board memory is needed? For the previous example, at least 307,200 bytes are needed. Memory boards are usually equipped with memory in increments of 0.5 MB (500 KB, 1 MB, or 2 MB); anything less than 1 MB is obsolete at present. This additional memory is used both for higher spatial resolution and higher color resolution. A common standard at present is 1024×768 resolution with 65,536 colors. This corresponds to 2 bytes of color information per pixel, and can produce almost perfect natural-appearing colors, but requires 2 MB of memory. Note that a natural result of the refresh requirement of computer displays is that they are well suited for display of changing information such as video, as well as for static information.

6.4.2 Printers and Similar Output Devices

Devices that produce their output on paper are referred to as hard copy output devices, or, more commonly, *printers*. There are several varieties of printers:

- *The facsimile machine.* The modern fax machine implements the so-called "Group 3" standard, which made the modern fax machine practical and affordable. It was optimized to give acceptable quality for a printed page while minimizing telephone transmission time with the modems then available (2400 or 4800 bps). The goal was 1 minute per page. The specifications are simple: black and white only (no gray scale), a vertical resolution of 3.85 lines per mm, and a horizontal resolution of 1728 pixels per line. A simple digital encoding technique is used to reduce transmission time by only transmitting data when black–white transitions occur, and skipping over the large amount of white space on a typical page.

- *The dot matrix printer.* Prior to the dot matrix printer, printers were essentially restricted to printing standard typographical symbols. Very crude graphics could be created with clever manipulation of these symbols, but they operated essentially as electric typewriters. The dot matrix printer brought added flexibility. It forms characters as sets of small dots created by tapping fine wires on a ribbon, thereby forming ink dots on the page. Typically, a vertical array of seven such wires is moved across the page, forming characters. The page is then advanced vertically as in a typewriter, and the process is repeated. If the page is advanced an amount equal to the height of the seven wires, then a matrix of dots (actually potential dots) is created over the whole page. Hence, a digital image is possible, with each dot representing a black or white picture element. The resolution of this type of dot matrix printer is approximately equal to that of a standard VGA display (without the color).

- *The laser printer.* This technology perfected the dot matrix approach by implementing a fast, quiet means to apply 300 dots per inch (dpi) to the page. That figure is now 600 dpi in most current laser printers. This resolution is fine enough to make lines that appear nearly perfectly continuous to the eye; the limitation for images is the black–white nature of the dots. However, good quality gray scale images may be generated by trading resolution for gray scale. That is, in a given region, a gray level can be generated by varying the density of black dots from near zero (white) to all present (black).

- *Color printers.* Some early color printers operated on the dot matrix principle, but with three ribbon colors (in the subtractive primaries). Modern ink jet printers operate on the same basic principle as the dot matrix printer—a vertical line of "dot formers" scanned line by line over the page—but instead of wires and ribbon, these use a small jet of ink at each dot location. This may be extended to three colors of ink at each location to form color images. A similar extension may be applied to the laser printer to provide color capability.

6.5 From Numbers to Images

A problem in early color display systems that still exists to some extent was the mismatch between the amount of stored color information for each pixel and the color dynamic range of typical displays. For example, while some of the VGA standard formats allow 256 different colors (1 byte per pixel), the video display has three inputs to determine the color of each pixel (red, green, and blue intensities, each of which can have at least 256 levels). Because the video display device is capable of $256 \times 256 \times 256$ (16,777,216) different pixel color values, the following question arises: "How should the 256 available codes be mapped into the 16,777,216 available display colors to provide a reasonable representation of the bit-mapped image?"

The practical answer is that the two quantities are mapped together via a look-up table with 256 3-byte entries. Each pixel code then indicates a location in that table that specifies a set of red, green, and blue intensities. The look-up table is often called a *palette* (or a color map) because it represents all the colors that are available to make the image on the screen. This overall system is referred to as *indexed color* or *pseudo-color*, because the stored data is used as an index into the available display colors. Note that the indexed color system can be used for any reduction of the ultimate set of over 16 million video display colors into the 256 which will be used. As an example, consider the default 256 color VGA format. While this specific format is essentially obsolete, the principle remains important. The default color palette is a look-up table that maps the 256 VGA colors into one of a subset of the 16,777,216 video display colors (each red, green, and blue intensity is stored in a 6-bit value, resulting in a total of 262,144 possible video display colors). The look-up table lists index values (1 through 256) in the left column. The

DEFAULT VGA COLOR MAP				
Index I	I + 0	I + 1	I + 2	I + 3
	R G B	R G B	R G B	R G B
0	0 0 0	0 0 42	0 42 0	0 42 42
4	42 0 0	42 0 42	42 21 0	42 42 42
8	21 21 21	21 21 63	21 63 21	21 63 63
12	63 21 21	63 21 63	63 63 21	63 63 63
16	0 0 0	5 5 5	8 8 8	11 11 11
20	14 14 14	17 17 17	20 20 20	24 24 24
24	28 28 28	32 32 32	36 36 36	40 40 40
28	45 45 45	50 50 50	56 56 56	63 63 63
32	0 0 63	16 0 63	31 0 63	47 0 63
36	63 0 63	63 0 47	63 0 31	63 0 16
40	63 0 0	63 16 0	63 31 0	63 47 0
44	63 63 0	47 63 0	31 63 0	16 63 0
...	...	...	...	...
252	0 0 0	0 0 0	0 0 0	0 0 0

next four columns list the corresponding red, green, and blue intensity values for the given index I, and for the three following indices $(I + 1)$, $(I + 2)$, and $(I + 3)$.

Inspection of the table will reveal that it contains three sections: Index values 0 through 15 point to 16 different color values spread throughout the color space. This is used for the original VGA mode, which only displays 16 colors. Index values 16 through 31 are mapped to 16 different gray intensity values. The remainder of the indices are mapped to color values distributed throughout the color space. For the 256 color mode, all three sections are useful because no color values (other than 0, 0, 0—black) are repeated for different indices.

The computer display begins with this default palette. Clearly, 256 color values represent quite a limited set, compared to the millions of possible video display colors. This limitation is partially overcome by allowing the palette to be changed to whatever is most appropriate for displaying the image at hand. In other words, each screen image can have its own, possibly different, color palette. By processing the image to be displayed, and identifying the colors that appear frequently in that image, we can choose the 256 colors that are most frequent. The 256-color palette is then constructed so that these important colors are included. This new palette must then be stored with the image so that it is available to use on the receiving and display system.

This is only a partial solution, for two reasons: (1) even choosing the best 256 colors for a given image may not result in a high-quality rendering of the original image, and (2) the palette must be the same for the entire computer display (that is, different images in different windows *cannot* have different palettes). Any approach that does not store full color information for each pixel represents a compromise in image quality, for the sake of cost reduction and/or speed improvement.

6.6 Virtual Reality Modeling Language

The concept of displaying (rendering) images from their stored format is quite straightforward. This concept may be extended to the rendering of images not from stored image data but from a stored model of the world that will produce the image. In other words, we don't just take a picture of something in the world and then display it. We first synthetically create a virtual world, and then take virtual pictures of that! This process is referred to as virtual reality. The Virtual Reality Modeling Language or VRML (pronounced vermel by those in the business) is a scene description language for creating navigable virtual 3D "worlds." This language was created specifically for use with the Internet, but has proven an excellent vehicle for all applications, including those that simply run on one computer and do not involve any Internet-based movement of the data. One of the ways in which VRML may be used to enhance the Internet experience is to provide an environment in which any number of people at various locations may view a single virtual world from their own vantage points. That is, while one computer synthesizes a description of the objects in a world and their locations with respect to each other, the computers the viewers are using generate a picture of that world that depends upon a position and orientation of a virtual camera that is freely and independently movable by each viewer.

A 3D VRML world is much more than a realistic 2D rendering of a 3D scene. A single VRML description is the basis for generating an infinite number of possible images based upon the infinite number of viewpoints that a participant in this world might have. The work of rendering a particular image from the world based upon the location of the participant is the work of the VRML-enabled Web browser or viewer. Using such a viewer, a person can move through a virtual 3D world and even interact with the objects that exist therein. Interaction and navigation is usually accomplished via manipulation of the computer mouse and keyboard; however, more sophisticated input devices such as track balls, space balls, and haptic input (gloves that sense the user's hand position and gestures) can also be used. The first version of VRML was based on Silicon Graphics' OpenInventor file format. Silicon Graphics is a computer hardware and software company that has long specialized in building systems that can quickly create highly realistic computer graphics renderings of virtual realities. OpenInventor is Silicon Graphic's 3D software toolkit for programming graphics applications in the C^{++} programming language. In other words, if you were the programmer responsible for generating detailed computer animations for a new science fiction movie, you might find yourself using this tool to simplify your job.

The VRML 1.0 standard, however, was not a direct copy of this system, but consisted of a subset of its features with extensions to support Internet transmission of VRML worlds and interaction between users within the virtual world. After the release of VRML 1.0, some of the VRML experts involved in initial development of the standard formed the VRML Architecture Group (VAG). VAG was responsible for creating VRML 2.0, which was officially released at Siggraph '96 (an annual multimedia and graphics conference) on August 4, 1996, and remains active in its development to date.

The word *language*, appearing in the acronym VRML, may lead one to believe that it is a programming language such as C or C^{++}; however, it is not. Unlike C and C^{++} programs, VRML descriptions are not turned into machine code for execution on a computer but are *interpreted* by a VRML viewer or VRML-enabled Web browser. The fact that VRML is an interpreted language means that the job of generating the rendering of the 3D scene is done on the fly each and every time a VRML description is loaded and each time the viewpoint changes. By comparison, a program written in compiled language will undergo a one-time process of *compilation*, in which the original syntax of the language is converted into a form directly useful for the target computer.

📖 **C and C^{++}**

6.6.1 A Comparison of VRML and HTML

📖 **VRML**

VRML files are similar to HTML files in that all of the data is stored as plain (human readable) text. Thus, even though many interactive VRML builder programs exist, all that is really needed to generate a VRML scene is a good text editor and a knowledge of the VRML syntax.

VRML is also similar to HTML in that, just as HTML is used to prescribe the content and behavior of a Web page with the duty of rendering in the context of the page left to the browser, VRML is used to prescribe the content and behavior of a 3D scene and not its rendering. For example, in HTML the tag pairs <B></B> and <I></I> are used to specify the appearance of text in the page; in this case <B></B> designates text that should appear in bold type while <I></I> designates text that should appear in italic type. HTML provides similar tags for specifying font type, text and image justification, text color and the behavior of hyperlinks. In a similar manner, VRML provides building blocks for describing objects in virtual worlds. VRML's capabilities include the ability to specify object geometry and location, object surface material and/or color, and object behavior. VRML provides the ability to create hyperlinks, just as HTML does; the hyperlinks of VRML lead from objects to Web pages or from objects to completely separate virtual worlds.

6.7 The Organization of a VRML Scene

To gain an appreciation of the way in which a virtual world can be represented as a textual description, we will take a look at the actual construction of some simple VRML worlds. A collection of descriptions of objects that make up such a world is typically called a VRML scene, and the computer file into which it is placed will be called a *source* file, as this is the only source of information that the computer will be using to form the renderings that we will view.

A typical VRML scene may contain many objects, each possibly having a different geometry, size, color, and position in space. Furthermore, some objects may be moving within that 3D space, while others are sitting still. There may also be objects that are capable of performing tasks as a result of user interaction (e.g., via clicking on an object with a mouse). From this description, we can see that a single VRML scene can contain an enormous amount of information. The way in which this information is organized is the topic of this section.

6.7.1 In VRML Everything Is a Node

The fundamental unit of organization in VRML is called a node. We can think of a node as an empty box with a blank tag on the outside. The information that is put inside of the box and the name that is placed on the tag define the type of the node. To define a node that holds the geometry of a cube, the width, length and height would be put in a box and the word "Cube" would be placed on the tag. The same method could also be used to define a node for a cone, a sphere, or any other geometric object that might come to mind.

In the computer, the information that defines a VRML scene is always represented as a text file. Thus, the concept of a "box" and a "tag" translate into a text structure that is used to define the attributes of a node. The following text shows the "Cube" node as it would appear in a VRML source file.

```
Cube {
    width    3
    height   3
    depth    3
}
```

This node defines a cube that is three meters in length on all sides. Note that VRML assumes that distances are given in meters, angles are given in radians, and all other values are expressed as percentages. For those not familiar with the unit of radians: If you draw a circle on a piece of paper that is 1 inch in diameter, the distance around the perimeter of the circle is 2π inches (approximately 6.283 inches); the angle spanned by a portion of that arc measured in radians is simply the number of inches of perimeter spanned by that arc. Hence a full circle spans the familiar 360° degrees or 2π radians.

In VRML, nodes are used to do everything from specifying the geometry and attributes of an object to controlling the ambient light intensity for the entire scene. That may sound like a lot of different node types to have to deal with; however, in general all nodes fall into one of three broad categories:

1. *Shape Nodes*—These nodes hold information about the geometry of an object. In VRML, geometries can be as simple as a box or as complicated as an automobile.
2. *Property Nodes*—Property nodes hold information that can be used to modify geometry. The color of an object, the material it is made of, and the texture

that should be applied to its surface are all examples of information that can be stored in a property node.

3. *Group Nodes*—Group nodes allow many nodes to be grouped together and treated as one. For example, the body of a car is composed of a hood, doors, a windshield, and a trunk. In VRML, each of these pieces can be created as separate geometry nodes and assembled using a group node to form the body of the car.

Typically, a moderately complex scene will consist of hundreds or even thousands of nodes. However, a list of nodes alone does not completely define a VRML scene. It is the way in which the nodes are arranged in the scene graph that determines the result produced.

6.7.2 The VRML Scene Graph

Nodes in scenes are arranged in a hierarchical structure called a *scene graph*. Conceptually, a scene graph looks like an upside-down tree with the "trunk" or "root" node located at the top of the tree, and the "leaf" or "child" nodes arranged below the root. Figure 6.3 shows the general structure of a VRML scene graph.

The nodes marked **S** are examples of a special type of group node called separator nodes. Separator nodes are used to group various types of property and geometry nodes while preventing the property information from propagating beyond the geometry nodes contained therein. The scene graph in Figure 6.3 contains two separator nodes. The separator node on the left contains one property and two geometry nodes. The property node specifies the material (in this case, the color blue) for the two geometry nodes (spheres) below the same separator node. The case is similar for the separator located on the right. Here the property node specifies that the geometry node (sphere) appears in red.

The positioning of the properties nodes (i.e., the order in which they are arranged from left to right) is of particular importance because it is this position that determines how each geometry node will be affected by each property. The VRML text corresponding to the scene graph of Figure 6.3 is given below. Notice the similarity between the organization of the text and the structure of the scene graph. The image that is rendered from it from the default position is shown in Plate 13.

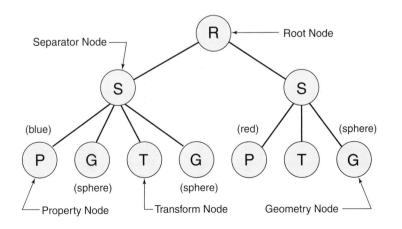

FIGURE 6.3 The general structure of a VRML scene graph.

```
#VRML V1.0 ascii

Separator {
    Material {
        diffuseColor   0 0 1   # Blue sphere
    }
    Sphere {
        radius        1
    }
    Translation {
        translation    2 0 0
    }
    Sphere {
        radius        1
    }
}
Separator {
    Material {
        diffuseColor   1 0 0   # Red sphere
    }
    Translation {
        translation   -2 0 0
    }
    Sphere {
        radius        1
    }
}
```

If the `Material` section appearing in the first `Separator` section of this text were positioned after the first `Sphere` declaration, only the second sphere in this separator node would appear in blue. The first sphere would appear in gray (no color). This shows how property nodes affect geometry nodes in the scene graph and how the positioning of nodes (from left to right in the scene graph) can affect the appearance of the resulting scene.

VRML also includes many predefined *geometric primitives* that can be used as a basis for creating more complicated objects. These primitives include spheres, cones, cubes, and cylinders, to name a few.

6.8 Placing a Surface on a Virtual Object

The many features of VRML certainly provide a robust set of tools for creating and coloring complex geometries, but its capabilities go far beyond that. VRML also supports *texture mapping*. By texture mapping we mean that we can *paste* any picture onto the virtual surface of an object. Without texture mapping, our objects would generally have relatively simple surface appearances, as if they were simply painted with a uniform color.

At first glance, this might not seem like a major feature, but consider the following example. A brick building is composed of thousands, maybe millions, of bricks. Initially one might be inclined to create a primitive "brick" element, complete with geometrically accurate texture and color, and then use thousands of these elements to create the brick walls of a virtual building.

However appealing this approach may seem, it is highly impractical for one simple reason. If a single brick element contains six polygons (one defining each side of the brick), then a single wall containing 20,000 bricks (not an unrealistic estimate for a real building) would contain 120,000 polygons. If the building has four walls, then the total polygon count reaches 480,000! Even the fastest computer would have to work overtime to render this many polygons in real time, and most of them would not be visible.

This is where texture mapping saves the day. Instead of creating a wall that is composed of thousands of bricks, we can create a single polygon with same dimensions as the entire wall. The texture of brick can then be placed or *mapped* onto this polygon (that is, the picture of a brick wall can be pasted to the polygon's surface) to achieve the same effect as creating a wall from individual bricks.

Conceptually, the process of texture mapping is not unlike that of placing a decal on a plastic model aircraft or car, only in VRML the model car or aircraft is equivalent to the polygonal geometry and the decal is equivalent to the image map. In the VRML standard an image map is defined as nothing more than an image in JPEG format. The VRML code shown below maps the image contained in the file my_image.jpg onto the surface of a sphere of radius 1.

```
#VRML V1.0 ascii

Separator {
    Texture2 {
        filename   "my_image.jpg"
    }
    Sphere {
        radius    1
    }
}
```

We will now look at some concrete examples in which texture mapping has been used as well as more advanced rendering features of VRML systems. In Plate 14 we show four images that were captured with a digital camera of real scenes and which will be used in our example.

In Plate 15 we see the image that results from mapping the brick and glass images onto the surfaces of two spheres that have been suspended in front of a plain wall with no texture. In Plate 16 no change has been made to the objects or textures, but the rendering has used a process in which each ray of light is traced from its origin from a virtual light source until it hits a surface. The result is that the objects now cast shadows onto one another.

In Plate 17 we have introduced several more objects including a cylinder and a torus. These have had the ivy and mulch images mapped onto them and the background has been changed. The use of textures can be seen as yielding a surrealistic atmosphere to what is obviously an artificial image.

On the textbook CD there is a link that will play an animation in which such a scene constructed from spheres and textures undergoes motion.

In addition to supporting texture mapping of still (nonanimated) images onto objects, the newer standard, VRML 2.0, also supports *animated texture mapping*. This process is almost identical to that of mapping still images, but a movie file (i.e., a movie in MPEG format) is used as the texture instead of a still image. The result is an object with a surface that changes with time depending on the animation that is used as the map.

Summary

The fundamental topic of this chapter has been the formation of images by computers. These images are always artificial because they are *images*, they are not reality! However, we commonly encounter two types of images: images taken from reality, and images created purely synthetically. The manner of display of these two types of images is exactly the same, but the manner of creation and storage may be very different. With images from real life (natural images) we are fundamentally limited to the data (usually intensity data on individual picture elements) which we extracted from the real world and put into storage. With the synthetic (virtual reality) images we have no such limitations. In fact, we are not even necessarily limited by the laws of physics. Virtual Reality languages allow complete freedom of apparent movement within a virtual world, rather than being limited by a single camera location as in conventional images (both still and video). Display devices are improving at a rapid rate, with increasing performance and convenience, and decreasing cost. High-quality, full color, full motion displays of moderately large size are now readily available. Technological limitations still exist for very large, high-quality display with reasonable prices, and for 3D displays.

Over the past ten years we have seen a progression of ever more striking examples of the use of virtual reality rendering in use in movies and television. It is not uncommon to see feature length movies that have entirely been rendered using virtual reality techniques. With the ever-increasing capability of computers and our growing expertise in learning how to engineer with information, it is a safe bet that within another decade we will see movies released that are artificially rendered but cannot be distinguished from actual reality-based filming.

Try These Exercises

1. An image storage format uses 2 bytes per picture element. How many different colors may be represented in the displayed image? Comment on the differences if this format is implemented as a pseudo-color format (using a color map), versus a direct (true color) format. In the pseudo-color format, how many output bits would most likely be provided to each of the red, green, and blue D/A converters? In the true-color format, describe one means by which the data bits (2 bytes) could be allocated to the R, G, B D/A converters.

2. Early color PC formats only accommodated 16 colors. With this very limited set, determine a color map that will take data values for each pixel that range from 0 to 15, and map them to "good" 6-bit data values for each of the three (R, G, B) D/A converters for the color display. Explain how you decided on the mapping. Your results should include a matrix with 16 input indices and R, G, B output (6 bits each) values for each input index. After making your map, compare to the sample map that is in the Web textbook. Comment on the differences (unless you cheat and look at the sample map first, there will certainly be differences!).

3. "Brainstorm" and list several types of data that could benefit from being rendered as images. Your ideas need not be completely original, but choose examples not already described in detail in this text. In each case, describe the process by which an image would be created, and how the aspects of an image (spatial position, intensity, color) will be related to the original data for ease of human interpretation.

 **Color Resolution**

4. The "Color resolution" applet simulates the range of color resolutions available on different display devices. For each of the test images, find the number of colors where image defects become clearly visible as the number of colors is reduced.

5. Explain in your own words the fundamental differences between bit-mapped and vector graphics image storage formats, including the advantages and disadvantages of each.

6. In general, images are stored without any knowledge of the display device which will be used. Explain, with examples, what types of processing would be needed to render a bit-mapped image on different output devices, including a computer monitor (which may have any of several resolutions), a black and white laser printer, and a color printer.

7. Draw a simple example image and use this to explain the difference in representation between the bit-mapped and vector graphics formats. Determine the number of bits which would be required to store this image in the two formats for good image quality. Explain your reasoning and calculations.

8. What determines the physical size of an image when it is output on the chosen device?

9. Explain in your own words how "virtual reality" is different from a series of stored images.

Data Compression

Staccato signals of constant information...

Paul Simon, "The Boy in the Bubble," Graceland

As you saw in the last part, the number of bits needed to represent an image with high fidelity is quite impressive. But that was only the tip of the problem. When the images are changing, as in a movie, we have to move many of these pictures per second; we need to move a staggering among of data per second. Yet we have all experienced Web downloads of individual pictures and sometimes small movies in fairly reasonable amounts of time with a computer connected by a relatively slow modem to an Internet provider. How is this done?

In this part we will continue our use of images and movies as a basis for a good intuitive introduction into some of the otherwise more difficult aspects of information infrastructure operation. You will see how it is possible to compress the number of bits in a representation of a picture or movie. It is this same compression technology that we will apply later to the human voice in order to reduce the number of bits that have to move in the course of a voiceover Internet Protocol (VoIP) exchange. We will need to: just as we had to send 25 to 30 pictures per second to make a movie look continuous and natural, we will have to send 8000 snapshots of a voice per second to achieve the same for your ear. Even though these voice snapshots are each much smaller in size than the pictures we were considering, the bandwidth still adds up to a challenge within the context of today's typical Internet data rates.

Compressing Information

Objectives

Given some information, an important question is "How much space does it take to store this information?" This leads us to learn about the following principles and processes:

▲ a way to measure precisely the amount of information in a given message;

▲ the fact that the amount of information in a given message may be expressed as a number of bits;

▲ that most messages are longer than they need to be to convey the information they contain (in other words, that they contain redundancy);

▲ that this redundancy can be removed, thereby shortening (compressing) the message;

▲ that methods exist for systematically removing redundancy from data to compress the data for storage or transmission; and

▲ examples of some practical data compression techniques.

7.1 Introduction

We have described many examples of powerful techniques for representing information in digital fashion. In most of these cases, the price we pay for flexibility, fidelity, and realism is that we need to use large amounts of digital information for the representations. This is especially true in cases involving information for visual purposes. Fortunately, the digital nature of this information makes it particularly amenable to methods for reducing the total number of bits to be stored, processed, or transmitted. In this chapter, we will discuss techniques for *compressing* digital information. These techniques are essential in providing useful, fast, and practical applications of information technology.

7.2 Why Can Information Be Compressed?

When large information files are moved around the Internet, they are often *compressed* prior to transmission and then *decompressed* after delivery, to reduce the time and resources needed for delivery. This often happens unbeknownst to the user; for example, it occurs every time that a picture is downloaded from a Web site. In fact, most computers today are equipped with modems (the devices, typically inside a computer, that send data through the telephone system to another computer) that apply data compression techniques to all information leaving or entering via the phone line.

How information that is coded as a series of binary digits (as introduced in earlier chapters) can be sent with fewer bits is a mystery to many newcomers. It seems that if a message is coded in a certain way, then exactly that number of bits will be necessary to send exactly that message and no other. The trick is to recall the power of "protocols." That is, with an appropriate system in place, mutually recognized, we can cut down on the amount of data that must be sent to deliver a message.

Suppose we agree with a friend that from now on, whenever we would have spoken the word "information," we will instead simply say "eep." And, in the odd situation in which we should ever actually need to say *eep* itself one or more times, we will simply tack on an extra *eep*, for example, saying *eepeepeep* to convey the unusual message "eepeep." Consider the benefits:

- We have reduced every occurrence of the common four-syllable word, information, into a single syllable word;
- We have a simple scheme that we can use to still convey an eep or even an eepeep when we really want to do so;
- The penalty is that we need to add a syllable to every eep utterance we make. But how often does it happen that we need to say *eep* or any of its derivatives?

In this way, we can obtain a substantial compression of utterances through careful substitutions of this sort. At the center of this approach to compression is an important differentiation between data, message, and information, which we have not addressed very directly in this simple example.

In this chapter, you will discover the difference between the number of bits of data in a message and the number of bits of information that the data represents. You will see that compression allows one to reduce the message size, in some cases down to the size of the information content itself, which provides a fundamental limit on how much one can compress the data in a message. You will learn how some typical compression mechanisms work, and be able to conduct such a data compression procedure on small amounts of data by hand.

7.3 Messages, Data, and Information

In the remainder of this chapter, we will discuss the *information content of a message*. We will find that efficient storage and transmission of information in the form of digital data comes about by removing *redundancy*. This removal of redundancy can take place at two levels. If there is some sequence of data bits that conveys the same message as another different sequence, then obviously we would choose to send the briefer (less redundant) data representation. But, there is also a kind of redundancy that applies to the message itself. Because certain messages are more common than others, recipients can make assumptions about receiving likely messages, and only corrections to these assumptions will then need transmission. We will also introduce means to remove redundancy so that less data is required to transmit a sequence of messages.

Let's begin by clarifying our use of the words *data*, *message*, and *information*.

Message: In formal language, we may define a message as the particular set of values being conveyed. For example, the message could be the sentence "The sky is blue." This message could be transmitted in several quite different ways. It could be spoken aloud, or it could be written down as in this textbook. Fundamentally it is a sentence in the English language composed of words. A message could be as small as a single binary bit or as large as an encyclopedia (or even larger). Messages need not be connected with any human language. For example, a thermostat sends a message consisting of the current room temperature to the controller for a heating system.

Data: By data, we refer to the actual stream of symbols (physical, electronic, optical, etc.) stored or transmitted to convey the message with which we are dealing. A stream of voltage levels representing ones and zeroes comprise the data in a binary encoded transmission of ASCII text, for example. A set of air pressure variations comprise the data in the spoken sentence referred to above. Sometimes the term "data" is used more broadly with digital transmission, to refer to *both* the physical symbols and the binary digits that those symbols represent.

Information: Information is a mathematical, descriptive characteristic of the message. Information, as you will see, can be mathematically defined as the average amount of *surprise* involved in receiving a long stream of messages from a source with particular, known characteristics. Qualitatively, we can say that the amount of information contained in the message "The sky is blue" is not large because that matches our previous knowledge, whereas if we received the message, "The sky is orange" there would be a larger amount of information (surprise) involved.

If we know that a given text consists of the first 100 digits of the number π, and we already know what those digits are, then there is *zero information* in this transmission so far as we are concerned. We would say that this source has zero information content relative to our previous (so called *a priori*, or prior held) knowledge (see also Figure 7.1).

Take the case of a mathematician who is discussing a new mathematical proof with a friend. There are several numbers that occur quite often in mathematics because of special links they enjoy with geometry, relationships between prime numbers, and so forth. Several of these numbers have decimal expressions that do not repeat and can only be written completely as a series of an infinite number of digits. For example: the ratio of the circumference of a circle to its diameter, 3.141592653589793...; the natural base of logarithms, 2.7182818284590...; Euler's

FIGURE 7.1 There is little information in a message that is expected.

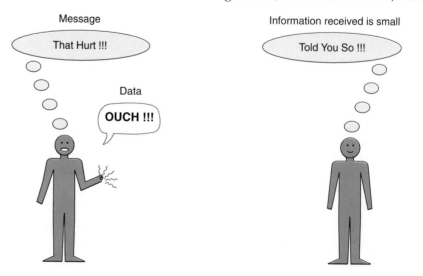

constant, 0.577215664901.... Because these numbers occur so often in mathematical proofs, mathematicians have given them names and symbols, respectively: π (pi); e; γ (gamma). Thus, through a single symbol or utterance, a message representing an infinite sequence of digits is conveyed.

Consider the implications of a message source that supplies messages with little information content for us. In simple examples we can see immediately how we can exploit the deficit of information (that is, lack of surprise) to reduce the amount of data we have to store or transmit to convey the same message. For example, in the case above, in which the number π is to be sent, we need to transmit nothing about the numerical content of π; we need only send a symbol, because we can always reconstruct the intended message from our previous knowledge. In other words, if a message stream has significant *redundancy* in the sense that we can often anticipate what the message will be, then we would expect to be able to transmit the same message with fewer (or perhaps zero) data bits through some form of *compression*, which removes the redundant content. If we could remove all the redundancy with our compression scheme, then the average number of data bits now needed would become our numerical definition of the average information in our message stream, because without any redundancy, we would be sending "pure information."

Now let's add a little more information to this message. Suppose we are testing new computer microprocessors by examining the first 100 digits of values generated by an algorithm that would yield π exactly *if* the floating point number processing unit in the chip were working properly. The failure of this portion of an Intel computer chip made headlines in 1994, and had a great deal of economic impact on Intel and companies that manufactured computers with this chip. (No one wants computers that return incorrect answers!)

Suppose we have asked hundreds of friends scattered all over the Internet to assist us in this work, and have provided them with software that would calculate π correctly on a correctly working computer. We have also provided each one with a copy of the correct value of π. We ask them to execute the π computing algorithm on their computers, and to send us the value they get so that we can assess the performance of each computer and collect a record of the exact values that were computed in each case.

Thus, the message to be transmitted in each case will be whatever 100 digit value a specific computer has generated. However, we expect almost all of the messages to contain the correct string of 100 digits for π, because the problem we are trying to detect is caused by highly infrequent manufacturing defects. That is, our *a priori knowledge* includes the fact that we have a high likelihood of receiving a certain known message. Furthermore, the senders also know what the correct value of π is, so we can immediately obtain a great deal of compression by having each person who computes the correct message send us mail with no data in it. That is, we will waste no actual data bits on these messages because they will be so frequent. Reception of an empty mail message will constitute the *code* for this common case.

Now, those friends who don't compute the correct value of π will still probably get values that agree for many of the leading digits of the number. (More flagrant errors would have been noticed during quality control checks at the manufacturer.) As infrequent as these messages will be, we can still achieve even more compression by taking advantage of the above fact. We instruct these friends to use the following code: if their value disagrees with the correct one, send data consisting of all the digits in your computed value starting with the first incorrect one, and nothing else. When we receive this data, we need only count the characters received, and use this count to correctly replace the last so many digits of our known correct value. Thus we can reconstruct the message from the data.

Now, consider that if we are even smarter about how we treat the above problem, we can achieve even greater compression. For example, the typical Internet mail message system uses ASCII codes for each digit (as treated in Section 3.4.4). That's an 8-bit code for each digit, because in general an ASCII character may be an uppercase or lowercase letter, or many things other than a numeral. Our friends, however, are never transmitting anything but one of 10 numbers. So, we could have used 4-bit codes (capable of representing our 10 digits with the 16 possible code values) and thus halve the data bits transmitted.

We can even take this further. The additional, unused code values in a 4-bit code (there were 6 unused code variations for each group of 4 bits we transmitted) result in a waste of data also! We can save even more bits on average by sending groups of two digits at a time. There are $10 \times 10 = 100$ combinations of two digits. So, we could transmit a pair of digits by transmitting a number between 0 and 99, which can be coded as a 7-bit binary value. That means we save one bit for every two digits transmitted over the previous coding. (We do send three additional bits for the whole message in those cases where the total number of digits is odd, but this is on average a small loss unless most of our disagreeing values of π only have very few wrong digits.)

Finally, why not just encode the whole tail of disagreeing digits as a single binary number with the appropriate value? This would be even more efficient on average.

This example raises many questions:

- Could we do even better?
- Where does this process of refinement end—what's the best we could do?
- How do we find schemes in other cases where the redundancy in the message is less obvious?
- What if we don't know anything about the message beforehand? Can we still compress it?

Luckily, there are good answers to all of these questions. These answers are contained within a field of study known as *information theory*. Information theory is an area of mathematics that finds many applications in electrical and computer engineering. In the next section, we will introduce the basic concepts of information theory; in the following sections we will describe how to exploit these concepts to compress data so that messages can be transmitted with an amount of data that on average is *equal to the information content measure*, and is therefore the smallest number of bits that can be transmitted to still convey the original message content.

7.4 Information Theory

In July and October of 1948, a pair of papers[1] were published by Claude E. Shannon of Bell Laboratories. This work created a new field at the intersection of mathematics and electrical communications theory, *information theory*, and forever shaped the means and mathematics of information transmission, compression, and coding.

---

[1]   Claude E. Shannon, A mathematical theory of communication, *Bell System Technical Journal*, Vol. 27, July, 1948, pages 379–423 and October, 1948, pages 623–656.

Shannon recognized the fundamental difference among the notions of data, messages, and information content. He went about systematically dividing and defining these concepts in absolute terms that set ultimate limits on the minimum average amount of data needed to convey messages with a previously known probability of occurrence. His work, and refinements of that work, resulted in practical methods to enact compression schemes to achieve these limits. The story of information theory is a story in which science, mathematics, and engineering come into play in a finely orchestrated fashion to address every aspect of a practical problem.

The crux of information theory is the realization that the information content of a stream (that is, a sequence) of messages is connected directly with the probability of appearance of each possible message. We can take advantage, on average, of any nonuniformity of these probabilities to reduce the data transmission burden. We will make this concept concrete by treating a few simple examples in the sections that follow.

7.4.1 A Little Probability

As hinted at above, the concept of information and the ability to compress data are fundamentally linked to the probability of occurrence of the messages that are involved. So, to fully grasp the following material, you need a least a small amount of understanding of the mathematics of probability. Luckily, all that is needed is a very small amount, which we introduce here.

You are probably familiar with the idea that if some event has a *probability of zero* of happening, we are unlikely to see such an event ever occur (although, this statement does actually leave the opening for the utterly unlikely to happen, as it is not the same as total impossibility). On the other hand, the statement that an event has a *probability of one* (or 100%) means that we believe this event will happen, with almost no room for surprise (though again it is not a statement of absolute guarantee).

The probability that an event will occur takes on values anywhere from zero to one. The best way to understand the meaning of a statement such as "this event has a probability of 1/4, or 0.25, or 25%," is to understand how one would determine this value of probability by observations of events. The determination of probabilities by observation is an exercise of an area of mathematics called statistics. The example below will clarify the difference between a statement of probability and a statement of statistics.

Suppose we study the outcomes of coin tosses. There are obviously two possible outcomes, or events: heads and tails. Now, if we toss a coin 100 times, and note that 48 times we obtain heads and 52 times we obtain tails, we are equipped to make an estimate of the probability of each of these events by a statistical calculation of what is called the *relative frequency* of each event. Relative frequency is simply the fraction of times that a specified event occurred, relative to the total number of trials of the experiment (in this case, coin tosses).

Thus, given the experimental data we obtain about the coin, we can state that the experimentally observed statistic: the relative frequency of the occurrence of heads is 0.48, and the relative frequency of occurrence of tails is 0.52. Because of the simple nature of the shape of the coin and the seeming fact that there is really no reason that it should fall one way more often than the other we might offer a judgement based on pure reason that the probability of either heads or tails arising is $\frac{1}{2}$. This statement agrees with our intuitive feeling that this would be the case for any *fair* coin.

FIGURE 7.2 Statistics from past observations would have led us to believe there was no chance of seeing a llama leave the room.

3 People and 3 Cats have been observed leaving the room

In fact, sometimes we feel the case is so strong for our intellectual arguments of equal distribution of outcomes (or other special properties that naturally arise from the geometry or dynamics of the situation), that even if the relative frequency of heads had been even less, say 42% (42 heads out of 100 tosses) instead of 48%, we would still find it hard to get ourselves to say that the probability of heads was 0.42, even though our only real evidence is the relative frequency. Hence statements of probability are sometimes strongly driven by our picture of how the world works.

However, not all coins and dice are fair, and caution should always be taken with statistics: the unexpected can happen (as illustrated in Figure 7.2.) If we perform many repetitions of the coin toss experiment and consistently obtain a statistic of relative frequency near 0.42 for the heads outcome, we may come to accept the idea that the heads side of the coin must be a little lighter or have some different aerodynamic quality than the tails side; that is, we may accept that the actual probability of heads is about 0.42.

The only other useful fact about probability that we need to develop here is connected with the idea of *independent events*. Events are said to be independent if the occurrence of one has no influence on the occurrence of the other, and vice versa. For example, the probability that it will rain today is *not* independent of the probability of rain yesterday or tomorrow, because rainstorms often last two or three days and hence the events are linked (although knowledge of one does not lead to complete knowledge of the other, just a "better guess" than we would otherwise have).

On the other hand, the events of which sides come up when we toss two *fair* (not fixed) coins are independent. That is, there is nothing that links these occurrences, and a heads on one coin does not influence in any way the result for the second coin.

The beauty of independent events is that the probability of both events occurring is obtained simply by multiplying the probabilities of the individual events. So, because the probability of a heads result on a single coin toss is 1/2, the probability of the result heads and followed by heads on two coin tosses is given by $\frac{1}{2} \times \frac{1}{2} = \frac{1}{4}$. Only when the two events are independent can we perform this simple calculation to determine the *joint probability*, or probability of both events happening.

7.5 Probability-Based Coding

Suppose we have a source of binary data—for example, a transactions at a point of sale terminal (electronic cash register) at a drugstore that notes and transmits the gender of each patron to a customer research database. After several months of research, we determine that this drugstore enjoys a rather homogeneous customer base; in fact, our collected data shows that there are exactly equal numbers of male customers, N_m, and female customers, N_f. If this is true, we can then say with some good statistical confidence that the probabilities of a customer being male, P_m, and female, P_f, are both equal to 1/2. That is, we have used the relative frequencies from the experiment to estimate the probability of each event.

Let's say that we want to store the data from this ongoing experiment using binary digits, using a 0 for each male patron and a 1 for each female patron. We will then have a string of bits that represents the genders of the customers, and we will continue adding to this string in the future as we collect more data.

How much information do we expect this stream of data to convey in the future? Shannon's theory showed that the average information content of a message stream, which is known as the *entropy* of the source of information, can be calculated.

The mathematical symbol for entropy is H. The entropy H of a source of information is a measure of how much *information* is contained, on average, in each piece of data produced by the source. This information is measured, perhaps a bit confusingly, in units of bits. That is, the entropy of a source tells us how many *bits of information* are contained in each message; yet in our case, the messages are 0 or 1, which are also thought of as bits! The difference is that each *bit of data* may or may not live up to its full potential to deliver one *full bit of information*.

Read the previous paragraph again and try to read "bit of information" as a single word which describes a very different thing than "bit of data," which should also be thought of as a single word. A "bit of data" is the 0 or 1 in a list such as 10101010. A "bit of information" on the other hand is a measure of how much we learn from the outcome of an experiment; a long string of data bits may comprise only one bit of information. This concept is difficult because a bit of information is not something we can point to; it is in the cause of the data and not in the data itself. It was Shannon who first understood this and then invented tools for us to quantify this idea of information bits.

For a simple case in which there are only two outcomes like the store patron gender example and our previous coin toss example, we can use the graph shown in Figure 7.3 to determine the entropy, H, from the probability of either outcome. Note that the symmetry of the problem allows us to look up the value of the probability of either event and still get the same answer.

Thus, on this graph we see that corresponding to the probability of male (or female) of 1/2, we have an entropy of 1 bit. This tells us that, because the probabilities of male or female customers are each 1/2, the amount of information received every time we register the gender of either a male or a female is a full bit. Therefore, in this particular case, each 0 or 1 that we send is conveying a full bit of information. This may make some intuitive sense; since male and female are equally likely, there is a maximum amount of surprise associated with each data point—we have no basis for guessing which gender the next client will have, and that client's gender provides us with the answer to a question (male or female?) which provides us with a consistent and maximal amount of information, regardless of the answer.

Now, let's move our system to another store, one specializing in the sale of men's wear. We certainly don't expect all customers to now be men, but the nature of the goods will skew the patronage in favor of men. Our initial study of 1000 customers reveals that the number of male patrons was 800 and the number of females was 200.

FIGURE 7.3 The entropy of a binary event (an event with two possible outcomes) as a function of the probability of one of the outcomes.

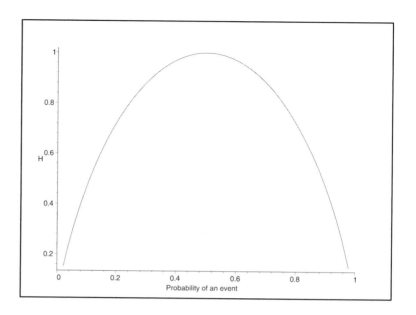

So based on these results we estimate the probability of males and females in this second store to be 0.8 and 0.2 respectively. Now, if we apply Shannon's entropy measure using the graph in Figure 7.3 we obtain a value of $H = 0.72$ bits.

How do we interpret and use this result? The result says that on average the experiment involving determination of the gender of a new customer in this store provides us with 0.72 bits of information. The fact that this is less than 1 full bit indicates that there is redundancy in our data, which causes each result to be less informative than each drugstore result in which males and females were equally likely.

The nature of the redundancy is that if we were to guess that each patron was male, we would be right more than half of the time. So, in some sense, we would be better off guessing "male" for each customer, and occasionally having our guess corrected. This indicates that we are not taking full advantage of each data bit we store or send, and that it should, in the view of our previous examples, take less data to make these corrections than to store the original messages.

The above result is quite specific and exact in nature. It says, that on average, we need only to save 0.72 bits per patron. Obviously, we can't store anything other than a whole bit at a time, so, we really mean, *on average*. Our scheme to store the information in fewer symbols (the 0 and 1 symbols) must exploit groups of results and not individual customer results to take advantage of the opportunity for compression that is being made available to us.

How can we take advantage of this redundancy and reduce the number of data bits stored? Suppose we store our results in groups of two. Let's look at the possible cases of ordered pairs of incoming patrons, the probability of occurrence of each pair, and the codes we will assign to each instance. In this case, we are defining a new experiment, in which we record the gender of two customers at a time. In all cases we are going to make the assumption that there is no relationship between the two genders; that is, we will assume that the gender of any customer is *independent* of the gender of customers before or after—whether the current customer is male or female, the probability of the next customer being male is still 80%, and the probability of a female customer is still 20%.

Event A, Male–Male: Because the probability of a male is 0.8, and the probability of independent events is the product of the pair of probabilities, we have that the probability of this event is 0.64. We will assign the very short code of a single 0 bit to send the message in this case.

Event B, Male–Female: By similar reasoning to that in the previous case, the probability of this event is 0.16, and we will assign it the 2-bit code 10.

Event C, Female–Male: Again, the probability is 0.16, and we will assign it the 3-bit code 110. While it doesn't seem fair to make this a 3-bit code in light of the similar previous pair's encoding, we have no choice but to achieve a property known as *unique decodability*. More will be said on this point below.

Event D: Female–Female: This event has a probability of 0.04. This rather infrequent event will have a 3-bit code also, 111.

In a complete derivation of the coding method at which we are hinting here, we would calculate entropies for each event and choose codes appropriately. Hence, the resulting coding method is called *entropy coding*.

The codes were assigned such that the longest codes were associated with the most infrequent events to the greatest extent possible, while maintaining unique decodability. What do we mean by unique decodability? We mean that given a string of information coded in this way, we can unquestionably break the string of bits into the correct code groups connected with the original events.

For example, consider that we use this new code and record data given by 01010110100. Careful examination reveals that this code can only be generated by the sequence of events ABBCBA as defined above for customer pairs. The reason we can do this is that the code we are using has the property that *none of the code groups is the prefix (the beginning) of one of the other codes*! It was to preserve this essential property that we had to use a 3-bit code for event C and not just arbitrarily use, say, 00 as the code; that could also be interpreted as two event As in a row. By ensuring unique decodability, we ensure that the data stream can be unambiguously interpreted.

So, how good is this code? That is, on average, how many data bits will we be using to represent the information about a patron? We can compute this using the definition of an average value, given the probabilities of our four new events, P_i, and the number of bits associated with each of those events, N_i. Because codes of Length 1 occur 64% of the time, and codes of Length 2 occur 16% of the time, and so forth, we have that the average code length is given by: $(0.64) + 2(0.16) + 3(0.16) + 3(0.04) = 1.56$ bits/event.

Because our events each contain information about two patrons, we are using two data bits to achieve an information content of 1.56 information bits. That is, we are encoding our patron information at a rate of 0.78 bits/patron. This is an improvement on the original scheme, which required 1 full data bit to encode each patron's gender. We certainly have improved our coding efficiency, but we have not achieved the 0.722 bit information rate we computed earlier. Why not?

The answer is that the code we used only exploited groups of two patrons to encode the information. If we had used groups of three, the rate would have been even closer to the information rate we computed. As the number we group grows larger, we gradually approach the ideal given by that formula. Given that we group enough data points together, we can eventually get as close to 0.722 bits per customer as we wish.

You should now have a better sense of what we mean by the information content of a message stream, what encoding and compression are, and how we can obtain information storage and transmission rates close to the computable optimum. The next question is: how does one find the *best uniquely decodable code* to use, given a set of events such as those which we constructed above. It would certainly be a difficult job if we had to guess at good distributions of code strings and then test the results. Luckily there are well defined means to not only generate the best entropy codes for a given size grouping of events, but also even automatically create uniquely decodable code strings.

The Huffman coding procedure[2] finds the optimum, uniquely decodable, variable-length code associated with a set of events, given their probabilities of occurrence. This procedure is straightforward to implement, and is outlined via an example in Figures 7.4–7.9. Here, a code is found for six possible events, with probabilities indicated in Figure 7.4. The construction of the code proceeds by successively pairing events with the lowest probabilities, until all events have been paired. Elements of the code (zeros and ones) are assigned as indicated, and the resulting codes may be read from the diagram. For example, the code for event A (the most likely) is 00 while the code for event F (the least likely) is 111. A more complete explanation of this procedure may be found on the CD.

● **Web Copy**

📖 **ASCII**

7.6 Variable Length Coding

A very important concept, that of *variable length coding*, was introduced in passing above, and deserves more complete treatment. The simplest codes are called *fixed length codes* and use the same number of binary bits to represent each possible symbol. An example is the ASCII code, the standard version of which uses 7 bits to represent 128 different characters. This is in contrast to a much older code, the Morse code, which uses patterns of dots and dashes to represent characters. For example, the letter z is represented by a dash and two dots, "–..", and the letter e is represented by a single dot, ".". The fact that e requires fewer code symbols than the letter z is not an accident. The letter e occurs much more frequently in English (the native language of the inventor of the code) than does z, so transmission time is shortened by assigning shorter codes to the more frequently occurring letters. This is another example of the principle of entropy coding described above (although it was developed heuristically, long before the formal development of information theory).

Variable-length codes introduce a potential decoding difficulty: the determination of how many bits should be grouped together when doing the decoding. With the Morse code this problem is avoided by the introduction of a short pause after the dot-dash pattern representing each letter. With binary codes this is not possible; what is received is an unbroken string of zeros and ones. If the code is fixed-length, it is only necessary to count off a fixed number of bits to identify each code word, assuming that a start point is identified. With variable length codes, each code word must be uniquely identifiable regardless of its length. For example, consider the code in the example from the previous section which we introduced to reduce the number of bits needed to encode our store patron gender values:

Event Name	Code
Male–Male	0
Male–Female	10
Female–Male	110
Female–Female	111

---

[2]   D.A. Huffman, A method for the construction of minimum redundancy codes, *Proceedings of the IRE*, Vol. 40, pages 1098–1101; 1952.

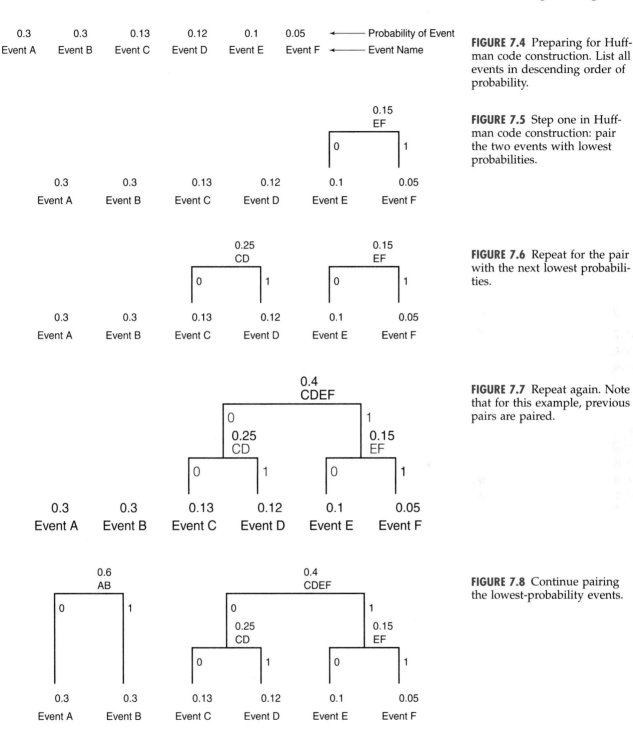

FIGURE 7.4 Preparing for Huffman code construction. List all events in descending order of probability.

FIGURE 7.5 Step one in Huffman code construction: pair the two events with lowest probabilities.

FIGURE 7.6 Repeat for the pair with the next lowest probabilities.

FIGURE 7.7 Repeat again. Note that for this example, previous pairs are paired.

FIGURE 7.8 Continue pairing the lowest-probability events.

Assume we receive the following data: 1100111100. So, who came into the store? To decode, start with the first (leftmost) bit and find the shortest bit pattern that matches one of the codes in the table. In this case it is 110 (1 and 11 are not found in the table). Hence the first two customers are female–male. Continuing from that point, 0 is found in the table, so the next two customers are male–male. Next, 111 is identified, for female–female. Next, 10 is identified (male–female), and finally 0 (male–male).

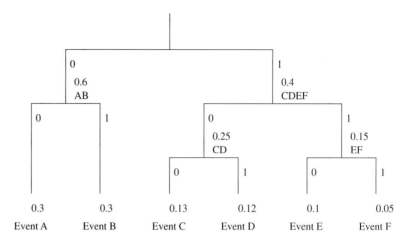

FIGURE 7.9 The complete Huffman code tree.

It should be noted that variable length coding will only produce a savings in total number of bits when some events are much more likely to occur than others. If all events are equally likely, a fixed length code is best because no codewords need to be "wasted" to provide unique decodability.

7.7 Universal Coding

Entropy encoding, as should be clear from the discussion above, depends upon a knowledge of the statistics of source events. This poses a few problems for the user:

1. What if a document is "one of a kind," and so it makes little sense to talk about representative statistics?
2. Are we supposed to keep collections of statistics about all the various kinds of documents, images and so on that we might choose to code someday?
3. How do I know what size of groups of events to code together so that I get reasonably close to the optimum compression?

It is important to consider these questions, because entropy codes can actually perform quite poorly, potentially increasing our bit rate instead of reducing it, if the actual statistics of the message differ from the assumed statistics!

Wouldn't it be great if there existed a *universal code* scheme that didn't require a knowledge of the statistics of the events to be coded, and that always provided optimum performance as given by the information rate calculation if the document were long enough? Lucky for us, such universal codes exist and have been found.

A universal coding scheme is based upon the realization that any stream of data with some measure of redundancy consists of repetitions of "typical" sequences for that data set. So, we can use these typical sequences as a natural event group—a sequence we expect to see frequently and should encode efficiently in the future. A universal code will realize optimum compression "in the limit" for large data sets. That is, the larger the data set being compressed, the closer the results will come to fulfilling the promise of the calculated entropy so far as average data rate required for transmission or storage. If the data set is large enough, we can store or transmit it using only as many bits of data, on average, as there are bits of information in the message, as calculated by the entropy formula.

The only disadvantage of using a universal code over an entropy code is that an entropy code may achieve better compression than a universal code for *small data sets* for which reliable statistics are available for construction of a good entropy encoding.

This relatively recent idea[3] in information theory from the mid 1970s generated a flurry of activity that resulted in the creation of several widely used universal coding schemes. We will examine the Lempel-Ziv scheme below, because it is particularly easy to explain and paints a good picture of the workings of these universal codes.

7.7.1 An Example of Universal Coding

The basis for *Lempel-Ziv universal coding* is the idea that we can achieve compression of a string (an arbitrary sequence of bits) by always coding a series of zeroes and ones as some previous string (the "prefix string") plus one new bit. Then, the new string formed by adding the new bit to the previously used prefix string becomes a potential prefix string for future strings. Compression results from reusing frequently occurring strings.

We shall present a more complete explanation as part of an example. Suppose we wish to code the data string: 101011011010101011. We will begin by dividing it into comma-separated "phrases" of bit strings, which can be represented by a previous string as a prefix, plus one bit.

The first bit, a 1, has no predecessors, so, it has a "null" prefix string (that is, the no-prefix prefix) and the one extra bit is itself: 1,01011011010101011.

The same goes for the 0 that follows because it can't be expressed in terms of the only existing prefix: 1,0,1011011010101011.

Now, the following 10 is obviously a combination of the 1 prefix and a 0: 1,0,10,11011010101011.

Continuing in this way we eventually parse the whole string as follows: 1,0,10,11,01,101,010,1011.

We will now assign codes to each of the phrases that appear, including the null phrase, with the exception of the last phrase. Because we found 8 different phrases, we will use a 3-bit code to label the null phrase and the first 7 phrases for a total of 8 phrases to be assigned a code. The ninth and last phrase, 1011, does not need to be encoded, because it is not needed as a prefix for any subsequent phrases, and can be built from some other prefix plus an additional bit.

The assignment of codes to the prefixes will be done using the following list. The actual order is arbitrary; the point is that each prefix gets its own unique code.

Prefix	Code
null	000
1	001
0	010
10	011
11	100
01	101
101	110
010	111

---

[3] Coding theorems for individual sequences, *IEEE Transactions on Information Theory*, IT-24, pages 405–412; 1978.

Next, we will write the data string using the code for each prefix phrase, plus the new bit needed to create the complete phrase. We will use parentheses and commas to separate these at first, to aid our visualization of the process. The eight phrases can be described by pairs of bit groups consisting of the 3-bit number code for the prefix phrase, followed by the 1 additional bit needed to complete that phrase. Thus we have in this case: $(000,1)$, $(000,0)$, $(001,0)$, $(001,1)$, $(010,1)$, $(011,1)$, $(101,0)$, $(110,1)$.

Thus the coded version of the above string (removing all the parentheses and commas, which were only included above for readability) is: 000100000010001 10101011110101101.

In this case, we have not obtained any compression; the encoded string is actually longer than the original! However, the longer the initial string, the more savings we get as we move along, because prefixes that are quite large become representable as small numerical codes. In fact, Ziv proved that for long documents, the compression of the file approaches the optimum obtainable as determined by the information content of the document. Following is a practical example with an actual implementation of the coder described above. The Lempel-Ziv encoder is the basis for the "compress" program that is typically distributed with the UNIX operating system. If we apply compress to the 22774-byte file of text that makes up this chapter of the book, we get a 11037-byte file as a result, thus achieving a compression ratio (11037/22774) of 0.484. On the other hand, if we apply the same compression technique to a file only containing the letter g, a 1-byte file, we get a 5-byte file, yielding a compression (actually expansion) ratio of 5. It is important to remember that the benefits of compression come about in those cases when we most need compression—when we have a large amount of data to store or transmit.

Summary

This chapter has introduced several major concepts in Information Technology:

- The concepts of *message*, *data*, and *information* are each important and distinct:

  - *Message*: the content being transmitted, such as a sentence, a book, etc.
  - *Data*: the physical, electrical, or optical quantity that actually transmits the message. Examples include ink on paper, optical data streams, etc.
  - *Information*: the amount of new knowledge ("surprise") contained in the message.

- Messages often contain some *redundancy*. That is, some portions of the message either repeat previous portions, or contain content that is already known to the receiver.

- This redundancy may be removed to send the message with a shorter set of data than would have been required. This is referred to as *data compression*.

- The amount of nonredundant information in a message may be quantified with a formula, and is referred to as *entropy*.

- There are many different means to remove redundancy from a message, requiring different amounts and types of knowledge regarding the message.

- The different compression mechanisms can be divided into two fundamentally different groups: those that require advance knowledge of some characteristics of the message (such as how often, on average, various events occur) and those that do not require any advance knowledge. The former group is easier to implement, but is infeasible in many practical situations.

- The data compression algorithms which were presented in this chapter can be applied to *any* binary data stream. Other types of compression (such as image compression) rely on specific characteristics of the data to be compressed.

Try These Exercises

1. Present an example where you can clearly identify the components of message, data, and information. Explain in your own words what these terms mean and why each is needed to explain and understand information technology.
2. The concept of variable length coding occurs very often in human experience. Find and explain two examples of such coding other than those in the text.
3. Determine the frequency of occurrence of each of the letters in this sentence. From these results, determine a fixed-length binary code and a variable-length binary code for the letters. Explain your procedure. Recall that variable-length codes must be designed for unique decodability. There are many appropriate codes which you may create.
4. The principle of transmission of differences rather than each complete item of information is key to data compression. Explain how this can work using stock market prices as an example. The normal way to transmit stock prices is to transmit the closing price each day. Assume that the price ranges from 0 to $500, in increments of 10 cents. Explain how it would be possible to transmit the complete price just once each week and then transmit shorter messages each succeeding day that can be used to determine the closing price. Why would it be a good idea to transmit the full price once a week, rather than just assuming that you can always start the next week with the price that you determined the previous Friday?
5. Find a coin, flip it 10 times, and report the results. Repeat this procedure four more times, reporting the results of each set of 10 trials. The application of probability theory to this situation results in a probability of one-half for the occurrence of heads and one-half for the occurrence of tails on each toss. Explain any disparity between your actual results and the probability value of one-half for heads and tails.
6. It is possible that in flipping a coin 10 times, the results of the first three flips will all be heads. If this occurs, explain what the probability of heads will be on the fourth flip.
7. Explain the use of probability theory in determining variable length codes to assign to various colors for the purpose of transmitting images of textbook pages. The book is printed with black ink on white paper, with occasional illustrations which make use of three additional colors: red, green, and blue. Give a possible variable-length code for this situation.
8. Explain in your own words how it can be possible to compress a message (a sequence of ones and zeroes) if we do not know anything about how the message was generated. Use an example data sequence in your explanation.

Image Compression

Objectives

Digital images are both very important and very large in terms of their storage and transmission needs. Hence, this chapter is devoted to the means by which images may be compressed, including the following aspects:

▲ a review of the amount of data storage needed for images;

▲ the distinction between lossless and lossy image compression;

▲ basic techniques for lossless image compression;

▲ an explanation of lossy compression, and the many tradeoffs it encompasses; and

▲ a nonmathematical introduction to the most popular lossy compression technique: JPEG coding.

8.1 Introduction

In the last chapter we discussed several ways in which the number of bits needed to store or transmit a given message may be reduced. We are able to do this, not by magic, but because of redundancy in the original data. We learned of several techniques to remove that redundancy, and once all the extra data has been removed, no further compression is possible without damage to the original message. For us humans, images are a very common, and a very important, type of data. Images also require much data storage space, so it is particularly important to investigate means to compress images.

We have seen in previous chapters that images can be sampled and quantized sufficiently finely so that a binary data stream can represent the original data to an extent that is satisfactory to the most discerning eye. We can represent a single picture by something between many thousands and millions of bytes of data, and we can apply the techniques of the last chapter directly to the task of compressing that data for storage and transmission. Fortunately, we can do even more than this! Image data is amenable to specialized compression methods that do not actually preserve the original message. We will discuss those methods in this chapter and see how we can benefit from applying these special techniques.

8.2 Image-Specific Compression Methods

In this chapter we will see that methods such as those described in the previous chapter are extensively used for the compression of images. However, we will also see the possibility and desirability for another new kind of compression that we would never want to apply to a textual document, a spreadsheet, or numerical value data set. High-quality images are represented by very large data sets. A high-quality image may require 10 to 100 million bits for representation. For example, a nearly photographic image requires approximately 1,280 rows of 800 pixels each, with 24 bits of color information per pixel; that is, a total of 24,576,000 bits, or 3,072,000 bytes. The large data files associated with images thus drive the need for extremely high compression ratios to make storage (particularly of movies) practical. Without compression, a CD with a storage capacity of approx-   📖 CD
imately 600 million bytes would only be able to store about 200 pictures like that above, or, at the 24 frames per second rate of a motion picture, about 8 seconds of a movie.

Applications that involve imagery are linked inherently to immediate human consumption, and so the need for fast access on computers and fast transmission. Television, movies, computer graphical user interfaces, and the World Wide Web are examples of applications in which imagery must be moved from storage or across some kind of distribution network very quickly for immediate human intake. Consider the fact that most home users of the Web connect through a telephone connection that provides at best a transmission rate capacity of 56,000 bits per second. At this rate, the picture we described above would take 439 seconds to download; that is, more than 7 minutes. Obviously the use of pictures on the Web would be unheard of if not for some kind of compression technology.

Two factors common to most imagery allow leeway for us to construct new kinds of coding techniques:

1. Imagery data has more redundancy than we can generally find in other types of data. For example, a pair of adjacent rows of picture elements in an image are usually nearly identical, while two adjacent lines of text in a book have essentially no commonality.
2. As we saw in preceding chapters, the human eye is very tolerant of approximation error in an image. We may decide to exploit this tolerance to produce increased compression, at the expense of image quality (that is, we may intentionally introduce some error into the image). This approach would never be applied to financial data, for example, but for imagery the information loss may be irrelevant.

The first factor indicates that compression ratios for imagery will generally be more favorable (much larger) than for other types of data we have considered. But there is also another key feature of images hidden here. We developed methods in the previous chapter to root out well-hidden redundancies in data to obtain theoretically optimum elimination of those redundancies and hence optimal reduction in data size. Despite this, the fact that redundancies are clearly available "on the surface" in the case of image data will have an impact on our systems. The motivation for greater compression is more efficient storage and, also, *faster processing of the data*. In the previous chapter we did not address the fact that some substantial amount of computation time is needed to code and then decode our data streams. Because images must often be encoded and/or decoded in real time, it is important to minimize the computational time as well as the size of the resulting data. The close relationships among neighboring pixels in an image can be exploited to reduce the computation time of the compression and decompression actions significantly.

The second factor, above, hints at how some special compression techniques may be possible that will take special advantage of the structure and properties of image data. How do these special advantages relate to the previously established fact that the coding techniques already described can achieve the maximum possible compression? We showed in the last chapter that our entropy and universal codes essentially achieve, for large data sets, the optimum compression ratio as given by Shannon's information measure, the entropy function. The second factor in the list opens up a new possibility: that by trading off some of the quality of the image we might obtain significantly reduced data size. When dealing with still or moving imagery, we may wish to compress data beyond the limit established by Shannon, because we are often willing to accept a loss of original data. This is a new form of compression unlike those we previously studied. We will classify the previous methods as *lossless coding techniques*. With lossless coding, we restore every detail of the original data upon decoding. Obviously this is a necessity for numerical documents, as well as many other types of data. Our tolerance of image approximation and need for high compression opens the opportunity to exploit a new form of coding: *lossy coding*. Lossy coding can only be applied to data such as images and audio for which humans will tolerate some loss of fidelity (faithfulness of our reproduction of an image after compression and decompression with the original image). Because we are no longer being held to the same requirements that underlie the reproduction of financial or engineering data, we should be able to realize greater compression of the data as we increase the allowed loss of information.

8.3 Lossless Image Compression

We noted previously that images are given to much more structure than arbitrary data. For example, take the case of facsimile (fax) images of typical office documents such as the one shown in Figure 8.1 (which is an image of the beginning of this paragraph). These two-color images (black and white) are predominantly white. If we spatially sample these images for conversion into digital data, we find

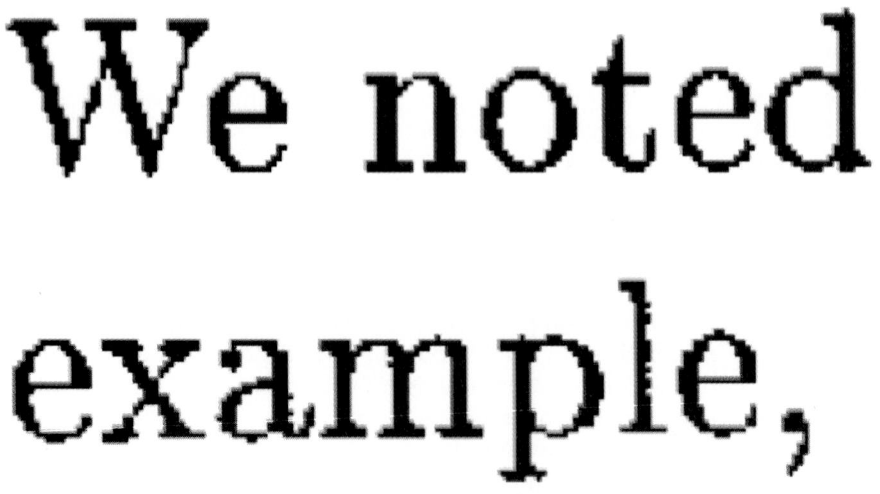

FIGURE 8.1 This is a close-up view of an image of the first paragraph of this section at fax resolutions. Note that the image clearly consists of mostly long horizontal runs of either black or white pixels.

that many entire horizontal lines of picture elements are entirely white. Furthermore, if a given pixel is black or white, the chances are very good that the next pixel will match it. We call these groups of identical picture elements "runs," and can assign codes to them that are much shorter than would be the case if the intensity and color of each individual picture element were transmitted. This form of data compression is called "run length coding."

While the fax is an extreme example, almost any kind of image data has similar characteristics. We say "almost" because we could certainly produce pathological cases if we wished to by having a computer generate an image with totally random and independent pixel values for an image. We will typically look at an image like this and conclude that it represents either random noise or a "texture," and not even attempt to appreciate it at the level of the extraction of content from each and every pixel.

Because most imagery is not so pathological, we should be able to somehow take advantage of the available structure to reduce our compression efforts. We will first examine a common method that does not attempt to achieve the maximum compression available, but that is simple to implement. The purpose of run length encoding will be to achieve compression by exploiting this special structure of images to the extent that is available only on this basis and at very little computational expense in the coding and decoding process.

8.3.1 Run Length Encoding

Run length encoding is a lossless compression technique well-suited to most types of imagery, and involves a fast and simple technique for encoding and decoding the image data. The idea behind run length encoding is that if a long series of pixels are identical, we can extract considerable compression simply by sending a special code that represents the entire string of pixels. Here is an example of how we might find ourselves applying the idea behind run length encoding in an everyday situation. Suppose you and a friend were given the task of counting the number of men and the number of women exiting a certain building. To make sure that no one is missed, you will simply watch the door and call out the sex of the person leaving. Your friend will make the appropriate notations in a notebook that you can later tally. After a half hour of calling out "man, man, man, woman, woman, woman, woman, man, woman,...," you are getting quite tired of talking so much and your friend is getting quite tired of making little stroke marks in the man and woman columns. Your frustration causes you to become innovative.

There is no reason to call out and write down a result at each and every event. You could have called out the same sequence we described above in this way: "Three men, four women, man, woman,...." This is called run length encoding. Your friend, knowing the two categories, does not confuse the numbers for genders. Hence, numbers can be intermixed in the stream of words to compress the amount of talking and writing involved in recording an unbroken sequence of one gender.

Note that run length encoding is quite a bit easier to understand than some of the data compression technology discussed in the previous chapter. That's partly a consequence of the fact that it is not nearly as good a compression technology! It's easy to understand because it is a common-sense thing to do if there are lots of runs in our data. As we said before, we can expect such behavior of pictures, but certainly have no right to expect it of more general data collections.

So, why use run length encoding if it need not be as good at compression as our previous methods? The simplicity we find in describing and understanding this technique translates into great simplicity for our computers to apply it. So, why should we care whether our computer finds it simple? After all, the computer is not going to complain about hard work, is it? In a way, our computer does complain. If the algorithm is too complicated, it takes longer for the computer to do it. While a better image compression technique might result in a smaller image file, so that transmission might take 1 second instead of 3, we may have to wait longer for the compressed image to be restored to its original form at our computer. So, instead of waiting for 1 second to see a picture displayed on our Web browser after it is received, we might have to wait 10 seconds. Thus, the total time from when we clicked on the desired image would be 11 seconds for the highly compressed image and only 4 seconds for the less compressed image. Of course, as available speeds for transmission of data change, and as the speed with which computers can do their job of compression and decompression increases, the tradeoff changes and hence the choice of compression technology that is best changes.

In the next subsection we will examine the details of how this simple idea is applied in a real-world lossless image compression scheme. This section may be omitted without compromising your grasp of the concept; it is intended for those who wish to know in more detail how a single stream of bits, all of which look the same (in some sense), can be broken into special run-length symbols (such as "three") versus the identity of the item in the run ("men").

Example of Run Length Encoding: PCX Format

Run length encoding is used in an image format called PCX, commonly used in personal computer software for the compression of images. The PCX format was introduced as part of the PC Paintbrush series of software for image painting and editing, sold by the ZSoft company. Now, the PCX format actually is an umbrella name for several possible image compression methods and means to identify which has been applied. We will restrict our attention here to only one of the methods, that for 256-color images, and that portion of the PCX data stream that actually contains the coded image and not those parts that store the color palette and image information such as numbers of lines, pixels per line, file, and coding method. The basic scheme is this: if pixels in a string are identical in color value, we will encode them using a special "flag" byte that contains the *number* of identical pixels followed by a byte with the color value of those pixels. If the pixel is not repeated, we will simply encode it as a color byte. Now, such simple schemes can often become more complicated in practice. Consider that in the above scheme, if all 256 colors in a palette are used in an image, then we need all 256 values of a byte to represent those colors. Hence, if we are going to use just bytes as our basic code unit, we don't have any possible unused byte values that can be used as a flag/count byte to indicate when we are using the special format. On the other hand, if we were to use two bytes for every coded pixel to leave room for the flag/count combinations, we might wind up increasing the size of certain images, instead of compressing them.

The compromise in the PCX format is based on the belief of its designers that many user-created drawings (which, after all, was the primary intended output of their software) would not use all 256 colors. So, they optimized their compression scheme for the case of up to 192 colors. Images with more colors will also probably get good compression, just not quite as good, with this scheme.

PCX compression codes single occurrences of colors (that is, of pixels that are not part of a run of the same color) 0 (binary 00000000) through 191 (binary 10111111) simply as the binary byte representation of exactly that color's numerical value.

Note that the remaining 8-bit codes, those for 192 (binary 11000000) and all higher values, are the only one-byte codes in which the two most significant bits (MSBs) are both set to a 1. We will use these codes to signify a *flag and count byte* for those cases when two or more adjacent pixels share the same color. If the two MSBs are equal to one, we will say that they have "flagged a count." The remaining 6 bits in the flag/count byte will be interpreted as a 6-bit binary number for the number of pixels of the same color. This byte is then followed by the byte that represents the color for all of the pixels in that "run."

If we have a run of pixels of one of the colors with palette code over 191, we can still code the color of the run, because the top two bits are not reserved in this second, color code, byte of a run coding byte pair.

If a run of pixels exceeds 63 (6 bits) in length, we simply use this code for the first 63 pixels in the run, and then code additional runs of that color with more byte pairs, until we exhaust all pixels in the run.

So, how do we code those remaining colors (192 to 255) for which we cannot directly use the binary value (because these binary numbers have been reserved to flag runs)? In fact, we will still code these as a run, and simply set the run length to 1. That means for the case of at most 64 colors—and we will choose colors that appear infrequently—when they appear as single pixels in the image and not part of runs, we expand the data for that pixel by a factor of two. Luckily, this rarely happens.

8.3.2 The JPEG Standard for Lossless Compression

As we said above, while run length encoding is suitable where moderate compression is sufficient and fast processing of the compression by a computer is desired, there are needs for better compression of images as well. For example, if data transmission rates are very slow, or if the amount of data storage that is available is very small, then high compression is needed even though it might take longer to compute.

One of the most commonly used image compression techniques fulfilling these needs is the JPEG system. JPEG is an abbreviation of "Joint Photographic Experts Group," the group of vendors and researchers that cooperated to design this industry standard for image compression.

The JPEG image compression standard[1] is actually not a single approach to compressing images. Rather, the standard describes 29 distinct coding systems for compression of images. The standard includes so many options because the needs of users vary so much with respect to quality versus compression, and compression computation time. The committee of experts developing these standards decided to provide a broad selection from which to choose.

These various approaches can be divided into two basic groups: those that are lossless, like the run length encoding method we just described, and those that are lossy. The lossy JPEG compression options are often used in practice, and are described later in this book. In this section, we discuss the lossless approach, which includes only two of the 29 JPEG versions. Both of these use a technique called predictive coding to attempt to identify pixels later in the image in terms of previous pixels in that same image. We saw in the last chapter that there are essentially two approaches one may use to obtain high degrees of data compression: Entropy coding and Universal coding. Both are capable of optimal (the best theoretically possible) compression for very large amounts of data. But performance differences

---

[1] Mark Nelson and Jean-Loup Gailly, *The Data Compression Book*, Second Edition, M& T Books, 1996; page 327.

will exist for any small, practical data set. Hence, the JPEG system offers the option of applying either kind. The Huffman code is used for the Entropy coding action and a code we did not examine in the last chapter, Arithmetic coding, is the choice for the Universal code.

Given that we have such theoretically optimal codes available to us, why would we have to apply any other processing to the images? The key again is that these lossless coding methods are only optimal for very large sets of data. By applying some simple preparatory operations to our images, we can greatly improve the compression obtained.

Looking back at previous examples, we can see how this would help. Suppose a set of 10,000 bytes in a file all had the same value, 0. Then, a Universal coding would replace successively larger runs of these zeros by special symbols, producing a very small file. But, if run length encoding had been applied first, the data would have shrunk to as little as three bytes in length and then might be reduced to still fewer bits by Universal coding. We tried the experiment just suggested and got the following results: the 10,000 byte file compressed to 162 bytes when a Lempel-Ziv Universal encoder was applied directly and to 6 bytes when it was first run length encoded and then Lempel-Ziv encoded. While run length encoding is a step applied before Entropy or Universal coding as part of the lossy JPEG encoding process, a more image-specific process is employed in the lossless encoding of pictures with JPEG. Run length encoding can be thought of as a predictive process. Our encoder is predicting that the next byte in an image will be identical to the last. This notion can be improved for images because there is a large amount of structure in most images.

There is not just a single prediction process that is used. The predictive process that is used in the lossless JPEG coding is varied automatically for any image on a line by line basis. The choice is made according to that prediction method that yields the best prediction overall for the entire line.

There are seven prediction methods available in the lossless JPEG coding standards. These may be divided into the following categories:

1. Predict the next pixel on a line in the image as having the same value as the previous pixel on that line.
2. Predict the next pixel on the line as having the same value as the pixel on the line directly above it.
3. Predict the next pixel on the line as having a value related to the values of three nearby pixels, such as the average of the three nearby pixel values.

The next encoding step after the predicted pixel value is formed, is to compare that value to the actual pixel value. The difference, if any, forms that output stream of information to be sent to the next encoder step. If these differences are large, nothing is gained by this prediction process. However, as a result of the smoothness and general redundancy of most pictures, the differences generally consist of a series of relatively small positive and negative numbers that represent the typically small errors in the prediction. The probabilities associated with these values are high for small error values, and are quite small for large errors. This is exactly the kind of data stream that compresses well with an entropy code.

The typical lossless compression that we can achieve in this way for natural images is 2:1, or a 50% reduction in image data. While this is substantial, it does not in general solve the problem of storing or moving very large sequences of images as encountered in high quality video.

8.3.3 GIF: Another Lossless Image Compression System

Because the two most often encountered compressed image formats on the Web today are the JPEG and GIF formats, we include a brief description of the GIF format here for completeness. GIF stands for Graphics Interchange Format and was developed by CompuServe. CompuServe was one of the pioneering companies in providing telephone-based computer network access, initially to its own bulletin boards and other services, and more recently to the Internet. Their interest in creating the GIF compression scheme was that of making the exchange of pictures via telephone connections to their system practical. The GIF compression process involves an application of the Lempel-Ziv-Welch (LZW) universal coding algorithm to the image data.[2] The standard includes additional prescriptions for the content of an image header, which indicates the name, size, and other features of the original image.

The LZW algorithm as implemented in GIF differs from the Lempel-Ziv (LZ) algorithm we encountered earlier in our discussion and Universal encoding and the *compress* program, in that we do not treat the data as a stream of individual bits coded with arbitrary break points. Instead, we treat each byte of data as a indivisible message (one of the 256 colors allowed by the GIF format) and code strings of these whole bytes. This allows the GIF compression to be much faster than would be a direct application of the LZ algorithm we studied previously. This approach takes advantage of the fact that our images are structured and that strings of color patterns will be quite common. Here again we see GIF as occupying a place between that of run length encoding and lossless JPEG encoding in the spectrum of possibilities between low complexity and low compression systems (RLE) and high complexity and high compression systems (JPEG).

8.4 Virtual Lab Demonstrations of Lossless Compression

In this section we will describe some simple algorithms for lossless compression and the results obtained from applying them. All of these examples have been provided as Java Applets in the virtual laboratory component of this textbook. Simply go to this section of the CD version of the textbook to access the laboratory experiments.

8.4.1 Run Length Encoding Java Applet

The first algorithm we will examine is the run length encoding (RLE) algorithm. This image compression algorithm simply looks for long runs of the same pixel value and encodes it into a single copy of the value and a number representing the number of times that value repeats.

◉ **RLE Algorithm**

Note that there is essentially no point in showing both the input and output pictures in this section because lossless encoding is being applied. That is, the pictures that result from decompression of lossless encoded pictures are guaranteed to be identical.

Using the default picture shown in this applet we find that an original image with a size of 76,800 bytes is reduced to a file of 65,954 bytes after compression. That is, a compression ratio of only 1.16:1 has been obtained. Thus, while run length encoding does reduce the file, the impact is not huge for this image. If we were to select an image that had more uniformly colored regions, however, we

---

[2]   Steve Rimmer, *Bit-Mapped Graphics*, Windcrest Books; 1990, pages 127–194.

would see much greater compression ratios. When we apply the same algorithm to the fax image shown in Figure 8.1 we obtain a much larger compression thanks to the greater structure (longer runs) in the picture. The original image has a size of 17,169 bytes, while the RLE compressed image has only 2,297 bytes. Thus a compression ratio of approximately 7.5:1 has been achieved. The accompanying CD contains some test images.

8.4.2 Predictive Filter Preprocessing Java Applet

The next algorithm to be examined first preprocesses the images using a simple predictive filter and then RLE encodes the resulting data. The predictive filter used is one of those used in the JPEG system described above. It encodes each pixel as the difference between itself and the one in the same horizontal position but in the previous pixel row. That is, in effect it predicts that each row will look just like the previous one.

Once again we will apply this technique to two images, that in Figure 8.2 and that in Figure 8.1. For the case of the photograph we obtain a compressed image size of 67,318 bytes for a compression ratio of 1.14:1. This is only a slight improvement over the RLE-only encoding of this image, but demonstrates the advantages of the predictive step in removing redundancy. In the case of the fax-like image we would expect to see little if any improvement (and in some cases, we might

● Predictive Filter

FIGURE 8.2 Applying only RLE compression to the default image in a virtual lab experiment, we obtain only a 15% reduction in image size.

see degradation). That is because this image is extremely well suited to RLE coding and any attempt to remove the line to line redundancy may actually increase the complexity of the coding, because some runs will be broken up by this step. We find that the compressed image size becomes 2,047 for a compression ratio of 8.39:1. Thus, the compression ratio has slightly improved. This is due primarily to the fact that many of the transitions along lines were well lined up with each other.

8.5 Lossy Compression

We have made the case in previous sections for obtaining greater compression of certain time critical or storage critical imagery at a loss in image fidelity. This calls for an entirely new kind of coding system based on making the tradeoff of lost image quality for improved compression. In this section, we will describe and examine the results of lossy image compression systems. As previously noted, lossy compression algorithms obtain greater compression by allowing distortion of the image that will be recovered on decompression. In effect, these systems simplify the image by removing information from them. The more the degree of simplification, the less the recovered image will look like the original. Because the allowable distortion varies according to the purpose of the image, the amount of compression is typically set by the user of the compression system. Thus, little if any lossy compression is typically acceptable for spy satellite and medical images, while considerable compression is applied to the screen saver and icon images that are displayed on one's computer.

We will begin by examining some simple approaches to lossy compression rather than the ones most often encountered on the Web or as part of PC application software. The reason is that, as you will see, commercial compression software algorithms are quite complicated. Examining the simplified cases will probably convey the central ideas to a greater extent than would treatment of more effective methods.

8.5.1 Simple Lossy Compression Methods

The first algorithm we will examine applies a small simplification to the image being compressed. It begins by subtracting from each pixel the value of the pixel before it in a line. Now, it scans the result looking for patterns of the form $(1, -1), (-1, 1), (1, 0, -1), (-1, 0, 1), (1, 0, 0, -1), (-1, 0, 0, 1)$ and replaces them with strings of two, three, or four zeros, respectively.

What this is doing is replacing changes in intensity that reverse themselves with no change at all. The pattern $(1, -1)$ for example would be caused by a string of pixels in which an increase in brightness by a single level is immediately followed by a decrease by a single level. Under our compression scheme, the change will not be found in the new, compressed, image. Thus we have simplified the picture, but in such a way that it would only be revealed upon extremely careful inspection. Next, a run length encoding is applied. Thanks to the simplification step, there ought now to be more long runs of similar pixel values. Hence the compression should be better than before at a small loss of fidelity.

As before, we can run a virtual laboratory experiment by using the applet found in the CD version of the textbook.

Virtual Laboratory Experiment

The resulting number of bytes needed to represent the image with this technique is shown in the applet window, and a new window comes up with the image after restoring it from the lossy compression operation. Applying this technique to the image in Figure 8.2 we find that the new file size is 59,963 bytes for a compression ratio of 1.28:1, a small improvement over RLE compression applied alone.

We can further increase the compression by increasing the simplification of the image. Another applet supplied in the virtual labs section of the CD version of the book does just that.

 **Median Filter**

This applet applies what is known as a median filter over an image to reduce detail. A median filter replaces a pixel with the most popular pixel value in a certain neighborhood around it. If we pick a neighborhood of 5×5 pixels, then it will be replaced by the value of the pixel closest to the median (the center of the ordered list of pixel values) of the group of 25 pixels that surround and include it.

A run length encoding algorithm is then applied to the result of the filtering process. The applet outputs a new window showing the image after the median filter process. As in the other image compression applets, the original size of the image is shown along with the size that results after the compression operation.

When this algorithm is applied to Figure 8.2 with a 5×5 neighborhood we find that the new file size is 48,879 bytes for a compression ratio of 1.57:1, a further improvement over RLE compression compared with the previous lossy compression system.

However, a glance at the resulting image shows that much fidelity has been lost to obtain this improvement. The point of this exercise is that ad hoc compression techniques do not produce remarkable amounts of compression and may produce remarkable losses in fidelity. However, a body of mathematics, practiced by information engineers, has grown up to support the development of extremely good lossy compression techniques. We will look at one of these in the next section.

8.5.2 The JPEG Standard for Lossy Compression

Because JPEG and GIF are the only two image compression technologies built into most Web browsers, JPEG is one of the most popular image compression technologies in use today.

The JPEG standard includes a set of sophisticated lossy compression options, which resulted from much experimentation by the creators of JPEG with regard to human acceptance of types of image distortion. The JPEG standard was the result of years of effort by the Joint Photographic Experts Group, which was formed as a joint effort by two large, standing, standards organizations, the CCITT (European Telecommunications Standards Organization) and the ISO (International Standards Organization). The JPEG lossy compression algorithm consists of an image simplification stage, which removes image complexity at some loss of fidelity, followed by a lossless compression step based on predictive filtering and Huffman or arithmetic coding.

Optional Discussion: JPEG Details

This section may be skipped unless the reader has a good mathematical background and deep curiosity about how advanced lossy compression systems like JPEG work. The lossy image simplification step is based on the exploitation of an operation known as the Discrete Cosine Transform, or DCT. We will not treat the mathematics of the DCT here, nor will we treat the reasonableness of the selection of this particular type of image transform. Rather, we will summarize in a factual and simplified nature the role of this operation.

Recall that to represent color images, three values per pixel are needed. These may be the intensities of the three primary colors (red, green, and blue), or three other values that can be related mathematically to the primary colors.

The lossy JPEG approach requires that color images be treated in such an alternative form. That is, the original color image is separated into three images, one of which represents the brightness of each pixel, and the others of which represent color information.

In the JPEG image reduction process, the DCT is applied to 8×8 pixel blocks of the image. Hence, if the image is 256×256 pixels in size, we break it into 32×32 square blocks of 8×8 pixels and treat each block independently. The 64 pixel values in each block are transformed by the DCT into a new set of 64 values. However, these new 64 values, known also as the DCT weights, form an entirely new way of representing an image than we have treated so far.

Imagine 64 slide projectors all playing light on a single screen. Further imagine that each of these projectors projects a different picture so that what we see is the result of overlapping all the pictures. Finally, imagine that we can control the brightness of each projector independently. The 64 DCT weights tell us how bright or dim to make each projector so that the overlapped image forms a desired picture.

The 64 images that the DCT weights refer to are 8 pixel $\times$ 8 pixel images that don't resemble anything from a particular image. However, it can be shown that *any* 8×8 image can be created by superimposing all 64 images with appropriate scaling of the intensities of each one.

It may be hard to imagine that anything good could come from this way of building a picture from other pictures, but information engineers have shown that most pictures can really be built with only a few projectors operating. Thus, we can send a few "weight" values instead of all the pixels in the original picture and still obtain a reasonably high fidelity version of the original picture on reconstruction.

If the basis images are well chosen, some will be needed much more strongly to reconstruct an image than others. Now, what is a good choice of basis images for most images? That is a question that can't be directly mathematically derived because it involves human perception. We also don't want to use representations that are very computationally costly to derive. The choice that was made by the JPEG committee was the set of basis images that are associated with the DCT transformation. We call the operation a transformation because it transforms the natural pixel representation of the image into this alternative basis image weight representation. The DCT has the following features:

- It is fast to compute compared to many other suitable image transformations,
- It usually tends to result in low values for the weights of some of its basis images.
- The image that results from deleting low weight components is generally pleasing to the eye.

The JPEG lossy compression algorithm next simplifies (throws away information) the DCT weight data to reduce the number of bits in the images while doing minimal damage to the image quality. The process used is as follows:

- First the smallest weights are eliminated, by setting them to zero.
- The remaining weights are rounded off so that they may be represented with few bits. The amount of rounding, and hence the number of bits transmitted, varies among all the DCT weights, according to observed levels of sensitivity of viewers to these degradations.

Now several lossless compression steps are applied to the weight data that results from the above DCT and quantization process, for all the image blocks:

- One of the underlying images for which we obtain a DCT weight value is actually a *flat* image of constant intensity. The weight for this particular image is just proportional to the average value of that 8×8 block of pixels. This particular weight tends to vary slowly from block to block, so prediction of this value from surrounding blocks works well. We replace each such weight with the difference from the previous weight.

- The coefficients for each block now tend to have many zeros and similar values. Run length encoding is then applied to the whole set.

- Finally, Huffman or Arithmetic (entropy or universal) coding is applied to the resulting data.

The Performance of JPEG Compression

What kind of compression can we expect to obtain from the JPEG algorithm? Typically quoted performance for JPEG is that photographic quality images of natural scenes can be preserved despite the lossiness of the method, with compression ratios of up to about 20:1 or 25:1. Usable quality (that is, for noncritical purposes) can result for compression ratios to 100:1, or more in special cases.

The following images demonstrate JPEG compression with increasing loss in quality as a tradeoff for increasing compression. The original image was generated with a digital camera and when represented in an uncompressed, 24 bit per pixel format, it occupies 921,600 bytes.

Compression with the lossless JPEG system reduced the file to 252,906 bytes without any loss of fidelity (Plate 18), a compression ratio of 3.6:1. In Plates 19–22 we see the effect of increasing the compression from 27.5:1 to 41.1:1, to 64.9:1, and finally to 102.6:1. We see that for the last image, we have passed the point of practical lossy compression for almost any purpose.

Summary

Image data may generally be compressed by a large amount for two reasons: images generally contain a large amount of structure that may be exploited to transmit the image information in a more compact form with no loss of information. This is called lossless compression. Also, the relative insensitivity of the human eye to certain types of image detail may be exploited to further compress the image. With this lossy compression, some detail and information is lost, but in such a way that to the human eye the image still appears to be of acceptable quality. The compression and decompression operations require some processing time at both ends, and the complexity and time required must be balanced against the compression obtained. Without these compression techniques, high-quality video storage and transmission would be almost completely infeasible.

Try These Exercises

1. The previous chapter introduced the general topic of data compression, and this chapter narrowed the focus to image compression. Explain why image compression merits a special discussion. Also explain why lossy compression was not presented as a possibility in the general data compression discussion.
2. Are there other types of information which could be amenable to lossy compression? Among other information types, consider text, financial data, and audio (music).

3. By hand, run-length encode the following fragment of one line of an image where the numbers in each box represent the intensity value at that pixel:

15	15	15	205	205	5	8	198	44	44

4. Apply predictive coding to the image fragment in the previous problem.

5. Comment on lossy versus lossless compression for the following images: a videotelephone call, a movie, a medical X-ray, and a construction drawing for an aircraft.

6. One Mbit/second is available for a portable video player. Explain what processing and compression would be necessary to display conventional TV video and HDTV video with this data rate. Comment on the amount of compression, the likely type of compression, and image quality.

7. Give examples of the use of image in your profession or possible profession, and comment on the impact of compression, particularly lossy compression.

8. Using the applet "Run-Length Lossless Image Compression," compress three different images. Give the image size in bytes before and after compression for each image and explain (from the image appearance) why these differences exist using this run length compression algorithm.

9. Using the applet "Predictive and Run-Length Lossless Image Compression," repeat the above problem. If you do both problems, comment on the different results.

10. Applet "Lossy Image Compression" implements a simple lossy compression algorithm where small differences in intensities of adjacent pixels are removed. With these differences removed, run-length coding can then more effectively compress the image. Apply this algorithm to the same images used above, comment on the compression results, and see if you can visually determine any degradation in the images from the lossy algorithm.

Run-Length Lossless Image Compression

Predictive and Run-Length Lossless Image Compression

Lossy Image Compression

Digital Video

Objectives

The addition of motion to images further increases the data requirements, and hence the need for compression. In this chapter we learn about:

▲ the fact that the appearance of motion is formed from a rapid succession of still images;

▲ the manner in which compression may be achieved by finding the (generally small) differences between successive still images;

▲ the insensitivity of the eye to fine detail in areas of rapid motion;

▲ MPEG video coding, which takes advantage of these effects; and

▲ the new and evolving world of Digital Television (DTV) which includes High Definition Television (HDTV) as a component.

While all of the techniques described in the previous chapter could be used to encode images, none addressed the issue of how to compress a sequence of similar images, such as would be found in the frames of a video stream.

We saw previously that to present the appearance of motion to a viewer, the eye must be presented with a sequence of still images in which the content of each changes only a small amount from the previous image. Also, the images must be presented rapidly, at least 50 times per second, to prevent a sense of image flicker or jerkiness of motion.

These very same characteristics make video quite amenable to data compression coding, both lossless and lossy. That is because these requirements make the information in a video sequence quite redundant; each image in the sequence closely resembles the previous image. Thus we would expect that high levels of data compression should be possible with video data, and that specialized techniques will have been developed to exploit the special structure that the redundancy has in the case of video.

Because the techniques that are used to obtain high levels of compression are quite involved, in this chapter we will only examine in detail a simple example of how the special redundancy in video is exploited. The remainder of the chapter will be devoted to listing the major attributes of some of the more commonly encountered compression technologies and examining their role in the developing field of digital multimedia.

9.1 Video Compression

If we examine two still images from a video sequence of images, we will almost always find that they are very similar. This fact can be exploited by transmitting only the changes from one image to the next. Many pixels will not change at all and hence require no data to be transmitted. For those pixels that do change, only the change in color and brightness needs to be transmitted. This is called *image difference coding* and is used extensively in the compression of digital video. Following the subtraction operation, the values that express the difference between two images can themselves be viewed as a kind of image. This *difference image*, if displayed on a computer screen, will mostly be black or at least dark, indicating the small values that remain on cancelation of everything in the original images but the changes in intensity. Any brightly valued pixels indicate large scale changes between two frames, which are typically confined to the edges of moving objects.

By applying the run length encoding methods of the previous chapter and other coding techniques (such as entropy or universal coding) that take advantage of the appearance of many similar values, we can obtain extremely large compression ratios.

9.1.1 Image Difference Coding Virtual Lab

The virtual laboratory section of the textbook CD contains a Java applet that uses simple RLE encoding to compress the difference between two images. We will apply this technique to the same image that appeared in the example shown in Figure 8.2 and a second frame that was taken a fraction of a second later. Only the human subject in this picture moved, hence we would expect a rather dark difference image and fairly high compression of that image.

⊙ **Java Applet**

When RLE compression was applied to the first image alone in the last section, we saw that the original image with a size of 76,800 bytes was reduced to a file of 65,954 bytes after compression, a compression ratio of only 1.16:1. However, as can be seen in Figure 9.1, the lossless compression of the image sequence results in a file of size 34,919 bytes, a ratio of 2.2:1. In the top right-hand side corner of the figure we see the difference image that resulted from the subtraction of the top left and bottom left images. As predicted, the image is nonzero (not black) only where the two images differed, which was confined to intensity edges in the single moving object.

The reconstruction of the bottom left image is obtained by decoding the RLE encoded difference image, and then adding that difference image to the first image. The result of this reconstruction is shown on the bottom right of the figure. When applied to a full video sequence, only the compressed difference images need to be transmitted. At the receiver, each difference image is added to the previously reconstructed frame to obtain a new frame.

You may experiment with image difference coding by using the CD version of the textbook to access the virtual laboratory applet.

9.2 MPEG Video Compression

In Chapter 8, we encountered the international standards committee (called the Joint Photographic Expert Group) that defined the JPEG standard for lossy and lossless compression of still images. In the case of motion picture compression another such group, the Motion Picture Expert Group (MPEG), performed the same duty and has developed a progression of standards for compression of video.

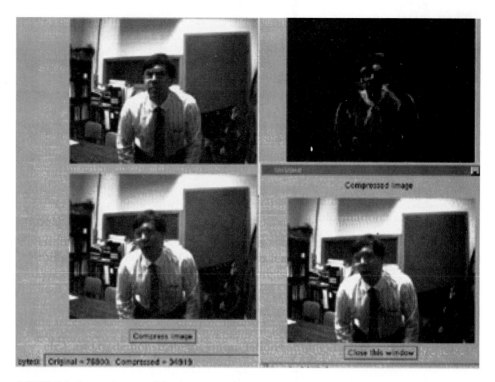

FIGURE 9.1 Screen image of the image sequence compression applet in action.

Why a *progression* of standards, and not just one? As we discussed in earlier chapters, there is an immense amount of data associated with video. And there are many applications in which people are interested in storing and viewing video, some of which are more amenable to holding or moving large amounts of data than others, and some of which are more sensitive to distortion as might result from heavy compression through lossy encoding. Consider the following applications of video and the sensitivity of each technology to the handling of very large data sets or to the effects of lossy encoding:

Digital Movie Editing: Most movies are put into digital format for editing because of the versatility of computer-based editing systems. Because of the very high image quality of motion pictures, little distortion is tolerated in this application. However, the digital tape recorders that are used provide immense bit rates for image transfer to and from the computer as well as enormous data storage capacity; hence, little compression is needed.

Digitized Television: The bit rates that are possible over television transmission systems are fairly high, and users are fairly insensitive to quality owing to the relatively low quality of existing nondigital television systems.

High Definition Television: New Digital Television (DTV) formats have recently become available on the market that will greatly enhance the quality of the picture seen on new TV sets at home. To obtain higher definition images requires significantly higher bit rates and use of less lossy compression technology.

Video Discs: A variety of video disc technologies have been created to provide consumers with the ability to purchase video in a form that is easily handled and cheap to manufacture. Here the video quality simply matches that of Digitized Television. However, the compression requirements vary widely according to the storage density of the media being used to hold the data, which include high capacity systems such as the DVD and low capacity systems such as the ordinary CD.

Internet Video Clips: Many Web sites today feature small, 10 to 60 second, video clips. Because these will usually be viewed in a small portion of a video monitor the quality of the displayed video need not be high. The video usually is displayed only after the full video file has been downloaded; hence, the only impact that compression ultimately has is in the amount of time that a typical user wishes to wait for the download. In general, the compression rates need to be fairly high but the low quality requirement allows this need to be met.

Video Teleconferencing: With commerce becoming more global each day, many businesses are resorting to the use of video teleconferencing over telephone and Internet connections as a substitute for travel. Here the quality requirements are about the same as in the case of Internet Video Clips, but the transmission must be made in *real time*. Thus, compression levels must be high enough to move entire frames of the video across the connection before the next frame is ready. To accomplish this feat involves the use of very low bit rate digital video, which implies extremely high levels of lossy video compression.

The various MPEG compression standards were created to span the breadth of needs demonstrated by the above examples. For example, the MPEG standards include:

MPEG-1, which was intended for the compression of video for storage on CD media to meet digitized television quality standards. Typically the full frame rate video stream is compressed into a digital data stream employing approximately 40,000 bits per frame, for a total of 1.2 Mbps on compression of a continuous stream. MPEG-1 is the most common video format in use today on Web pages as the means to encode and transmit video clips. The is also a common selection for the storage of longer video sequences (up to entire movies) on CD discs.

MPEG-2 is directed at higher quality, high bit rate applications. With a target bit rate between 4 and 10 Mbps, MPEG-2 addresses the needs of high definition television and studio editing systems. MPEG-2 is the format used today to encode feature length movies for the DVD-Video disc market.

MPEG-4 addresses the needs of video teleconferencing systems that must sacrifice video quality for the need to obtain very low bit rates. The bit rates addressed by this compression scheme range from 4.8 Kbps to 64 Kbps, rates that are supported by telephone connections and many Internet connections.

9.2.1 Some Examples of MPEG Encoded Video

In this section we will examine the tradeoff between quality and file size (or equivalently, bit rate) associated with the compression techniques used in the MPEG-1 system. Because the tradeoff is very much a function of the content of the video sequence, we have applied various levels of compression to a single video for comparison. While we can only show individual images taken from the compressed video sequences in the paper copy of the textbook, the CD version of the textbook contains hyperlinks to the full video files. These videos will actually be launched by your computer if an MPEG-1 compatible "media player" program has been installed on it. (A quick search of the Web will reveal sources for free media players if you do not already have one installed.)

Plate 23 shows a single frame from a 5.26 second video sequence that was compressed from its original size of 5.648 Mbytes to a size of 2.437 Mbytes with the MPEG-1 compressor set to preserve essentially all of the quality of the video.

In Plate 24 the same frame is shown but taken from a video file that results upon setting the compression to obtain a file of 405,520 bytes. Even at this level of compression, the distortion of the image is quite small.

Finally in Plate 25 the same frame is shown as it appears in a video that results from setting compression parameters to obtain an MPEG-1 file of size 145,424 bytes. As can be seen, considerable distortion has been added to the video sequence. However, the file size accommodates rapid transfer of the video across the Internet.

9.3 Digital Television

For many years there has been talk about changing the system used to transmit television to our homes to provide higher quality video than that provided by the fully analog (National Television System Committee, or NTSC) transmission system that has been in use since December 17, 1953, when it was last changed by the Federal Communications Commission (FCC) to allow the transmission of color pictures. On February 17, 1998, the FCC adopted the final rules for the creation of a new Digital Television (DTV) service based upon general principles that were described in a report issued in April, 1997. Prior to the adoption of the final DTV standard, the quest for a better television standard, called High Definition Television (HDTV), was driven in part by the desire to offer a higher quality image on the home television. But two other factors were also important: aspect ratio and digital technology. Aspect ratio is the name given to the ratio between the width and height of an image. The NTSC television video aspect ratio is 4:3 (1.33:1). That is, if a picture is 12 inches wide, then it will be 9 inches high. Unfortunately this choice was made in the earliest hours of the invention of television, when most motion pictures were filmed using 35-mm film (which had this aspect ratio). In 1953, with the threat of color television looming over the motion picture industry, 20th Century Fox released the first wide screen motion pictures featuring an aspect ratio of 2.35:1. Since then various formats have been used, ranging from 1.85:1 to the full wide screen format. One of the thrusts of HDTV was to provide an aspect ratio on the home TV display that would more closely match these wider formats.

The second thrust was conversion to a digital technology. By using digital transmission technology it would become possible to transmit the higher quality video in the same bandwidth as the original signal. (See Chapter 14 for a discussion of bandwidth and the allocation of bandwidth channels in the radio spectrum.) Another reason to use digital technology is the insensitivity of digital transmission to many effects that produce "snow" or "ghosts" in an NTSC video.

United States standard NTSC video provided the television viewer with an image consisting of 525 lines (of which 486 are visible on most screens) transmitted in two interlaced parts so that a complete new picture is rendered 30 times a second: *the frame rate.*

One cannot directly state the resolution of a current NTSC picture, because, it is in fact not digitized into separable pixels. However, by comparison of image quality with digital pictures, and given the 486 visible lines in the picture, it is generally accepted that it produces an image with the quality of a 720 × 486 pixel image. What is less generally appreciated by the public is that the color information in a color TV picture is actually quite blurred compared to the monochrome picture onto which it is painted. The colors are in a sense painted with a broader brush and if a picture were formed with no intensity variation, just color variation, it would appear to have a resolution of approximately 360 pixels across and not 720.

The new DTV standard addresses the desire for HDTV by both increasing the frame rate to 60 frames per second and increasing the full color pixel resolution. It provides an image with a resolution of 1920 × 1080 pixels in an aspect ratio of 16:9 (2.11:1). Thus DTV provides more than four times as many pixels in an image than current technology.

The actually technology that is used in DTV was discussed earlier in this chapter. The new Advanced Television Systems Committee (ATSC) standard requires DTV to use the MPEG-2 compression scheme and transmission format. Furthermore, sound will be broadcast using the Dolby Digital AC-3 audio encoding system and will provide four sound channels (quadraphonics) was well as a separate channel for a subwoofer unit for accentuated bass reproduction.

The FCC has set a fast schedule for the phasing in of DTV. An estimated 53% of U.S. households will have some DTV channels available by the end of 1999 and everyone in the country will have access by May 1, 2002. The existing NTSC service will continue to be available till the year 2006.

Summary

In this chapter we have taken our investigation of image data compression to the next level and considered its application to digital video. We saw that image compression is an essential technology in making digital video a practical consumer product. But we have also been exposed to the fact that other information technologies have been developed to handle the still copious amounts of data that result from compression of long streams of digital imagery. We have also hinted at the important role that bit rates and bandwidths will play in determining the commercial viability of information technologies.

In the following chapters we begin our discussion of the digital representation of nonimage data. This will lead eventually to our introduction of the concept of bandwidth, how it is connected to bit rate, and how each is determined by characteristics of a wire, cable or radio/TV channel.

Try These Exercises

1. The "Image difference compression" Applet in the textbook CD implements a very effective means of lossless coding for image sequences (such as television or other video). Apply this algorithm to the two image sequences that are provided. Explain why the amount of compression is so different between the two image pairs.

   ⊙ Image Difference Compression

2. In mainland China a popular medium for movies is the ordinary CD (that is, not the DVD). Find out what format is used. Explain why this format was chosen in terms of the descriptions given in this chapter.

    DVD

3. In this question you will explore the reason that online home delivery of video selections on demand through the telephone is not available. In Chapter 17 you will discover that the storage capacity of a single-sided, single-layer DVD-Video disc is approximately 4.7 GB (4.7 billion bytes). Using a bit rate of 56 kbps for a high speed telephone modem connection, how long would it take to download this amount of data? If it takes you 10 minutes, roundtrip, to drive to the local video store, rent a DVD and bring it home, what is the bit rate of your car in this application?

4. Using Web-based and library research, sketch the history of the television standard from the first demonstrations of black and white television through to the acceptance of the new DTV standard.

5. Initially, the move to digital television was driven by the desire to improve the image quality (resolution and aspect ratio) of conventional television, resulting in the HDTV standard. However, one of the benefits of the move to a purely digital transmission format was the possibility to support a variety of image qualities, as well as compatibility between a range of image qualities and a range of display device qualities. As a result, the move to DTV does not necessarily imply a move to HDTV. Given that the standard HDTV image contains four times the number of pixels as standard television, how many standard TV signals could be transmitted in one HDTV channel? What are the cost implications to the broadcasters and the implications on number of available channels to the viewer if such an option is chosen? All of this relates to the question: "How much more will the viewer pay for a higher-quality image?" What do you think?

6. The topics discussed in this chapter are evolving very rapidly. Perform some background research and report on the current state of HDTV and DTV. Address questions such as: how many DTV stations are broadcasting over the air? What percentage of cable companies are broadcasting DTV? What percentage of DTV signals are in high-quality HDTV format? What about the direct broadcast satellite services? How many HDTV receivers are being sold annually? What percentage is this of total TV sales?

Bandwidth and Information Theory

A loose affiliation of millionaires...

Paul Simon, "The Boy in the Bubble," Graceland

Having finished the treatment of image and motion picture coding, we can finally turn our attention to the matter of capturing, sampling, digitizing, transmitting and storing audio. We will have an opportunity now to take a second look at the matters of bandwidth, fidelity, and representation but within the context of this less familiar territory.

What you will discover is that the way for digital representation of audio has already been well paved by several systems with which most consumers are already quite familiar from an outside view: parts of the existing wired and wireless telephone system and the music CD.

10

Audio as Information

Objectives

Just as we live in a visual word (the subject of the previous chapters), we also live in an audio world, with similar needs for representation, processing, storage, and transmission of audio signals. That world is introduced in this chapter, including the following topics:

▲ the physical principles underlying sound in the natural world;

▲ the idea of a signal, and examples of some specific sound signals;

▲ the concept of frequency, and its relationship to bandwidth of audio signals;

▲ the ways in which signals can be represented graphically and mathematically; and

▲ the special characteristics of sinusoidal signals that make them very useful.

10.1 Introduction

Many of the first applications of electronic technology involved *audio signals*—electronic representations of audible information. Early systems for recording, transmitting, and recreating audio signals included phonographs and radios, and these systems quickly grew in popularity and acceptance. This is no surprise, because much of what defines the human experience, including conversation, music, and the sounds of nature, involves the exchange of information in audible form. As technology has advanced, we have constantly developed new and better ways to convey audio for purposes such as entertainment, business, and interpersonal relations.

In this chapter, we will take a look at how audio signals are created, and how the limitations of human hearing help define the useful information content of an audio signal. This will lead to an introduction to the concepts of *frequency* and *bandwidth*, important issues in information technology that have implications extending to every type of information. This will provide a way to formulate the tradeoffs that must be made between audio quality and the amount of information needed to represent audio information.

10.2 The Physical Phenomena Underlying Sound

If you drop a book on the floor, one of the results will be the *sound* that is created upon impact. What is the nature of this phenomenon? When the book strikes the floor, energy is expended; much of this energy is used to move air around. *It is this motion of air that we perceive as sound.*

Sound is created by the motion of air particles in space. To create sounds, we must provide a *mechanical force* to the surrounding air. In response to this force, the air is compressed, and the difference in pressure between the compressed air and the uncompressed air causes the compression to propagate away from the source of the sound. This is similar to the effect that occurs when a stone is dropped into a pool of water. First, the water is compressed in the vicinity of the stone. Then, due to the difference in pressure between the area where the stone has landed and the surrounding pool, the compression begins to propagate outward, causing the familiar concentric ripples.

Like water, air is a fluid, and sound propagates through air in a similar manner to ripples propagating in a pool of water. An important difference is that the ripples we see along the surface are propagating in two dimensions, whereas sound moves away from its source in three dimensions; that is, in all directions.

Consider a stationary observer in the pool (say, a frog on a particularly stable lily pad). When a stone hits the pool some distance from our frog, she will not necessarily notice anything, unless she is watching. But after some time, the ripples that have been caused will reach her, and she will begin to sense the movement of the water. Because the frog is stationary, she will experience the peaks and troughs of the ripples as they propagate past her. These peaks and troughs are caused by changes in the pressure of the water at each point. The frog perceives the effect of the stone as a series of motions of the water—up and down, up and down—which gradually die out.

Similarly, we do not instantaneously perceive sound when our book hits the floor. Areas of compressed and expanded air propagate toward our ears, and we, as stationary observers, perceive the changes in air pressure as the "peaks" and "troughs" reach us. These changes in the air pressure at our ears cause the air to move, and we sense this when the moving air comes in contact with the moving parts of our inner ear. In this way, sound is a measurable, quantifiable thing. We can measure sound by recording the changes in air pressure at a particular location using, for example, a *microphone*. Like the human ear, a microphone has sensitive moving parts that respond to the motion of air caused as sound propagates past. These moving parts can convert the motion of air into electrical signals—voltages or currents—which can then be used to represent the sound. Fortunately, we do not need to discuss the nature of voltage and current to describe how the sound is recorded and stored.

10.3 From Sound to Signals

As was mentioned above, a device such as a microphone can be used to sense the changes in air pressure—the peaks and troughs—at a particular point in space, just as the human ear does. The result is an electrical signal, known as an *audio signal*, which describes the local changes in air pressure at the microphone as a function of time. Figure 10.1 shows an example of an audio signal that is an idealization of one that would be created by a transient sound source, such as that from a book striking the floor and recorded with a microphone.

In this figure, the measurement of pressure has been converted into an electrical voltage, and the waveform shown depicts the voltage as it changes in time. The vertical axis shows the voltage (proportional to air pressure) at any instant, and the horizontal axis represents time in tenths of milliseconds. Louder sounds

FIGURE 10.1 A signal such as would be created by a transient audio source upon transformation by a microphone into an electrical signal. The horizontal scale represents time in tenths of milliseconds.

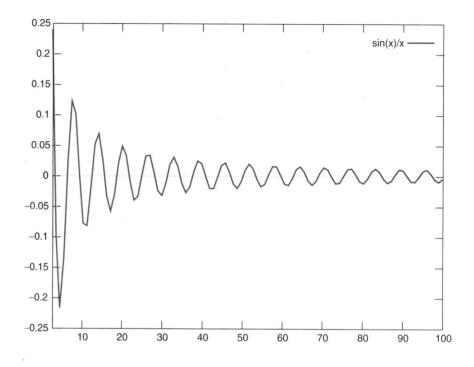

will create a greater vertical displacement; that is, the swings in air pressure due to loud sounds are greater. Similarly, rapid changes in the vertical displacement, as we see in this figure, correspond to rapidly changing air pressure. In this case, the sudden, rapid changes in air pressure caused by the book striking the floor have propagated toward the microphone, and the air pressure at that location has changed quickly with time. This is depicted by the rapid changes in voltage evident in this figure. This representation of information in the form of a *voltage signal changing as a function of time* is a common one used for many types of measurable quantities that change with time. The variations in the signal are then seen to die out gradually. This is often called *decay* of the signal. This represents, in this case, the dying out of the vibrations of the face of the microphone as the effects of the sudden blast of air are dissipated through the mechanics of the microphone and the surrounding air space. Another sound, this one less jarring, is depicted in the form of an audio signal in Figure 10.2. This audio signal, with its regular, sinusoidal peaks and valleys, represents a *pure tone*—in this case, the tone corresponding to the note A above middle C on a piano. The peaks of this sound wave are separated regularly at intervals of 2.27 milliseconds, or 1/440th of a second. This means that the wave repeats itself 440 times per second. We say that this wave has a *frequency*, or rate of repetition, of 440 hertz. The unit hertz, abbreviated Hz, is equivalent to cycles per second, and is used to measure the rate at which electric signals (and other cyclic phenomena) repeat themselves. The frequency, in hertz, is a measurement of how rapidly the audio signal is changing.

Our ears are quite sensitive to changes in frequency. The rate at which a sound wave repeats itself, in fact, is perceived as *musical pitch*. If we were to play and record the note A *below* middle C on the piano, the resulting audio waveform would appear as shown in Figure 10.3. This wave repeats more slowly than the previous note; it cycles at a frequency of 220 Hz, or 220 cycles per second. This is why we perceive it to be a "lower" musical tone. Although it would travel to our ear about as quickly as the higher note, it would cause the air to vibrate at a rate just half as fast as the higher note would.

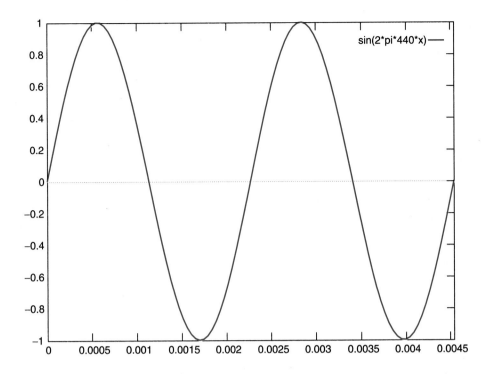

FIGURE 10.2 A 440-Hz sinusoid.

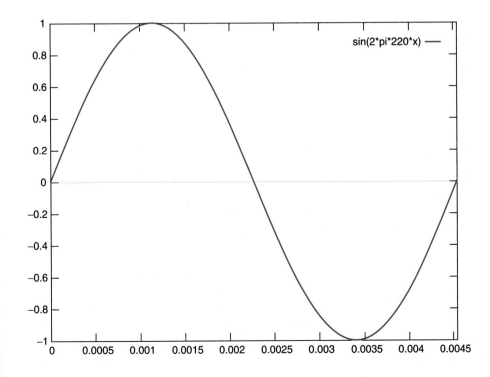

FIGURE 10.3 A 220-Hz sinusoid.

10.4 Limitations on Human Hearing

In Chapter 5, we described how visual latency—the inability of the human eye to respond quickly to changes—determines how much information is necessary to create the illusion of smoothly moving video images. Similarly, the amount of information we require to represent audio information is determined by the limitations of human auditory perception. It is also determined by the type of audio signal we are interested in representing.

In Figures 10.2 and 10.3, we saw that pure tones can be represented by simple *sinusoidal* signals. These sinusoidal signals have a frequency of repetition that determines the pitch of the tone. What is the range of pitch, or frequencies, which humans can hear? Although it varies from person to person, the standard range used by manufacturers of audio systems is from a lowest frequency of 20 Hz to a highest frequency of 20 kHz, or 20,000 Hz. The lowest audible frequency, 20 Hz, is a low, rumbling "bass" note, experienced as a vibration by the entire body, not just the ear. The highest audible frequency, 20 kHz, is actually beyond the range of most humans—if you listen to a lot of loud music, you probably can't hear much beyond 15 kHz—but some people and most dogs can hear this high pitch. Notice that the ear can respond to a stimulus that is changing up to 20,000 times per second! This is a much more impressive *dynamic response* than that of the human eye, which cannot discern changes at a rate of much more than 40 or 50 times per second. Accordingly, we will need to take this into account when we attempt to convert audio information into digital form. We will need to use far more samples per second of information to represent the audio information than we need to use for video. Fortunately, each of these samples is a single air pressure measurement, instead of an entire image! So, as we will see, the total amount of information in an audio signal—even for very high fidelity—is far less than that needed for video. Also, much useful audio information, such as voice signals, can be conveyed with far fewer samples per second than are required for music.

10.5 Sinusoidal Frequency Components

Recall the pure tone for the note A above middle C (440 Hz) as shown in Figure 10.2. When an orchestra tunes to this note, each musician creates a musical sound at that same note. Yet each instrument sounds different. We can discern the difference between a piano, a guitar, and a saxophone, *even if they are playing this same note*. How is it that these sounds are at the same frequency, yet different? In Figures 10.4 through 10.7 four sound waveforms are shown. Figure 10.4 shows the *pure tone*, or sine wave, at 440 Hz. Figures 10.5, 10.6, and 10.7 show the waveforms created by an alto saxophone, a tenor saxophone, and a vibraphone, all playing that same note. Each waveform has different details that cause the characteristic sound of the instruments; however, each waveform *repeats at a rate of 440 times per second*. Thus, we perceive each of these to be the same note, even though the characteristics of the sounds are distinct.

These sounds are interesting and pleasing to the human ear due to their differences and complexity. In fact, each one of these sounds can be created by *a sum of pure tones*—of sinusoids—at different frequencies. Thus, even though these notes are all thought of as "at" 440 Hz, each one also has *frequency components*, or sinusoidal content, at other frequencies as well. Thus, we could describe the differences between the notes of these instruments by their *frequency content*, or by which tones they possess. Now, there are also important differences in the way in which each instrument starts, or *attacks*, each note, and the way in which the note decays, or

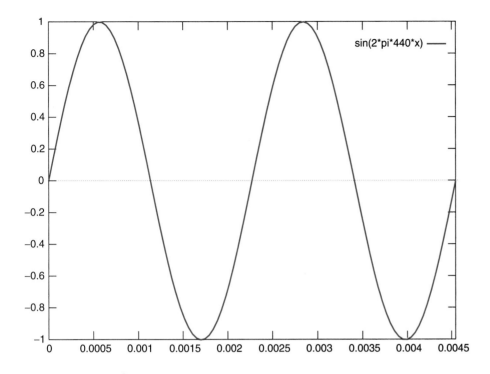
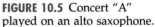

FIGURE 10.4 A 440-Hz "A" concert pitch sinusoid.

is *sustained*. But these figures show us significant differences in the air pressure patterns that occur as the instruments are producing the notes. These differences depend on the frequency content of the waveforms. In the early 19th century, the French mathematician Fourier proved that *all waveforms*, whether musical or not, *can be constructed out of a sum of pure tones*. The implications of this are that *every au-*

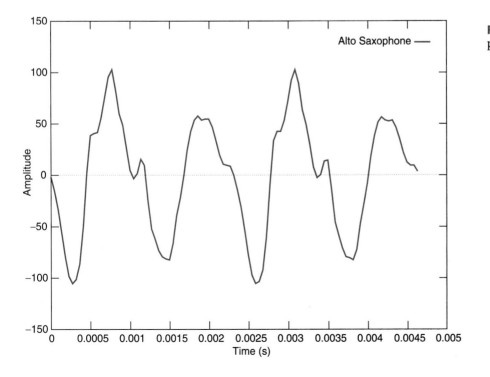

FIGURE 10.5 Concert "A" played on an alto saxophone.

FIGURE 10.6 Concert "A"
played on a tenor saxophone.

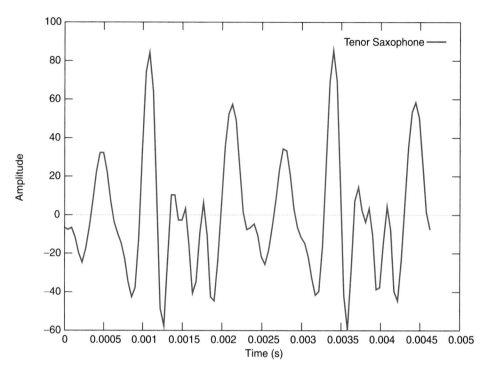

FIGURE 10.6 Concert "A"
played on a tenor saxophone.

*dio waveform—whether speech, music, or any other sound—can be built out of sinusoids
at certain frequencies.* The different frequency components (or pure tones) which are
added together to produce a complex waveform are called *the frequency spectrum*
of that waveform. The frequency spectrum tells us which frequency components,
and in what proportions, are needed to construct the waveform in question. Every

FIGURE 10.7 Concert "A"
played on a vibraphone.

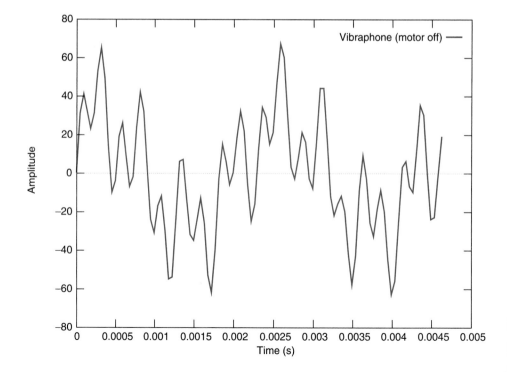

FIGURE 10.7 Concert "A"
played on a vibraphone.

audio signal has a frequency spectrum, and this tells us what tones make up that particular audio signal.

10.6 The Frequency Content and Bandwidth of Audio Signals

This idea that every signal is made up of a sum of simple sinusoidal tones—known as the *Fourier decomposition* of the signal—is very helpful to us. This is because the simple sinusoid is a useful signal for testing audio systems, including the human hearing system. In fact, the range of human hearing that we discussed earlier, from 20 Hz to 20 kHz, is determined by subjecting human subjects to pure, sinusoidal tones of every frequency. The limits of human hearing were thus established to be within this range, so every sound we can hear—every sound we care about—consists of frequency components in this range. Thus, if we build systems that can reproduce all of the sinusoidal tones between 20 Hz and 20 kHz, *the system can reproduce any audible waveform*. However, not all audio signals use all of these frequency components. Such a wide range of frequencies is usually unnecessary unless we are dealing with high-fidelity music signals. Many useful and important audio signals, such as human voice signals, don't possess as wide a range of frequencies as music signals. The frequency spectrum, or content, of most human voices contains no significant (for purposes of intelligibility) frequency components higher than about 3000 Hz, or lower than about 100 Hz. So, human voices can be recreated nicely by systems that can handle frequencies between 100 Hz and 3 kHz. In fact, the telephone system does not recreate frequency components even as high as 4 kHz. As a result, although we can still understand what we hear using such systems, we perceive the quality of the sound to be low. This is because some of the higher frequency components—the ones that give each sound its distinctive character—are not recreated by these low-fidelity systems.

Typically, we are much more interested in the *highest frequency* we will need to represent than in the lowest frequency. This is because the amount of information we must capture and represent—the rate at which we must *sample* the waveform—is determined by the highest frequency component. This highest frequency component tells us (in a sense) how fast the waveform can change, which is related directly to how often we must sample its value to represent it faithfully in all cases. The highest frequency component in an audio signal is referred to as the *bandwidth of the signal*. Thus, the bandwidth of voice signals is about 3 kHz, and the bandwidth of high fidelity music signals is about 20 kHz. The term "bandwidth" refers to the width of the range—or *band*—of frequencies that the signal occupies. For audio signals, we just assume that the lowest frequency is very low—near 0 Hz—and measure the bandwidth from 0 Hz to the highest frequency component. As we will see, the bandwidth of a signal is closely related to the amount of information it can convey, and therefore also closely related to the amount of storage it will require when digitized.

10.7 Frequency Content of Audio Signals

Because all audio signals are comprised of a sum of different pure tones, each at a different frequency, we can describe a given audio signal in two different ways. One way we have already seen—we can use the waveform that describes how the audio signal varies with respect to time. This waveform is sometimes referred to as the *time-domain description* of the signal. The second way to describe an audio signal is by its *frequency spectrum*—that is, by specifying which frequency compo-

⊙ Frequency Spectrum

FIGURE 10.8 A concert "A" 440Hz sinusoid.

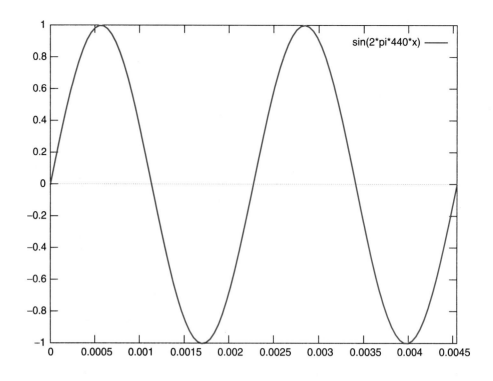

FIGURE 10.8 A concert "A" 440Hz sinusoid.

nents the signal contains, and in what amount each frequency or pure tone occurs. This description of a signal is referred to as the *frequency-domain description*.

In Figures 10.8 and 10.9 two time-domain waveforms are shown, for a pure tone at 440 Hz, and a musical note at that same frequency, respectively. Although both of these audio signals are at the same "pitch," the pure tone consists by definition

FIGURE 10.9 Concert "A" played on a vibraphone.

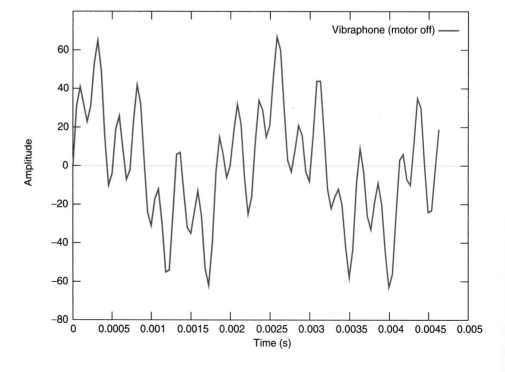

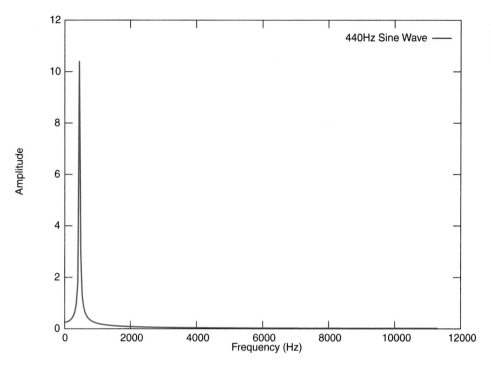

FIGURE 10.10 The frequency spectrum of a concert "A" 440Hz sinusoid.

of a single sinusoidal frequency component; that's why we call it "pure." The musical note, however, is more complex, as can be seen by its waveform. What might not be obvious from this time-domain waveform, however, is *which additional frequency components are contained in this musical note, and in which quantities*. This is important, for it is these extra components that make the note more "complex" and more interesting to listen to than the pure tone. And, it's these extra components that allow us to distinguish whether the note was played on a Hammond organ or a Les Paul guitar.

In Figures 10.10 and 10.11 are shown the *frequency-domain* descriptions, or *frequency spectra*, for these two same sounds, respectively. Note that Figure 10.10, the spectrum for the pure tone of Figure 10.8, consists of a *single frequency component*—in this case at a frequency of 440 Hz. The spectrum in Figure 10.11, corresponding to the note whose waveform is shown in Figure 10.9, on the other hand, shows additional frequency components at a number of higher frequencies, in addition to a strong component at 440 Hz. By looking at these frequency spectrum plots, we can determine the *frequency content* of these signals. Not only does this help us understand the difference between them, but it will also provide the key for us to know how to digitize these waveforms for purposes of processing, storage, and transmission.

Not every signal of interest, of course, consists of a musical tone. As we have mentioned, a voice signal has a bandwidth, or highest frequency, of about 3 kHz. Figure 10.12 shows the time-domain waveform of a voice signal; this particular voice signal consists of a male speaker saying the word "information." In Figure 10.13 the frequency spectrum of this signal is shown. As you can see, this voice signal has a very different type of frequency spectrum than the musical notes above. As can be seen from this example, voice signals contain many different frequency components, all in different quantities. The same is true for pieces of music and other complex audio signals of interest.

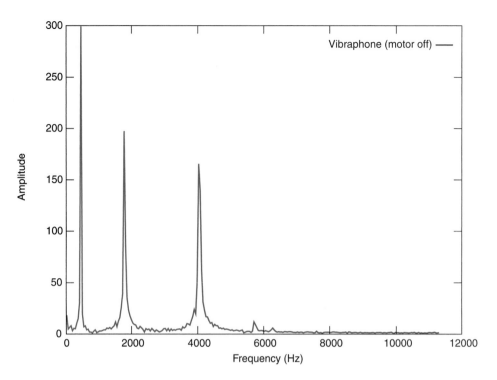

Fortunately, we do not need to know the specific frequency content of a signal to build equipment for digitizing and processing it. All we need to know is the *bandwidth* of the signal, so that we know the *highest frequency component* the signal might contain. Because this is a voice signal, we are not surprised to see that almost all of the frequency content lies within the range between 100 Hz and 5 kHz. In fact, because this male speaker's voice contains low frequencies, there really is

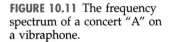

Bandwidth

FIGURE 10.12 A male saying "information."

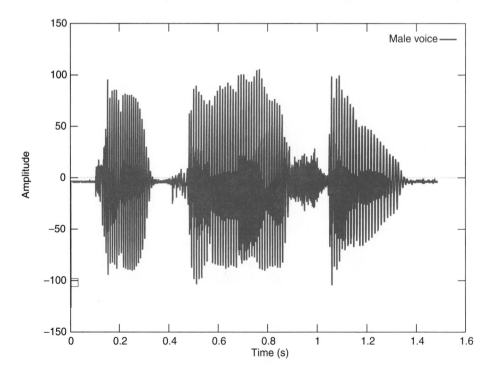

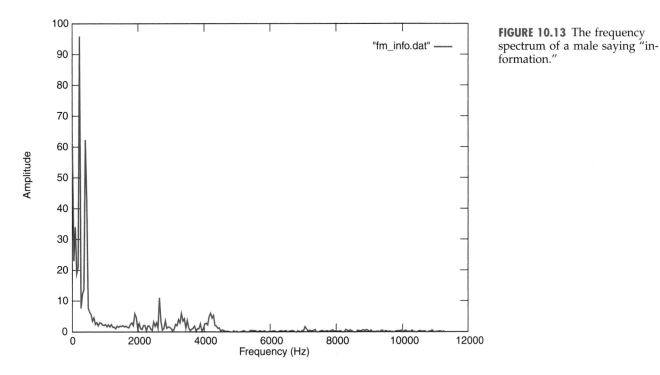

FIGURE 10.13 The frequency spectrum of a male saying "information."

not much frequency content above 1 kHz. Figures 10.14 and 10.15 show the time-domain and frequency-domain descriptions, respectively, of a female speaker saying the same word: "information." Two aspects of the frequency spectrum should be noted. First, it is apparent that the spectrum for both speakers is within the standard bandwidth for voice signals. Thus, any equipment we design with this

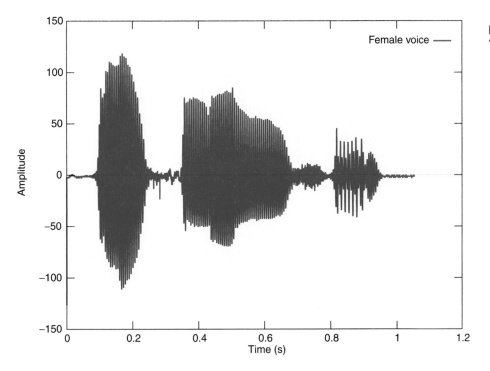

FIGURE 10.14 A female saying "information."

FIGURE 10.15 The frequency spectrum of a female saying "information."

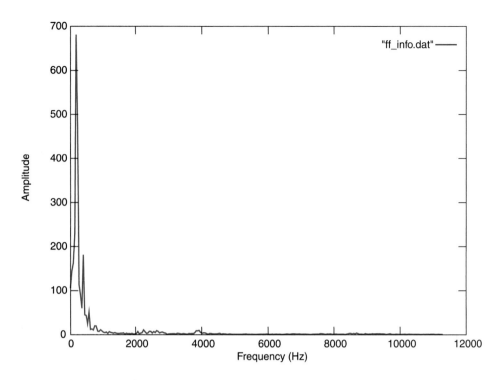

bandwidth in mind can be used to process either signal. Second, it is evident that the details of the spectra for the two speakers are quite different. It is these differences that distinguish one person's voice from another's.

Summary

In this chapter, we have taken a look at the phenomena underlying the creation of sound, and how audio signals can be captured and represented using electrical waveforms. We've discussed the idea of frequency, and discovered that all audio waveforms are comprised of a sum of pure tones at different frequencies. The range of possible frequencies for a signal, also known as the signal's bandwidth, determines how quickly the signal might change.

In the next chapters, we will see how this signal bandwidth directly affects the way in which we digitize and store audio signals. We will discuss practical issues regarding the representation of audio signals in binary form, and also explore some of the issues involved in recreating an audible signal from a binary representation.

Try These Exercises

1. Describe and explain some ways in which the sense of hearing is like the sense of sight, and some ways in which it is different. In a general sense, compare the bandwidths of the two senses.
2. Explain why two musical instruments playing the same note may sound entirely different.
3. How is sound different in outer space?
4. Explain the concept of bandwidth in your own words.

5. Explain what Figure 10.11 tells you about the frequencies contained in the sound from the vibraphone.

6. How many syllables does the word "information" contain? Try to match those syllables to the graph of the signal in Figure 10.12. Draw a sketch of the figure indicating where each syllable is represented.

7. In the applet "Frequency Spectrum (FFT) of a signal," the frequency spectra of four signals are calculated and displayed. Two of these may be called simple signals or fundamental frequencies; one may be called moderately simple, and the fourth signal may be called complex in form. By observation of the spectra, indicate which signals fit in which categories, and explain your reasoning.

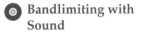

Frequency Spectrum (FFT) of a Signal

8. Use the applet "Frequency Spectrum (FFT) of a signal" to find the frequency spectra of the four sample signals. What is the bandwidth of each signal? Explain how you reached your conclusion in each case.

Frequency Spectrum (FFT) of a Signal

9. The descriptions of sound perception in this chapter are actually quite simplistic because they do not include important real-world effects such as binaural sound arriving at our two ears, and multipath effects as sound waves bounce off of objects and arrive at our ears after traveling multiple paths from the source. Assume that the waveform in Figure 10.5 represents what one ear receives for the sound arriving directly from the saxophone. Now assume that a wall is put in place behind the listener, and the sound wave bounces off it and is reflected to the listener, in addition to the direct sound. Sketch the new waveform in comparison to the original waveform, and explain your sketch. Assume that the wall is 50 feet behind the listener, so that you can be quantitative in time.

10. Figures 10.10 and 10.11 display the frequency spectra of two signals with the same fundamental frequency: 440 Hz. What are the approximate bandwidths of the two signals, from the figures?

11. Using the applet "Bandlimiting with Sound," with the chirp signal, observe the effect as the bandwidth is lowered. Explain the observation. Repeat for the other three signals.

Bandlimiting with Sound

12. Using the applet "Bandlimited Music," listen to the music samples at the indicated bandwidths. Comment carefully on the differences at the various bandwidths. Note that the frequency ranges start near zero Hz in each case. Beyond stating which versions sound "better" or "worse," comment on the specific differences. Are certain aspects of the sound missing in some cases?

Bandlimited Music

11 Sampling of Audio Signals

Objectives

In the previous chapter we learned about sound and audio as an important class of signals. These analog signals must be converted into digital form for processing, transmission, and storage. This process provides the opportunity to describe several important concepts:

▲ the concept of sampling, where a signal that is continuous in time is observed only at periodic intervals;

▲ the determination of an appropriate sampling rate (the Nyquist rate) based on the bandwidth of the signal, which guarantees that all of the information in the original analog signal is preserved; and

▲ the way in which a signal may be exactly reconstructed from knowledge only of its samples.

11.1 Introduction

Pixels

In Chapter 5, we discussed how continuous images are digitized via a two-stage process. First, the images are broken down into pixels, or small regions. Then, a measurement of brightness or color is taken at each pixel location and quantized, or converted into a finite-length binary data representation. A similar two-stage process is employed for the digitization of audio signals. The first step of this process, in which a continuous audio signal is made discrete in time, is called *sampling*. This is because we choose to sample, or evaluate, the audio waveform at specific instants in time, rather than to attempt to represent its value for all moments of time. The second step is then identical to the quantization of the video samples; each audio sample is converted into a sequence of binary digits. This process is depicted in Figure 11.1, which shows a block diagram representing the process of digitizing an audio signal. In a block diagram, quantities such as signals and information are represented by arrows, and system components such as hardware

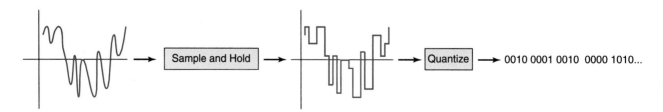

FIGURE 11.1 A block diagram of an audio sampling system.

and software processes are represented by blocks. In this diagram, the original audio waveform is first converted to samples, and then the samples are quantized into binary digits. These binary digits are then suitable for storage, transmission, or other processing. Note that when we wish to retrieve the signal, we must be prepared to undo the effects of this system and rebuild, or reconstruct, the audio signal into a form we can use.

In this chapter, we will discuss some of the theoretical and practical issues associated with sampling audio waveforms. We'll present guidelines for ensuring that a signal has been sampled properly, and give illustrations of what happens if the rate of sampling is not appropriate.

11.2 Sampling an Audio Signal

An audio signal is a continuous function of time. When we convert sound into an electrical voltage, the voltage takes on a particular value at each moment of time. Because there are an infinite number of different time instants, there would appear to be an infinite amount of information in this signal! We must decide how to capture systematically the *necessary* information from this signal to digitize it. An example of an audio signal from the previous chapter is shown in Figure 10.12, and the frequency spectrum of this signal is shown in Figure 10.13. This is a voice signal; from our discussion of frequency in the last chapter, we know that the highest frequency in this signal may be no more than several kHz. From Figure 10.13 we see that there are indeed no frequency components higher than about 4.5 kHz. This is significant, because the bandwidth of the signal tells us that the voice signal will never change more abruptly than a 4.5 kHz tone. This will allow us to determine how often we must sample it.

11.2.1 Sampling Intervals and Sampling Frequency

In order to digitize the signal in Figure 10.12, we must first choose particular instants of time when we will "look" at the signal and attempt to represent its value. It will be easier to understand sampling and its effects if we begin with a simple audio signal, a sinusoidal wave. Plates 26, 27, and 28 demonstrate the effects of three different sampling rates on a sinusoidal wave of 125 Hz frequency. In each figure, the top graph shows the original input waveform, the center graph shows the results of sampling the waveform, and the lower graph shows the result of reconstructing the input signal from the samples.

The center graph bears some explanation because it captures the essence of the sampling operation. The location of each vertical line in the center graph indicates the time at which the input signal was "looked" at. The height of each line represents the amplitude of the input signal at that time. It is important to note that all of the other information between sampling points on the input signal is discarded! In Plate 26 a sampling rate of 1 kHz is chosen. This is considerably higher than is actually needed to represent the input signal, and the resulting samples provide a pleasing view to the eye, making it easy to recognize the original signal. In the lower graph the reconstructed signal is shown, and as expected, it is a perfect replica of the input signal. Plate 27 represents the case where the sampling rate is the minimum value that provides complete information about the input signal. That rate is twice the frequency of the signal, or 250 Hz. This principle will be explained further later in this chapter. Note how little information is retained by the samples, as shown in the center graph! Nevertheless, as the lower graph shows, exact reconstruction is possible. Finally, Plate 28 demonstrates the effect of a sampling rate that is too low, in this case 187.5 Hz. The most important aspect to note is that a completely incorrect signal is reconstructed in this case. This situation is called "aliasing." This name comes from the fact that the components of the signal are completely changed, and have a new identity—an alias—which hides their original form from us.

Plates 29 and 30 demonstrate the effect of sample rate or more complex (and useful) signals such as music. In Plate 29 the sampling rate is sufficiently high that all the information in the input signal is retained. Plate 30 demonstrates the aliasing (errors) that occur with a sampling rate that is too low.

⦿ Sampling Applet

The figures produced above are taken from the Sampling Applet that accompanies this text. More example signals are available on the applet, as well as control of the sampling rate.

Assuming that we are going to sample a signal *uniformly*—that is, with sampling instants evenly spaced at regular intervals of time—we need to decide how often, or at what rate, we are going to sample the signal. This can be indicated either by the *sampling interval*, which is the amount of time separating the samples, or the *sampling rate*, which is the number of samples taken per second. The sampling rates for Plates 26, 27, and 28, respectively, are 1000, 250, and 62.5 samples per second. The corresponding sampling intervals are simply the reciprocals of these values, or 1 millisecond, 4 milliseconds, and 16 milliseconds.

Because sampling occurs at regular intervals, and because these intervals are typically small fractions of a second, we usually find it more convenient to describe how often we are sampling by specifying the *sampling rate*. We see that this rate describes the frequency—literally, how frequently—we are sampling. For that reason, it is also called the *sampling frequency* being used for the signal. We can describe this sampling frequency, or sampling rate, in samples per second, but usually we will use the familiar unit hertz to represent this. You will recall that when measuring the repetition rate of pure tones, we used this unit to represent cycles per second. When we express a sampling rate in hertz, the interpretation is *samples per second*. In either case, we see that hertz is used to describe a frequency, or rate, in terms of how many times per second an event (a cycle or sample) occurs.

It is easy to convert back and forth between sampling rate and sampling period. These quantities are reciprocals of each other:

$$f_s = \frac{1}{T_s} \qquad T_s = \frac{1}{f_s},$$

where f_s is measured in hertz, and T_s is measured in seconds. For example, in Plate 26, the 1000 Hz sampling rate is equivalent to a 1 millisecond sampling period.

By looking at the waveforms and sampling intervals, we can attempt to get some intuitive feel for whether we are sampling the signal often enough. For example, in Plate 28, we see that the samples are widely spaced, and the waveform undergoes changes in between the samples that do not seem to be represented or "captured" by the sample values. We might therefore suspect that 187.5 Hz does not appear to be a sufficiently high sampling rate. This is verified when we look at the reconstructed signal and see that it is different than the input signal.

On the other hand, if we look at Plate 26, we may conclude that 1000 samples per second seems to be adequate; the samples are closely spaced, and so we might expect that this is a sufficiently high sampling rate. Plate 27 represents a sample rate between these two values. The sample rate of 250 Hz is, in fact, the minimum

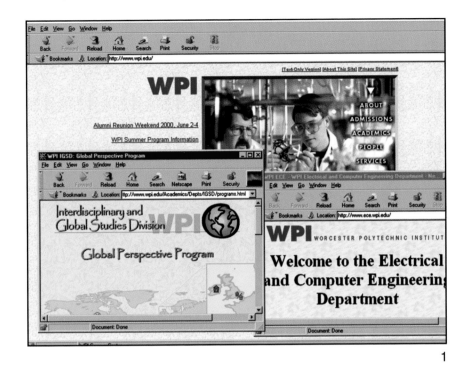

1

2

Plate 1 Screen image of a typical web browser session

Plate 2 A picture of a flower bed, represented as a collection of tiny pixels and a close-up view of a small section of that flower. The close-up view reveals the pixels that were small enough not to be noticed before.

3

4

5

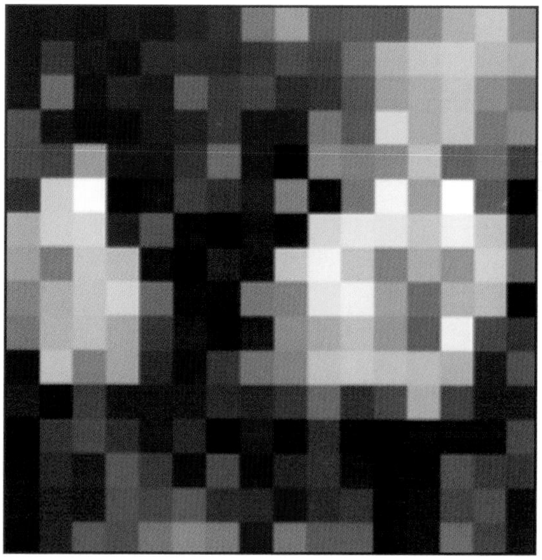

6

Plate 3 A 256 x 256 pixel image.
Plate 4 A 128 x 128 pixel image.

Plate 5 A 64 x 64 pixel image.
Plate 6 A 16 x 16 pixel image.

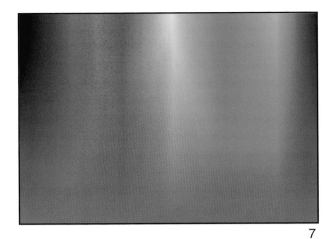

7

8

9

10

11

12

Plate 7 Diagram showing the colors corresponding to the full range of hue (along horizontal axis) and saturation values (0% saturation at bottom and 100% saturation at top).

Plate 8 An image with 24-bit color (8 bits each for red, green and blue).

Plate 9 An image with 8-bit color resolution.

Plate 10 An image with 4-bit color resolution.

Plate 11 An image with 4-bit color resolution in which a dithering process has been used to obtain a better representation on average.

Plate 12 Stereoscopic shutter glasses are shown being used to view a #d display of terrain. The operation of electronic shutters in this case is synchronized with images shown on the computer screen via an infrared link (note the small box on top of the computer monitor) between the computer and the glasses.

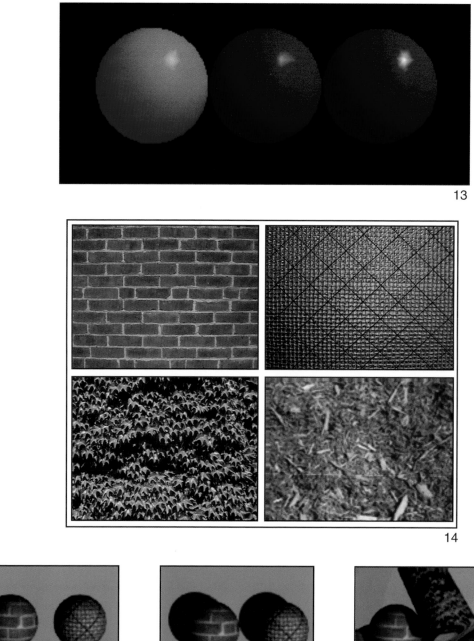

13

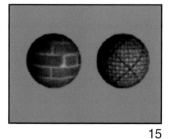

15

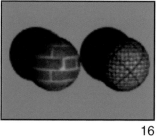

16

17

Plate 13 An image rendered from the VRML file describing three balls.

Plate 14 Four images of natural material are shown; from the upper left and clockwise: brick, a wire reinforced glass window material, black mulch and ivy.

Plate 15 Two balls onto which brick and glass images have been texture mapped.

Plate 16 Shadowing has been added to the rendering of the two balls.

Plate 17 Several objects, onto each of which one of the previously shown textures has been mapped.

18

19

20

21

22

Plate 18 The test image file compressed va JPEG lossless compression to 252,906 bytes.

Plate 19 The test image file compressed va JPEG lossless compression to 33,479 bytes. This is the first level of lossy compression at which a change in the picture from the original can be detected by a person.

Plate 20 The test image file compressed va JPEG lossless compression to 22,418 bytes.

Plate 21 The test image file compressed va JPEG lossless compression to 14,192 bytes. At this level of compression, the distortion of the image becomes quite noticeable.

Plate 22 The test image file compressed va JPEG lossless compression to 8,978 bytes. The image is essentially unusable at this compression level.

23

24

25

Plate 23 Single frame from a high quality, high bit rate MPEG-1 encoded video sequence.
Plate 24 Single frame from a medium quality, medium bit rate MPEG-1 encoded video sequence.

Plate 25 Single frame from a low quality, low bit rate MPEG-1 encoded video sequence.

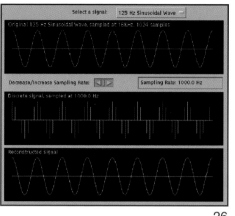

26

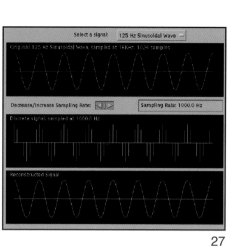

27

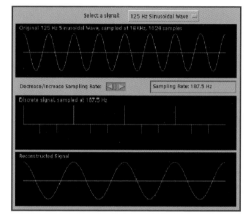

28

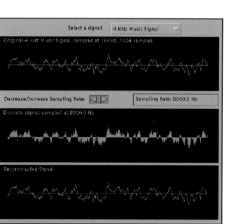

29

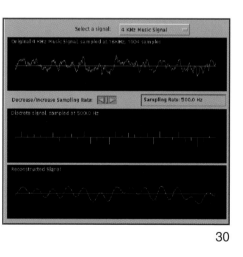

30

Plate 26 The effects of sampling a 125 Hz sinusoidal wave at 1 kHz.

Plate 27 The effects of sampling a 125 Hz sinusoidal wave at 250 kHz.

Plate 28 The effects of sampling a 125 Hz sinusoidal wave at 187.5 kHz. Note the erroneous reconstructed signal!

Plate 29 The effects of sampling a music signal at a sufficient rate (8,000 Hz).

Plate 30 The effects of sampling a music signal at an insufficient rate (500 Hz).

31

32

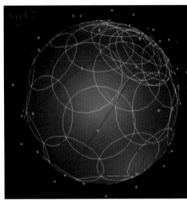

33

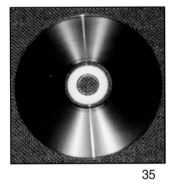

35

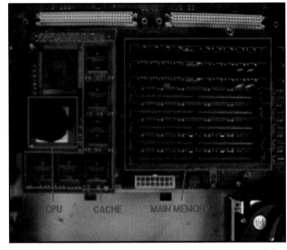

34

Plate 31 Two cellular telephone antenna towers erected by competing cellular phone service providers at the top of a solitary hill.

Plate 32 The cellular telephone has made it possible for people to stay in contact over most highly populated regions of the world.

Plate 33 This picture depicts the orbits of the 66 satellites that make up the spaceborne portion of the Iridium satellite telephone system. (Courtesy of Patrick Worfolk [www.ee.surrey.ac.uk/Personal/L.Wood/constellations/]), based upon Lloyd;s satellite constellations, rendered using SaVi, by the Geometry Center at the University of Minnesota (www.geom.umn.edu/locate/SaVi/).

Plate 34 Main computer circuit board of a mid-90s generation workstation that employed cache memory to improve information access speeds.

Plate 35 A standard CD.

rate that will capture this waveform accurately. Note how few samples are necessary! This is an aspect that makes the processing of signals digitally so attractive.

11.2.2 The Minimum Sampling Frequency

Because we want our samples to reflect accurately the original waveform, we see that we must sample the waveform often enough to capture all of the important changes and fluctuations in the signal. If we sample less often than is necessary, we will get a corrupted and incorrect representation of the signal.

How can we know if a sampling rate is fast enough? Communication and information theory provided this answer in the first half of the 20th century, when such pioneers as Harry Nyquist and Claude Shannon developed a mathematical framework to determine how often a signal should be sampled. Their result, known as the *sampling theorem*, states that: IN ORDER TO BE PERFECTLY REPRESENTED BY ITS SAMPLES, A SIGNAL MUST BE SAMPLED AT A SAMPLING RATE EQUAL TO AT LEAST TWICE ITS HIGHEST FREQUENCY COMPONENT.

You may be surprised to see the word *perfectly* in this theorem; the implications of this word are worth noting. This theorem states that if we take samples of a signal frequently enough, then no information is lost, and the signal can be perfectly reconstructed from these samples. This remarkable result is based on the fact that because we know the signal's bandwidth, we know the highest frequency—the maximum rate of change—which the signal is capable of attaining. Thus, we can determine how often we must sample its values to avoid "missing" any important information. The minimum sampling rate (or lowest acceptable sampling frequency) for any audio waveform is, according to this theorem, equal to twice the bandwidth of the signal. For our 125 Hz audio signal, we see that we should sample it at a rate which is at least

$$f_s = (2) \times (125 \text{ Hz}) = 250 \text{ Hz},$$

or 250 samples per second.

Knowing this, we can return to the waveforms of Plates 26, 27, and 28. Because the minimum sampling rate for this signal is 250 Hz, we see that the samples in Plate 28, taken at a 187.5 Hz rate, are, as we suspected, inadequate. The samples in Plate 26, taken at a 1 kHz rate, are more than sufficient to represent the signal. And the samples in Plate 27, taken at a 250 Hz rate—the minimum rate for this signal—are just right. As we will see, just as it is best to eat porridge that is neither too cold nor too hot, there is also an advantage to sampling at a frequency that is not too slow, and not too fast, but "just right."

11.3 Reconstructing Audio from Samples

At some point it is usually necessary to reconstruct the analog signal from its digital version. The figures in the previous section have demonstrated that exact reconstruction is possible if the sampling rate is sufficiently high. Now let us look at the reconstruction process in more detail, first from a very simple point of view.

Figure 11.2 shows a short section of a speech waveform. The bandwidth of this waveform is 2,500 Hz, so a sample rate of 5,000 Hz is required to represent it accurately. First, we will show the reconstruction result with a sample rate of 1,000 Hz, which is too low. This case is shown in Figure 11.3. This figure shows the sampled values only, connected by some horizontal line segments. This method of building a signal from sample values—assuming the signal maintains each sample value until the next sample occurs—is called *zero-order hold* reconstruction. Although

FIGURE 11.2 A short section of a speech waveform.

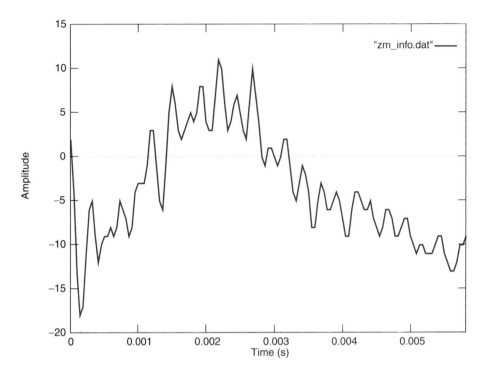

this is a very simplistic method, it is often used as a first step, and sometimes the only step, in rebuilding a signal from its sample values.

In Figure 11.3, we see that the reconstructed version of the signal bears little resemblance to the original signal. Many of the detailed excursions in the signal have been lost due to undersampling. What remains after reconstruction is not simply

FIGURE 11.3 The reconstructed speech waveform, based on a 1 KHz sampling rate.

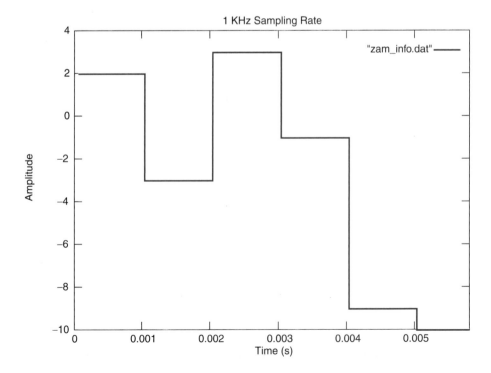

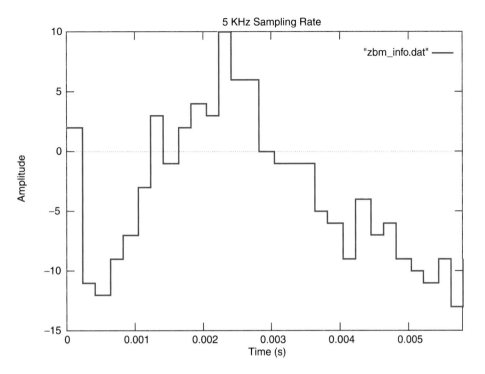

FIGURE 11.4 The reconstructed speech waveform, based on a 5 KHz sampling rate.

a somewhat distorted version of the original signal, but a completely new signal that bears little resemblance to the original. If we attempt to listen to it, we may not even be able to detect the original signal's content at all. As was mentioned above, this effect is called aliasing. It is important to note that this aliasing is a permanent effect; we cannot "undo" the effects of sampling too slowly, because the original information has been lost forever.

In Figure 11.4, we see the signal that has been sampled properly, at the minimum rate of 5,000 samples per second, as reconstructed from its samples using zero-order hold reconstruction. Although the zero-order hold creates a "staircase" effect that is artificial, we see that enough samples have been retained so that the original signal's details are not lost. In Figure 11.5, we see the zero-order hold reconstruction of the version sampled at 10 kHz. In this case, it is very easy to see that enough samples have been taken, because the reconstructed signal closely resembles the original.

In the next chapter, we will go into more detail about other methods of reconstruction, and also describe how the reconstructed signal can be converted exactly back into the original form (as shown for example in Plate 29).

11.3.1 Oversampling

We have seen that there are dangers to *undersampling*, or sampling at a frequency that is not high enough. When we undersample, the information in the signal is aliased into a new form, and we lose the information in the original signal. It would seem better to "play it safe" and sample at a high rate. Sampling at a rate higher than the minimum rate required is known as *oversampling*. As we will see, oversampling can be a good thing, but like many things, it is good only in moderation!

Recall why we are sampling: so that we can convert each sample into a binary form and create a digitized version of the audio signal. The more samples we

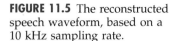

FIGURE 11.5 The reconstructed speech waveform, based on a 10 kHz sampling rate.

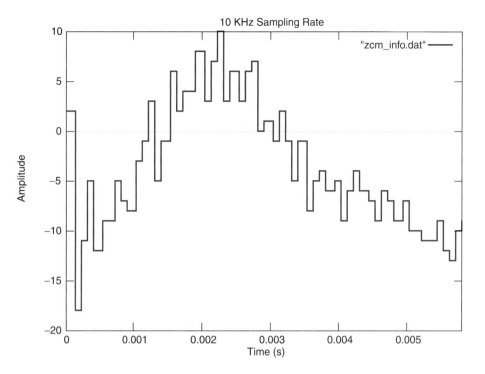

create, the more values we will need to digitize and process. When we sample more often than is necessary—that is, at a higher sampling frequency than is needed—we will generate additional, unnecessary samples, which must be digitized, stored, and/or transmitted. In other words, sampling faster than is necessary (oversampling) will increase the amount of storage and transmission needed for the digitized signal without providing any extra information about the signal. This would result in a waste of storage and transmission resources; in other words, it would be more costly.

So why would we ever wish to oversample? The answer lies in the fact that the faster we sample, the easier it is to reconstruct the original signal in a simple and inexpensive way. An oversampled signal allows us to recreate the original signal from the samples using less sophisticated methods. Indeed, if we sample a signal at exactly the minimum rate, we effectively require perfect equipment to reconstruct the original signal in its exact form. However, if we oversample by some modest amount, our equipment and methods for reconstruction can be much simpler, and therefore less expensive to design, build, and use. We conclude that there is a tradeoff that must be made when choosing a sampling rate. A modest amount of oversampling allows for simpler reconstruction, but also creates more samples to be digitized. In the next chapter, we will present some typical examples of sampling rates for common applications, such as digital telephone and audio CDs.

Summary

In this chapter, we have presented an overview of how audio signals are sampled prior to digitization. We have discussed how the choice of sampling rate affects our ability to accurately reconstruct a signal from its samples, and found that the minimum rate of sampling, in hertz or samples per second, is equal to twice the highest frequency of the signal—the bandwidth of the signal—also measured in hertz. We have discussed the problem of aliasing, which results from sampling a signal at too low a rate, and have discussed some of the advantages and drawbacks of oversampling—that is, sampling at a rate higher than necessary.

In the next chapter, we will continue with this topic, and explore how these samples are digitized and reconverted to their original form. We'll talk more about reconstruction, and give some examples of common applications of digitized audio signals.

Try These Exercises

1. Explain in your own words what each graph in Plate 26 represents. Explain the differences for each graph between Plate 26 and Plate 28.
2. We wish to digitally record (in stereo) high-quality audio with a 20 kHz bandwidth. How many samples must be taken in each second?
3. Explain why the reconstructed waveform (as in Figure 11.4) does not look exactly like the original waveform (Figure 11.2).
4. Use the applet "Sampling and Reconstruction with Sound" with the chirp signal and a sampling rate of 2 kHz. Describe the reconstructed signal and explain why it has the shape that you observe. What part of the reconstructed signal matches the original chirp signal and what part does not? Explain.

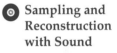
Sampling and Reconstruction with Sound

5. Use the applet "Sampling and Reconstruction with Sound" with the 375 Hz sine wave signal. Using sampling rates of 4000 Hz, 2000 Hz, 1000 Hz, 687.5 Hz, and 500 Hz, observe the reconstructed wave and listen to the audio. As the sampling rate is lowered, at what rate do the reconstructed waveform and reconstructed audio begin to deviate from the original? Explain.

Sampling and Reconstruction with Sound

6. Using the applet "Sampling and Reconstruction with Sound" with the music signal, gradually reduce the sampling rate from its maximum value and note where the reconstructed signal begins to deviate visually from the original signal. Also, can you explain why the reconstructed audio never sounds like music? Note that the audio is generated by taking the visible section of signal and playing it repetitively.

Sampling and Reconstruction with Sound

12

Digital Audio

Objectives

The process of sampling a signal, as described in the previous chapter, moves us only half way toward the digitization of an analog signal. The remainder of the process is presented here, and contains the following aspects:

▲ the concept that a digital signal must be represented by a series of integers, each of finite length;

▲ the process of quantization by which each sample of an analog signal is approximated by an integer of a given length;

▲ the concept of an analog-to-digital converter that performs sampling and quantization;

▲ the concept of quantization noise and the trade-off between fidelity and the number of bits used to represent the integer value of each sample; and

▲ the process of digital-to-analog conversion by which the digital signal is converted back to analog form for use by humans.

12.1 Introduction

In the last chapter, we introduced the idea of sampling an audio signal. This is the first step toward digitization of the signal, and we saw that the sampling rate, which determines how many values of the signal we choose to retain, must be chosen according to the signal's bandwidth. In this chapter, we will discuss the rest of the digitization process, and talk about how the audio signal can be reconstructed from the digitized version. We will also provide some examples of how this is done in familiar audio systems.

12.2 Digitization of Audio Samples

Audio signals, being continuous in both time and amplitude, must be digitized in both time and amplitude before they can be represented in binary form. These digitization processes are typically accomplished separately: first, the signal is made to be discrete in time by sampling, and then it is made discrete in amplitude by quantization. This two-step digitization process is depicted in the block diagram shown in Figure 12.1. The sampling process, which was discussed in detail in the previous chapter, must be done at a rate equal to or greater than the minimum, or Nyquist, sampling rate to retain all of the information in the original signal. For a signal bandlimited to a highest frequency content of B Hz, this means we must

 Nyquist

172

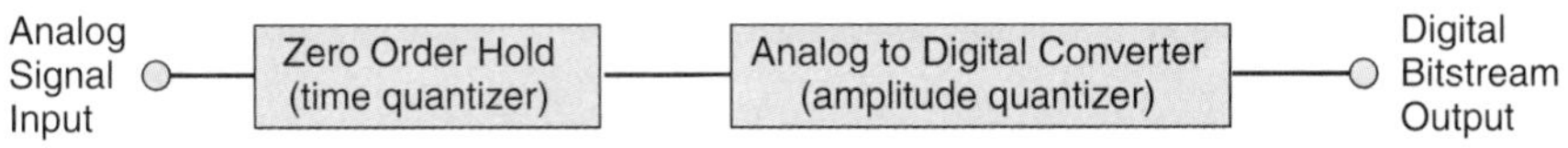

Analog
Signal O─── [Zero Order Hold (time quantizer)] ─── [Analog to Digital Converter (amplitude quantizer)] ───O Digital
Input   Bitstream
                                                                                                                Output

FIGURE 12.1 The two-step sampling process.

take at least $2B$ samples per second. As we mentioned, in practice we will over-sample, using a somewhat higher rate to allow the use of inexpensive equipment for digitization and reconstruction.

Once these samples have been captured, they must be discretized in amplitude to allow a digital representation. The reader may recall that we faced the same problem when digitizing images; after an image is segmented into pixels, each pixel must be represented by a gray level (for black and white imagery), or a set of color values (for color imagery). In either case, the values associated with each pixel must be represented by a finite number of bits; because the actual brightness values are continuous, this requires a rounding process that introduces some amount of error into the representation. The more bits used to represent the brightness, the smaller the average error will be. This process of rounding off a continuous value so that it can be represented by a fixed number of binary digits is known as *quantization*, and the devices we use to accomplish it are called *analog-to-digital converters* (ADCs). This is the task with which our audio digitizing system is faced after sampling: each audio sample must be digitized and converted into a finite string of bits. We recall that N bits can be arranged in 2^N different patterns; this means if we use N bits to represent each audio sample, then each sample can represent any one of 2^N different audio signal amplitudes. The choice of N is the most important decision to be made in the process of quantization, and it must be made according to the criteria of fidelity; that is, how much error are we willing to introduce?

12.3 The Process of Quantization

Obviously, we would prefer to introduce as little error as possible into our audio representation. However, as we have learned from image and video examples, we must accept some amount of error based on a trade-off, or compromise, between performance (in this case audio quality) and cost (in this case, equipment, storage, and processing speed). And, unlike sampling, quantization will necessarily involve introducing some error and losing some amount of information. As we did with gray-level quantization of images, we will consider two important issues when determining how to quantize audio samples: the limitations of human perception, and the specific application being developed. It does not make sense to worry about errors that are so small as to be imperceptible to humans, if the ultimate goal for the information is human perception. Additionally, the specific use to which the information will be put is also an important consideration. We will be more concerned with the fidelity of music to be recreated in a home entertainment system, for example, than we will be with the fidelity of voice signals to be sent across noisy, low-quality telephone equipment.

In any case, we must determine the relationship between the number of bits used to represent each sample and the maximum possible error we will make in that representation. This means we must determine the system we will use to assign different audio sample amplitudes to specific binary codes. Audio signals, as we have mentioned, are usually captured by equipment that converts them into time-varying voltages. Thus, each audio sample will represent a particular voltage measurement taken at a specific time. Depending on the equipment used,

FIGURE 12.2 A time quantized
audio waveform.

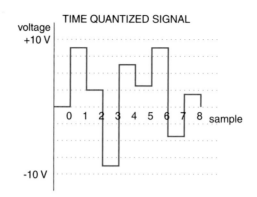

there will be a certain range of voltages between which the audio signal might take
on values. Figure 12.2 depicts a set of audio samples, for example, which take on
values between -10 and $+10$ volts.

If we choose, for example, to represent each of these samples by 4 bits, then we
have $2^4 = 16$ different binary codewords to represent different voltages. Clearly,
because there are an infinite number of voltages between -10 and $+10$, we will
have to assign a range of voltages to each codeword. The simplest way in which
to do this is to divide the entire range of voltages from -10 to $+10$ into 16 evenly
sized ranges, or intervals. In this case, each voltage interval will cover a range of
voltages equal to

$$\frac{10 - (-10)}{16} = 1.25 \text{ V}.$$

Then, we can assign one of the 16 codewords (0000 through 1111) to each of these
intervals, starting with the lowest voltage range and proceeding to the highest. Finally, we can represent each audio sample by the code corresponding to the range
within which that sample falls.

TABLE 12.1   QUANTIZATION CODES AND QUANTIZED VALUES

Range	Code	Range Center
$8.75 \rightarrow 10.0$	1111	9.375
$7.50 \rightarrow 8.75$	1110	8.125
$6.25 \rightarrow 7.50$	1101	6.875
$5.0 \rightarrow 6.25$	1100	5.625
$3.75 \rightarrow 5.0$	1011	4.375
$2.50 \rightarrow 3.75$	1010	3.125
$1.25 \rightarrow 2.50$	1001	1.875
$0.0 \rightarrow 1.25$	1000	0.625
$-1.25 \rightarrow 0.0$	0111	-0.625
$-2.5 \rightarrow -1.25$	0110	-1.875
$-3.75 \rightarrow -2.5$	0101	-3.125
$-5.0 \rightarrow -3.75$	0100	-4.375
$-6.25 \rightarrow -5.0$	0011	-5.625
$-7.5 \rightarrow -6.25$	0010	-6.875
$-8.75 \rightarrow -7.5$	0001	-9.375
$-10.0 \rightarrow -8.75$	0000	9.375

This coding is specified in Table 12.1, where each of the 16 ranges from −10 to +10 is indicated, with its assigned code. Note that the assignment of these codes is arbitrary. We simply chose to assign the code 0000 to the most negative number, and then to proceed in order to the largest value with the highest code. It is important to recognize that some information has been irretrievably lost in this coding process: we no longer have any idea where within the range interval each original value lay. It is also interesting to note that at the boundaries between each range there is a small region of uncertainty where the code for either the larger or smaller range could be assigned. Note that our input signal took on a value that appears to be zero volts in Figure 12.2 for the first sample. In fact, the signal was some small amount greater or less than zero, and this small deviation will determine the assigned code.

12.4 Quantization Noise

Because all of the voltage values within any interval are represented by the same codeword, we are clearly making an approximation and losing information when we use this 4-bit code to represent the sample. To see this, consider the process by which we could attempt to reconstruct, or rebuild, the original sample values of the audio signal from just the binary codes. What voltage value would we use to represent an entire range? The most obvious answer is that we would use the value in the middle of the range. Indeed, if any voltage within the range is equally likely to have been the actual value, then using the middle or mean value of that range will minimize the average size of the error we will make in recreating the sample value. This is the approach taken in Table 12.1.

Figure 12.3 shows the reconstructed sample values from the previous example; as can be seen, each sample value takes on the mean value within its interval. Given this understanding of how we will have to attempt to "undo" the effects of quantization, we can see that when we quantize, we are effectively "rounding off" each sample value to the center, or mean value, of each of our 2^N voltage intervals. The difference between the original sample value and this rounded value is called the *quantization error*. In effect, when we quantize we are introducing this amount of error to each sample. Unwanted distortion added to any signal is usually referred to as *noise*; thus, quantization error is also referred to as *quantization noise*. The extent to which this noise will degrade the signal quality depends on the relative sizes of the signal values and the errors. This comparison is usually

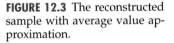 Quantize

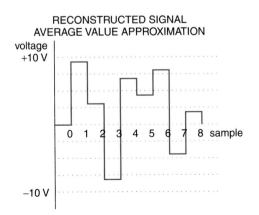

FIGURE 12.3 The reconstructed sample with average value approximation.

expressed as a quantity known as *signal-to-noise ratio*, or SNR. The higher the SNR, the smaller the average error is with respect to the signal value, and the better the fidelity of the reconstructed signal can be.

12.5 Adding Up the Bits: Home CD Players

Let's consider a common example of digitized audio to examine how an audio signal is converted into binary form. A common compact disc (CD) contains a purely digitized representation of an originally continuous audio signal, and our home stereo systems are able to recreate the audio signal with what most people consider to be excellent quality or fidelity. An examination of the standards used for CD systems will easily help us make the connection between a certain interval of music and the number of bits needed to represent it on the CD. The music created at the recording studio must be sampled and quantized according to some standard specifications so that all CDs can be played using the same equipment. The standard value within the audio industry for the bandwidth, or highest frequency, of a high fidelity audio signal is 20 kHz. Thus, the minimum (Nyquist) sampling rate is 40 kHz, or 40,000 samples per second. However, it is desirable to oversample so that reconstruction can be achieved with affordable equipment. The standard sampling rate for digital audio is 44.1 kHz, which represents a rate about 10% higher than the Nyquist rate.

Each sample must then be quantized. CD systems use 16 bits to represent each sample, meaning that each sample value will be represented by one of $2^{16} = 65,536$ different 16-bit codes. This would suggest that each channel of the audio stream is converted into bits at a rate of

$$44,100 \text{ samples/sec} \times 16 \text{ bits/sample} = 705,600 \text{ bits/sec};$$

in actuality, there are some extra bits used for purposes of error detection and correction as well.

Ignoring these extra bits, this means that a CD with 60 minutes of music on it has 60 minutes × 60 seconds/minute × 44,100 samples/second × 16 bits/sample × 2 channels = 5,080,320,000 bits—over 5 billion bits—encoded on its surface as a pattern of shiny and dull areas to be read by a laser detector. Note that when you buy the CD, the amount of information on it is fixed by this standard. CD players that advertise "oversampling" are not actually in a position to provide you with the extra samples that word would suggest. Instead, these CD players use signal processing techniques to artificially insert extra sample values into the stream of samples, thereby making it possible to reconstruct the signal with less effort. This technique produces the desirable result of facilitating accurate reproduction in an efficient fashion; however, it cannot actually provide you with extra information about the music you listen to!

12.6 Reconstruction

Up to this point, we have alluded to the fact that the audio signal can be acceptably reconstructed from the quantized samples, but we have not provided any in-depth discussion of how this can be done. Indeed, the theory that proves that a signal can be perfectly reconstructed from samples, as long as they are taken frequently enough, is beyond the scope of this text. And the fact that quantization adds in a loss of information that must be quantified using probabilistic arguments complicates a technical discussion of reconstruction. Nonetheless, a simple consideration of the techniques used can provide a useful qualitative understanding of how reconstruction is achieved, and why it might be expected to work. As we have seen from applications to image and video, it is a fairly straightforward matter to convert binary codewords back into voltage signal samples, using a device called a *digital-to-analog converter* (DAC). The DAC effectively reverses the process of analog-to-digital conversion performed by the quantization process. This process of digital-to-analog conversion is often accompanied by a technique known as a zero order hold (ZOH), which creates a "staircase" signal that is continuous in time, but not a good representation of the original, smoother, audio signal. Figure 12.4 shows a ZOH signal that might be generated from binary sample values by a DAC.

The difference between this ZOH signal and the original audio signal (ignoring for the time being quantization noise, which may have been introduced) consists of unwanted high-frequency information present in the ZOH signal. These very high frequency components are evident in the sharp discontinuities between samples, the "risers" of the staircase, if you will. Fortunately, it is a fairly straightforward matter to remove this unwanted high-frequency information without destroying the audio signal using a system known as a *filter*. The filter literally filters out, or removes, the unwanted frequency components from the ZOH signal, much as an oil filter removes undesirable particles from your engine's lubricants. Moreover, just as the oil filter lets the cleaned oil through to the engine, the audio filter lets the desired audio frequency spectrum through, resulting in a reconstructed signal, as shown in Figure 12.5.

In fact, it is this process of filtering to remove the unwanted high frequencies while retaining the audio frequencies that motivates oversampling. If a signal is oversampled, then it is simpler to retain all of the desirable audio components while removing all of the undesirable higher frequencies via filtering.

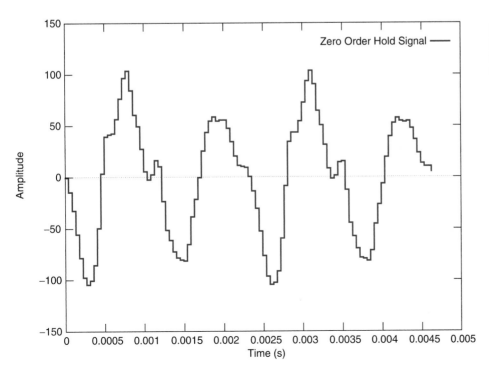

FIGURE 12.4 An audio waveform that has been passed through a zero order hold device.

FIGURE 12.5 The reconstructed
audio signal.

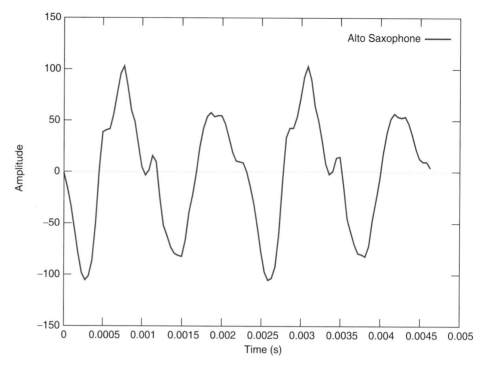

12.7 Other Applications, and a Few Tricks

In addition to digital audio for entertainment purposes, there are numerous applications of discretized audio signals. Perhaps the most familiar of these is in telephony. Most telephone calls, including any which use equipment installed recently, are digitized and reconstructed during their transmission. Because digitized signals make more efficient use of system bandwidth, they are the choice for any application involving an expensive communication resource, such as a satellite link. Also, because information in digital form is much more amenable to encryption and encoding, digital audio is used for military and other applications for which security is desired. In practice, there are techniques that can be used to minimize the effects of quantization noise on audio signals. For example, an approach known as *companding* can be used to improve the signal-to-noise ratio of a quantized signal without requiring additional bits for representation. This is accomplished by using nonuniformly sized intervals for the voltage ranges, with smaller intervals used for small voltage values, and larger intervals for larger values.

Furthermore, there are approaches that minimize the size of each sample to be quantized by exploiting the similarity that is apt to occur between successive sample values. These approaches use previous values to *predict* future values, and encode only the differences between the predictions and the actual values. Because these differences fall within a smaller range of voltages than the original sample values, fewer bits need be used to achieve the same signal-to-noise ratio, and therefore, the same fidelity. These techniques are especially useful in wireless applications and other situations in which it is desirable to transmit digital audio using as few bits per second as is possible.

Summary

In the last two chapters, we have taken a close look at the process by which audio information is digitized for purposes of storage, transmission, and processing. This chapter has focused on the necessity to *quantize* analog information for digital representation, on the effects of that quantization, and on the means by which digital information is converted back to analog form for use by humans. The digitization of other signals proceeds in a similar fashion. Although the requirements for sampling rate and quantization error will vary according to the application, the essential processes of sampling, quantization, and reconstruction via filtering are common to all applications in which continuous information is temporarily digitized. This digitization allows use of efficient, fast, and inexpensive digital systems for processing, transmitting, storing, and reproducing the information. As a result, we benefit in our professional and personal lives from more efficient, inexpensive, and better-performing information technology.

Try These Exercises

1. We desire to digitize the outdoor temperature for storage and transmission with a precision of one-half degree. The desired range is from −20° C to +40° C. Determine how many temperature levels we will have and how many bits will be needed to represent all the levels.

2. Continuing the problem above, if the temperatures in successive hours are the following: 18.1, 18.5, 19.2, 20.1, to what values will these temperatures be quantized? Carefully explain your procedure.

3. Explain why quantization, and hence quantization error or quantization noise, is inevitable in digitizing signals.

4. Based on what you have learned, determine the amount of storage needed to record a normal telephone call of one hour in duration.

5. Using the applet "Quantization and Reconstruction with Sound," with the 375 Hz sine wave and a sampling rate of 2000 Hz, vary the number of quantization bits and observe the quantized and reconstructed signals. How many quantization bits are needed to produce a signal which appears identical to the original signal? At what number of quantization bits can you hear a change in the audio signal?

   ◉ **Quantization and Reconstruction with Sound**

6. Determine an appropriate value for the data rate for digitized voice in a telephone system, without data compression. You will need to determine two pieces of information: the rate at which the voice should be sampled, and the number of bits to be used to represent the value of each sample. Each of these values should be no larger than necessary, since any increase beyond the necessary bit rate will raise the transmission cost without significantly improving quality.

13

The Telephone System: Wired and Wireless

Objectives

Now that we understand the fundamentals of what information is and how it can be represented, we are ready to begin investigating one of the oldest and most useful electronic information systems: the worldwide telephone system. In this chapter you will learn about:

📖 Analog
📖 Digital

▲ the five fundamental components of the original analog telephone system: the microphone, transmission system, receiver, switching system, and signaling system (some of these will be discussed in more detail in Chapter 18);

▲ the present telephone system, which is a hybrid of analog and digital technologies;

▲ the principles of the cellular telephone system and the ways in which it differs from the wired system;

▲ the many different "flavors" of cellular systems, and the technical and marketing reasons for the many variations; and

▲ satellite telephone systems, and their advantages and disadvantages.

13.1 Introduction

The telephone system was introduced briefly in Chapter 1 as an example of an important communications system (Figure 1.3). Some more important details will be presented in this chapter, as well as an overview of the ways in which "POTS" (Plain Old Telephone Service) has evolved into a ubiquitous, global, multifaceted communications system. Still, at the core of all the new technologies and services is the capability to put two people in instant, real-time audio communication.

13.2 The Original (Analog) Telephone System

Recall that any form of telephone system has five major components:

* The microphone, which responds to input sounds and converts it to electrical energy,

* The transmission system, which conveys information representing the sound from the microphone to the receiver;

* The receiver, which converts the received information (which may be in many forms as described below) into sound waves;

- The switching system, which makes appropriate connections among pieces of the transmission system to create an unbroken (real or virtual) path from transmitter to receiver (and also in the reverse direction for two-way communication); and
- The signaling system, which indicates to the switches the connections that they should make.

The original telephone system was entirely analog, and substantial pieces remain analog as this book is written. However, this 125-year-old system is about to change fundamentally as it becomes just one piece of a general-purpose digital communications system. It is worth understanding the "classic" telephone system, however, as the principles and technology remain valid. Moreover, the two endpoints (microphone and receiver) *must* remain analog because we humans, for whom the system is designed, remain analog. It is instructive to consider the components out of which a working telephone system can be constructed. They are incredibly simple:

- *Microphone*: a small amount of carbon granules, a container for the granules, a diaphragm making up one side of the container, and two metal contacts. The action of sound waves on the diaphragm alternately compresses and relaxes pressure on the granules, varying their electrical resistance in synchronism with the sound waves. Hence, a mechanical quantity (sound or air pressure variations) is converted into an electrical quantity (resistance).
- *Receiver*: a permanent magnet and a coil of wire attached to a paper diaphragm. When an electrical current passes through the coil, a magnetic field results, which interacts with the permanent magnet field to cause the diaphragm to move. If the electric current varies at the same speed as the sound pressure waves for voice, the diaphragm moves at that same speed, and produces new air pressure variations also at the same speed, and hence with the same sound. This describes the operation of all loudspeakers.
- *Transmission System*: two lengths of wire and a flashlight battery. The wires, the battery, the microphone, and the receiver are connected into an *electrical circuit* so that the current caused by the battery varies due to the variation in resistance of the microphone in response to sound waves. The receiver (loudspeaker) moves in synchronism with the electrical current and hence produces new sound waves that match the original sound waves.
- *Switching System*: the system described above is a working telephone (actually one direction of a telephone, but adding the second direction is easy to understand) but it does not permit the transmitter and receiver to change. The switching system breaks the electrical wires from one end and connects them to the desired telephone at the other end. In fact, this connection generally happens with many intervening switches as various point-point transmission systems are connected together to reach between the two desired telephones.

13.3 The Digital Telephone System

While the description of the analog telephone system given above provides an accurate overview of the principles of current telephone systems, it is a fact that most telephone calls today are really *digital* telephone calls. How can this be? It is quite simple: the two ends of the call are analog, and the middle section is digital. Conversions from analog to digital, and back to analog, are made in such a way that it is essentially impossible to determine that they were made at all.

 Digital
Analog

At present, most telephone calls are analog from the telephone in the home to the first telephone switching office. In areas of moderate or greater population density, most telephones are within about five miles of the telephone central office. At the central office, most incoming telephone lines are connected to equipment that converts the incoming voice to digital (A/D conversion) and converts the outgoing (to the telephone set) voice to analog (D/A conversion). This process of A/D and D/A conversion has been described in Chapter 11. For voice, the signal is sampled at 8,000 Hz (for a 4 kHz bandwidth) and quantized to 256 levels at each sample. Eight bits are required to represent 256 levels. Hence the bit rate for the digital telephone call (in each direction) is 8,000 times 8, or 64,000 bits per second. If the telephone call needs to be routed from one central office to another (across town or across the world) the call is combined (using time division multiplexing) with many other calls for efficiency. The smallest unit of channel combination (in the U.S.) is 24 channels, which corresponds to a data rate of 1.544 Mbits/second. This is the so-called T1 rate, which has become well known. Actually, some bits are "stolen" from the voice data so that synchronization bits may be included in the 1.544 Mbits/sec rate. This is also referred to as the DS1 rate in the hierarchy of digital transmission. At present essentially all of the transmission facilities among telephone central offices are digital. One of the major advantages of digital transmission is that after digitization one signal is exactly like another: they are all just bits. Hence T1 or other digital transmission facilities may be used to carry telephone calls, Internet data, or any other data that will fit in the bit rate.

The nature of the digital revolution appears to be to constantly expand the realm of the digital signal, replacing more and more cases where analog signal processing or transmission has been done. Within the first years of the new millennium, most telephones will become purely digital, with A/D and D/A conversion being done within the telephone set to accommodate the analog beings (humans) who are using the telephone.

13.4 Cellular Telephone Systems

In some ways, conventional telephone systems and conventional radio systems could not be more different:

- Telephone systems connect two users for a private conversation; radio by its nature is broadcast for many people to hear.
- Telephones are connected via wires; radio is a wireless medium.
- Radio systems are limited in range; telephones can connect everyone on earth.
- Telephones are private (at least reasonably private); radio is open to eavesdropping.
- Telephones limit access because a physical connection is required; the radio waves are open to anyone with a transmitter.

In spite of these differences, radio has had a place in telephone systems for many years because of its fundamental difference and advantage compared to wired telephones: it is wireless! The fundamental purpose of the telephone system is immediate, real-time access from one person to another. Wires are just a means to that end, and they are clearly not a perfect means because they do not reach every person at every time. Hence, an integration of the best aspects of radio with the best aspects of conventional telephone transmission could greatly extend the utility of the telephone system. "Radio-telephones" have existed for over 60 years, but until the invention of the "cellular radio system," the number of users in a given area such as a city was severely limited (on the order of only a few hundred users!). There are several factors that created this limit:

- The radio spectrum is limited in size (frequency range), and hence in the number of telephone signals that can be active at any given time.

- The *ultimate* upper limit of the spectrum, and hence the number of telephone channels, is determined by physical laws. For example, as the frequency becomes very high, the signals can no longer pass through heavy rain.

- The *practical* upper limit of the spectrum is affected by current technology. Until recently, the electronic equipment for very high frequencies was quite expensive.

Given these principles, the early radio-telephone systems were designed so that one radio base station covered a city, with some number of channels allocated to it (in the United States) by the Federal Communications Commission (FCC).[1] This might have represented 100 channels, each 20 kHz in width. The base station transmitted with enough power to cover the entire city. Naturally, the mobile stations also were required to transmit with similar power to reach the base station. This power requirement, as well as the lack of integrated circuit technology, typically made hand-held units impractical, and required mounting in a vehicle. This system had several flaws: large mobile stations due to the power requirement; "dead spots" in coverage due to buildings, hills, and so forth; and in particular, the very limited number of users. All of these problems were addressed by the Cellular Telephone System, which the Bell Telephone System (these were the days before the breakup of the Bell System and AT&T) began to deploy in 1979.[2] The fundamental breakthrough of the cellular system is that it made the limited range of low-power radio an advantage rather than a disadvantage! Rather than one base station for an entire city or region, many low-power base stations are distributed over the service area. The region covered by each station is referred to as a cell. Within each cell the number of active users is still restricted by the basic principles of the RF spectrum, but this is less of a problem because the area is small. A large city may have several hundred cells, and all of the frequencies can be reused in other cells. Hence, the total number of allowable active users is much larger than when one cell covers the entire city. This is true because the given frequencies can be reused in other cell sites! The power is kept low because the area of each cell is small, and we do not want a given signal to reach much beyond the boundary of that cell.[3] With low power, hand-held radio-telephones, small and convenient cell phones (Plate 32) are possible. Figure 13.1 shows a diagram of the cellular system layout. Individual cell sites are connected together by conventional wired (or fiber or point-point microwave radio) technology, and computerized switching equipment keeps track of all the users and makes the correct connections for the complete circuit between two users. The preceding paragraph describes all of the fundamentals of cellular telephones, and contains no revolutionary ideas. Hence, a reasonable question might be: Why has it only been within the last few years that cell phones have become so common? The answer has two parts:

- While the cell system is straightforward in concept, it was a completely new system and hence required substantial time and money for design and con-

---

[1] The FCC is an agency of the U.S. government that regulates many aspects of communications, particularly the use of radio frequencies.
[2] William Webb, *Understanding Cellular Radio*, Artech House; 1998.
[3] The antenna height may be kept low (Plate 31) which makes installation of cellular base stations relatively easy.

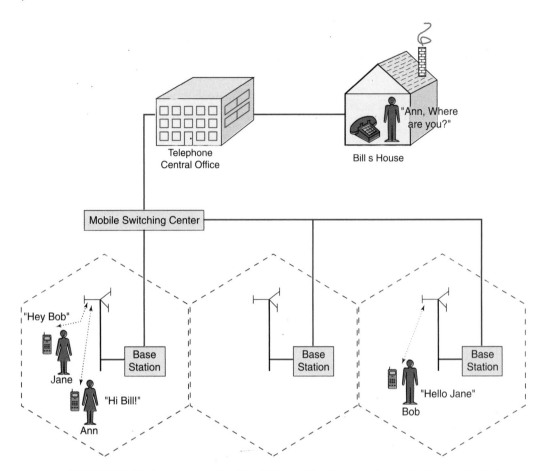

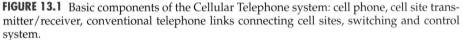

FIGURE 13.1 Basic components of the Cellular Telephone system: cell phone, cell site transmitter/receiver, conventional telephone links connecting cell sites, switching and control system.

struction. Also, until there are many users, the overall costs must be shared by few customers, raising the average cost, and hence slowing market penetration.

- The cell system makes use of much higher technology than the conventional telephone system (all of whose major pieces would be quite recognizable to Alexander Graham Bell) and initially all of the components (base stations and cell phones) were very expensive. As in almost everything else electronic, costs have fallen rapidly, so that equipment costs are now quite reasonable.

The lower costs stimulated more cellular customers, and this generated further economies of scale, so that a chain reaction has resulted in cell service quickly moving from a luxury to an everyday item.

13.4.1 The Cellular Telephone System: How It Works

Perhaps the best way to describe the operation of the cellular system is to follow a typical call. Begin with the user's cell phone. It has a number associated with it, just like any telephone. This number serves several purposes, including getting the monthly bill to the correct person. However, its main purpose is to identify the user and associate him or her with the specific telephone equipment. Calling *from* a cell phone is more straightforward than calling *to* a cell phone. First the user turns on his or her phone. After a few seconds the phone generally indicates that it is in service. If no cell site is within range, the phone indicates "no service." What happens in that time is that the phone has automatically communicated with at least one cell site base station to confirm that communication is possible, and (very importantly) to let the telephone system know where the cell phone is now located. If more than one cell site is within range, the one with the strongest signal is selected, and the control system directs the other cell site(s) to ignore the call. When the user enters a number on the cell phone and presses "send," a channel is dedicated to that user, and the number is processed at the cell site and sent into the regular telephone network (called the Public Switched Telephone Network, or PSTN). Assuming the called number is a wired telephone, the call is completed in the normal manner. If it is another cell phone, the cellular system control center is queried to determine whether the called cell phone is in service, and if so, what cell site (nearby or around the world) it is currently accessing. If the cell phone is not located, the calling party is notified via a tone or recorded message. What happens if either (or both) cell phones in a conversation move from one cell site to another? The call must be "handed off" from one site to another without losing the connection. This (usually) works correctly, and the user may notice (with traditional analog cell phones) that the connection first becomes noisy, and then becomes clear again when the transfer is made. This hand-off is possible because each cell site continuously monitors all the cell phone signals it hears, even if that site is not handling the call. As the signal becomes weaker at the active site, the central control unit searches for another site that is receiving that phone's signal with more power. Upon locating such a site, the controller makes the hand-off. What about "roaming?" This mode reflects a combination of nonideal technical design of the cell system, and the competitive nature of telecommunications! When your cell phone indicates that it is in "roam" mode, it means that you are not within range of the cell system to which you subscribe (to which you pay your monthly bill) but you are within range of another system. Your calls will go through with no problem, but you may be charged extra for using that different system. In the past, a greater problem was in receiving calls in this mode. When you were off the home system, there was often no way to know where the cell phone was located, and hence no way to connect an incoming call. This problem has essentially been eliminated at present, with better real-time communication of cell phone status and location among systems.

13.4.2 The Alphabet Soup of Competing Cellular Systems: AMPS, GSM, TDMA, CDMA, and PCS

The cell phone concept originated in 1947, but commercial service in the United States did not begin until 1979. Shortly thereafter, the original system design was improved, and this design (still in wide use today) was referred to as AMPS (Advanced Mobile Phone System). Today, the "A" is often defined as referring to "Analog" because this is in fact an analog system, and the newer systems are all digital. AMPS was the only system in the United States until about 1997, and as of 2000 is still in common use in the U.S. The voice transmission part of the AMPS system is completely conventional, essentially the same as could be used in any "walkie talkie." AMPS uses the 800 MHz frequency band. It was the cellular system design and the overall control functions that were technically novel. The analog format made cell phone conversation almost completely nonprivate. Anyone with a simple scanning receiver could listen to the conversations.

The next major cellular system to be developed, and the one with the greatest worldwide use, is referred to as GSM. Originally this stood for the name (in French) of the committee that approved the system design, *Groupe Special Mobile*. This was originally a European standard, but has spread worldwide (including the U.S.) and the initials have been redefined to represent *Global System for Mobile Communications*. This is a digital system, meaning that the voices are digitized and processed to minimize the bit rate (using some of the techniques described in this book) before transmission. The digital signals are transmitted over similar RF channels as in the analog case, in the 900 and 1800 MHz bands. The frequencies for AMPS and GSM are different so that both systems may operate simultaneously in a given area. As we have seen, straightforward digital coding of a voice signal (for speech, not music) requires a sampling rate of about 8,000 Hz and on the order of 8 bits (256 levels) per sample. This produces a bit rate of 64,000 bits per second, which requires a rather wide radio channel for transmission. Because minimization of the radio bandwidth per user is one of the most critical aspects of cellular system design, sophisticated voice coders have been designed that produce good speech quality with much lower bit rates, on the order of 13,000 bits per second. These coders operate by simulating the manner in which the human vocal tract creates speech. They require a lot of digital processing power, but that is now readily available on a small chip. Another difference between AMPS and GSM is worth noting: the means by which individual calls are kept separate during radio transmission. In AMPS, each user is simply assigned an individual frequency (actually two frequencies, one for each direction of voice transmission) for the duration of the call. This is exactly the same as the manner in which individual radio stations are separated in the frequency spectrum and on the radio dial. This is called *frequency division multiple access* or FDMA. It is conceptually simple, but has some technical drawbacks. An alternative used by GSM is called *time division multiple access* or TDMA. In this scheme the radio spectrum is not divided into channels for each user. Rather, each user occupies the entire radio spectrum, but only for a brief time. After one user transmits a burst of information, that user is quiet for a time and another user transmits a burst. This continues for all the users until it is time for the first user to transmit again. Because speech is continuous, this system obviously requires a means to store the information for each user during the periods in which that user cannot transmit. With digitized voice data, this storage is quite easy. TDMA lends itself naturally to digital signal processing.

The final basic type of common cellular system is called CDMA, referring to its channel separation scheme, which is *Code Division Multiple Access* rather than FDMA or TDMA. In CDMA each user occupies the entire radio channel as in TDMA, but the user also transmits all the time, as in FDMA. In other words, the users are not separated in either time or frequency. What does keep the users separate? Each user is assigned a unique digital code (the "Code" in CDMA) which is used to encode the data from the voice digitizer before transmission. At the receiver the same code is used to decode the incoming signal, and the result contains two terms: the original voice coder data bits, and a (hopefully) small amount of interference from the other users with different codes. In FDMA the number of available radio channels determines the number of simultaneous users. Similarly, in TDMA the number of available time slots determines the number of simultaneous users. In CDMA the maximum number of users is determined by the amount of interference that can be tolerated (the total interference is the sum of the interference contributions from all the other users). In practice this number of users is somewhat greater than would be the case with FDMA or TDMA on a given piece of radio spectrum. This is the fundamental advantage of CDMA; the principal disadvantage is greater system complexity. There is also considerable controversy over just how great the extra capacity is. Claims of a channel gain on the order of a factor of 10 have been made, but in actual use the increase appears to be somewhat less than a factor of two, but still significant.

Finally, what is PCS? This stands for Personal Communications Services, and it was intended to encompass an overall vision for telephony as distinctions among wired service, cellular service, and paging disappeared. For example, a person might have a small handset which he or she always carried, and a telephone number associated with the person rather than with a conventional telephone. The telephone system always keeps track of the person's location for call delivery. In the home or office, the handset operates as a *cordless phone* working inside buildings, and not taking up expensive cellular bandwidth. Outside it operates as cell phone. At all times it also incorporates paging functions. It may also work in planes and trains in a *microcellular* mode. This range of functions requires digital capability, and the various digital standards have become somewhat synonymous with PCS.

13.4.3 The Three Generations of Cellular Systems

The various digital cellular systems described above represent the *second generation* of cellular service. Analog systems were the first generation, and these first generation systems are still in widespread use, and will remain so for some years. The digital services are superior to analog in essentially all ways, and so over time analog will disappear. This change of generations is facilitated by the availability of dual-mode cell phones, which can operate on two systems, such as analog AMPS and digital-GSM. From the service provider's point of view, greater capacity represents the major benefit of the second generation digital systems. From the users' point of view, along with better audio quality, the second generation systems add some features such as Caller ID and integrated paging. There is still substantial room for improvement, however, and that is where "third generation cellular" comes in. Desired features include higher (much higher) data rates for video, Internet access, Web browsing, complete worldwide operability, and usability inside aircraft and buildings. Widespread introduction of third-generation systems is expected to begin by 2005.

13.4.4 Cellular System FAQs

The following frequently asked questions (FAQS) and answers summarize some of the interesting and important characteristics of cellular telephone systems.

- Why are base station cellular antennas so ugly? The antenna on a handheld cell phone is a simple rod, about 6 inches long. Base station antennas could be as simple and unobtrusive as this, but technically they work better if they are arranged in groups of three so that each antenna transmits to one third (120 degrees) of the complete cell. Each antenna must be physically separate from the other antennas. Hence we see rather complicated arrangements of equipment on top of most cellular towers.

- Why are some antennas on high towers, while some are fairly low to the ground? This relates to the desired size of the cell. As you drive along the Interstate highways in the midwest of the United States, you will see occasional high towers with cellular antennas on top. These serve large (long and narrow) cells along the highway, that may be 20 miles or more in size. Conversely, in cities the cells must be small to handle the large number of users, and it is desired to keep the radio energy from propagating outside those cells. Because the energy travels only in straight lines, keeping the antennas low accomplishes this goal.

- Why aren't all telephones wireless? Until recently, a simple answer to this question is that it would have been too expensive. Cost is becoming less of a factor, and in some circumstances cell phones can be cheaper to install and use than wired phones. However, it appears that the fundamental limit of frequency spectrum capacity may not permit all communication to be wireless.

- What is the difference between a cell phone and a cordless phone? A cordless phone is more properly called a "cordless handset" because it must be connected to regular telephone service. The cordless handset must stay within range of its base station, which in turn is connected to the wired network. The cordless phone has no capability to travel from one base station to another.

- Why is it illegal to use a cell phone in an airplane? There are two answers to this question: First, during critical phases of flight, the use of any devices that can emit radio energy is not permitted because of possible (highly unlikely) disturbances to the aircraft control and navigation systems. Specifically for cell phones, the problem is that from a high altitude the signal would be received by many cell sites, potentially causing confusion, and certainly tying up channels on unneeded sites. Of course, similar problems can occur from tall buildings or mountains, but the FCC has not found it practical to regulate these uses!

- Are cell phones safe to use? There is a potential concern whenever radio frequency energy is absorbed by humans. The concern increases as frequency increases. As we reach X-ray (so-called ionizing) frequencies the danger is quite serious. However, cell phone frequencies are well below the ionizing range, and the limits are stated in terms of how much heating of tissue the energy creates. Hand-held cell phones (and all other cell phone equipment such as base stations and car-mounted phones) meet this limit. It should be noted that distance from the antenna is the most significant factor, with any risk falling off rapidly with distance. Hence, any possible concern relates to the users of hand-held cell phones (because the antenna is within inches of the brain), *not* to cellular base stations in the neighborhood!

13.5 Satellite Telephones

What about those situations where there is no wired telephone, and not even a cellular system is within reach? A good example is on a large ship or small boat out at sea. Not too many years ago, the only alternative would be use of some sort of two-way radio system. In fact, since the time of the *Titanic*, and continuing until 1999, all commercial sea-going vessels were required to have a licensed radio operator on board, who could communicate in Morse code as well as voice. A skilled operator was required because the type of radio that was used was very different in its operation from a telephone system.

The system was called "HF" because it used so-called "high frequencies." These frequencies lie between the AM and FM radio bands (between about 1 MHz and 30 MHz in fact), and are not high at all by today's standards. In the days before satellites, however, these frequencies had one important, and unique property: under the correct conditions they can travel all the way around the world, and hence can support communications between any two points on earth. At any given time a few frequencies would perform much better than any others for communications between the desired points. The selection of the proper frequency was one of the reasons for requiring a trained operator. This long-distance communication was possible because with the proper frequency, the radio energy would not just travel in a straight line (out into space) but would reflect off of the ionosphere, which envelopes the earth above the atmosphere. This reflection would enable some of the energy to travel beyond the horizon of the transmitter, and the energy might reflect off the surface of the earth and head back for the ionosphere. Several of these reflections may occur if conditions are just right, resulting in around-the-world propagation. It is interesting to note that this ionospheric reflection is analogous to the total internal reflection that occurs inside optical fibers, with dimensions many orders of magnitude different. The ionospheric conditions described above are constantly changing, requiring constant retuning of the radio transmitter and receiver, and may permit only poor-quality communications. All of this changed with the advent of the communications satellite. Now a ship at sea is as easily reachable as any point on land. For some years a corporation called INMARSAT (for International Marine Satellite) has provided satellite radio communications for ships at sea, and somewhat as a sideline has made their facilities available to other users, typically those in very remote areas. This system has two disadvantages: the ground terminals are rather bulky (by today's standards) and service is expensive. The smallest available terminal is the size of a briefcase, and it requires that an antenna be set up and aimed at the satellite. Taking this system to the next step is the *Iridium* system, which was conceived by Motorola Corporation. This system was planned to consist of a constellation of 66 satellites in low earth orbit, 780 km high (Plate 33). The low orbit was selected (rather than high-altitude geosynchronous orbit) to reduce the power required to reach from handset to satellite. This reduces the battery power required, as well as the antenna size, and makes a hand-held satellite telephone possible (though the handset is substantially larger than today's terrestrial cellphones).

The Iridium system would operate in a manner quite similar to that of terrestrial cellular systems, the difference being that the cell sites are overhead, and are moving! The voice signals are digitized in a manner similar to that used in the GSM cellular system. Frequencies of about 1.6 GHz are used between the cellular telephone and the satellites, and frequencies of 20 to 30 GHz are used between satellites, and between satellites and ground stations. These latter frequencies are very high, and suffer rain attenuation, but this can be compensated by extra power because these frequencies are not used to the handsets.

The Iridium system began operation in 1999, and represented the first generally available global telephone system. It had two significant drawbacks: the relatively high cost of service and the fact that it was intended for analog voice, not data transmission. After operating commercially for about a year and attracting few customers, the Iridium system went into bankruptcy and ceased operations early in 2000. With the service's high cost and inability to handle data transmission, it could not attract a viable customer base in competition with the rapidly-spreading celllular systems across the globe.

Summary

This section provided an overview of the various forms of the worldwide telephone system, which today would barely be recognizable by Alexander Graham Bell and his colleagues. In the middle years of the twentieth century, the AT&T company provided most of the telephone service in the United States, and much of the international service via its Long Lines division. At that time its motto was "universal service." That meant getting wired telephone service to every home in the U.S. Today, that slogan could be resurrected to mean telephone service to every person (not just every fixed location) anywhere in the world!

We have seen how this is accomplished with an interconnected network of wired telephones, cellular telephones, and satellite telephones. Each of these three systems has distinct advantages and disadvantages, both technically and economically, and all three are likely to play significant roles for many years. A key component in the cellular and satellite systems is the efficient use of the radio spectrum, made possible by inexpensive integrated electronics, and efficient computer control of the overall system.

Try These Exercises

1. For a given power, a cell site in open country could communicate for a fixed distance in all directions. This distance would correspond to a circle surrounding the site. Why are the areas for each cell site not in fact circular? To help determine the answer, draw circles around an array of cell sites so that the circles just touch. What problem is created?

2. The boundaries between cell sites in a diagram of a cellular system do not exist in actuality (there are no dotted lines on the ground). What do these lines in the diagram represent?

3. Cellular system diagrams typically show the cell boundaries as hexagonal. Draw two other possible geometric arrangements for boundaries using polygons with different numbers of sides. Comment on the three arrangements (hexagons and the two versions that you created).

4. One fundamental way in which a cell phone differs from a wired phone is that it can move around, even around the world. Explain how this makes the connection of a caller to a given cell phone more complex than a connection to a wired phone.

5. What factors do you think are at work that are causing some advancing third world nations to implement only cellular telephone systems instead of wire-based telephone systems?

6. Perform some online or library research, and report on the commercial history of the Iridium system, including the subscriber costs, the maximum number of subscribers, and the reasons for its failure. Report on the fate of the orbiting satellites.

7. Digital cellular systems are rapidly replacing the original analog systems. Perform some Web research and determine the number of cellular phones in use today in the United States (or your home country). How does this compare to the number of wired phones? Also, attempt to determine the ratio of analog to digital cell phones and the ratios among the various competing digital systems.

PART

VI

Transmission and Storage Technology

These are the days of lasers in the jungle
Lasers in the jungle somewhere...

Paul Simon, "The Boy in the Bubble," Graceland

The information revolution began in the mid-19th century with the first transmission of pulses of electricity on a wire. Before the turn of the 20th century we had learned to transmit information with electrical pulses, flashes of light, and beams of radio energy; every means that we use today. Yet despite living in the age of information transmission technology, most users have only an outsider's view of it.

In this part we will examine the origin of the limits of bandwidth of transmission systems. We will get to the root of the question: if bandwidth is so necessary to information infrastructure, what's stopping us from just turning it up?

It will turn out that the only way that the Internet can subsume the telephone system, television system, etc., is to first greatly expand the bandwidth of the links that interconnect its components. We will take a close look in this part at fiber-optic technology which is the transmission revolution behind the modern information revolution.

We will also examine the nature of radio transmission, because at the same time that the Internet is becoming the telephone system, the cell phone is becoming the universal telephone handset, computer interface, Web browser and general information companion.

Finally, we will take an in-depth look at the only alternatives to moving information in digital cables that can compete for total bandwidth: moving information in boxes packed in aircraft and trucks! The optical technologies that are at the base of the Internet revolution have had considerable application in the storage of information in physical media such as the CD and the DVD.

14

What Is Bandwidth and How Is It Used?

Objectives

Recently, words such as "bandwidth" have moved from the vocabulary of engineers into everyday conversation. This chapter begins with some basic physical principles and explains several important concepts and constraints of the world in which we live and communicate. These include:

▲ the fundamental limits imposed by the speed of light, and the fact that in modern-day communications and computation, "light speed" is not all that fast;

▲ the implications of the speed of light on long-distance (satellite) communications and on short-distance data transmission, such as within a computer;

▲ the distinction between data transmission rate and data latency (delay);

▲ the fact that everything in the world has a limited bandwidth, and the reasons for this fact;

▲ similarities and differences of the three fundamental communications media: free space (radio), wires, and optical fiber;

▲ the principles by which optical fiber transmits signals, and its advantages over wires; and

▲ methods of transmission of information over a given bandwidth, through the use of modulation and pulses separated in time.

14.1 Introduction

Up to this point, our discussion has been limited to the representation of information in the abstract form of binary data, or by the waveforms associated with audio signals, which can ultimately also be reduced to digital data by sampling and quantization operations. The transportation of this data from one location to another via a floppy disk or a CD is rather easy to understand now, and involves no additional complicating concepts. This is, unfortunately, not the case if we wish to transport the data in "real time" from one location to another. This chapter will reveal the complications that are involved and introduce some of the concepts that information engineers must encounter that ultimately put a price on the movement of data! In this chapter we will encounter and explain the concepts of *latency* and *information rate* as they apply to the movement of data. Latency is another word for delay; specifically, it is the time delay involved in the movement of a message from one location to another. The definition varies from application to application, but for the purposes of this discussion, we will simply take it as the time that it takes to move 1 bit from source (origin) to sink (destination). Information rate is the number of bits that can be sent at the source or received at the sink per second. We can have communication channels that suffer huge latencies (seconds, or even minutes) while moving data at a rate of billions of bits per second, because in most systems there is no need to wait for a bit to be delivered to the sink before inserting another for delivery at the source.

This discussion will cause us to uncover one of the more mysterious quantities that information engineers measure or specify, that of *bandwidth*. Finally, we will discuss at great length the physical origins of the limits that prevent zero latency, infinite bandwidth, and infinite information rates.

14.2 Real-Time Data Transmission

What do we mean by real-time transmission of data? In the context of any data transmission or processing scheme, *real-time* transmission means that the data is available soon enough after its creation to be of as much use as it would be if no processing or transmission delays had been involved. For example, if a human voice is delayed by 0.1 second, the average listener will never notice the difference in a conversation as compared to undelayed speech. This audio could be said to be delivered in real time. On the other hand, if the delay is increased to one half second, we would not only notice an annoying delay between statements and reactions, but we would also find ourselves tripping on each other's interruptions! For other applications, acceptable time delays differ. Professional photographers often use "slave" flash units to enhance their lighting. The slave flash has a photoelectric sensor that detects the flash from the photographer's hand-held camera. The slave unit then flashes its light soon enough so that it contributes to the light seen by the camera during the open shutter time. To do this, the slave flash must light within less than 1/200th of a second, or within 5 milliseconds. Traffic engineering involves changing the electronic signs on highways and streets to route traffic so as to minimize traffic tie-ups. To do this, traffic engineers require real-time data regarding the occupancy of streets and the flow of traffic. Sensors planted in the streets can count cars and relay information every minute over low-speed (low-cost) special-purpose telephone connections to centrally located computers, where it can be processed and displayed within a couple of minutes. This information arrives sufficiently quickly to appear to be immediate reactions to traffic conditions as perceived by the drivers.

As these examples illustrate, the definition of real time is quite application-specific. The delay that is allowed within the context of a use of the information system determines a maximum delay time, or latency, that we allowed in that application. While the impact of latency is quite specific to the application, the source of latency is often outside our control!

14.3 Delay Time and the Speed of Light

There is an ultimate limit as to how small a delay can be achieved in the movement of data. This irrevocable limit is due to the finite speed of light and the now well-verified theory by Albert Einstein that no information can be relayed at speeds that exceed the speed of light.

That the movement of information has a speed limit may seem rather difficult to believe. One may readily imagine how poorly received the idea was when originally presented by Einstein. In fact, it might have hardly been discussed if it hadn't supplied a reason for some difficult-to-explain observations that had been made in laboratory experiments. The theory, if true, indicates that a host of other even stranger behaviors of the physical world would be found if certain experiments were conducted. Many such experiments have been conducted to date and others are still under construction. The results have been unanimous: Einstein's theory successfully predicts the sometimes bizarre and utterly unanticipated outcomes of each experiment that has been tried.

Does the speed of light actually impact practical human communications? It certainly does. Following are a few examples.

14.3.1 Geosynchronous Satellites

Prior to the use of fiber-optic cable as the means of choice for connecting remote locations on Earth for telephone communications, the geosynchronous satellite was a common means for telephone information transmission. A geosynchronous satellite orbits the Earth at a height of 22,300 miles. At this height the time for one orbit of the Earth is 24 hours (see Figure 14.1). Because the Earth itself also rotates

FIGURE 14.1 A communication satellite in geosynchronous orbit above the Earth.

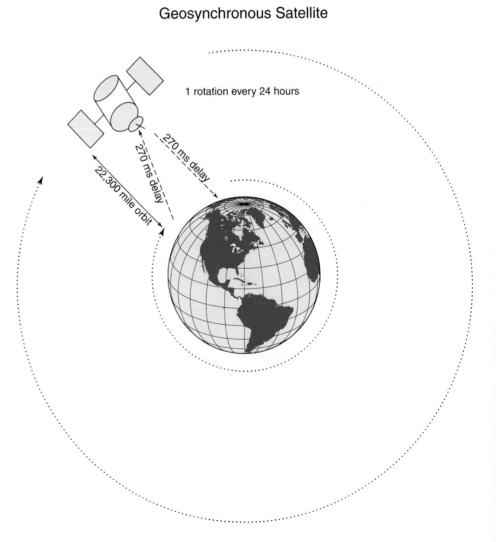

Geosynchronous Satellite

1 rotation every 24 hours

270 ms delay

270 ms delay

22,300 mile orbit

once every 24 hours, if the satellite is rotating in the same direction as the Earth, the satellite appears to stay still over the same spot on Earth. Thus, a geosynchronous satellite is always in the same place with respect to antennas on the ground, a very useful attribute for simple, low-cost and continuous communications coverage.

Now at this distance from Earth, due to the travel time of a radio signal moving at the speed of light, there is a delay from one side of the connection to the other of 270 milliseconds. Thus, the delay between when you say something and when you hear the other person's response is 540 milliseconds—over half a second. Anyone who has ever had a conversation over a satellite link can attest to the annoying quality of this delay time.

14.3.2 Interplanetary Communications

The moon is 240,000 miles from Earth. The finite speed of light introduces a round-trip delay time of 2.6 seconds in any conversation with an astronaut. Is it any wonder that these conversations sound very unnatural? (See Figure 14.2.)

We have placed robots on the surface of Mars that are controlled from Earth. The manipulators of these robots, however, have quite a difficult job working the robotic arms to pick up rocks even though they have a "live" video feed from the robot. Now, the distance between Mars and Earth is constantly changing because both are in elliptically shaped orbits with different orbit times (the martial and terrestrial years). The average (over many orbits) of the distance between Mars and Earth at the point in any year when they are closest to each other in their orbits is 50 million miles. The round-trip time between them at the speed of light is, in this case, 9 minutes. Not exactly real time for almost any purpose! This explains why it was so difficult to jockey the Mars Rover around rocks and to free it from

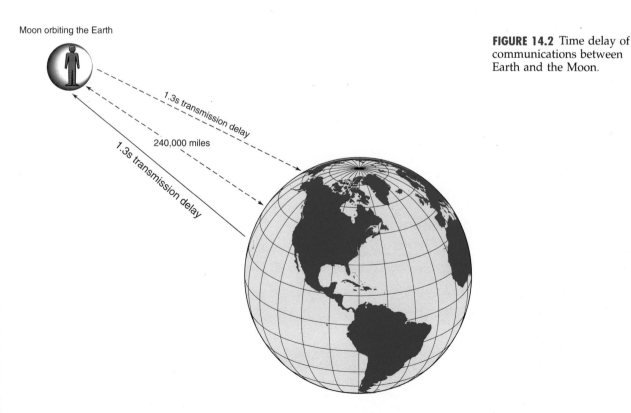

FIGURE 14.2 Time delay of communications between Earth and the Moon.

Moon orbiting the Earth

1.3s transmission delay

240,000 miles

1.3s transmission delay

occasional traps. The controller on Earth needs to wait at least 9 minutes before the result of a command is evident.

14.3.3 Internet Distributed Computing

It is not uncommon to hear on the nightly news about some new success by certain groups in cracking ever more complicated, ever more supposedly secure encryption systems. Quite often, we hear that the key was the use of thousands of computers scattered throughout the country, cooperating in a massive brute-force effort. It makes sense that if a lock has a huge number of combinations, then huge numbers of people can cooperate in finding the right key by simultaneously trying different keys on many identical copies of the lock.

We say that such a problem has a *parallelizable solution.* That means that we can solve the problem N times faster by having N people (or computers as the case may be) working in parallel to solve it. Unfortunately, many interesting and important problems do not have parallelizable solutions. Consider, for example, looking up a word in a dictionary. If the word has 10 letters, it does not help in any way for 10 people to be using 10 dictionaries in this effort, because the letters must be searched in order. Each would accomplish the entire task in the same amount of time as a single searcher.

Some problems are *piecewise parallelizable*; that is, a step in the solution process can be parallelized. But, all the results obtained from the N participants must still be brought together at one place before the next step can be taken. Many real problems fall into this category, and some improvements in solution time can be obtained by dividing the workload among many computers. Unfortunately, the limitations introduced by the speed of light may again intervene to make the parallel solution slower than the one-computer solution.

Figure 14.3 illustrates the relationships among several locations in the United States and the time it takes to move information between them at the speed of light. Consider a problem in which a single step may be parallelized, and suppose

FIGURE 14.3 The speed of light greatly impacts the ability of computers distributed across the Internet to cooperate in the solution of large-scale problems. It takes at least 20 thousandths of a second (20 ms) to move data from Illinois to California.

Distances and round-trip times (speed of light)

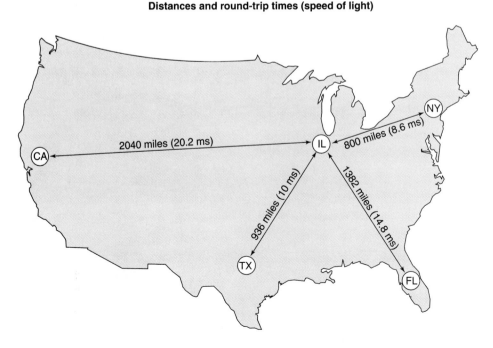

that one of the parallel elements of that step takes 1 millisecond to solve. Then, a single computer can solve five such elements in 5 milliseconds, doing them one at a time, or *serially*. If we were to distribute the step to four other locations to get a hand, we would find that the total time to a complete solution is at least 20 milliseconds now, the time for the farthest result to make its way back to the home system. Of course, we have just taken light-speed travel time into account in this illustration. On the real Internet, our information packet may have to wait in line with others to use the communications channel, incurring further delay. Hence, even in the heyday of the Internet, it is still true that often the fastest way to solve a problem is with one very fast computer.

14.3.4 Personal Computers

The speed-of-light limitation applies to all information transmission, regardless of the means or medium. Thus, the movement of data inside a computer between its *brain* (the central processing unit, or CPU) and the memory, display, and disk storage devices is also subject to light-speed induced delays. The actual speed at which information travels along the wires on circuit cards in a computer is actually less, equal to about one half the speed of light.

A fundamental action in the operation of a computer is the retrieval of information from the memory for use in the CPU. You can think of a computer as being the electronic equivalent of a postal clerk in front of a wall of addressed (street names and numbers for example) pigeonholes, with an index card in each pigeonhole that can be either read or written upon. The useful action of the computer is obtained by a programmer arranging for the cards in the pigeonholes to contain simple directions for the clerk to follow and data (information) that will be used to generate still other information that will be written back onto some of the cards.

Now, the act of obtaining a piece of information from memory by the CPU is a two-step operation that we liken to the postal example, as follows.

1. The CPU must first send a message to the memory that indicates the numerical address of the information to be read—the postal clerk extends a hand to the pigeonhole that has the address of the information that is needed.
2. The memory device responds by sending the information contained in the addressed memory slot—the postal clerk withdraws his hand from the slot with the card that was in it.

Obviously the speed of our postal clerk is determined by the distance that her hand must travel and the speed with which she can move it. So it is with our personal computer (PC). Here the speed limit is the speed of light (or less), and the distance is the distance between the CPU and memory components inside the computer.

Now, the typical distance from a CPU to a memory device (measured along the entire path of the wire) is 1 foot. The speed of light is approximately 1 foot per billionth of a second (one billionth of a second is referred to as a nanosecond, or ns). Hence, at half the speed of light, the round-trip time for the above transaction is about four billionths of a second. Thus, if no other delays were involved, the fastest that this operation could be repeated over this distance would be at a rate of 250 million instructions (that is, operations) per second, also referred to as 250 MIPs.

Real electronics, however, take time to operate. That is, the memory chips cannot respond in zero time, and it also takes time for the CPU and memory to recognize the presence of new information and to issue it. Thus, the 4 ns delay above is just part of the total time for these interactions, and real computers cannot achieve speeds even near 250 MIPs when these distances and delays are involved. In 2000, you can purchase PCs with processing speeds of 400 MIPs, and some more costly workstations boast speeds of 600 MIPs. How are these speeds achieved? The solution to our problem is to minimize the distances involved, on average! Today's PCs typically have a *cache* memory located within an inch or two of the CPU. Information is moved in large blocks from the main memory unit rather than in single address slots into the cache.

Thus, the CPU now can typically communicate over a much faster connection with the cache, and the slower transactions occur only when the cache needs to be updated with a new region of the main memory content.

Plate 34 and Figure 14.4 show the circuit board inside of a computer that has a particularly easy-to-see memory layout, and a diagram that helps you visualize the path that the data must take from memory to CPU. In this computer, the cache memory chips have been arrayed around and near the CPU to minimize the travel time to and from this temporary store of information. Furthermore, this cache memory typically is constructed of circuits that are themselves faster than ordinary main memory chips, with the tradeoff being cost, larger size for a given amount of memory, and total power usage. Because only a small amount of information is stored in this temporary cache memory, the speed advantage outweighs the various disadvantages.

Current PC technology presses this tradeoff even further by incorporating two so-called cache levels. In addition to fast, power hungry Level 2 cache memory situated near the PC, are even smaller amount of so-called Level 1 cache is located on the silicon chip with the CPU. This space on the chip is costly to include, because chip production costs grow very rapidly with increased chip size. However, this addition of only a small amount more of cache memory means that at a relatively low cost, the speed of light apparently can be beaten, because the most needed information sits so much closer to where it is needed than in the main memory chips.

FIGURE 14.4 Diagram of the main computer circuit board shown in Plate 34.

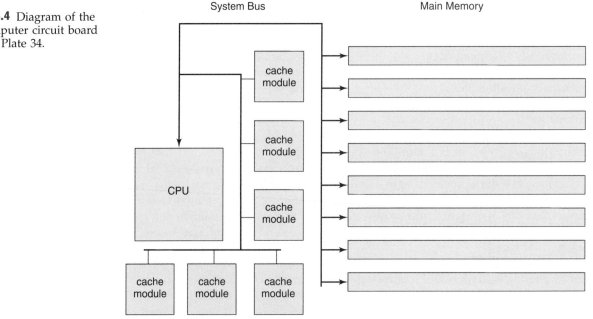

14.4 Finite Data Rate and Real-Time Transmission

In the previous discussion, we have made it clear that the definition of real-time transmission of information is dependent on the time-delay sensitivity of an application, and the minimum time delay is determined absolutely by the finite speed of light. But this unavoidable delay time is not the only roadblock in the path of the information engineer with regard to providing real-time communications. The other roadblock is the finite data rate allowed by any real communications channel. Suppose we were to create a very slow and crude communication system that links two rooms located 20 feet apart using a conveyor belt, as shown in Figure 14.5. Let the conveyor belt have small dividers on its surface spaced about 1 inch apart, so that a ping pong ball can nicely rest within and stay within each slot. Further, suppose that the conveyor belt moves at about 1 inch per second (any faster and the balls might fall out because of the wind generated by their movement).

Now we can transmit a message that has been coded in binary by placing a ping pong ball in a slot to indicate a 1, and by leaving the slot empty to indicate a 0. Obviously the delay time from transmission of one of these binary bits to reception is 240 seconds. But our communication system is so simple that we can also quickly determine the maximum data rate (the number of bits per second) that it allows us to transmit. Because the conveyor allows us to drop a new bit into a slot every second, and one is delivered at the other end every second, the data rate is 1 bit per second, or 1 bps. Now suppose that we wanted to transmit a digital music signal via this system and did not mind the 240 second delay. If we further suppose a CD-like encoding scheme in which a stereo pair of signals is sampled at 44 kHz each and encoded as 16 bits per sample, then our outgoing bit rate is approximately 1.4 Mbps. Thus, immediately after sending the first bit, we would begin generating a backlog and have about 1.4 million bits ready to send by the time the second slot was available, a backlog of 2.8 million bits by the third slot time, and so on. If we were transmitting a song with a 3-minute duration, we would accumulate 2.5344×10^8 bits at the transmit side and wouldn't be able to deliver them until as many conveyor slots rolled by. This would take a total of 8 years to happen. However, at the end of those 8 years we could finally enjoy the song in crystal-clear stereophonic CD quality!

What this example illustrates is that transmission latency, sometimes called transmission propagation delay, determines message delay only if the *source rate* of data is below the *information rate capacity* of the communications channel. If the source rate exceeds the channel capacity, we have an ever-increasing backlog of

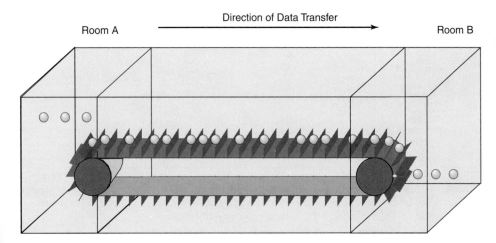

Room A   Direction of Data Transfer   Room B

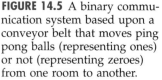

FIGURE 14.5 A binary communication system based upon a conveyor belt that moves ping pong balls (representing ones) or not (representing zeroes) from one room to another.

data that can only be delivered some time after the source message has finished. Any real communications channel has a finite channel capacity associated with it. In what follows we will discuss the physical origins of this capacity limit. Obviously, anyone who deals with real-time transmission of information must be cognizant of the source data rate and provide a channel with sufficient capacity. Furthermore, higher-capacity channels will, for reasons to be explained, cost more to construct, install, maintain, and power. Hence, for economic reasons, there is typically a fairly tight fit between source rates and the capacity of channels that are chosen for the transmission scheme.

14.5 Physical Origin of Bandwidth Limitations

When we discussed the human ear earlier in this text, we explained the physical origin of what we called the band-pass response behavior of the ear. We introduced the idea of Fourier decomposition and the frequency response curve to justify and quantify a very important description of this limitation. You will now see that the human ear as a communications channel provides a good model for understanding any other communications channel; there are similar limitations due to physical phenomena, and these limitations can also be described by frequency response curves. Information engineers typically transmit information in one of three ways (Figure 14.6):

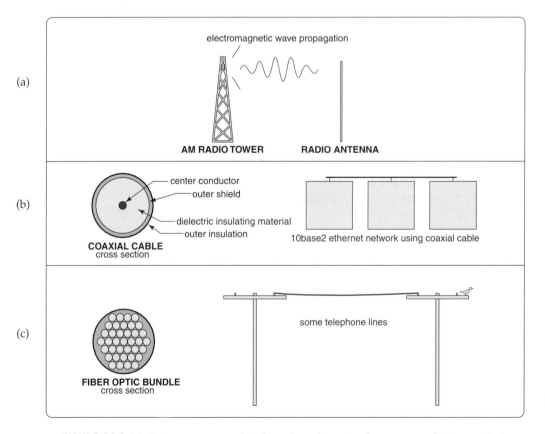

FIGURE 14.6 (a) Antennas are used to launch and receive free space radio transmissions. (b) Examples of coaxial cable used for cable television and data networking. (c) A bundle of fiber-optic cables, which may be buried or strung on poles.

1. As a free-space electromagnetic wave. Examples of this approach include radio, television, cellular telephones, wireless modems, and microwave telephone and data links.
2. As a variation of a current or voltage on a pair of wires (a cable). Examples of this approach include cable television, the telephone local loop (the part of the telephone system that enters your home and links it to nearby central offices), and cable-based local area computer networks such as Ethernet and AppleTalk.
3. As a variation of light intensity in a fiber-optic cable. Examples of this approach include the telephone *long lines* system (the part of the telephone system that links distant central telephone offices and provides overseas connections).

📖 **Ethernet**

An electrical engineer who specializes in electromagnetic field theory would be quick to explain that in all these cases the *stuff* being transmitted is actually the same: an electromagnetic field. What is the difference between an electromagnetic field and electricity, which you have probably been taught is the fluid-like flow of tiny particles called electrons? There is a strong connection between the two, but they are most certainly not the same thing. However, you have daily experience with a similarly related pair of physical concepts: mass and gravity.

We learn in introductory physics courses that Isaac Newton realized that every material object has some *mass* associated with it. This property of mass means that it emits an invisible gravitational force field that causes it to attract other masses through what has been called action-at-a-distance. That is, every piece of matter attracts other pieces of matter to it, and is attracted to the other pieces of matter through the action of this field.

Now, we can use this effect to send information between two places in two different ways. I can use matter itself to send the message by letting gravity propel it, or I can use gravitational action at a distance directly.

Suppose I am standing on a ladder and wish to send a message to the surface of Earth below me. If I bring a bag of marbles with me, I can exploit the mutual attraction between the marbles and the Earth to cause a marble I drop to fall to the Earth. Using a pattern of marbles being dropped, I can send the message. So as to not run out of marbles, I could even set up a continuous elevator that brings the marbles back up to me (closing the marble circuit). This arrangement is like that used in electrical circuits, in which electrons both are the cause of electromagnetic fields and are moved by electromagnetic fields. Any conductor-based transmission system, like a wire cable, uses this approach.

Alternatively, I can send a message from the Moon to the Earth without dropping pieces from the Moon onto the Earth. The force of gravitational action at a distance produced by the Moon's gravitational field is well known to be the cause of lunar tides in the ocean. When the Moon moves around the Earth, it moves the ocean waters with it, causing tide elevations to increase or decrease. Thus, the Moon sends a message regarding its position to us on the surface constantly. However, in this case, we do not need a "circuit," because no matter what is changing hands, only the remote influence of the otherwise insubstantial field is being used to communicate. When we use radio waves or light waves to communicate, we are using the electromagnetic field in just this way. Of course, as in the case of the matter that makes up the Moon and Earth, electrons, as a source of electromagnetic fields, are being manipulated at the source to create the communication, and by the field at the destination to sense it.

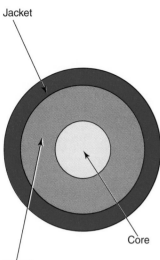

FIGURE 14.7 Cross section of optical fiber cable showing the coaxial arrangement of optical conductors of different indices of refraction, and a protective jacket.

The primary difference in the three transmission systems we introduced above is the way in which the field was contained and directed. In the three cases above we have unguided (free space), transmission line, and so-called dielectric waveguide guidance of the wave, respectively. We will not dwell on the differences here, but rather emphasize the similarity so that a single treatment will suffice to explain the frequency-response behavior in all three cases. As there is no way to contain or guide a gravity field, you will not have an easy reference for this field phenomenon in your day-to-day life.

However, because we all have some daily experience with the electromagnetic field that we call light, it is fairly easy to intuit the operation of a fiber-optic system. Hence we will discuss it in some detail next.

14.6 Fiber-Optic Transmission

A fiber-optic cable is a coaxial arrangement of glass or plastic material of immense clarity. Figure 14.7 illustrates the typical construction of a fiber-optic cable. As can be seen, a clear cylinder of optical material, called the *core*, is surrounded by another clear wrapper of optical material called the *cladding*. These two materials are selected to have different indices of refraction (a term that will be explained below). Finally, the fiber is surrounded by a plastic or Teflon jacket to protect and stiffen the fiber.

The index of refraction of a material is a measure of the speed of light in that material, which in turn affects the angle by which a light ray is bent on passing through the material; hence, the name of the measure. In Figure 14.8 we see a ray of light striking the surface of water in a tank from its origin in air above the tank. The indices of refraction for air and water are such that the light ray is bent, as shown, toward a more vertical path. This phenomenon is the cause of the apparent

FIGURE 14.8 A ray of light is shown passing through a material interface as it moves from the air into the tank of water. The bending or refraction of the ray of light is determined by the velocity of light in each material.

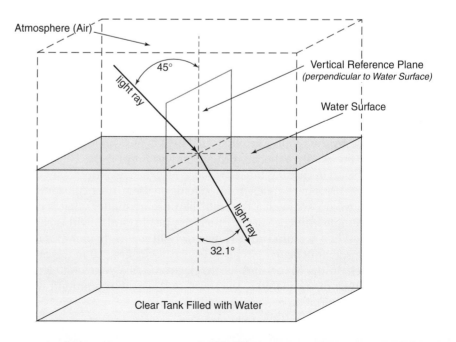

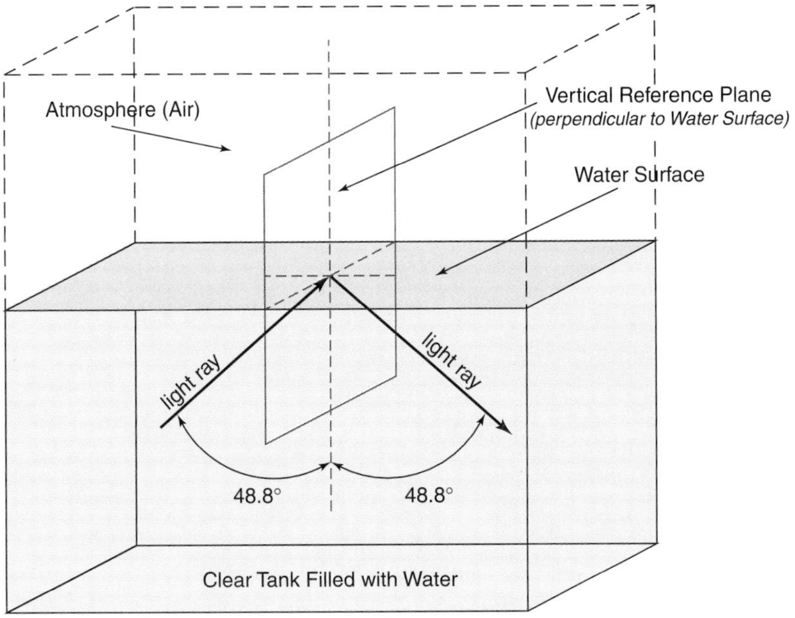
Atmosphere (Air)
Vertical Reference Plane
(perpendicular to Water Surface)
Water Surface
light ray
light ray
48.8°
48.8°
Clear Tank Filled with Water

FIGURE 14.9 A light ray that strikes the air–water interface from the water at an angle larger than the critical angle is totally reflected.

bend we see in a stick that passes through the surface of water when viewed from above.

Regardless of the angle at which the light hits the surface of the water, it will be bent closer to the vertical, with vertical rays passing through unbent. The situation is quite a bit different for light rays that originate below the surface of the water.

Light striking the underside of the water surface at an angle sufficiently close to the vertical will be bent further away from the vertical on exiting into the air. More interesting is the fact that when light strikes this boundary at a sufficiently shallow angle, it is totally reflected as if it had struck a mirror, as shown in Figure 14.9!

This *total internal reflection* phenomenon occurs only if the light is in the *denser* medium (that is, the one with the higher index of refraction and hence slower speed of light) and strikes an interface with the less dense medium. The maximum grazing angle at which this will occur is called the critical angle of the interface. The reflectivity provided by this effect is essentially perfect, making it much better than any real mirror, which has substantial loss (not that you would notice in the usual use to which you put a mirror).

You can experience this phenomenon the next time you are in a dense medium looking out at a less dense medium. For example, when you are next swimming underwater, place your eyes just below the water line and keep very still. When the surface of the water is still, you will see the floor of the pool reflected in the interface of the water–air interface as clearly as if by a mirror. How does a fiber-optic cable work? The operation is quite easy to visualize with the aid of Figure 14.10. As illustrated, any rays entering the fiber-optic cable at an angle shallower than the critical angle will bounce off the core-cladding interface and go on to strike another side of the cable at the same angle, repeating until it comes out the far end.

Making this apparently simple scheme work is of course not easy, or else it would have not been until the past decade that it was widely exploited for the transmission of data over long (intercontinental) distances. To preserve the light intensity requires optical material of incredible clarity.

FIGURE 14.10 Side view of an optical fiber cable showing the paths of light rays that enter the face at different angles. Note how different the path lengths are of the two rays that are shown. The rays labeled (a) and (b) propagate through the fiber, but with different path lengths. Ray (c) is lost in the cladding.

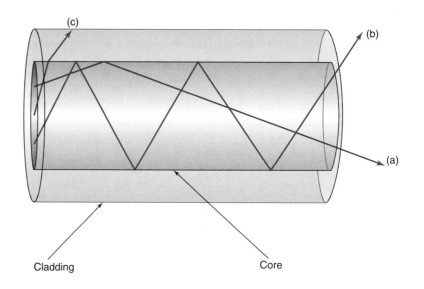

Cladding   Core

The amount of light that a fiber-optic cable loses is measured in terms of decibels per kilometer (dB/km). A decibel is a measure of loss that engineers love to use because it is additive. That means that if 1 km of fiber loses 1 dB of light, then 2 km will lose 2 dB of light and so on. A good way to translate figures in decibels into nonengineering terms is to remember that a 10 dB loss means that 1/10 or 10% of the original light is still left. Thus, dividing the loss in dB/km into 10 we would obtain the number of km of cable that would be needed to lose all but 10% of the original light.

So, because the clarity of fiber-optic cable is about 0.1 dB/km for the best fibers in production today, only 1/10 of the light that entered would exit the far end of a cable with a length of 100 km (or 62 miles).

Now that we have some explanation of the operation of a fiber-optic transmission system, we will explain the origin of low-pass behavior in such transmission systems.

14.6.1 Talking Through Your Pipe

We can construct a very simple and intuitive analogy of the fiber-optic system that you certainly have encountered in your day-to-day activities. A hollow cardboard tube presents such an example. When we speak into one end of such a tube (Fig. 14.11), the air pressure waves from our voice bounce back and forth between the walls of the tube in the same manner as occurs for light waves in fiber-optic cable. The path that any component of our voice-induced pressure waves takes is of course determined by the angle of entry into the tube. As we saw in the fiber-optic cable system, each path has a different path length. Hence, the complete pressure waveform that exits the end of the tube is the sum of many copies of the entering wave, each delayed by different amounts determined by the path it took.

What happens to a waveform when it splits up into smaller copies of itself and then these are added back together after introducing various delays to the various components? Let's find out by examining what would result by applying this *processing* to a special waveform known as a chirp waveform, shown in Figure 14.12. A chirp waveform is obtained by continuously varying the frequency of a tone from one frequency to another. The name chirp is descriptive: if the frequency range involved fell inside the range of human hearing, it would indeed sound like

FIGURE 14.11 When you speak into a long tube, your voice exits with most of the higher audio frequencies attenuated. As a result your voice sounds muffled and baritone.

 Figure 14.11

a chirp if the tone variation took place quickly. Or, if the variation were slow, it would sound like the result of moving the arm on a trombone from full extension to least extension: a siren-like sweep from a low note to a high note on the musical scale.

In Figure 14.12 we see the waveform depicted as usual as the variation of air pressure versus time. Note that on the left, that is at first, the variation is very slow corresponding to a low-frequency audio note. As time progresses, toward the right of the graph, the variations occur closer together; that is, the frequency of the note increases.

Because the peak height of the graphed waveform indicates the amount of peak air pressure at any moment, it should be clear that the *amplitude* (or loudness) of the waveform remains the same as the frequency increases with time. This will be the perfect waveform with which to demonstrate the effect of adding many

FIGURE 14.12 Chirp waveform that will be used in our experiment with summing waveforms delayed as if by various path lengths in a tube.

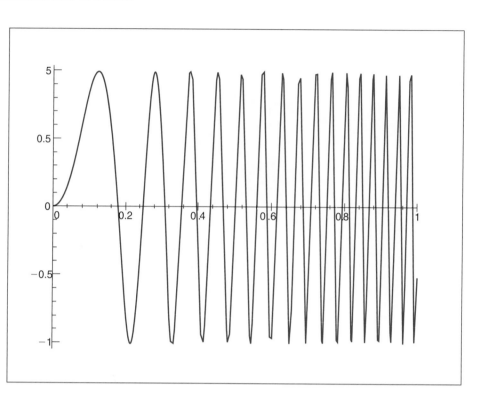

echoes. If such a composite waveform favors one frequency over another, making it louder, we will see this reflected as an increase in the amplitude for that portion of the waveform at which time that frequency is present.

Now we will add together 50 copies of this waveform (each with a fair share of 1/50 of the original waveform's amplitude) to form a new waveform in which each copy is delayed by a small and increasing amount of time. The resulting waveform is shown in Figure 14.13.

Note that the result has air-pressure peaks of decreasing height! What we see is that the higher-frequency components of the chirp waveform were suppressed by this process, and increasingly so with increasing frequency of the waveform. That is, the lowest frequencies pass through with all the loudness of the original, but the higher frequencies are muffled by the process.

Can we supply a simple and reasonable explanation for this behavior? Yes. The delayed versions of the signal we used were placed with staggered start times all lying in the first 0.025 seconds of the waveform displayed in Figure 14.12. At the left-hand side or low-frequency end of this waveform, the waveform hardly changes over this period of time; hence, all the components added constructively to almost the original waveform. On the other hand, at the right-hand side, the waveform undergoes major variations from one moment in time to the next. In fact, the air pressure often changes sign (from an increase to a decrease in pressure relative to the average air pressure) over that interval. Hence, many of the components destructively add; that is, they cancel each other out. Thus the loss of amplitude at this end of the waveform is to be expected.

Thus we have illustrated the fact that a distribution of arrival times of components of a launched signal leads invariably to a low-pass response in which higher-frequency components of a signal are degraded, while lower-frequency components pass with little loss.

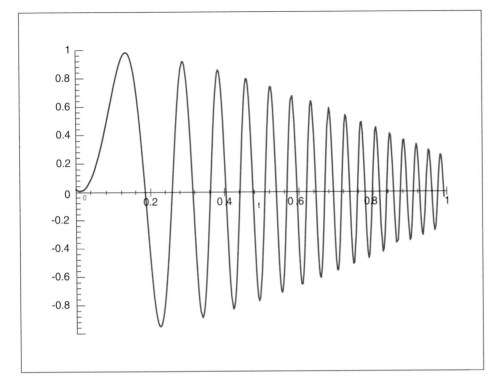

FIGURE 14.13 Result of summing 50 copies of the waveform in the previous figure. Note that the frequency components of this waveform are suppressed progressively with increasing frequency.

Any real transmission system is subject to the same sort of low-pass response characteristic because of the *smearing* of the transmitted waveform brought about the existence of a distribution of travel times for a waveform rather than a single travel time. Hence, any real transmission system has a maximum usable *bandwidth* associated with it. That is, these systems become practically unusable for waveforms with frequency components above a certain frequency because of the loss of signal amplitude due to the smearing.

14.7 Human Laws Set Limits Too!

A given finite bandwidth is sometimes not a physical limitation but rather defined by convention or convenience. For example, the finite bandwidth of radio and TV channels is determined by the government. We will briefly explore this situation here. There exists an information technology that was known and has been exploited since the 1920s to create an electrical signal that simply transports all of the information in a given signal to a new *center* frequency. This *translation* of the center frequency is called *modulation* and is depicted in Figure 14.14 for a simple modulation scheme known by the technical name of "Double Sideband Suppressed Carrier Amplitude Modulation" (DSBSC-AM). This is commonly just called "AM" as in AM radio. If the original signal (we call this the *baseband* signal) occupies a certain finite bandwidth, then the new signal is also finite in bandwidth but, as can be seen, centered at a new frequency.

When multiple signals are translated to different center frequencies and then placed onto the same medium (like the cable for cable TV or the airwaves for AM and FM radio), the process is called *frequency division multiplexing* (FDM). In fact, this is exactly how an AM radio transmission and channelization system works. The signals in the voice and music signal is translated via AM to the desired lo-

FIGURE 14.14 Audio signals undergo the modulation process described in the text to obtain AM radio signals, which are arranged into evenly spaced channels that we can tune to with our AM radios.

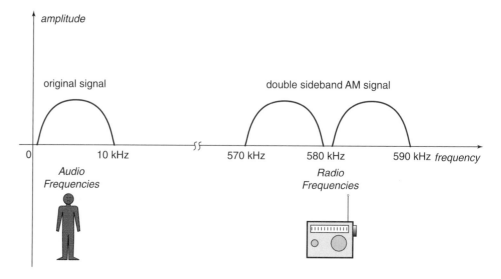

cation (actually to the location licensed by the FCC) in the AM band, along with the other radio stations. The AM receiver then filters out the portion of the signal to which you have tuned and reverses the modulation process through a process known as *demodulation*.

To understand how this process works consider this silly analogy. Two men and two women are sitting at a dinner table attempting to have two simultaneous conversations. However, because the pair of men who are trying to talk and the pair of women who are trying to talk are facing the wrong partners to make this easy, they can hardly separate the two conversations. To remedy the situation they decide to use FDM technology. The women speak in a high-pitched falsetto while the men move their voices into a more baritone mode. By dividing the available audio bandwidth into high and low channels, and by using their hearing ability to separate these channels, they succeed in having two simultaneous conversations.

The importance of FDM frequency translation is that it allows us to divide any available bandwidth into channels of finite bandwidth and then to fill those channels with the modulated baseband signals. So, many users can share a single transmission system whether it is a cable (such as in cable TV or short haul telephone transmission); the free-space electromagnetic spectrum (as in AM, FM radio and TV); or a fiber-optic line (as used for long haul telephone transmission). The use of FDM in this fashion to transmit many channels of television signals is illustrated in Figure 14.15.

So, returning to the original point of this section: finite bandwidth requirements on a baseband signal may be legislated to allow FDM translation into mandated channel widths.

For example, commercial AM radio stations must filter out any content in voice and music above 10 kHz so that the FDM processed signals will fit within 20 kHz assigned slots in the AM band. It is the fact that FM transmission requirements are much less stringent, allowing an 18 kHz original content bandwidth that makes FM music sound so much better even when not played on a stereo receiver, which uses the fact that two channels are effectively used for each FM stereo source. (The arrangement and use of these channels, by the way, are quite unintuitive. Suffice it to say for this treatment that the left- and right-side sound sources are not simply transmitted independently in separate and adjacent channels.)

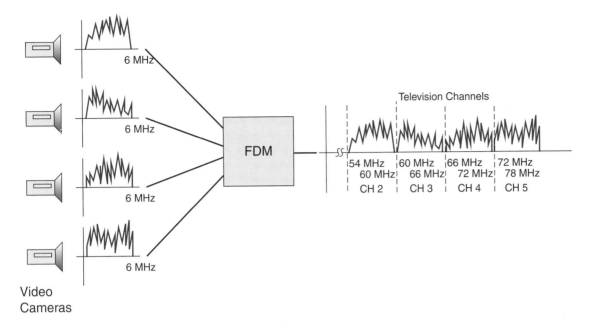

FIGURE 14.15 FDM is used to transmit many channels of television information to users simultaneously over the same cable or radio spectrum.

14.8 Pulse Transmission Limits and Bandlimits

This section contains a level of detail that may be above and beyond the call of duty for many users of this textbook. The brave of heart can read this to discover in some detail how bandwidth determines the amount of digital data that can be transmitted over a channel with a given amount of bandwidth. For the other readers let it suffice to say: There is a maximum data rate (that is, a maximum number of bits per second) that can be sent and received across a channel that is proportional to the available bandwidth, but is also a function of the amount of noise to be found on that channel.

So far our discussion of bandwidth and channels hasn't directly connected bandwidth to any kind of limitation associated with the transmission of digital information. However, there is an interesting and important limitation that was discovered and loosely proven by the Bell Laboratories electrical engineer Harry Nyquist. He showed that a finite channel bandwidth leads to a limitation on the number of pulses, of a given fixed shape, we can transmit per second. We call this maximum rate the Nyquist pulse rate (not to be confused with the Nyquist sampling rate introduced earlier). His assertion was rigorously mathematically proven later by Bell's Claude Shannon. Nyquist showed that it is impossible to transmit more than $2B$ pulses per second through a B Hz bandwidth channel and to unravel those pulses at the other end into $2B$ pieces of information again. If an attempt is made to increase the bit rate beyond this value, the pulses must be made narrower. Nyquist showed that the rate of $2B$ pulses per second represents the narrowest pulses that can be transmitted without the pulses becoming hopelessly smeared with each other in transmission. Furthermore, only one pulse shape permits transmission at the ultimate Nyquist pulse rate. For a finite bandwidth channel, the optimum such pulse is known as a sinc pulse (Figure 14.16). A good question at this point would be: "Does

FIGURE 14.16 The pulse shape that allows the greatest number of separable pulses to be sent over a finite bandwidth channel is shown. This pulse is zero periodically except at one distinguished point in the otherwise unbroken pattern.

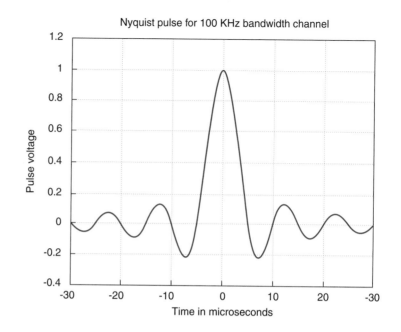

the pulse in the figure represent a one or a zero?" The answer is that it can represent either bit value, and the opposite value is represented by the negative of that pulse. In other words the shape is the same, but every point is made negative.

Information can be sent by superimposing many such pulses with each staggered in time such that at certain moments only one pulse of many has a nonzero value and hence can be separated from the others. In Figure 14.17 we see that two ones have been transmitted (with zeros to either side) by the transmission of two of these sinc pulses.

FIGURE 14.17 Two bits represented by two sinc pulses, one at Time −10 and one at Time 0. Note that the peaks are distinct, and that at the time when one pulse is at its peak, the other pulse amplitude is zero.

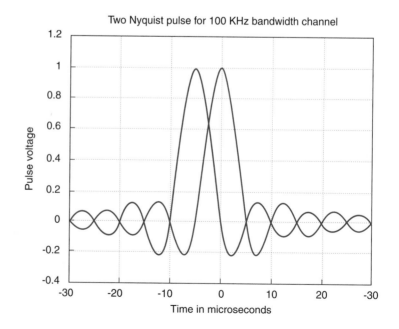

This best possible pulse is also impossible to use in reality because it literally lasts forever. To transmit this pulse requires that you begin the act in the infinite past and continue it into the infinite future.

While this optimum pulse is unusable, we can approximate it with practical pulses that approach the Nyquist pulse rate asymptotically with our effort and the complexity of our pulse generation system.

So, with this theory in place it is clear that if we associate a zero with no pulse in a given time slot and a one with a pulse in that time slot, that we cannot transmit more than $2B$ bits/second through a B Hz bandwidth channel. So, because our telephone system supports 4 kHz bandwidth to the home, we could never transmit more than 8 kbps with a modem. But that runs counter to your experience as a consumer! You probably own a computer with a modem with a signaling rate well over 8 kbps. Today 33.6 kbps modems are quite common. In the next section we will look at the loophole in the Nyquist limit and the actual ultimate signaling rate for a channel.

📖 **Modem**

14.8.1 Information Rates above the Pulse Rate

We can send more information than the Nyquist rate seems to imply by using more than just one pulse shape! The simplest such scheme merely involves sending a given "basic shape" with different heights. Let's turn to an analogy to understand this better before we proceed. The Nyquist pulse rate limit that we have encountered is analogous to the limit that we would find imposed upon us in a simple communication scheme like that of turning a flashlight on and off to communicate with a friend who lives across the street. Even with a lot of practice, we are not going to be able to flash the light and have our friend jot down a record of more than about one flash per second.

To increase our signaling rate we introduce a small modification. Instead of turning the light on and off, we hold one of four transparencies in front of the light. One is opaque (no light flash), one is completely clear (full brightness flash), and the other two are semitransparent to different degrees (low and medium brightness flashes). Thus, while I can only still flip about one card per second, each time I can convey two bits of information, doubling my information rate. For example, the brightest light would represent 11, the next brightest would represent 10, the darkest (but not black) would represent 01, and no light would represent 00.

Now take for example, a small modification of the pulses used in Figure 14.16, shown in Figure 14.18. Here, each pulse is transmitted with one of 16 heights. These pulses are still perfectly separable but now each one carries 4 bits of information, corresponding to the 16 possible levels with which it was transmitted.

So, could we transmit each one with 256 levels and get 8 bits per pulse? How about 65,536 pulse levels for 16 bits per pulse? In theory yes, but at some point the complexity and cost of properly and reliably detecting so many heights actually becomes impractical. Just consider what our friend across the street would say if we proposed using 256 different transparencies, each with a different level of transparency. Is the impracticality of detecting so many heights our only limitation to the amount of information that a channel can carry? No, it is not. We have to introduce two other real concerns in a real communication system: noise and power.

Any real communications channel is noisy. There are many possible causes for noise, but one is inescapable: the movement of subatomic particles caused by the energy in heat represents a disturbance of any and all signals traveling through

FIGURE 14.18 Two $\sin(x)/x$ pulses of different heights.

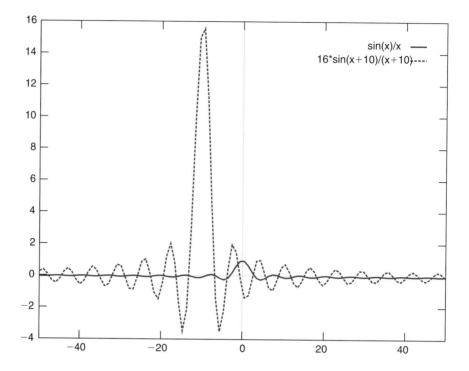

that system. Thus, in the same way it becomes impossible to hear a person who speaks too quietly in a noisy room, we can't discern exactly the height of a pulse riding in a noisy system. If the person speaks up, putting more power into their voice, we will again be able to hear them. If a transmitter puts more power into its pulses so that they become widely separated, we can once again discern their original values.

Thus, to use more pulse levels in a given system typically means having to increase the power that is transmitted, because the noise level in that system (dictated often by its temperature) requires some minimum amount of separation of the levels.

Now, some systems have limited power resources. For example:

- A satellite that extracts its power from solar batteries has a finite power budget.
- Telephone circuits were built to deal only with a power level associated with the signals generated by a voice in the telephone's microphone. To have made them capable of more would have made the telephone system cost much more.
- A laser diode in a fiber-optic transmission system will melt down if driven above a certain power level.

Thus, when we combine the limitation on the available signal power with the need to separate pulse heights due to unavoidable noise in the transmission channel, we see that a new ultimate information rate limit must exist. It was Claude Shannon (again) who discovered and rigorously proved this limit, which we call the Shannon channel capacity theorem. Furthermore he described how we can approach this capacity in practice by a sophisticated set of steps that involve not just well chosen pulse shapes but also the application of special error correcting codes.

It was many years after his discovery that electronics with sufficient sophistication to apply these ideas became commercially practical.

If we apply the channel capacity theorem to a typical telephone line, we discover that about 40 kbps is the maximum we will ever be able to squeeze out of the existing phone system. Thus, modern modem technology, as of the mid 1990s, finally hit the ceiling imposed by the nature of noise, power, and information. In fact, to obtain a slightly higher rate of 56 kbps, it was necessary to change the ground rules in use and to modify the telephone equipment so as to lower the amount of noise that corrupted the typical phone connection.

Summary

The *bandwidth* (and its derivatives, such as *broadband*) has recently come into widespread popular usage. It is an important concept that indicates the rate at which information can flow. The bandwidth of human hearing is about 15,000 Hz, for example. All real systems (natural or man-made) have a finite (noninfinite) bandwidth. In this chapter we have seen how bandwidth is defined and how the physical limitations arise. We have also learned about other important parameters such as delay time or *latency* in data transmission.

Given a certain bandwidth (call it B Hz) we learned that best data transmission rate that we can hope to achieve with simple binary pulse shapes is $2B$ bits per second. However, we then learned that this limit can be broken if we transmit pulses with more than two amplitudes. This is the mechanism by which a data rate of about 56 kbits per second is achieved over a telephone connection with a bandwidth of about 4 kHz.

Try These Exercises

1. Given the speed of light, determine the transmission delay for a telephone call from New York to Los Angeles, from one side of Los Angeles to the other side, and from New York to Tokyo. Is this significant for human conversation? Why or why not?
2. In one form of data transmission, each ASCII character is acknowledged by the receiver before the next character is sent. Assume that the data rate of the channel is 10,000 bits per second. For standard 7-bit ASCII, determine the transmission rate in characters per second with no acknowledgment. Now find the rate for each of the three cases in the problem above.
3. Explain in your own words the reason that bandwidth is never infinite. Use a specific example.
4. The FM radio band extends from 88 MHz to 108 MHz. Determine how many telephone conversations could fit in that bandwidth. State your assumptions and explain your reasoning.
5. Assume that a personal computer must get two pieces of data from its memory for every operation (one piece of data indicates which instruction to perform; the other is the information which is operated on). If the computer is the size of a typical PC, how long does it take to get these pieces of data? From this, what is the maximum rate at which the PC can execute instructions? Explain your assumptions and procedure.
6. Repeat the above question, but assume that now the memory from which the data must be retrieved is on the same chip as the processor. Explain your procedure and assumptions.

7. Two sinusoidal signals are set to be 180 degrees out of phase if the relative time delay between the two signals is equal to one-half of the period of the signals (or odd integer multiples of this value). In this case the signals cancel each other out and disappear! This is one of the origins of bandwidth limits. For a 1 GHz signal, to how much time delay difference does this 180 degree phase shift correspond? For a 1 GHz radio signal, to how much distance does this correspond?

8. Using Frequency Division Multiplexing, how many analog telephone channels will fit in the portion of the radio spectrum between 90 MHz and 100 MHz? Explain your calculations.

9. Use the applet "Bandwidth-limited Data Transmission Simulation" to simulate the transmission of the bit string: 10101110101. Start with a bandwidth of 20 kHz. Then try bandwidths of 10 kHz, 5 kHz, 2 kHz, 1 kHz, and 500 Hz. Explain what you observe. It would be good to include the signal plots in your answer. At what bandwidth does it become difficult to determine whether a one or a zero was transmitted?

15 Wire and Fiber Transmission Systems

Objectives

In this chapter, wire and optical fiber-based transmission systems are investigated in detail. Even though optical and wireless systems seem more "high-tech," wires in various forms are still a cost-effective communications medium for many purposes. In this chapter you will learn:

▲ about the important distinctions among various types of wires and cables, including shielded and unshielded twisted pair, and coaxial cable;

▲ about the interference rejection and transmission characteristics of these various wire and cable types;

▲ about the interference rejection and transmission characteristics of fiber optic cable; and

▲ about future advances in fiber transmission leading to both higher speeds and greater transmission distances without amplification.

15.1 Introduction

There are two fundamentally different ways to transmit information: using some communications medium (wire, fiber optics, etc.) and using no communications medium! The latter method is the case with all forms of radio communication, and merits its own chapter. In this chapter we introduce some of the important aspects of the various forms of wire and fiber optics for information transmission.

15.2 Wire as a Transmission Medium

Wire was the original medium for the electronic transmission of information; today it is still the most common and versatile medium. As mentioned in a previous chapter, transmission systems can involve both guided and unguided movement of electromagnetic waves. The wire-based transmission scheme guides electromagnetic waves, either between a pair of separate wires, or inside a coaxial arrangement. A coaxial cable (often called coax for short) has both a "center" conductor and a second "shield" conductor. These conductors are separated by some insulating material, such that the shield conductor entirely surrounds the center conductor, as seen in Figure 15.1. In the case of noncoaxial transmission, the pair of wires may be held either parallel to each other by an appropriate stiff insulating material, or individually insulated and twisted around each other. Finally, some arrangement of surrounding shield conductor may be placed around the resulting

FIGURE 15.1 Four common types of transmission cable: parallel wires, UTP, STP, and coaxial.

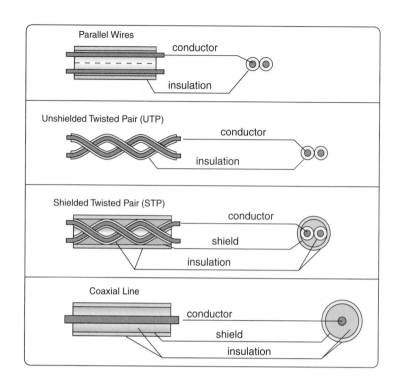

twisted pair to form a shielded twisted pair (STP). Implicit in this construction is that the physical arrangement of the shield conductor is not nearly as accurate as in the construction of coax. The unshielded twisted pair is called TP or often UTP to distinguish it clearly from STP. All of the above wire-based transmission media are called cables, not just the coaxial cable.

The cost of a cable is a function of the cost of the materials and the manufacturing process. Thus, cables with larger diameter, involving more copper conductor and more insulation, are more expensive than those with small diameter. Likewise, cables that have twisted pairs of conductors are more expensive than those that do not, while STP is more expensive, and coaxial is even more so (see Table 15.1). This of course leads to the question: why not use the smallest, simplest cable for all applications? We will address this question in the following discussion.

TABLE 15.1   THE TABLE SHOWS COSTS OF VARIOUS CABLE TYPES DISCUSSED IN THE TEXT. CATEGORY 3 AND 5 UTP ARE TWO GRADES OF CABLE DISTINGUISHED BY THE TYPE OF MATERIAL USED FOR INSULATOR AND THE PRECISION OF THE GEOMETRIC RELATIONSHIP OF THE CONDUCTORS. RG-58/U AND RG-8/U ARE LIKEWISE SMALLER AND LARGER DIAMETER COAXIAL CABLES, RESPECTIVELY.

Cable Type	Cost Per Foot for Large Bulk Purchase
Parallel Pair (4 pair, 24 AWG)	$0.09
UTP Category 3 (4 pair, 24 AWG)	$0.15
UTP Category 5 (4 pair, 24 AWG)	$0.17
STP (2 pair, 24 AWG)	$0.20
Coax, RG-58/U (Thin Ethernet)	$0.29
Coax, RG-8/U (Thick Ethernet)	$1.12

15.2.1 Cable Characteristics

As mentioned in the introduction and in our previous discussion of guided wave transmission, a cable moves electromagnetic (E&M) waves by providing a channel in which the pair of conductors act like a pair of mirrors between which the wave bounces back and forth until it reaches its destination. (To be precise, E&M waves may be confined in such as way that they can traverse the cable moving parallel to these conductors, that is without bouncing, yet still interacting with the conductors.) The E&M wave interacts with the free electrons in the conductors, which are responsible for the guiding of this wave. Think of these electrons, which are free to move within the conductor but confined there, as ball bearings, and think of the E&M wave as a package of energy riding on those ball bearings, guided to its destination by the shape of the conductor that holds the ball bearings. Now, no one can make a perfectly frictionless ball bearing! So, we would expect in this analogous system that our package would eventually slow down and stop on the conveyer if it offers no other source of energy for the packages.

The electrons in our conductor also are subject to a friction-like energy loss mechanism that we call resistance. However, in our case, our E&M energy packages act a little differently. By the theory of special relativity, our E&M packages (which are made of the elementary particles called photons) cannot slow down! They must travel at the speed of light. But because our packages "are" energy, they themselves can be consumed to provide the power needed to sustain their speed in the face of the losses due to the electrons. In effect, our electron ball bearings are eating away the package as it moves along. Thus, at the end of the trip, any pulses of E&M energy we have transmitted will be found to be smaller in size. Or, in terms of the kinds of graphs of light intensity or voltage and current we have been using throughout the preceding chapters, the height of all the transmitted pulses will be reduced. We call this loss of energy and related reduction in the size of transmitted pulses *attenuation*. As you might suspect, the longer the cable that we are using, the greater the attenuation. On the other hand, the larger the conductors we use, the less this attenuation will become, up to some limit. Hence, larger, more expensive cables will have less attenuation and be more desirable if this attenuation has negative effects on our ability to move information.

Because we will still be dealing with the problem of noise that is determined by the temperature of the receiving system at the far end, the reduction in the size of our pulses directly reduces the rate at which we can transmit information over a certain cable, as explained in Chapter 14. In Table 15.2 we see typical attenuation figures for various cables. These figures alone explain the willingness to pay more for STP and still more for coaxial cable in applications that require the highest information transmission rates.

TABLE 15.2 THE TABLE SHOWS THE ATTENUATION OF VARIOUS CABLE TYPES DISCUSSED IN THE TEXT. THESE ATTENUATIONS ARE GIVEN IN DECIBELS (DB), A LOGARITHMIC MEASURE. FOR EXAMPLE, 20 DB ATTENUATION CORRESPONDS TO A 10:1 REDUCTION IN SIGNAL LEVEL.

Cable Type	Attenuation per 1000 Feet in dB at 100 MHz
UTP Category 3 (4 pair, 24 AWG)	56
STP (2 pair, 24 AWG)	37.5
Coax, RG-58/U (Thin Ethernet)	60
Coax, RG-8/U (Thick Ethernet)	20

15.2.2 Why Some Cables Are Better than Others

While the previous section explained the desirability of some cables owing to their low attenuation characteristics, it did not explain why they possess these different characteristics other than with respect to behavior versus conductor size. Here we will discuss the role of the "geometry" of the cable.

In a vacuum, each of the above cables would perform nearly as well as the others. However, cables tend to be routed next to each other, and near other metallic objects and generators of E&M energies. The "open" nature of untwisted cable presents a problem in that nearby conductors can steal some of the energy that it carries and can insert unwanted E&M noise. UTP cable still is subject to the loss problem but is less affected by noise pickup because the twists cause interfering pickup signals to cancel themselves when picked up inside of adjacent twists! STP reduces the losses by better confining the E&M to the inside of the shield.

The coaxial cable, because of the complete confinement of the E&M wave, is not subject to the level of loss and noise problems found in other wired cables. Furthermore, because its geometry is very tightly held in position, the signal itself undergoes less distortion in shape while traversing it. In a very rough extension of our analogy of the last section, we can think of the coax as presenting very well manufactured mirrors for the transport of our signal, versus warped mirrors in the case of STP.

15.2.3 Common Uses of the Various Cable Types

Where might we find applications of each of the cable types described above? Here are some examples:

Parallel Conductor Cable Applications

While parallel conductor cable is used extensively for power delivery, about the only signal-carrying application you will find this cable being used to support is as the short extension cord leading from your telephone wall plug to the telephone itself. The short distance and small bandwidth of the signal involved allow use in this application, in which the flat nature of the cable makes it more attractive to the eye in its very visible role.

UTP Cable Applications

UTP cable is found extensively in the so-called *local loop* of the telephone company. The local loop is that wiring that connects your house to the telephone company's local "switch" building. This cable is typically under 18,000 feet in length and suffices for transmission of telephone signals. New kinds of special digital modems for ISDN and XDSL data services can sometimes (depending upon the length and nearby interfering sources) be used to move data at higher speeds than a telephone-signal–based modem. For example 128 kbps (ISDN, bidirectional) to 1.544 Mbps (HDSL in one direction) can be achieved using (now) relatively low cost and very sophisticated special connection devices. Rates as high as 52 Mbps (VDSL in one direction) can be obtained if the length of the local loop is below 3,280 feet.

The telephone companies also make extensive use of UTP for movement of digitized groups of voice signals between their switching stations. The T1 signal unidirectionally carries groups of 24 voice channels in a 1.544 Mbps digital format

📖 XDSL

over 6,000 foot distances between regenerator circuits. We will be discussing this T1 signal at great length in a later chapter.

UTP is also found in the walls (in spaces called plenums) throughout most buildings. It is used to complete the local loop from the building entrance to the telephone wall plates in the rooms.

UTP has found extensive use as a cheap medium for the distribution of medium-speed computer network data connectivity. Ethernet data is routinely transmitted in a signaling system known as 10Base-T Ethernet in which UTP cable is used for distances up to 100 m (328 feet).

UTP can be made with a variety of materials, sizes of conductors, and numbers of pairs inside a single cable. A particularly high quality UTP is called UTP-5. This cable type has been used to support 100 Mbps Ethernet transmissions over distances of 100 m.

STP Cable Applications

STP is used to some extent by telephone companies for moving groups (96) of digitized telephone conversations over distances of 6,000 feet between "repeaters" that receive and retransmit the signal for the next such hop, to span the distance of several miles between telephone company switching stations. The so-called T2 connection involves digital data transmission at speeds of 6.312 Mbps. High-quality STP has been applied by the telephone companies for transmission rates as high as 8.448 Mbps in Europe.

Coaxial Cable Applications

As seen before, coaxial cable is used wherever there exists a need for long-distance, low-attenuation, and low-noise transmission of information.

Probably everyone is familiar with the use of coaxial cable for the transmission of a hundred TV channels into the home via CATV coaxial cable, because 70% of all homes in the United States have CATV service. These cables provide a bandwidth of nearly 1 GHz (that is, 1,000 MHz) into the home. These same cables are capable of transmitting many Gbps of information into those same homes. In fact, the research and test deployment of CATV-based Internet delivery systems is currently a growth industry.

Until recently, coaxial cable has been the major delivery system for 10 and 100 Mbps Ethernet computer network data signals, for hop distances of 500 m (1,640 ft) and 185 m (607 ft), respectively, for the larger and smaller diameter cables. Coaxial cable for this purpose is being rapidly supplanted by UTP cable.

The telephone companies also resort to coaxial cable to bridge larger distances with higher-rate digital connections. One example is the use of coaxial cable to transmit 140 Mbps data signals between telephone switch buildings with a hop distance of up to 2 km (6,562 ft).

15.3 Fiber-Optic Cable

In Chapter 14, we described the construction of fiber-optic cables. This means of guiding an E&M wave has an immense advantage over the use of wire-based wave guides: this system does not depend upon the quality (low resistance) of the conductors to obtain low attenuation propagation of the E&M wave. In fact, the reflecting surface of the waveguide is formed by the surface of an insulator. In effect

FIGURE 15.2 Side view of an optical fiber cable showing the paths of light rays that enter the face at different angles. Note how different the path lengths are of the two rays that are shown.

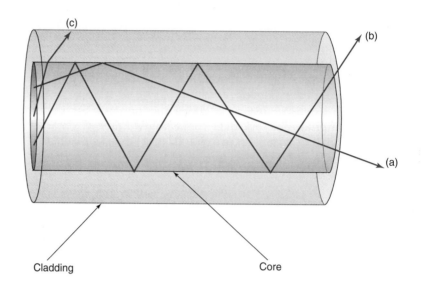

the boundary between two layers of glass or plastic (the core and cladding of the fiber) acts as an ideal (no loss) mirror (as shown in Figure 15.2).

The mirror behavior of this boundary derives from a property of such boundaries and E&M waves that strike them at shallow angles. If an E&M wave strikes such a boundary at an angle below the "critical angle" it undergoes "total internal reflection." You may be familiar with this phenomenon as it can be seen in operation by looking at the bottom side of the water-air boundary at the top of an aquarium from a position at the side of the glass enclosure. If your eye is near enough to the boundary, you see an exceedingly clear mirror view of the scene out the other side of the aquarium.

Thus, the attenuation of a fiber-optic cable is essentially only dependent upon the clarity of the optical material used in the core, and exceedingly high clarities have been achieved.

Other benefits of fiber-optic cable include:

- The total confinement of the E&M wave means that surrounding materials do not increase the attenuation of the wave.

- Because there are no free electrons as would be found in a conductor-based cable, no interference can be generated even by large surrounding magnetic fields.

- Being an insulator, the fiber insulates the connected systems from each other. This is a major factor in cable systems in which atmospheric potentials and ground potentials can cause interfering and sometimes destructive currents to flow parasitically along communication cables.

- For a given attenuation, a fiber cable is exceedingly lightweight and small in diameter. This means that many fibers may be placed in a cable where once only one wire-based cable may have been possible.

15.3.1 Fiber Attenuation Characteristics

Relatively low cost fiber-optic cable available off-the-shelf today exhibits attenuations of less than 0.5 dB/1,000 ft while offering usable bandwidths of hundreds of MHz. A cable exhibiting these characteristics containing four separate fibers, for example, could be purchased in 1999 for under $1.50/foot. Compare this attenuation and cost with that of even high grade coaxial line (see Tables 15.1 and 15.2). Higher cost fiber cables that achieve as little as 0.03 dB/1,000 ft attenuations and usable bandwidths in excess of 1 Tbps (1 Tera bps = 1,000,000 Mbps) have also been constructed.

As exciting as the above numbers are with respect to the capabilities of fiber-optics, there are two new technologies currently being introduced in practice that are simply breathtaking! Fiber integral optical amplification and soliton transmission will be described briefly in the next sections.

15.3.2 Fiber Integral Optical Amplifiers

A new technology is rapidly coming into commercial application and is revolutionizing the long-distance fiber-optic transmission of data. By adding a small amount of *Erbium* additive to a fiber during its manufacture, it is possible to turn the fiber itself into a laser amplification system! By simply passing an optical signal through a short piece of Erbium-doped fiber (typically 10 m) and *pumping* that length with light from another laser, the optical signal will be strengthened and can be returned to its original levels without ever leaving the fiber-optic cable for separate electronic processing. The Erbium-doped fiber amplifier (EDFA) is being incorporated in all of the newest transoceanic cable runs to interconnect the continents with very high-speed, low-maintenance, data service.

For example, a transoceanic cable from the United States to England that uses EDFA technology was completed in September of 1996. This cable holds four fibers each providing 2.5 Gbps of data service, for a total of 10 Gbps of data. It is anticipated that the achievable data rates can be increased by improved methods of signaling and upgrades that will bring each fiber's bit rate to 20 Gbps or greater.

Prior to deployment of this cable, the connection was served by a fiber-optic cable, deployed in 1988, which used electronic repeaters and provided a total of 280 Mbps of data service. Thanks to the immutable undersea electronic repeaters, no upgrades in data rates were possible despite significant new capabilities in fiber transmission and reception systems since that time.

15.3.3 Solitons

A remarkable property of special materials has been discovered that promises to have an impact like that of the EDFA on the speeds and distances achievable with fiber-optic cables. A soliton is a special packet of optical energy within such a cable that does not "disperse." That is, it is immune to the low-pass phenomenon that we have previously said characterizes all physical systems that transmit waves. Thus, a fiber using soliton transmission can achieve fantastic data rates over large distances.

Nippon Telephone and Telegraph (NTT) of Japan, for example, has demonstrated soliton transmission of a 10 Gbps data stream over a distance of 50,000 km (over 30,000 miles). Laboratory tests show that soliton technology may provide data rates in excess of 1 Tbps (10^{12} bps, or 1 million megabits per second) in the future over transcontinental and intercontinental distances.

15.3.4 How Fast Can Data Be Delivered to the Home?

As the previous section makes amply clear, high-speed data transmission needs some combination of high-quality cable and sophisticated electronics. As we have seen previously, the theoretical and practical maximum for data transmission using the normal telephone connection is about 56 kbits/second. However, several new technologies are competing to provide much higher-speed data service to the home. For many years, the telephone operating companies have been planning for Dial-up data service based on the system called Integrated Services—Digital Network, or ISDN. In most larger cities today, an individual or business can purchase special ISDN equipment and ISDN service from the telephone company (which means that the telephone company connects your line to special digital equipment and not the usual analog voice signal handling equipment). This provides up to 128 kbps bidirectional data services. Unfortunately, this may be a case of "too little, too late" in the bandwidth wars, as modern modems can provide almost 56 kpbs without special arrangements, and even 128 kbps is seen as quite slow compared to local area network speeds on the order of millions of bits per second. Some telephone companies are experimenting with the higher-speed XDSL (various Digital Subscriber Loop) technologies. These provide asymmetric services (high-speed movement of data to your distant computer and low speed away from it) that are suitable for World Wide Web-like uses in which users typically point and click their way through information-rich documents. However, many users do not live close enough to telephone switch buildings to enjoy the benefits of the highest-speed versions of this technology. Meanwhile, CATV companies are upgrading their equipment to take advantage of the very high potential of their cable connection into your home. This is often referred to (somewhat incorrectly) as "cable modem" service. Much CATV equipment in place now can only move information in one direction: into your home. However, initial demand appears to be demonstrating that sufficient customers exist to warrant upgrading the cable electronics for two-way data communications. Data rates on the order of at least one Mbps into homes are quite feasible.

Finally, there is the possibility of new "cable" being brought into each of our homes: fiber optic cable. This form of cable is cheap (in comparison to the number of other cables necessary to deliver the same services) and promises nearly inexhaustible bandwidth (multi-Gbps speeds) for all applications.

Summary

In this chapter we have seen how changes in small physical details of the construction of a pair of wires, or a fiber of glass, can have tremendous impact on their information-carrying capability. To electrical engineers, the recent advances in the technology of simple twisted pairs of wires to enable them to transmit millions or even billions of bits per second is amazing. Given these rapid advances in capability of each medium, it is safe to predict that wire, fiber, and radio transmission will all coexist well into the third millenium.

Try These Exercises

1. Find examples of at least three different signal-carrying wires or fibers in the place where you live or work. Describe the wire or fiber and explain what type of information it is carrying, including the bandwidth or bit rate if possible.

2. Explain the concept of attenuation in cables, and describe two different ways in which this problem can be dealt with.

3. Clearly, the home represents a very large market for high-speed data communications. Briefly describe several specific uses for that data service, and contrast the differences in those uses (for example, two-way vs. one-way, real-time requirement, equal or unequal data rates in each directions, etc.) which may relate to the type of home data service provided, and who provides it (telephone or cable company, etc.).

4. Compare the use of unshielded pair (UTP) cable, RG-58/U coaxial cable, and fiber-optic cable for the following data transmission use. In this application the maximum distance between terminals is expected to be 700 feet, and the maximum allowed attenuation at 100 MHz is 40 dB. If that attenuation is exceeded, then a "repeater" which costs $100 must be installed in the line. Use the costs and characteristics of the three cable types from the text. Determine the total attenuation, total cost, and necessity of a repeater for the three cable types for the maximum distance. Repeat for a distance of 200 feet. Comment on other factors such as installation costs.

5. If a maximum attenuation between repeaters of 40 dB is allowed for a fiber-optic system, determine the maximum repeater spacing for the two fiber attenuation characteristics (0.5 dB/1,000 ft and 0.03 dB/1,000 ft) mentioned in the text. How many repeaters would be required for a fiber-optic system of each attenuation characteristic circling the Earth at the equator?

6. High-speed Digital Subscriber Line (DSL) systems use existing copper wiring ("loops") from the telephone central office to the customer. The characteristics of this wiring are similar, but inferior, to the UTP wires discussed in the text. With some simplifying assumptions, determine what percent of its customers a central office could serve. Use the following assumptions: all of the customers are uniformly distributed at a density of 600 customers per square mile, at distances from the central office ranging from 0 to 5 miles. At 1 MHz the loop attenuation is 7 dB/1,000 ft. The maximum usable attenuation is 80 dB. No repeaters are permitted.

16

Radio-Frequency and Satellite Systems

Objectives

Wireless information transmission is the subject of this chapter. While commercial radio communications is over 75 years old, it has recently been experiencing explosive growth in new applications. We will learn about the following important principles and applications of radio:

▲ the fundamental design parameters for a wireless system, including signal bandwidth, transmission distance, transmitter frequency and power, and limitations on antenna location;

▲ limitations of "line of sight" in communications system design, including satellite systems;

▲ basics of antenna design; and

▲ the Global Positioning System as an example of a wireless information system.

16.1 Introduction

Radio communications has been in existence for over 75 years. In the period after World War II, its uses multiplied rapidly, with applications ranging from entertainment broadcast (AM and FM radio, television) to point-point application-specific communications (military, police, air traffic control, and space exploration) to long distance telephone links, to hobbyists (amateur and CB radio). The past few decades have seen another explosion of radio applications, driven by several related technical developments: Earth satellites, particularly geosynchronous satellites, and cheap high-performance, high-frequency electronics.

Prior to the emergence of the satellite, essentially all of the radio-frequency spectrum space was in use in populated areas. Satellites orbiting above the Earth provided a new direction to point microwave antennas: *up*. This new direction produced no interference with existing signals, and in addition enabled signals to propagate (via the satellite) almost halfway around the Earth. Previously, high-frequency radio signals had been restricted to line-of-sight distances on Earth (about 40 miles maximum). Radio signals in the lower frequencies (such as AM broadcast) and somewhat higher can travel long distances because of reflection off the ionosphere, but this phenomenon is not stable or reliable. Also, these low-frequency signals do not permit the transmission of wide bandwidth messages.

16.2 Overview of Radio Communications System Design

It should be noted that the terminology for various sections of the radio spectrum was developed when the technology was in its infancy, and electronic equipment could only work properly at the low-frequency end of the spectrum. At that time, signals in the 100 MHz range were labeled Very High Frequencies (VHF), and the region above that (400 MHz) was called Ultra High Frequency (UHF). Above that comes the "microwave" region, referring to the shorter wavelength of these higher frequency signals. The wavelengths are actually not at all microscopic, being in the centimeter region. All of these terms are still in common use (as in VHF and UHF television).

Cheap, high-performance radio transmitters meant that we could now think of producing many low-power transmitters and receivers. A benefit of low transmitter power is that the signal does not travel very far; this allows other users who are relatively nearby to use the same frequency. The distance limitation may be overcome by putting a sufficient number of base stations in strategic locations so that one is always within range of the users. This is the principle of the cellular telephone system.

There are a few basic parameters in the design of RF (radio-frequency) systems:

- Transmitter power
- Transmitter frequency, which determines the characteristics of signal "propagation" (how far the signal will travel, whether it goes in all directions or is beamed like a searchlight, the types of interference likely to occur)
- Receiver sensitivity
- Desired bandwidth and/or bit rate
- Limitations on antenna size, location, etc.
- Desired transmission distance

We have already learned a little about the cellular telephone system, which is actually one of the more complex RF communications systems in existence. This system would not be possible without current computer technology, which makes it possible to manage a complex, distributed system of wired and wireless links, and keep track of calls in progress, switching them among transmitter sites as appropriate. Another requirement for the cellular system, of course, is the availability of inexpensive, miniature RF electronics.

Let's look at the design of a simple point-point RF communications system, as might be used by police personnel either in automobiles or with hand-held radios. The same principles apply to the design of each cell in a cellular system. Following are the parameters:

- *Desired transmission distance*: While more is usually better with respect to this parameter, other considerations will limit the distance, so it is important to consider the purpose to be served. For example, consider coverage of a small city for police radio; in this case, a radius of 10 miles would be more than adequate.
- *Transmitter frequency*: Often this is given. We will assume that this service will be using a Federal Communications Commission (FCC) frequency allocation in the 800 MHz region; this means that the FCC has assigned us a particular band of frequencies around 800 MHz.
- *Transmitter power*: There are two quite different transmitters in this situation: one or more "base stations" and the mobile units. The transmitter power of hand-held units will be limited by two factors: available battery power, and

biological concerns because the antenna will be quite close to the user's head. The latter factor is a function of frequency, with more power being permitted at lower frequencies. At 800 MHz, 1 watt of transmitted power meets the biological limit, and also permits convenient battery size with reasonable life (on the order of 1 hour of transmission time). It should be noted that the power used while receiving is a small fraction of the transmitter power. For the base station, higher power is certainly possible; powers on the order of 25 watts are typical. More power would be of little use, because while the range in one direction would be increased, there would be no increase in the other direction, and the system requirement is for two-way communication.

• *Receiver sensitivity*: The receiver parameter corresponding to transmitter power is receiver sensitivity. This represents the amount of power at the receiver antenna needed to produce a usable signal (audible speech in this case). This quantity should be quoted on a "per unit bandwidth" basis, but often the bandwidth is assumed, as in an AM or FM radio receiver. A typical value would be about one picowatt (10^{-12} watt) for audio bandwidth (about 4 kHz). One picowatt is a very small value: 0.000000000001 watt; for comparison a standard electric light bulb consumes about 100 watts. For larger bandwidth systems (such as televison), the required power would increase in proportion to the bandwidth. For example, a system with 40 kHz signal bandwidth would require about 10 picowatts at the receiver.

• *Limitations on antenna size and location*: For a given frequency, there is a direct correlation between antenna size and the amount of power received. Also, for a given amount of power there is an inverse correlation between frequency and antenna size (i.e., at higher frequencies antennas may be smaller). Practical considerations limit the antenna size for the hand-held unit. This is not so much a limitation on the base station. Antenna size is often measured with respect to the wavelength of the RF frequency in use. For this case (800 MHz) the wavelength is about 0.4 meters. A reasonably efficient antenna has a length of one quarter of the wavelength, so our hand-held antenna need only be about 10 cm, or 4 inches, long.

Now the system has been specified, but one question remains: "Will it work?" To answer that question, we must determine whether for 1 watt transmitted, an antenna 10 miles away will intercept at least 1 picowatt of power. A precise answer to this question requires some rather detailed calculations, and a knowledge of the terrain and other obstructions between the base station and all possible locations of the hand-held units. Given the possibility of a hilly topography, and the fact that 800 MHz signals travel essentially in straight lines, and do not penetrate most obstructions, the answer is almost certainly, "No." But let's assume that the base station antenna is mounted high enough that it can "see" all of the locations within 10 miles. We can then apply a few very simple principles to get an approximate idea of the received power. To a reasonable approximation, we can assume that the 1 watt of transmitted power propagates equally in all directions, so that if we put the transmitter in the center of a sphere we would observe two things: (1) at any spot on the surface of the sphere, we measure the same power; and (2) if we add up the power per unit surface area over the entire sphere, the result is 1 watt, the transmitted power. The percentage of the total power on any specific surface area is given by the ratio of the given surface area to the total area of the sphere.

Another reasonable approximation is that the equivalent area of a linear antenna is that of a circular disk with diameter equal to the antenna length. For our case this is 0.03 square meters. The total surface area of a sphere of 10 mile

(16,000 m) radius is 3.2×10^9 square meters. The ratio of the antenna equivalent area to the total spherical area (and hence the ratio of received-to-transmitted power) is approximately 9×10^{-12}. In other words, for 1 watt transmitted, we will only receive about 9×10^{-12} watt. This is more than sufficient to meet our receiver specification of 1×10^{-12} watt. This gives us some confidence that in the actual situation, even with attenuation from vegetation, buildings, and so forth, the system will operate as designed.

16.2.1 Antenna Improvements

Practically, this result means that we will need more than one transmitter site to cover all of the desired area. There might be other possible approaches, such as the use of larger antennas at the receiver, and/or *directional* antennas (which focus all of the available transmission power in particular directions, resulting in a stronger signal that only goes to certain locations). Generally we would like the transmitted energy to follow straight paths along the surface of the Earth; we are unlikely to be transmitting vertically (unless this were an aircraft communications system) and we almost certainly will not be transmitting into the ground.

It is possible to design fairly simple antennas that radiate most of their energy in a plane, rather than a sphere. This obviously represents a great increase in efficiency. This concept may be carried further with antennas that radiate energy in narrow beams, like searchlights. In fact, for frequencies such as in this example, and higher, such antennas may look like searchlight reflectors. This is obviously impractical for hand-held units, and for base stations where signals may need to go in all directions, but it is very practical for applications such as wireless voice or data links between fixed sites. Another advantage is that because the energy is confined to a narrow beam, other users nearby may make use of the same frequency. An important concept of antennas that has been alluded to here is that they are *reciprocal*; that is, they behave the same way with regard to direction (and all other characteristics) for both transmission and reception.

16.3 Satellite and Other Long-Distance Communications Systems

Communications satellites provided the first long-distance, wide-bandwidth communications service. Before the advent of communications satellites it was not possible to broadcast live television around the world. Why not? Consider the two alternatives: conventional radio and cables. To accommodate television bandwidth (approximately 5 MHz), the necessary radio frequency would have to be many times 5 MHz, perhaps 100 MHz. These frequencies travel only in line of sight, so they require transmitting stations approximately every 40 miles to accommodate the curvature of the Earth. Such systems were in place across the United States, and some other continents besides North America, but were obviously not feasible across the oceans. Coaxial cable systems did span the oceans, but they were of very low bandwidth (less than 5 MHz) because coaxial cables have substantial attenuation at higher frequencies, requiring frequent amplification of the signal. These amplifiers were in place along the submerged cable, but the distance between them was maximized so that only a few would be required in the ocean span. With the launching of communications satellites (Telstar I was the first commercial satellite), high-frequency, line-of-sight frequencies could be used. Earth stations use large dish antennas to beam energy to the satellite, and the satellite receives the signals and transmits them back to Earth via its dish antenna. Satellites in low Earth orbit (typical altitudes are on the order of 100 miles) complete one orbit approximately every 90 minutes. In this case the Earth station would have to constantly adjust the direction of its dish antenna to keep its beam pointed at the satellite.

A more serious problem is that that the satellite would only be in view of the ground station for about 15 minutes before it would "set" (like the sun). This problem could be addressed by orbiting a large number of satellites, so that at least one is always in view, but this is obviously costly. A yet more serious problem is that the distance between two ground stations that can both see the same satellite for a significant period of time is rather limited, and certainly not the Earth's diameter, as we would like. The simple solution is to make the orbital diameter very large (approximately 23,500 miles). At this altitude, the period of each orbit is 24 hours, and hence the orbital rate can match the Earth's rotation rate. Then, the satellite will appear to remain above the same spot on the Earth at all times.

This high orbit causes two problems: the radio propagation distances are very long, resulting in both a great power loss and a significant time delay. The power loss represents an engineering challenge that has been overcome. The delay is immaterial for some purposes such as many types of data transmission, but is a significant impediment to telephone conversations.

Shortly after communications satellites were established, fiber-optic communications were developed. They provide much higher bandwidth than either radio or cable systems, have low attenuation, solving the repeater spacing problem, and are relatively inexpensive to install. Hence, for locations with large communications needs, fiber has become the system of choice. However, satellites will remain in considerable demand because they can provide immediate service to any spot on the globe where a small Earth station can be set up. Indeed, these "Earth stations" will soon be as compact and easy to operate as a cellular telephone (although the cost per minute will be much higher).

16.4 The Global Positioning System

The Global Positioning System (GPS) is an excellent example of a modern radio and satellite based information system, which demonstrates technology and capabilities that would have been inconceivable a short time ago. It is a good example for this book because it incorporates diverse types of information technology and it serves a breathtakingly broad range of purposes, from guiding smart bombs to locating fish. Following is a list of the major technologies that GPS involves:

- satellite communications
- powerful, miniature computers
- high-performance microwave radio receivers
- inexpensive graphics displays
- large digital memories
- geographic databases with fine detail
- very high-accuracy timekeeping

The basic function of GPS is quite simple: to determine the position of the GPS receiver anywhere on (or above) the Earth. This position is determined in terms of latitude, longitude, and elevation above sea level. The only basic limitation on the system is that the receiver must have a relatively clear view of the sky so that it can receive signals from at least three (preferably four or more) GPS satellites at different locations in the sky. Once the receiver has determined position in the units mentioned above, the processor may then convert that location into something more useful to the user. This may be anything from a street address to a location displayed on an electronic map. To be precise, with signals from three satellites, the GPS system can determine a location anywhere on the surface of the Earth. With signals from four (or more) satellites, the altitude can also be known, so that the position in 3D space may be determined. No other navigation system can perform this 3D positioning!

16.4.1 How Does GPS Work?

The principle of operation of the GPS system, *triangulation*, is very simple. On the surface of the Earth, if you know your distance from a given point, you know that you are somewhere on a circle with that point in the center. If at the same time you also know your distance from a different point, you know that you are on another given circle. Those circles cross at (at most) two points, so you have narrowed your position down to one of two points. With a known distance from a third point, you can identify your unique location. With GPS you can actually identify your location in three dimensions, so the circles are replaced with intersecting spheres.

Given that simple principle, how does the GPS receiver determine these distances, and the locations of the points from which the distances are measured? This last detail is particularly tricky because the points GPS uses are actually satellites in constant motion! The distance determination is easy, at least in principle, by making use of the known speed of light. Each satellite broadcasts a known signal at a known time, and the GPS receiver determines the time at which it receives the signal. The delay between the transmission and reception times, together with known speed of radio wave transmission (essentially the speed of light) may then be used to determine the distance from the satellite to the GPS receiver. This calculation is performed for all of the satellites from which the GPS can receive signals. Given that information, some trigonometric calculations in the GPS's microprocessor (as described above with the intersecting circles or spheres) can determine the GPS receiver position, assuming that the satellite positions are known. Even though the satellites are moving, their positions at each instant of time can be determined precisely because they follow the laws of celestial mechanics. Small perturbations are constantly monitored and updated from the GPS operations center (controlled by the U.S. Department of Defense). These updates are constantly transmitted by the satellites along with identification and time information.

The set of 24 GPS satellites are in orbits arranged so that at any given time the satellites are distributed fairly evenly above the Earth, so that four or more satellites are always in view. Use of more than the minimum number of satellites improves the accuracy of the position calculation. The satellites orbit at an altitude of approximately 11,000 miles. This is a high orbit and results in an orbital period of about 12 hours. Hence, the satellites move with respect to the receivers, but at a slow speed compared to low-altitude satellites, which complete an orbit in 90 minutes. Each satellite has an expected lifetime of about 10 years, and replacement satellites are launched on a regular schedule. The first GPS satellite was launched in 1978. It is interesting to note that while the technology is over 20 years old, it has only been since about 1995 that the cost has become low enough for widespread adoption outside the military. This book contains examples of many other technologies where this delay between concept and market acceptance occurred.

Each satellite transmits four types of information:

1. an identifying number (from 1 to 32 to provide for spares among the operational group of 24);
2. its location in astronomical terms;
3. time information; and
4. maintenance and "health" information so that receivers can identify unreliable data.

All of this information is coded using the principles described elsewhere in this book, and transmitted on a frequency of 1,575 MHz. This high frequency is necessary to provide the needed time accuracy. It is also convenient in that it allows the use of very small antennas.

16.4.2 Components of the GPS System

The overall GPS system contains only three elements: the satellites (described above), the receivers (described below), and the system control center, which monitors the health and accuracy of the satellites. This GPS system is elegant, useful, and free to the user, who must only pay the cost of a receiver (which may be as low as $100 or even less). A typical portable GPS receiver is shown in Figure 16.1. Who pays for the satellites, the system monitoring and control, and so on? The U.S. taxpayer pays, through the Department of Defense. The GPS system was originally developed and implemented purely for U.S. defense, and the U.S. military is still a major user. Recognizing that such a worldwide system could be useful to enemies of the U.S., the system implements a feature called *selective availability*, which purposely degrades the accuracy available to non-U.S. military users. Further, the U.S. military can turn the entire system off at a moment's notice if need be. As civilian uses are becoming more common and important, and as some uses (particularly in marine and aircraft navigation) become based solely on GPS, this degradation is being phased out, although ultimate control of the system remains with the U.S. government.

Typical civilian accuracy is on the order of 100 feet, with occasional errors up to 300 feet. For many uses that is more than adequate. However, for some purposes (ranging from aircraft landing to surveying, excavation, etc.) that much error is unacceptable. For these situations, several types of enhancements are available that provide accuracy down to the 1 centimeter level.

Prior to GPS, the existing navigation and position-determining systems were much more limited. These systems were intended for either maritime or aircraft navigation, but they did not provide complete coverage of the Earth, did not provide 3D (position and elevation) information, required larger and more expensive receivers, and hence were of much more limited usefulness. GPS is an excellent example of a breakthrough invention, which generates many new products and capabilities. Following is a partial list:

1. aircraft navigation;
2. marine navigation: exact position information is now easily available to all boaters at a very low cost (a few hundred dollars);
3. hiking, hunting, and other outdoor activities;
4. driving: for route finding, emergencies;
5. surveying;
6. construction; and
7. farming (yes, literally each seed may be placed in a farmer's field guided by GPS)

FIGURE 16.1 A portable GPS of the type used by general aviation (private) pilots. This unit will display a detailed aviation map and shows the current location of the airplane on that map as well as a depiction of the route to be flown.

The GPS receiver contains five major elements: an antenna, a sensitive radio receiver, a microprocessor, a database, and a display. The function of the radio receiver is to deliver the four types of information described above to the processor. The microprocessor performs the distance calculations as described above, as well as many other functions that greatly increase the usefulness of the GPS. These additional functions include: speed of travel, direction of travel, route to follow to get to a desired destination, time required to reach the destination, and so on. The database ranges from nothing to a complete topographical and street map of a large geographical area or a complete listing of all the airports and navigational facilities in North America. The database is typically updatable to keep it current.

It should be noted that formally GPS is a "positioning" system, rather than a "navigation" system. What is the difference? A positioning system tells the user where the receiver is located at the present time. A navigation system tells the user which direction to go in order to get to a desired location. A simple navigation system is the compass. It shows the user which direction to go to reach the magnetic north pole. However, it provides no direct information on the actual location of the user. Clearly, with a database (map), a positioning system may be used for navigation by comparing the known location to the location of the destination. However, the reverse is not true, at least not in a simple way.

Summary

The basic principles of radio communications system design are rather simple, and follow from the fundamental properties of radio propagation. Because the radio spectrum space is strictly limited, good system design to make most efficient use of this limited resource is essential. Broadcast radio, communications satellites, the Global Positioning System (GPS), and two-way, point–point communications systems are examples of very different radio communications systems, each designed for a specific purpose. It is important to realize that not all communications are human–human communications. The Global Positioning System makes extensive use of communications, but its output is a *position*, not a message conveyed from one point to another.

Try These Exercises

1. Explain why it would be impractical to use the AM radio band for television transmission.
2. Fairly large antennas are necessary for reception of signals from geosynchronous satellites (examples include the direct broadcast satellite services which compete with cable TV). Determine how much power a geosynchronous satellite would need to transmit (assuming it transmitted equally in all directions) in order for an antenna on Earth of 1 foot radius to receive 1 picowatt.
3. How many geosynchronous satellites are needed to achieve worldwide coverage? Explain your answer and use a diagram.
4. In GPS, errors in timing result in errors in position determination. In two dimensions show the result of these timing errors. Explain in writing and with a diagram.
5. The output of a GPS unit is the location of the receiver. How can GPS be used to *navigate* to a desired destination?

6. In the text the received power for a radio transmission distance of 10 miles with 1 watt of transmitted power is approximated, and is determined to be adequate for communications. Determine approximately how much power a cellular handset would have to transmit if we wished to communicate over a distance of 100 miles. Note that other problems such as the earth's curvature would arise with this distance, but we will ignore these other effects here.

7. Assume that we desire a position accuracy of ±100 feet with the Global Positioning System. What accuracy in time measurement is required to accomplish this? For satellites positioned as in the actual system, what is the total time delay from satellite to GPS receiver, and what is the percent accuracy required in this time measurement to achieve the desired position accuracy?

8. The radio spectrum that is available for practical use extends from about 100 kHz to about 30 GHz. How many 10 MHz data channels can be transmitted simultaneously? Given that this spectrum is all that is available, and that your answer to the first part of this question is a rather small number, explain why wireless transmission can meet a large portion of our data communications needs. Explain how you could determine whether there is any chance of wireless systems meeting all of our communications needs from a spectral space point of view.

17

Large-Capacity Storage

Objectives

An important component of most information systems is some form of data storage facility. This chapter introduces the physical principles and technologies of modern storage devices. You will learn about the following concepts and practical systems:

▲ magnetic storage systems, including tapes and discs;

▲ the Compact Disc (CD) which stores digital data optically, and which has found widespread use both for data and music storage; and

▲ the DVD (Digital Versatile Disc or Digital Video Disc) which extends and enhances CD technology, allowing more data to be stored on one disc.

17.1 Introduction

In this chapter, we will discuss options for storage of "large" amounts of data. It is interesting to note that the definition of "large" in the computer and information world changes constantly. Only a few years ago, data sizes on the order of 1 Mbyte were considered large. We have now moved to the Gbyte range (a factor of 1,000 larger), with no end in sight. To some extent this growth reflects the tremendous information-processing capability of humans, which the computer and information world is just now catching up with.

The various storage media, the formats they use, and their capabilities will be described. We will also give some insight into trends for the future of large-capacity data storage. This chapter will address devices intended for permanent or semipermanent storage of information, and will not address the internal memories of computers, which are generally reloaded each time the computer is turned on from one of the devices described here.

17.2 Magnetic Disks and Tapes

Magnetic disk and tape storage is almost as old as the computer itself. Magnetic recording was invented in the middle of the twentieth century, initially as a means to record the human voice. It was a more flexible and easier-to-use medium than the phonograph, which was the only sound recording device previously available.

The basic principle of magnetic recording is quite simple: a thin coating of a magnetic material is deposited on a surface such as a plastic tape. The tape is moved under an electromagnet (simply a coil of wire) in which an electric current proportional to the sound is flowing. This electromagnet magnetizes the material under it with strength proportional to the current at that instant, which is also proportional to the sound intensity at that instant. Hence, the tape contains a linear record of sound pressure intensity. This record may be read by passing the tape (at the same speed at which it was recorded) under a magnetic pickup. We are all very familiar with tape recorders from the music cassette.

Digital magnetic tape recording operates exactly as above, except that instead of a smooth (analog) variation of magnetization with sound level, only two magnetic levels are recorded, representing binary one and zero. From this basic principle, many technological enhancements have been made, primarily to maximize the amount of data that can be recorded on a given length of tape. These enhancements include making the magnetic recording head (the electromagnet) as small as possible, and recording multiple tracks of bits in parallel with each other down the tape.

Having explained magnetic tape recording, we can invoke the phonograph analogy to explain that a magnetic disk stores the same information as the tape, but in circular tracks around the disk. So-called "floppy disks" are quite familiar, and the "hard disks" inside computers operate similarly, but at higher speeds and with smaller tolerances to provide higher capacity. A high-capacity hard disk will have multiple "platters" inside the case. The operation of a hard disk looks quite similar to that of a phonograph, with a pivoting arm above each platter (actually each side of each platter) carrying the read/write head.

Chapter 4 contains more details about the way in which the data is organized on disks and tapes for ease of access.

17.3 The Compact Disc

The Compact Disc (CD, Plate 35) provides a standardized medium for the storage of digital data. A single CD-ROM containing computer data can accommodate up to 650 MB of data, over 450 times the capacity of a conventional 1.44 MB floppy diskette, on a 1.2 mm thick disc only 12 centimeters in diameter. Audio-CD technology has, for the most part, replaced analog phonograph technology among not only high-fidelity enthusiasts but the general populace. The fundamental reason for this transition is the ability to represent the audio signal digitally. In addition to providing high and nondeteriorating quality, digital representation provides unprecedented searching, editing, storage, and transmission capabilities. CD-ROMs are identical to Audio-CDs, but to facilitate computer access, a different standard is used to arrange the data on the disc.

Physically, a CD is composed of a thin film of aluminum embedded between two discs of polycarbonate plastic. Information is recorded on the CD as a series of microscopic pits in the aluminum film arranged along a continuous spiral track. If expanded linearly, the track would span over three miles. Using a low power infrared laser (with a wavelength of 780 nm[1]), the data is retrieved from the CD using photosensitive sensors that measure the intensity of the reflected light as the laser traverses the track. Because the recovered bit stream is simply a bit pattern, any digitally encoded information can be stored on a CD. Figure 17.1 illustrates the physical composition of a standard CD.

In the early 1980s, Phillips and Sony published the Compact Disc Digital Audio Standard, the first in a series of CD technology standards. The Compact Disc Digital Audio Standard is commonly referred to as the "Red Book," and defines several parameters fundamental to Audio-CD technology, including the physical

---

[1] nm is the abbreviation for nanometer, which is equal to 0.000000001 meter.

FIGURE 17.1 Physical composition of a standard CD.

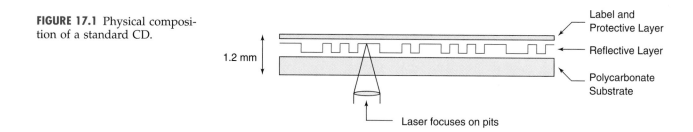

📖 **Frame**

disc size, rotational velocity, data arrangement, track size, frame size, and so forth. Audio-CD data is organized as one or more variable length tracks, with each track usually corresponding to a song. To conform to the Red Book specification, a maximum of 99 tracks is allowed on a single Audio-CD disc. Audio-CD data is divided into fixed-length units as follows:

- A frame consists of 24 bytes of user data (plus 1 byte of subchannel coding and 8 bytes of ECC code).
- 98 frames make up a block, each with $24 \times 98 = 2,352$ bytes of user data.
- 75 blocks make up a larger storage unit called a "second" for reasons that will be obvious later.
- 60 seconds make up a "minute."
- 74 minutes make up one complete CD of storage for an audio CD.

When playing an audio CD, the rotational velocity of the CD is constantly varied so that 75 blocks are read per second. That is, one "second" is read per second. Thus, $75 \times 2352 = 176,400$ bytes are read per second. The standard sampling rate of an analog audio signal in preparation for Audio-CDs is 44,100 Hz. Each sample is then quantized and represented digitally using 16 bits. Because an Audio-CD provides two channels, the data rate is:

$$R = 44,100 \frac{\text{samples}}{\text{sec} * \text{channel}} * 2\frac{\text{bytes}}{\text{sample}} * 2 \text{ channels} = 176,400 \frac{\text{bytes}}{\text{second}}.$$

So, there is exactly enough data read to drive two audio channels for exactly 74 minutes saved as 783,216,000 bytes (747 MB[2]).

Soon after the publication of the "Red Book," Phillips and Sony recognized the potential of using CDs for computer data storage, and thus published the "Yellow Book" standard in 1984. The Yellow Book defines the CD-ROM (Read Only Memory) standard. Because computer applications are far more susceptible to errors in data than most audio and video applications, the previously defined sector was redefined to increase the error detection and correction capability.

A standard CD-ROM sector, also called a *block*, contains 12 bytes of synchronization data, 4 bytes of header information, 2,048 bytes of user data, and 288 bytes of Error Detection and Correction Codes (EDC/ECC). Optionally, the 288 bytes can be allocated to user data for applications that are not as sensitive to corrupted data; for example, some audio and video applications. The Yellow Book defines both 63 and 74 "minute" CD-ROMs. Similar to Audio-CDs, 75 sectors make up a "minute." Table 17.1 summarizes the capacities of standard Yellow Book CD-ROMs.

In 1985, a common format for the presentation of user data files was agreed upon, and the ISO 9660 standard was shortly thereafter released. This standard ensures interoperability between various vendors' CD-ROM drives and CD-ROM disks. Because CD-ROMs and Audio-CDs are physically identical, a typical CD-

---

[2] MB represents (2^{20}) bytes.

TABLE 17.1   YELLOW BOOK CD-ROM CAPACITIES

Minutes per disc	63	74
Sectors per second	75	75
Sectors per minute	4,500	4,500
Bytes per sector (EDC/ECC)	2,048	2,048
Sectors per disc	283,500	333,000
Bytes per disc	580,608,000	681,984,000
Disc capacity	553.71 MB	650.39 MB

ROM drive can play Audio-CDs with only the need to use appropriate software for the interpretation of the different standards.

In 1986, Philips published the "Green Book" standard. The Green Book is the basis for CD-Interactive (CD-I) and provides a complete hardware and software specification for interactive audio and video. Although a CD-I disc is physically identical to a CD-ROM disc, CD-I uses an Adaptive Pulse Code Modulation (ADPCM) compression scheme and requires an appropriate decoding module. Therefore, CD-I is not compatible with standard CD-ROM drives. The Green Book makes interleaving data possible; thus, audio, video, and data can be intermixed on a single track on the CD.

Published by Philips, Sony, and Microsoft as an extension to the "Yellow Book" in 1989, the CD-ROM eXtended Architecture (XA) standard provides both CD-I and CD-ROM functionality. CD-ROM XA allows both computer data and AD-PCM audio, video, and picture data to be interleaved on the same track. CD-ROM XA drives are capable of reading standard CD-ROM discs, but standard CD-ROM drives are not capable of reading CD-ROM XA discs.

Photo-CD, defined in the "Orange Book," standardizes the storage of still photographs at a variety of resolutions using a proprietary storage format on a recordable CD. In addition to Photo-CD players, the images can be accessed using CD-ROM XA and CD-I players and the appropriate Photo-CD read software.

Also defined in the Orange Book, CD-Recordable (CD-R) is a special CD that can be written once using a CD recorder. Once written, data contained on the CD cannot be altered. Also defined in the Orange Book, CD-Rewritable (CD-RW) allows the disc to be erased and written more than once. Both CD-R and CD-RW discs can be read using a standard CD-ROM drive.

In addition to the standards listed above, several other CD standards have been published, including CDTV, CD+G, and CD+MIDI. As can quickly be noticed from this section alone, the development of CD technology has been an active area of research throughout the 1980s and 1990s. Table 17.2 summarizes the features and capabilities of some of the more common CD standards.

Currently, CD-ROM technology is the most common method for software distribution. Pirating, or illegal copying of software, results in the loss of billions of dollars for software distributors. These costs are ultimately transferred to the end users, and accordingly, some form of secure software distribution is necessary. Several approaches are available today, including both hardware and software solutions. Typically, the software-only approach employs an access code distributed at the time of purchase. This code is then used to unlock the software. However, once unlocked, access to the disk is usually unlimited and thus, the data can easily be copied.

TABLE 17.2 COMMON CD TECHNOLOGY STANDARDS

Medium	Specification	Features
Audio-CD	Red Book	defines fundamental parameters to CD technology
CD-ROM	Yellow Book ISO 9660	standardizes CD computer data storage, ensures interoperability across multiple vendors
CD-ROM XA	Yellow Book	provides both CD-I and CD-ROM capabilities
CD-I	Green Book	specification for interactive audio and video, provides for the interleaving of data
CD-Photo	Orange Book	write once capability, standardizes still photographs, supports a variety of resolutions
CD-R	Orange Book	write once capability
CD-RW	Orange Book	erase and write many times capability

A more secure approach employs a hardware and software hybrid scheme. The hybrid approach typically involves a software encryption algorithm and a hardware decryption device, often referred to as a hardware lock. Most hardware locks attach to a port on the computer, usually the printer port, but can be interfaced directly with the computer's motherboard. One approach used is to encrypt all sensitive data on the disk prior to distribution, and decrypt the data on the fly via the hardware decryption device. Other schemes involve electronic fingerprints, expiration timers, and metering services.

17.4 Digital Versatile Disk

In 1995, the DVD Consortium was founded by 10 companies to specify and promote standards for a high-capacity disc technology, known as the Digital Versatile Disk (DVD). Actually, the acronym DVD has changed its meaning. It originally stood for *Digital Video Disk*, but when this new technology was determined to be quite useful for data other than video, the meaning of the "V" was changed. In April 1997, the DVD Consortium renamed itself the DVD Forum. Currently, over 100 companies are members of the DVD Forum.

DVD is capable of storing audio, video, and data using a single digital format. Similar to CD technology, DVD records data in a spiral track of pits and the data is read using laser technology. Using a smaller-wavelength laser (635/650 nm), DVD offers increased data capacity over conventional CD technology by decreasing the pit size and track spacing. Further, additional capacity is gained by reducing the overhead of error detection and correction. Data can be recorded in as many as four layers, up to two layers per side. A single layer is capable of holding approximately 4.7 billion bytes of data, about seven times that of conventional CD technology.

When data is stored on two layers per side, a semireflective layer is used. Because the second layer has a lower reflectivity, the capacity is only 3.8 billion bytes, as compared to the fully reflective layer, which is capable of storing 4.7 billion bytes. Thus, a single side of a DVD disk is capable of storing up to 8.5 billion bytes of data. Because double-sided DVDs are available, a single DVD is capable of holding between 4.7 and 17 billion bytes of digital data. Table 17.3 summarizes the capacities of DVD-ROM.

TABLE 17.3 STANDARDIZED DVD-ROM CAPACITIES

DVD-ROM	Capacity (billions of bytes)
single sided, one layer	4.7
single sided, two layers	8.5
double sided, one layer per side	9.4
double sided, two layers per side	17

Figure 17.2 illustrates the physical composition of a single-sided DVD disc with two layers for a total disc capacity of 8.5 billion bytes. The second side of the disc is simply a 0.6 mm polycarbonate layer, resulting in a 1.2 mm thick disc.

To conform to the DVD specifications, DVD players and drives must be capable of reading discs with two layers per side. By simply flipping over the disc, both sides may be accessed. Largely due to the increased capacity, DVD offers capabilities not possible with conventional CD technology, including video captured at multiple camera angles, interactivity, and multiple language support. Provisions for parental control, pay-per-view, security assurances, and a variety of other features are being incorporated directly into the standards.

DVD video is based on MPEG-2, a variable bit rate compression scheme. Common DVD audio formats include Dolby Digital (formerly AC3) and MPEG-2 digital audio. Dolby Digital provides six independent audio channels, and MPEG-2 provides up to eight. By carrying completely separate signals, these channels can be used to achieve a surround sound effect in which the center channel is used for dialog, the left and right channels for music, and the rear channels for special audio effects and bass. In short, DVD audio rivals theater quality presentation.

Standard picture dimensions are 720×480 pixels at 29.97 frames per second, as defined by the NTSC standard, or 720×576 pixels at 25 frames per second, as defined by the PAL and SECAM standards. Because each picture is subsampled, allocating on average 12 bits per pixel, the uncompressed video source has a data rate of 124 million bits per second (bps). On average, the video source can be compressed approximately 36:1, resulting in the commonly referenced DVD video data rate of about 3.5 million bps. For MPEG audio and Dolby Digital, the average bit rate per soundtrack is approximately 384,000 bps. Therefore, for a single video and three soundtracks, a DVD layer can accommodate approximately 135 minutes of studio quality audio and video. If only one soundtrack is included, a single DVD layer can accommodate 160 minutes of audio and video. For this reason, it is expected that single layer DVDs will be most common.

Until 1999 there were two competing DVD standards, ordinary DVD and Divx DVD. Digital Video Express, Divx, was essentially a pay-per-view form of DVD,

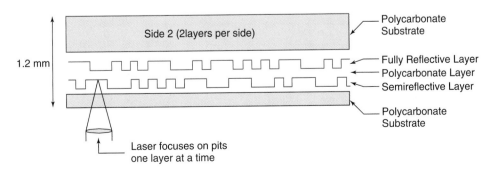

FIGURE 17.2 Physical composition of a single-sided DVD disc with two layers.

requiring the viewer to first purchase the disk, which allows access over a finite viewing period. During this period, the disk may be viewed without additional cost. Upon expiration of the initial viewing period, additional viewing time may be obtained using a modem communication link. To achieve this, the Divx player is plugged into a standard phone jack to communicate billing information with the appropriate Divx provider.

When compared to ordinary DVD, Divx provides additional safeguards to prevent unauthorized viewing and video piracy. Divx employed multiple layers of security, including individual serial numbers, triple DES (Data Encryption Standard, published in 1977 by the National Bureau of Standards) encryption, and watermarking. The use of triple DES encryption introduced possible exportation restrictions. Also, because Divx communicated billing information "behind the scenes," critics argued that Divx would enable providers to know exactly what the viewers were watching and when. Nevertheless, Divx was initially adopted by about half the industry, including Disney, Dreamworks, and Paramount. Although Divx players were able to play ordinary DVDs, DVD players were incompatible with Divx DVDs. As a result, introducing Divx as a competing format clearly slowed the initial deployment of DVD. This situation ended in 1999 when market resistance to the features described above caused the Divx format to be pulled from the market.

Similar to CD-ROM, DVD-ROM can be used to store computer data and is accessed using a DVD-ROM drive. Most new computers with DVD-ROM drives are capable of playing DVD videos. Further, most DVD-ROM drives are capable of reading conventional CD-ROMs, providing a forward migration path for the deployment of DVD technology. DVD-R (record once) and DVD-RAM (record more than once) standards were published in August 1997. Similar to CD-R, DVD-R uses a dye technology and is compatible with early DVD players. Although DVD-RAM has been standardized by the DVD Forum, several incompatible DVD-RAM technologies are under development by a variety of vendors, and it is still unclear which format will gain widespread acceptance.

With many competing electronic and hardware vendors involved, DVD technology is rapidly changing and the standards are in a state of flux. The introduction of Divx and many incompatible DVD standards has, without question, slowed the widespread deployment of DVD. Nevertheless, the increased capacity offered by DVD makes it an attractive solution for many high-capacity applications.

Table 17.4 summarizes the physical differences between CD and DVD technology.[3]

TABLE 17.4 CD AND DVD COMPARISON

Characteristic	DVD	CD
Disc Diameter	120 mm	120 mm
Disc Thickness	1.2 mm	1.2 mm
Laser Technology	Red (635/650 nm)	Infrared (780 nm)
Minimum Pit Size	0.40 μm	0.83 μm
Track Spacing	0.74 μm	1.60 μm
Layers	1, 2, or 4	1
Capacity per Layer	4.38 GB	0.64 GB
Maximum Capacity	4.38–15.90 GB	0.64 GB

---

[3] MB means megabytes (2^{20}) and GB means gigabytes (2^{30}). Thus, a single DVD layer has a capacity of 4.38 GB or 4.7 billion (10^9) bytes of data.

17.5 Future Digital Data Storage Media

Although DVD offers up to 17 billion bytes of digital data storage per disc, the search for media with greater capacities continues. Hitachi is an example of one vendor researching the use of smaller-wavelength lasers to increase data capacity per layer. Using blue lasers, current efforts have shown that up to 14 billion bytes of data can be stored on a single layer. Further, data access times have been reduced by a factor of five when compared to conventional DVD technology.

Summary

Large-capacity storage is dominated by two technologies: magnetic discs and optically read discs. Both forms continue to advance in speed and density, and neither appears likely to completely replace the other. Magnetic media excel for tasks that require frequent erasures and rewriting. Optical media excel in density, ruggedness, and cost per bit stored. Magnetic tape continues to play a role, primarily for backup purposes.

Try These Exercises

1. How many 1.44 Mbyte 3.5-inch discs would be needed to store a typical motion picture as encoded for DVD?
2. How many minutes of telephone-quality audio could be stored on a CD?
3. Determine the approximate diameter of the pit that represents a zero or a one on a CD.
4. Within the period 1990 to 2000, disc capacities have increased approximately 100-fold. Comment on whether this trend will continue in the future. Is there a need for larger storage capacity?
5. There are currently three popular general forms of data storage systems: disks, tapes, and solid-state. In your own words, summarize the advantages and disadvantages of each. Solid-state storage appears to have several advantages over the other two since it is totally nonmechanical. Why has it not taken over the marketplace? Tape appears to be declining in popularity. Why might that be?
6. To some extent, storage and data communications are competitive technologies. Rather than storing data (such as a movie) locally, it may be possible to download it as needed if transmission speed is adequate. Summarize the factors which determine the relative practicality and likely consumer acceptance of each approach. Use one or more specific examples.

PART

VII

Networks and the Internet

Maybe I've a reason to believe
We all will be received...

Paul Simon, "Graceland," Graceland

In this part of the book we come to the home stretch: the organization and operation of networks of interconnected computers and information appliances. We will begin by comparing and contrasting telephone and data networks of the type that predominate today: the Public Switched Telephone System and the Internet.

To understand all the issues involved in the convergence of all communication systems toward a single universal system, we will have to expose a number of the details of the behaviors of these networks. One of the revelations will be the nature of the secret codes that are used to insure the security of everything from telephone conversations to financial transactions on the Internet.

Finally, with the rest of the book behind us and its lessons learned, we can discuss the technological problems, future solutions, cost of and advantages of the convergence of telephone and Internet.

18 Telephone and Data Communications Networks

Objectives

The essence of communications is the ability for any two or more terminals to send and receive data among themselves at any time, regardless of their locations. This requires a communications network. In this chapter you will learn about:

▲ the two fundamental types of networks: circuit-based and packet-based networks;

▲ the means by which circuit-based networks establish a path between two endpoints for communication;

▲ the public switched telephone network (PSTN);

▲ digital transmission systems (including T1) used on the PSTN;

▲ the ways in which packet-based networks get data from transmitter to receiver without a dedicated path between the two terminals; and

▲ some types of data communications protocols, including Frame Relay and Asynchronous Transfer mode.

18.1 Introduction

Any discussion of networks should begin with an explanation of their basic function. The function of a network is to allow two or more endpoints to communicate information. This definition is very broad and very incomplete. It would logically bring up the following questions:

- What sort of information is to be communicated?
- Is the communication to be one-way or two-way?
- Must the communication be in real time?
- How many simultaneous users must the network handle?
- Are all users to be connected in pairs (like a normal telephone call) or in some other arrangement?
- Are the user–user connections permanent, or do they change frequently?
- What is the typical period of time that a connection is maintained?

The answers to these questions help define the design and physical arrangement of the network. To demonstrate this, we will examine a few cases with which almost everyone has familiarity.

Most of the existing telephone network was designed to provide a communications connection which is:

Two-Way: Each party can speak to the other; that is, this is a system meant for conversation and not presentation or publication.

Real-Time: A delay in excess of about 1/3 of a second is disrupting to conversations, as it is a large enough a time period to be confused with vocal gestures (pause, doubt, surprise).

Pair wise: The conversation is an exchange between two people and not an open forum for anyone to join.

Circuit Switched Connection: Voice connections are set up and taken down frequently under control of the user (by dialing a number) as opposed to being permanent (in which case we would need a telephone in our house for each party to whom we ever intended to speak).

The telephone network is used today for many purposes other than voice conversations, of course, but these applications are supported with varying degrees of efficiency that may fall far from the best possible, with specifically engineered networks having attributes that more closely match the needs of that type of communication.

How different can these needs be? Let's now take the case of a cable television network. Most of the cable television network was designed to provide a communications connection which is:

One-Way: The television programming provider sends its video product to your home and not vice versa.

Not Real-Time: As a viewer you don't really care or notice if the program you are watching is 10 seconds late or more. Because the communication is not two-way, there is no sense of delay, and hence the provider can use slow channels (satellites) or even manually mounted tape recordings to provide the video feed.

One-to-Many: The provider does not individually package and transmit TV shows to each user. A single launch of information is made of all the TV shows to all users. Users, of course, can independently select which information in the information stream to show on their screens (and with some modern TV sets, several of these can be watched at the same time).

Permanent Connection: The connections between the provider and the users are not switched or directed. As noted above, the same information is transmitted on one network to all viewers. When the viewers switch channels, they are only selecting what part of the information to view and are not altering what is being sent.

18.1.1 Circuit and Packet-Based Networks

There are many means by which a network can be implemented, with large variations in operation such as in the choice of the type of signal used (electrical, radio, light, etc.). A very significant difference, determined by the information engineering involved in its design, is whether the network is said to be circuit or packet-based.

Short definitions of these two types of networks are:

- *Circuit-based networks* are those in which a path is maintained between the users for the duration of the call; and

- *Packet-based networks* are those in which individually addressed packets of information are sent into a communications system, and are individually forwarded until they reach the recipient.

The circuit-based network with which the reader might be best acquainted is the telephone system. After a number has been dialed, a circuit is established. That is, a path has been created between your telephone and that of the person you called. You can think of the telephone circuit and any other circuit-based network connection as a hollow tube running between two endpoints. Anything you drop in one end of the tube will come out the other end (for example, your voice in the case of the telephone network). If you want to communicate with a second person, you need to establish a second circuit. The destination of your message is determined by the tube into which you drop the message. In the case of cable television networks (which are circuit-based) the provider drops the same messages into all the tubes.

The packet-based network with which the reader is probably most acquainted is the postal system. To send a packet of information (a letter) to someone, you must put an address on an envelope. Then, you drop the letter into a mailbox. This mailbox no longer acts like a tube following a single path to the destination. In fact, you can drop many messages with different addresses into the same mailbox and they will each be directed to the correct recipient, in stark contrast to the telephone example above. In fact, not only do you not need a separate box for each possible recipient, you can actually use any mailbox you find on any street to send the same piece of mail.

This apparently simple division is often complicated and confused, since many technologies have been implemented that blur the line in an effort to capture the advantages inherent to both types of networks in a single system. More confusion derives from application of simple rules to an endpoint of the communication system without a full understanding of the complete underlying network technology. For example, suppose we placed a special machine over the opening of a mailbox that has three slots. We can label these three slots with names of destinations (say, specific addresses in New York City, Chicago, and Houston). Our machine prints the address associated with a slot onto an envelope when it is dropped into that slot.

To the user of this system, it appears that the network is circuit-based because separate and *dedicated* (meaning one slot sends messages to one and only one recipient) paths have obviously been created. In reality, a packet-based infrastructure (the post office) has been made to appear to provide a circuit-based service.

In the remainder of this chapter we will treat the circuit-based approach in greater depth, and discuss several of the circuit-based systems that are available today for the network service customer.

18.2 Circuit-Based Networks

The term *circuit* originally referred to an unbroken pair of copper wires that connected one endpoint in a communications connection to the other endpoint. Thus a circuit here refers to the same kind of electrical circuit we associate with a light bulb, a switch, and the wires that connect them and a power source. When we flick a switch, we expect that only the light to which it is connected (and always has been connected) will turn on and off. Thus the circuit represents one of the simplest means of establishing electrical communications between two points.

How do circuits for communications come into being? A user might lay, or buy/rent an existing cable between the two points. Obviously, the two endpoint users in this case are the only users of the circuit. Thus the circuit formed by the cable provides the source user with a dedicated (unshared, unmovable), permanent (always available), and invariant (constant bandwidth) connection to the destination user. Systems that provide these attributes are now considered circuit-based systems whether or not they are based on wire-cable, and whether or not they are truly a single piece of cable or a vast network of electronics that simply provides the same interface and capability.

Originally such circuit connections were provided by physically laying a cable between every source and destination (the telegraph network and very early telephone systems). This is an extremely costly system when a high level of connectivity is desired. If N parties want to each be able to connect to any other party in the group, then $N \times (N-1)/2$ wires need to be laid. So, the number of wires need is proportional to approximately the square of the number of parties in the group.

Furthermore, the cost of this process goes beyond the cost of the cable and the labor for placing it. The true cost must include the time and money associated with acquiring the rights to place the cable on a right-of-way which may be owned by many individuals, corporations, and municipalities. Thus, a solution is sought that minimizes the number of wires needed while still allowing anyone to connect to anyone else.

The next step in the evolution of this system took place with the recognition that efficiencies could be gained by enabling a small number of existing wires to be reconnected as the desired user pairs changed. This led to the development of telephone central offices so that cables were laid from all potential users to the central office, rather than from user to user.

At first, telephone operators manually made the electrical connections by moving small connecting cables between points on a switch panel that connected to all the end users. To make a call, you *rang* the operator and asked him or her to make a connection between you and the desired party.

That system was soon replaced by the telephone dial mechanism (originally rotary and now pushbutton) and automatic switching system that allowed the user to make the connection without an operator's assistance. In a small town, a system in which all homes and businesses were connected by cables to a single central office was sufficient to connect all users to all other possible users.

In larger cities, many central offices were necessary because the distance between users at the outskirts and a centrally located office were such that the lengths of connecting cable became prohibitively costly, and effects of attenuation and dispersion of signals mentioned earlier in this book reduced the quality of the voices that were received below acceptable levels. Thus many central offices (called exchanges) needed to be placed in the city, serving smaller groups of parties.

But, it was altogether likely that within one city, people connected to different exchanges needed to talk to one another. So, these central offices were connected with cables that were similar or identical to those that ran to the users. These cables are called *trunks* to distinguish them from the user cables, which are called *loops*.

📖 **Loops**

In time this system was expanded further, introducing a hierarchy of telephone switching offices that enable any two telephones in the world to communicate by putting together a single circuit formed of two loops (one at each customer end), and any number of trunks between intermediate central offices. This switching function will be discussed in more detail in the next section.

FIGURE 18.1 Uninterrupted permanent circuit created by connecting existing cable plant between two customer premises.

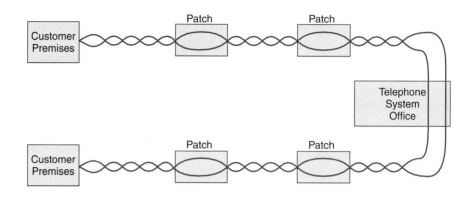

18.2.1 Telephone Circuits Are More than Just Wire

The advent of widespread telephony and the fact that cabling rights were negotiated on a wholesale scale for the popular telephone service, made the telephone companies a source of *circuit services* for purposes other than telephone calls. Thus, a circuit customer can rent a permanent circuit between two points directly from the telephone companies involved along the source-to-destination path. The telephone company makes use of its extensive and excessive (beyond its current telephony needs) in-place cable resources to patch together a continuous circuit from pieces of cable already in place by connecting these pieces at telephone switching offices where they come together. While composed of many pieces of cable, this configuration is still essentially a single unprocessed signal conduit in form (Figure 18.1).

However, to deliver better voice transmission services, the telephone system itself does not simply use the raw capability of wire cables to move electrical signals representing human voices over long distances. As mentioned above, attenuation and dispersion grow with increasing cable length. A sufficiently long cable would so much distort a voice as to make it unrecognizable.

To extend the transmission distance achievable with cable circuits, the telephone companies insert special electronic circuits called repeaters between segments of a long cable path. These repeaters receive and retransmit the signals present on the circuit lines at periodic intervals to strengthen and restore them. Thus, while no longer a simple copper-wire cable circuit, this system acts exactly like a low signal-loss single-cable circuit (Figure 18.2).

FIGURE 18.2 Permanent circuit using repeaters to achieve greater bandwidth and reduced attenuation of large signaling distances.

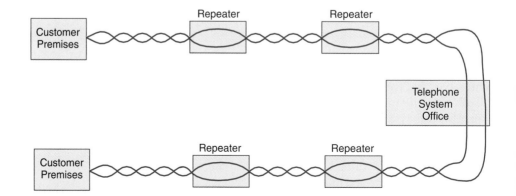

Even though the telephone circuit is now more complicated than a simple loop of wire, it can still be used as a conduit of signals other than those voice signals created by a telephone set. Thus, a system that is designed to carry signals generated by telephone microphones to telephone earpieces is actually a more general device: a virtual electrical pipe between two places.

The telephone system has continued to evolve due to changes in electronic and photonic (light communications) technology, and at present almost all of the telephone networks beyond the local loop actually make use of digital signals, and hence have a form radically different than the wire cable and repeater system described above. But even in this new form, the concept of the circuit connection may still be applied because the mechanisms in use create a switched, dedicated, fixed-bandwidth path between the users.

18.2.2 Public Switched Telephone Network Digital Services

The telephone companies comprise what has commonly been called the Public Switched Telephone Network, or PSTN. The PSTN has traditionally been in the business of providing temporary circuit-based connections on demand for voice communications.

It has come to pass many times in the history of business and technology that if a resource is made available with few constricting rules, someone will find new ways to exploit it for their benefit. For example, some users choose to use special devices known as telephone data modems for the transmission of data on analog telephone connections. The modem transforms the data bit stream into a signal that resembles a voice signal sufficiently that it can pass through the system and be recognized by another modem at the other end.

Unfortunately, the limitations imposed by a network designed for the transport of voice information greatly limited the practicality of large-scale, high-speed data transmission. Such applications were technically feasible by using many simultaneously operating *voice-grade* connections, or by obtaining use of the wire cable from the telephone system with all electronics removed or replaced by different electronics better suited to the purpose. Thus, while possible, the economics of the situation worked against direct high-speed data links.

The economics, however, began to change as dramatic drops in the price of digital electronics made high-speed long-distance digital interconnection less costly than analog circuit lines. Today, for example, fiber-optic lines connect many distant points in the PSTN with digital signaling speeds of 622 Mbps from end to end. Thus, very high bit rate digital circuit channels can be sliced out of the available connection bit stream for resale to digital services subscribers. In effect, the PSTN merely dedicates some bit stream locations that would have served some number of telephone conversations to the transport of the digital data for customers of digital data transport services.

Thus users may now exploit the telephone system for transport of data at certain digital data speeds and formats that conform to PSTN standard interfaces. The formats and speeds are rather specific, as the PSTN needs to be able to absorb the subscriber's data and to introduce it into the well-organized train of continuously generated bit streams from the thousands of digitized telephone conversations sharing the same transmission system. On the other hand, while the interface is specialized and the connection is certainly in no electrical sense a single circuit any more, the service available to the user still presents all the features of the original circuit:

- On arrangement with the PSTN it can be a permanent circuit.
- It makes a fixed transmission data rate available at all times exclusively for that user.

Suppose a user only has need for transmitting bursts of digital data separated by large periods of nonuse, and that furthermore, the user needs to transmit this data not just to one recipient but to a variety of endpoints depending upon an ever-changing situation. Then we are back to a situation like that created by the user of voice telephone service, except that data rather than voice is being transmitted. In that case, even though the backbone circuits that make up the telephone system are digital, the PSTN still provides an analog connection on request for use by ordinary telephones. So, our user with variable endpoint digital service needs can make use of the switched nature of the all-digital telephone system.

A customer can contract with the PSTN to provide a switched digital data circuit, which does not provide a permanent connection to a single endpoint, but rather provides a service for data just like the one we use for ordinary phone calls: a telephone number is used to make a connection (call set-up) when it is needed to the desired endpoint and then disconnected (tear-down) when we are finished. The rates associated with this service can be considerably less than that with a permanent circuit because we are only charged for connect time.

The downsides to this approach include:

- the time delay involved with call set-up and tear-down;
- the possibility of getting a busy signal;
- the possible higher cost than that of a dedicated circuit if the line is in use much of the time.

As will be shown later in this chapter and in the next chapter, these *downsides* are opportunities for other network architectures to address.

18.2.3 An Example of a Digital Transmission System: The T1 Carrier

One of the first and most popular digital permanent circuit services sold by the PSTN in North America was the so-called *T1 carrier*. This transmission system was devised originally to transport sets of 24 simultaneous digitized phone conversations over simple pairs of copper wire over distances of up to approximately 50 miles. Repeaters were placed 6,000 feet apart along the path of the cable to regenerate the signal, which otherwise would suffer severe degradation due to cable losses. The overall bit rate of this digital data transmission system is 1.544 Mbps per channel.

It is typical telephone parlance to refer to the format of the digital signal involved in T1 transmission not as a T1 signal, but rather as a DS1 (Digital Services 1) signal, because this same format can be used on essentially any kind of cable. Thus, T1 refers to both the physical medium (the twisted pair cable) and the DS1 format of the digital data being used to move the data on that cable.

The digitized voice telephone signals transmitted by a T1 carrier are represented by 8,000 samples per second quantized to 8 bits per sample. Actually, some of these data bits are "stolen" to provide synchronization information and "signaling" information, which is for routing the data at the various switch points. Also, one additional bit is inserted into the stream for every 192 bits (24 voice channels × 8 bits), which is used to establish overall synchronization of the channels within the stream. Thus, 193 bits × 8000 samples/sec = 1.544 Mbps are transmitted.

TABLE 18.1   THE NORTH AMERICAN DIGITAL MULTIPLEX HIERARCHY

Service Name	Bit Rate	Number of Voice Channels
DS1	1.544 Mbps	24 ch
DS2	6.312 Mbps	96 ch
DS3	44.736 Mbps	672 ch
DS4	274.176 Mbps	4032 ch

As summarized in Table 18.1, a variety of data services, originally conceived as bundles of digital voice data, are available from the PSTN. These services are very much the backbone of long distance Internet services provided by Internet Service Providers (ISPs) such as America Online, Compuserve, and Prodigy. (The transmission hierarchy is different in Europe, where groups of 30 voice channels rather than 24 are the basis for the hierarchy.)

With the advent of still higher data rate requirements and the means to provide them through fiber-optic transmission media, new standards for digital data transmission have been devised by the PSTN on a global basis. Table 18.2 summarizes the North American and European (CCITT) standards for digital transmission over fiber-optic cables.

📖 CCITT

18.2.4 Integrated Services Digital Network (ISDN)

In the late 1980s, the PSTN gave users direct access to a switched digital service. This service, which parallels the regular voice telephone network, became widely available in a form that has been named Integrated Services Digital Network, or ISDN. However, for reasons of cost (high), data rate (not very high), and installation difficulties, ISDN has not been widely accepted, and will likely be eclipsed by cheaper and/or faster data transmission alternatives.

ISDN services are available in a number of versions with various cable connection types and bit rates. We will briefly discuss the two forms are now readily available in most larger cities throughout the world. In particular, we will discuss the formats used in North America. ISDN BRI (basic rate interface) is available worldwide and offers a 192 kbps digital service divided in a fashion that separates it into one 16 kbps signaling (call set-up, etc.) data streams and two 64 kbps data streams that can be used as two computer data streams, two digital phone streams, or one of each. The BRI service is often called the 2B+D service, indicating that two "B" channels and one "D" channel are available on a single connection.

TABLE 18.2   THE NORTH AMERICAN SYNCHRONOUS OPTICAL NETWORK (SONET) HIERARCHY

North American Name	CCITT Name	Bit Rate
OC-1		51.84 Mbps
OC-3	STM-1	155.52 Mbps
OC-9	STM-3	466.56 Mbps
OC-12	STM-4	622.08 Mbps
OC-18	STM-6	933.12 Mbps
OC-24	STM-8	1244.16 Mbps
OC-36	STM-12	1866.24 Mbps
OC-48	STM-16	2488.32 Mbps

ISDN BRI services are delivered via the local-loop wiring that had been used before to simply provide the analog telephone technology connection for your home and office phone. (Actually, not all existing telephone wiring is "good enough" to support these data rates, and the PSTN company with whom one contracts for ISDN service will test the lines prior to selling the service.)

Once ISDN services have been purchased, users can connect a special interface box to their telephone wall plate for connection to computers, printers, telephones, and so forth. This device will support the call set-up function and allow users to enter (either on the front panel of the device or through a computer communications link and user interface software) the telephone number of another ISDN device anywhere in the PSTN. Thus, just as with analog telephone service, many endpoints can be serviced from any one line. In fact, the two B channels can be dialed into two different endpoints simultaneously.

Users who need higher speed direct data access with control signaling (to exploit switched circuit access) can purchase a T1 line to support the North American PRI (primary) service with 23B+D channels. That is, 23 64-kbps digital voice or data channels and 1 signaling channel.

Together, BRI and PRI ISDN services are now commonly called *Narrow Band ISDN*. Faster *Broadband ISDN* or BISDN services have been on the drawing boards for several years, and promise eventually to deliver SONET hierarchy switched digital data services to users. The ultimate goal of the telephone companies is to make BISDN the transport mechanism of choice for all data from bursty computer communications to continuous very high bandwidth television and future multimedia systems.

18.3 The Packet-Switched Connection

Early in the growth of point-of-sale terminals in large retail chains and ticket sale counters, a need became apparent that was dramatically different than that provided by permanent and switched circuits. What was needed was the ability to have hundreds, if not thousands, of terminals, spread across the country, send small, spaced streams of transaction data to central locations and to receive replies from those central locations, with rapid response time.

The solution came in the form of a new kind of data service known as a *packet-switched* delivery system. The components of this new system were:

- permanent circuits from the endpoint to a local PSTN switch office;
- the use of a packet interface protocol at the endpoints that transmits small packets of data encapsulated in a "data envelope" containing the address of the sender and desired recipient of the data;
- a packet "node" at the local PSTN office that receives these packets, determines the route to another packet node that would bring the packet closer to the destination, and stores the packet until space on a shared permanent circuit to the next node becomes available, at which time it is forwarded; and
- a small number of permanent circuits upon which the packets are transmitted among nodes.

In effect, a packet-switched network emulates the operation of the post office, except that packets of data rather than paper are stored and forwarded to destinations. As with the post office, great economy is obtained by concentrating the flow of traffic over well-defined and highly optimized routes. If a route becomes too busy over time, the PSTN can devote additional permanent circuit bandwidth (an additional line) to support the route. The users are charged on a per-packet basis, and obtain service with a speed that is generally much faster than that associated with circuit set-up, tear-down, and potential busy connection delays.

A key aspect of packet-switched networks is that many users share a packet channel. This is good from an economic point of view, but it also generates the possibility that the channel may become full if many users send data at the same time, delaying (or in some cases eliminating) the delivery of the packet.

18.3.1 X.25 and the Virtual Circuit

In 1976 the CCITT (International Consultative Committee on Telegraphy and Telephony) announced the definition of a standard for packet-switched communications known as X.25. X.25 provided the packet-switched capability for multipoint delivery of sporadic data as described above via an approach that has come to be known as a *virtual circuit*. A virtual circuit means that a path has been established (via some type of call set-up) between endpoints, but that path may not be uniquely dedicated to those users.

An X.25 service network provides a standard digital interface between a computer (or other digital device, such as a sales terminal) and a single PSTN node. However, at any given moment, the source endpoint could direct data to one or more destination endpoints without the need for call set-up and tear-down before changing endpoints. Instead, several "virtual circuits" could be established simultaneously by call set-ups with several destinations. Then a small "address" is affixed to each message to indicate to the X.25 network nodes which of the destinations previously selected is to receive the data.

A user's cost in using X.25 is determined both by the connection time of all virtual circuits, and by the amount of data transmitted to each of those destinations. This reflects the costs to the PSTN both of keeping the lines open and of handling the data.

A number of new X.25 based network systems arose that were not outgrowths of the telephone industry in response to the popularity of the X.25 virtual circuit packet service. These companies are often referred to collectively as the Public Data Networks (PDN). The maximum data rate available via X.25 services at this time is about 64 kbps. The reasons for this maximum rate and means to go beyond it in a packet-switched network are treated in the following section on Frame Relay.

18.3.2 Wider Bandwidth Data Transmission: Frame Relay

A relatively new entrant in the virtual circuit packet network market is the Frame Relay service. The distinguishing characteristic of Frame Relay is that, unlike in the X.25 service, there is no guarantee that a packet once sent will be delivered. Now this would appear to be a relatively useless service at first. However, the guarantees provided by X.25 result in low speed and high cost! Frame Relay services allow the end-users to apply their own strategies for replacing lost data and throttling data usage so as to make effective use of the service. In return, Frame Relay provides up to 2 Mbps data rates at lower costs than X.25 for moving data in virtual circuits.

The higher speed and lower cost associated with Frame Relay derives from the fact that in an X.25 circuit, a great deal of processing must take place at every node in the network. Hence, high-speed computers must be employed at each node. In turn, the amount of data that can be handled is driven by the availability, or lack thereof, of this computational power. A Frame Relay data packet is simply passed on to the correct connection if received from the previous one. A "dumb" piece of fast, cheap, dedicated, easily duplicated hardware can handle this transaction.

18.3.3 Asynchronous Transfer Mode

The highest practical rate for Frame Relay, approximately 2 Mbps, is quite fast compared to X.25, but is small compared to the speeds achievable on dedicated permanent circuits today. Furthermore, this is too slow for the transmission of multimedia data, such as might be generated by on-demand movie delivery services and interactive high definition TV. We have seen in the progression from X.25 to Frame Relay that the key to moving packet-switched data more quickly is simplification of the data handling at the network nodes. This is taken to the extreme in the most recent packet-switched offerings from the PSTN companies: ATM (Asynchronous Transfer Mode).

ATM further squeezes overhead out of the process of handling data streams by making the following additional concession: every packet (now called a cell) is of fixed size—53 bytes—with 48 bytes devoted to data and the remainder to addressing and controlling the virtual circuit.

By breaking the data into small cells it becomes possible to pack those cells into standardized cell-divided data streams, "on-the-fly." Furthermore, the small cell size leads to a lessening of the storage needed in the store-and-forward architecture of the network. As in Frame Relay, we also abandon any guarantees of packet delivery and let the end-users apply their own techniques to recover from missing cells.

ATM-based virtual circuit packet transmission services for speeds up to OC-3 SONET, 155 Mbps, are readily available from PSTN companies. ATM equipment is now commercially available that handles data at speeds associated with the OC-12 SONET system, 622 Mbps. And, new integrated circuit chips have also been previewed that handle ATM data rates up to OC-96 SONET speeds of 5 Gbps.

Summary

Communications networks can be characterized in several different ways including: speed, type of transmission (analog vs. digital), one-directional or bidirectional, physical arrangement of facilities, means of getting information to the correct location, and intended uses. Fortunately, as the number of different uses for communications networks explodes, it has *not* been necessary to design and build special-purpose networks for each use. The most fundamental characteristic of networks is their configuration as either *circuit-based* or *packet-based*, as described in this chapter. But this distinction is blurred by the use of circuit switched connections in the implementation of packet-based networks and the creation of virtual circuits through packet-based networks.

Another distinction, that between analog and digital information, has almost completely disappeared, as essentially all communications networks are digital with conversions to and from analog as needed.

Finally, it is important to note that the type of network is not defined by the physical facilities (wire, optical fiber, radio transmission) that actually carry the data. A given transmission facility may simultaneously carry some packet-switched data and some circuit-switched data. The equipment (routers, switches, etc.) in the communications hub sorts everything out appropriately. Hence, as we move from a predominance of telephone-generated data to other forms of

 Routers

data sources, it will not be necessary to discard all the long-distance transmission facilities already in place.

Try These Exercises

1. Examine the list of characteristics given at the beginning of the chapter for telephone and cable networks. Develop a similar list for the Internet, based upon your Web viewing experience.
2. Your company works with customers to produce t-shirts with custom-designed graphics. This requires you to communicate with the customers regarding details of their order (number of shirts, sizes, means of payment, etc.) as well as the graphic design. Then you must transmit the graphic and associated information digitally to the plant (you work with only one plant) that actually manufactures the t-shirts. Assume that you have 50 customers to deal with each day, at various stages in the process. Describe the data communications needs, being as specific as possible, with regard to circuit or packet switching, and so forth.
3. Design a packet-switched system, considering the following parameters: packet size (number of bytes per packet), necessary address information on each packet, and virtual circuit set-up information (specific information to set up each virtual circuit). Assume that the terminals are used for surfing the Web, with 50% of the requests representing graphical information.
4. Pretend you are Alexander Graham Bell and design the first telephone network for a city of 10,000 households. Assume that each household has one phone line, and calls only within the city, placing four calls per day. Assume that each call lasts 10 minutes.
5. For your professional area, identify a data transmission need, and comment on the applicability of packet-switched versus circuit-switched methods for handling that data.
6. Assume that 10 terminals are generating packets of data, each at a rate of 100 packets per second, and that the packets are 100 bits in length. All of these terminals are connected to a router which has a single data connection to the Internet. What minimum data rate would be required on the Internet connection? Would this minimum data rate be acceptable in practice? Explain.
7. Continuing from the above question, assume that the average packet rate is as given above, but that the rate is not constant. Assume that the rate can vary from 0 to 1,000 packets per second from each terminal. Now what data rate is required from the router to accommodate all of the packets in the worst case? Given that the average data rate from the terminals has not changed, how much of the capacity of the new line will be unused, on average? Is there a way (with some extra equipment in the router) to transmit all of the packets with a line of capacity smaller than that just calculated, but larger than the minimum from the previous question? Explain.

19 The Local Area Network

Objectives

When computers became numerous, so that many were often housed in a single building, the need for communications among those machines developed. This situation is very different than the person-person, relatively long distance communications need that drove the development of the telephone network. In this chapter we discuss the Local Area Network designs which resulted, including the following concepts:

▲ basic design characteristics, including short length and relatively short bursts of data transmitted between random pairs of terminals;

▲ virtual circuits as a compromise between circuit-oriented and packet-oriented networks;

▲ protocols for assigning addresses and performing routing based on addresses;

▲ the Datagram;

▲ Ethernet as an example of a shared-medium LAN which allows "collisions" between data packets; and

▲ principles by which order is maintained in an Ethernet-type LAN with no central controller.

19.1 Introduction

In the previous chapter, we discussed the respective virtues of circuit-switched and virtual circuit-based packet-switched data transmission technologies. However, neither of these technologies is well suited for use in moving data among a very dense, highly malleable collection of computational devices, such as might be encountered in a large business complex or university setting. In this chapter we discuss the general nature of the Local Area Network (LAN), which was an outgrowth of these needs.

As will be revealed in this chapter, a LAN is an interconnection of computers and other devices for digital information exchange that:

- is limited in size, typically spanning no more than a mile;
- is very fast, moving data with speeds from 10 Mbps to 1 Gbps;
- requires very little wiring, typically with a single cable connecting to each device; and
- permits any device to send messages to any other device, without the overhead of creating and tearing down virtual connections.

258

While circuit switching has certainly been used to address the interconnection of very large numbers of people within the telephone system, it implements a one-to-one circuit between any two such parties (Figure 19.1a). The concept of creating many concurrently open connections from any source and to any destination is not within the scope of this technology. That is, suppose you have a single phone line connecting your home with a telephone system central office. In that case, you can't start using your computer to connect to the Web at the same time as you are having a telephone conversation. That single connection can be used only for a single purpose for the lifetime of the connection (from when you dial until you hang up the phone).

ISDN connections, made through your telephone connection to the central office, allow two computers or a computer and a telephone to open two independent connections to other locations. However, two limitations have prevented widespread acceptance of ISDN technology:

- The relatively low speeds of ISDN technology, which are linked to its relationship with telephone wiring and the need to centrally (at the packet-switching node) handle the movement of each packet.

- The fact that endpoints are identified in part by their wired connection (in effect, the telephone number of the connection). Hence, moves from one wall to another, for example, mean a change of telephone number about which every other user must be notified.

Virtual circuit-based packet technology has also been used to provide this kind of multiple-party interconnection service. But, virtual circuits are point-to-point and connection oriented. That is, while a single computer might be able to access a handful of other computers, there is a substantial and time-consuming process involved in making and breaking these connections. This style of connectivity would not be amenable to today's Web-driven rapidity of access to many different computers. Almost every time you click on a Web page hyperlink, you can potentially be jumping to another computer. There are many services that can be provided for computers and users of computers that don't match the virtual circuit style of connection and are better served by *multicast* and *connectionless* communications. In multicast operations, a single transmission by one computer is received by any and all interested listeners. In connectionless communications a self-contained message can be transmitted or received by any member of the net-

(a) Circuit Switching Based System

(b) Packet Switching Based System

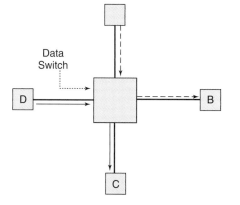

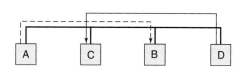

FIGURE 19.1 (a) Node A communicates to node B via a circuit created by the data switch; the same for Nodes D and C. (b) All nodes talk on a shared medium where they take turns sending information via packets, which contain addresses of both the communicating nodes.

work, which identifies the source and destination and requires no further set-up or tear-down handling.

To address the special needs of such businesses and campuses, a new packet-switching technology was developed that uses a special packet addressing scheme named the *datagram*. We explore datagram packet switching in the next section.

The most popular LAN is called the Ethernet. In this chapter we will focus exclusively on this technology, though certain concepts such as the datagram are common to other LAN technologies. Ethernet LAN technology is our focus because it has enjoyed such overwhelming commercial success that many readers of this book may never encounter any other LAN in their professional endeavors.

19.2 Datagram Packet Switching

The term *datagram* is derived from the word telegram, a now almost extinct form of paper communication. A telegram is an addressed letter that is transmitted electronically over several long distance hops into the local area of the destination. At that point a printed copy is rapidly and personally delivered by a special messenger service to the doorstep of the recipient. That is, the idea behind the telegram was fast service, multiple retransmissions, and rapid direct delivery to a specified address. Along the way, the movement and handling of the message was determined (much like mail) by the address on the telegram. At no time was an arrangement made for a future delivery (a connection). In fact, telegrams were used in the past not only when speed was needed, but also before the time of universal telephone and mail service.

Because no connections were made, it was also possible for the telegram service to discover that the telegram was undeliverable! In that case, a message was rapidly returned to the originator. While a seeming disadvantage in these cases, the benefit is that most messages arrive more quickly because of the removal of interactions that would otherwise be needed. Furthermore, the end station in the telegram service would often try several times to locate the recipient before giving up. Thus, the sender could be worrying about other communications rather than waiting for the destination availability to be verified.

The concept and handling of the data network datagram is rather parallel to the paper telegram. A datagram is a packet of information that is self-contained. That is, in addition to the message content itself, it contains the entire *universal address* of the sender and recipient. These datagrams are then delivered on a "best effort" basis. In other words, the delivery service takes responsibility for getting it there, but will abandon the attempt after a certain amount of time has passed or a number of attempts at delivery have been made. In the usual datagram implementation there is not even feedback in case of failed delivery.

The datagram is the basic message transfer unit used in both LANs and internetwork communications, such as in the operation of the Internet (Figure 19.1b). In the remainder of this chapter we will focus on an example of LAN operation; the next chapter will review Internet operations.

19.3 The Ethernet

One of the first LANs and by far the most successful to be developed is the Ethernet and its progeny. In 1976 a paper[1] was published by members of the Xerox Palo

---

[1]   Robert M. Metcalfe and David R. Boggs, Ethernet: Distributed packet switching for local computer networks, *Communications of the ACM*, July 1976, Vol. 19, No. 7.

Alto Research Center (Xerox PARC) group, which outlined the concept for a communications scheme that could link 256 computers and other office equipment for the purposes of sharing documents and other information. The approach, called the Ethernet in this paper, was improved upon and published as a proposed industry standard in September of 1980 by the team formed by Digital Equipment Corporation, Intel, and Xerox. This standard is now known as Ethernet DIX. A slightly tightened version of this standard (reissued by the three companies soon after and now known as Ethernet II) is the basis for most LAN implementations in use today. The Institute of Electrical and Electronic Engineers (IEEE) modified the specifications for Ethernet protocol and published it as IEEE Standard 802.3 in 1984.

The Ethernet was originally intended as a backbone for the operation of the office of the future. In such an office, no unnecessary paper changes hands, and paper is not used as the universal medium of exchange between office equipment. Instead, after a letter is typed and stored as data, that data could be transferred to a printer, a copier, an overhead projector, or to the archive file system. To make such an office possible, it would be necessary for all office equipment manufacturers to absolutely agree upon data formats and to make equipment that could be pulled out of a box and instantly plugged into the network anywhere and without difficult administrative set-up by specially trained network technologists.

When compared to these goals, it is obvious that the Ethernet and literally all of today's network technology have been an utter failure (some would say disaster). On the other hand, thinking and development based on such lofty goals has resulted in the creation of one of today's greatest growth industries and a change in business and lifestyles that is almost unrivaled in history. Not a bad job for a miss.

Ethernet II provides means of transmitting 10 Mbps data streams among large numbers of computers distributed over a 2.5 km (1.5 mile) diameter area. Later revisions of the Ethernet scheme have realized data speeds as high as 1 Gbps. Figure 19.2 shows an Ethernet card and cabling in the original "daisy chain" configuration.

It may seem that a 2.5 km diameter is rather limiting. But, as you will see in the following, efficient operations arise from keeping this size small. To transmit information over larger areas these smaller LANs can be interconnected with other schemes that allow information to be shared selectively. These interconnections, which we will discuss in more detail in the next chapter, make up the Internet.

There are two components of the Ethernet architecture that are of interest to us here. The first is the datagram itself. We will take a brief look at what is packaged inside this electronic telegram. The second, to be treated in the following subsection, is the means that the Ethernet uses to move datagrams to and from many users efficiently and without the need for prearranged connections.

19.3.1 The Ethernet Datagram

The Ethernet datagram is a collection of data composed of the following (Figure 19.3):

Preamble: An 8-byte sequence that is always the same. This acts as a flag that a receiving system can watch for and synchronize itself with, so that the body of the message can be properly identified. The preamble provides an important protocol service: it stands out in a way that cannot be mistaken for any other part of a message. Every recipient knows what information to expect and in what order immediately after seeing the preamble.

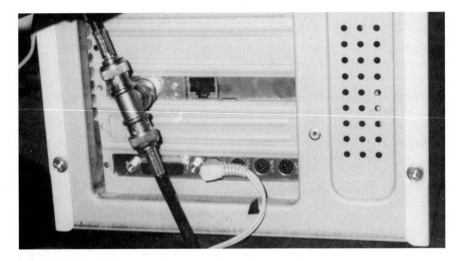

FIGURE 19.2 This computer is connected to a 10 Megabit per second Ethernet LAN, which uses a thin coaxial cable to communicate datagrams between the members of the LAN. The computer in this case attaches by means of a *T* connector, which simply allows it to place its transmissions on the cable and listen to transmissions from all the other computers on its LAN. The use of coaxial cables is rapidly being phased out in favor of the use of more cost effective Unshielded Twisted Pair (UTP) cables. The Ethernet card in this picture has a socket for a UTP cable connector just above the coaxial connector.

Destination Address: A 6-byte address that uniquely identifies the recipient of the datagram from all recipients throughout the world. That's right: A 48-bit number is big enough that every computer can have its own address without overlap.

Source Address: Another 6-byte address that identifies the sender of the datagram.

Type Field: A 2-byte identifier of the type of handling that this datagram should receive by the recipient. There are groups that issue standards regarding how this number is used. For example, a type value of 0800 Hex identifies an Internet Protocol packet as would be generated by Internet-related services.

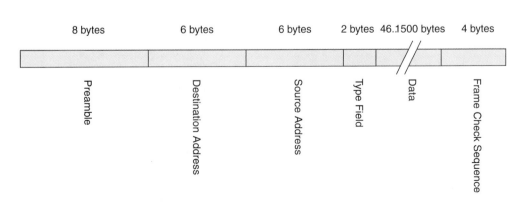

FIGURE 19.3 Diagram of an Ethernet data packet (datagram).

Data: From 46 to 1500 bytes of data intended for use by the destination system. This would contain perhaps a fragment of a picture being moved through the Web or a piece of text from an e-mail.

Frame Check Sequence: A 4-byte number constructed from processing of all the data that follows the preamble in a certain way. The chances that the same number would result from similarly processing an altered version of this data are very, very, small. Thus, the recipient can process the received data in the same way and check its FCS calculation with the one that was received. If they differ, the message can be discarded as being in error.

The Ethernet addresses, which are the key to datagram operation, are uniquely issued and permanently attached to Ethernet hardware (the piece of electronics in your computer that attaches to the network wire). The IEEE was given the duty in January of 1986 to issue these addresses, which they renamed Organizationally Unique Identifiers (OUIs). Every manufacturer of Ethernet equipment submits a request to the IEEE, which grants the use of blocks of these addresses. The manufacturer then installs each address exactly once into each device manufactured. Thus, no two Ethernet devices ever built, or ever to be built, share the same OUI. Hence, a datagram launched from one machine to another cannot be misdelivered.

With a 48 bit address size, there are approximately 3×10^{14} addresses available— that is, about 20,000,000 addresses per person on the face of the Earth. Thus, even though addresses are never used, there is an almost inexhaustible supply. In Figure 19.4 we see the electronic chip on an Ethernet LAN connection card that holds this card's unique address.

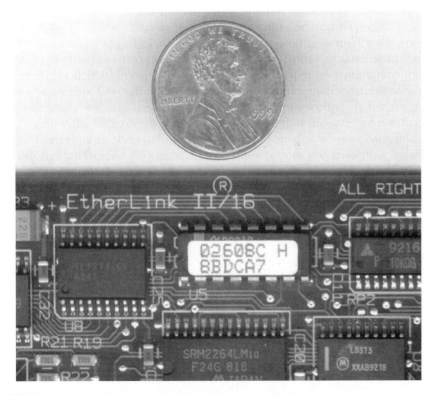

FIGURE 19.4 On this Ethernet network interface card (NIC) a chip holds the Organizationally Unique Identifier for this card. The 48 bit OUI, which is written in Hexadecimal format on the chip label, 02608C8BDCA7, will never be minted again!

Ethernet Cable

FIGURE 19.5 Ethernet Local Area Network technology is based upon an efficient message delivery scheme (for small collections of computers) in which all messages are simply transmitted on a single shared cable and the unique addresses (names) on the datagram alert the desired recipient.

Now that we know what goes into a datagram, we need to discuss how these datagrams are delivered to the correct destination.

19.3.2 Datagram Transmission and Delivery

Now, let's consider how we might deliver information most quickly between any two parties from among a large group. Imagine 30 people with unique names who may each occasionally need to send information to another person from the group. Suppose each person has a desk placed somewhere in a large room, but we don't tell anyone where they must sit and they occasionally change positions to get better window views or to sit closer to the coffee machine. For this example, suppose the names of the people are Alice, Bob, Carol, and so on. Now, suppose Dave has a message for George. Dave could write a telegram, write *George* on the outside of the envelope, and hand it off to a delivery person who circulates the room. The delivery person has no idea where anyone will be seated in general, so at each point in a delivery round, he has to check the nameplate on the desk and look through all the telegrams. Eventually every telegram gets delivered, but the system is not exactly fast.

Here's another approach to our delivery problem: Dave stands up and shouts "George!" and then reads the message (Figure 19.5). George receives the message instantly. Everyone else hears but ignores the message. The seating arrangement had no impact and all that mattered was that the names of the people were unique.

Of course, this delivery approach would have a problem if there were many more people in the room. With enough people trying to send telegrams in this way, at some point there will not be any empty time between shouts to add any more telegrams.

The Ethernet is based on exactly the scheme just described. All the computers in an Ethernet LAN are connected to a single piece of cable (it may be broken into smaller pieces for convenience, but these are hooked up to act like a single piece of wire). When one computer wishes to send a message to another, it simply transmits the datagram by causing a variation of the voltage on the wire. This variation can be seen by all the computers attached to that wire. It is as if the computer shouted the telegram in a room (the cable) occupied by all the computers.

The Ethernet hardware in each computer observes the destination addresses for each datagram and only passes on to its computer those datagrams that are addressed in a way that matches its own address. (There are other special "broadcast" addresses that mark information of interest to all parties. The parallel would be the messages "Fire!" or "Lunch!" shouted in our example office.)

Thus we see that the uniqueness of the OUI addresses assigned to Ethernet hardware is essential to the proper operation of this networking scheme. We also see that the single cable that connects all the computers is actually being shared by those computers. Thus, when a sufficient number of computers are connected to a single LAN, the *network performance* or perceived available bandwidth begins to drop. We also see here one reason that LANs need to be kept relatively small in size.

19.3.3 Collision Detection Multiple Access

Ethernet avoids the bottleneck of a circuit switch; that is, of a device that has to direct each packet from its input connections appropriately to the correct output connection by distributing the packet-switching function to all connected devices. When a datagram is transmitted, all connected devices see it and only the addressed recipient extracts the data from it and processes that data. This, however, raises an interesting question: How do we know when we can transmit a packet without interfering with someone else's transmissions? When is our computer allowed to shout?

The problem is actually harder than one might at first imagine. Because it takes time for a transmission to reach us, and no transmission can move faster than the speed of light, if we begin a transmission before someone else's transmission reaches us, we will corrupt their signal with ours.

Returning to our analogy based on office communications: suppose the office was 1,000 feet across. It takes about 1 second for sound to cross 1,000 feet. That means if Dave yells "George!" from the right side of the room, and Hank yells "Alice!" from the left side at the same time, neither one will know that the other was yelling at that moment. But, Alice and George, who are both at the center of the room, will hear neither of their names because the two shouts will overlap.

The solution in the case of Ethernet is not unlike that which our office workers might devise after some thought:

- We wait till the cable seems unused and begin transmitting.

- Every computer connected to the cable watches to see if two transmissions overlap. This is called a collision.

- If anyone sees a collision they "yell" an announcement of the fact. (This is called *jamming* in Ethernet lingo.)

- If anyone who is transmitting hears a collision or jamming announcement while they were transmitting, they stop.

- Each individual who aborted a transmission now rolls a pair of dice and waits that many seconds (in Ethernet it is actually a certain number of nanoseconds, or billionths of a second) before trying again.

- Whoever got the low roll obviously goes first and the *contention* for the use of the cable is resolved.

In the actual Ethernet specification there are many more details with respect to such things as the number of faces on dice thrown; that is, the range of possible wait values used. Furthermore there is an escalating scale of waiting times that increases the range of the potential random dice-roll outcomes as a function of how many times have we successfully tried to send the same message and still had a collision with someone.

This odd sounding and somewhat ad hoc approach to sharing a connection is remarkable in its robustness. Theoretical and practical studies[2] show that almost 100% of the bandwidth of a cable gets fairly used (every participant gets a fair share) even when very busy with many users competing for the bandwidth.

---

[2] David R. Boggs, Jeffrey C. Mogul, and Christopher A. Kent, Measured capacity of an Ethernet: Myths and reality, *Proceedings SIGCOMM '88, Symposium on Communication Architectures and Protocols*, 1988; pp. 222–234.

Summary

LAN technologies, such as the Ethernet, solve the problem of fast and efficient distribution of messages with the following favorable attributes:

- There is no need to tie each computer to each other computer with as many cables as there are pairs of computers. A single cable connects to each computer and the bandwidth of a single cable is shared by all.
- There is no bottleneck for information flow created by the need for a single device like a circuit switch to be involved in the connecting of computers or routing of messages. Each message is heard by all and selected on the basis of universally unique addresses.

While this scheme works very effectively for small groups of computers (up to a hundred or so) it could never be used to span a whole city, let alone the whole world. In the next chapter we will explore the construction of the Internet, which solves this large-scale interconnection problem.

Try These Exercises

1. Explain in your own words some of the advantages and disadvantages of the LAN compared to circuit-switched networks. (You might want to use the example of the circuit-switched network, to which a typical computer in the home belongs when it uses its modem and a phone-company-provided connection, to motivate your answer.)
2. LANs are appearing in homes as part of the behind-the-wall wiring of new and renovated houses. Explain how and why we might want to interconnect the home computer, telephone, television, burglar alarm, lawn sprinkler, coffee pot, clocks, and furnaces by a LAN.
3. The allowable amount of data in one Ethernet packet ranges from 46 to 1500 bytes. Why is there an upper limit? Explain in terms of the behaviors we might want to discourage in an office message delivery system based on the *Ether-shout* analogy described in this chapter.
4. Find a computer connected via a LAN at your school, library, or other location. Find out to which kind of network it connects from the markings on the network interface card, or from personnel responsible for that computer. Is it an Ethernet? What kind of cable does it use, coaxial or UTP? What data transmission speed does it provide (1, 10, 100, or 1000 Mbps)?
5. One of the alternative LAN technologies that was not a commercial success is called Token Ring. In this approach the random quality of Ethernet's collision and retransmission system is replaced by a more orderly system. A special packet, called a token, is handed from neighbor to neighbor on the wire. You can only transmit if you currently hold the token. Illustrate the difference between Ethernet and Token Ring with a set of drawings and a description, or demonstrate each of a group of classmates posing as computers.
6. Clearly, packet-oriented communications must include the destination address information in each packet. Explain why the source address is also needed.
7. A possible problem with packet-oriented data transmission is that packets may not be received in the order in which they are sent. This seems to be a serious problem, but the Ethernet protocol does not appear to have a field where the transmission order of each packet can be placed, to assist in reordering the packets. Is there a way to fix this apparent problem? Explain.

8. One potential problem with a multiple-access protocol such as Ethernet is that with high demand, the system can fail completely. This is because of continuous "collisions" among multiple users trying to communicate simultaneously. This is addressed with a process called "back off" in which users who find their access is blocked by a collision do not try to immediately repeat their transmission. Rather, they remain silent for some length of time. Explain why this helps, and how the length of time should be determined for each user. Specifically, should everyone wait the same length of time?

20 Organization of the Internet

Objectives

Now that we understand the types and principles of operation of transmission systems, both connection-oriented and pack-oriented, what is left to discuss regarding data transmission? The Internet has not been explained, and that is the topic of this chapter. Specifically, you will learn about:

▲ what the Internet is and is not;

▲ the systems design process that led to the Internet standards which have proven so broadly useful;

▲ specific Internet addressing schemes: OUI and IP addresses, and DNS host names;

▲ the central role of routing in the Internet;

▲ the makeup of the Internet backbone; and

▲ the role played by Internet Service Providers (ISPs).

20.1 Introduction

The Internet is not a single entity or even a uniform collection of entities. The Internet describes a system with the complexity and dynamics of the "Government." In this introduction we will explore this analogy. Without this comparison it might not be at first apparent that a technological entity could be as complicated and as vaguely organized as a social construct. But, that is indeed the case. Where would you begin to describe the government of the United States? Some might begin with a historical perspective: The government began as the result of the work of a small group of activists who chose to experiment with a structure of governance based on the inherent equality and freedom of all people and as determined by a rule of law and not of particular men in power. The Internet began as an experiment based on the freedom to interconnect any device based on rules of protocol and not on the particular wires and signals used to carry that information. In either case we could examine how each system flourished and multiplied in size and influence thanks to the great power for personal and commercial success that was granted to parties involved in each.

Another approach would be to describe the government by the laws that have been adopted and the process by which those laws are ratified, new laws are proposed, and conflicts are resolved. Likewise the Internet may be described by details of the protocols that are used to transfer the data. The first of these protocols were drafted by the small group of founders, but eventually grew to meet the needs of new kinds of communications (such as the Web) and to resolve weaknesses that were identified from the experience of users. Eventually a system for evaluation of proposals and adoption of new protocols arose to meet the needs of this dynamic entity.[1]

Still another approach involves describing the bodies and organizations that make up the government. One would have to describe the operation of city and town governments, how they are related to county and state governments, and how these are affected by the federal government. Next one would have to deal with the operations of many overlapping jurisdictions and systems such as local, state, and federal law enforcement officers, the federally sanctioned mail system versus independent package delivery companies, and the tax system that supports the cost of this large enterprise.

Likewise the Internet may be described in terms of a similarly loosely knit, overlapping but coordinated collection of backbone, national, regional, and local access providers. The routing of information on the Internet may vary from minute to minute and may involve transmission over many different subsystems chosen on the basis of available bandwidth and rate structures. One would have to explain how you and your neighbor might purchase access from two entirely different Internet Service Providers (ISPs), yet be able to share information without knowledge of either's choice. There is also a structure of fees that are invisibly exchanged by these various access providers for each other's interconnection services. In this chapter we cannot hope to explain the whole of the Internet at any significant level of detail. What we shall do instead is provide a broad picture of its operation and how we can understand it in terms of common systems such as the mail system.

20.2 How Would You Organize Universal Mail Delivery?

In the last chapter we saw that LAN technology, which is well suited for rapid delivery of datagrams over a minimum of wire connections, is poorly suited for delivery of information over large distances involving very large collections of possible senders and recipients.

📖 **LAN**

To understand how a large-scale system might be devised, we can look to existing mail delivery systems for a hint. Along the top of Figure 20.1 we see a depiction of a set of events that might take place in the delivery of a piece of mail from one organization to another. We will step through this example and explore the parallels between it and the delivery of an e-mail message via the Internet. First we will step though the case of the mail delivery.

1. Suppose we (the authors) want to send a piece of mail to our friend David Coldera's office at his place of employment. We address an envelope to him via a well known protocol for paper mail. The address describes the broad geographic region on the last line, and narrower and narrower destination descriptions as we work our way up the lines.

2. We then stick the mail in a mail pick-up tray in our department's office which is labeled: OFF CAMPUS. An interoffice mail handler will come by and toss this tray into a sack with the "Off Campus Mail Services" address for delivery to the office that handles mail leaving the university. This first delivery has

---

[1] The Internet Society (ISOC) (http://www.isoc.org/) is the overseer of the operation and evolution of the Internet. The Internet Architecture Board, a technical advisory group within the ISOC, is responsible for oversight of the protocols and procedures used by the Internet and administers the adoption and appeals procedures related to new protocols.

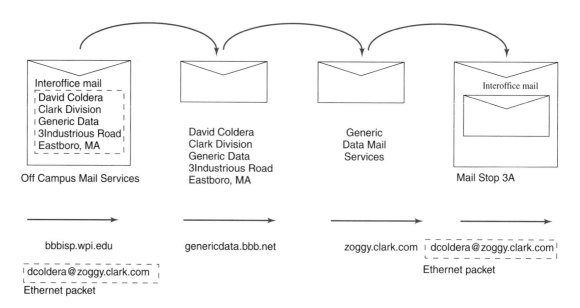

FIGURE 20.1 As explained in the text, there are deep parallels between the routing of mail between organizations and the routing of e-mail between individuals on the Internet.

nothing to do with the address we wrote on the envelope, but simply is determined by the internal code implied by the tray we used and the label on the sack it was placed into.

3. Once it arrives at the Off Campus Mail Services office, the letter is removed from the sack and routed into the U.S. Mail sack versus one of the sacks used for exchange of mail between a few local universities. This choice is made on the basis of the destination address we wrote on the envelope.

4. At the post office, our friend's name and division are altogether ignored. The post office forwards the letter to other post offices, based first upon the city and state (and finer zip code information, in reality) and then finally on the company address.

5. Once it arrives at the company, interoffice mail workers place the envelope in a box destined for a particular building and jot the room number on the envelope based upon the division location and the person's name. The detailed delivery information is obtained by looking up the name in a company mail directory.

6. Finally, a mail delivery person places the letter into our friend's in-box based on the match of the room numbers (after all, they can't be expected to remember everyone's name in a large company).

Now we will describe the sequence of events that take place during the delivery of an e-mail. The steps with corresponding numbers in the two descriptions are associated with related actions.

1. We will now send a piece of e-mail to our friend David Coldera's PC at his place of employment. We will address the e-mail via a well known protocol. The address describes the broad category of recipients (.com) in the last segment of the address, and narrower and narrower destination descriptions as we work our way toward the beginning of the line with our friend's computer name and account name last in this right-to-left reading of the address parts.

2. Our computer checks the tail end of this address and determines that it is destined for an off campus location. (It would have to have ended in *.wpi.edu* to remain on campus.) So, our computer sends it to a *router* (bbbisp.wpi.edu), which handles all data packets going off campus. A router is an electronic device that will handle data that arrives and departs from the Internet Service Provider's (ISP's) network. Our computer sends the data there by wrapping it in an electronic sack with the router's LAN address. The sack is an Ethernet packet and the OUI for the router is the label on the sack. This first movement of the e-mail has nothing to do with the detailed address of the destination, and is simply based on the fact that the destination is off campus.

3. Once it arrives at the router, the e-mail is removed from the original Ethernet packet and routed onto one of several high-speed digital telephone T1 cables. In this case it is routed to one that connects this router with our ISP's network. The decision is again simply based on the fact that we have no direct connection to the final destination.

📖 T1

4. Within the ISP's network, our friend's account name and computer name are altogether ignored. The ISP's routers forward the letter to other routers based upon the broadest parts of the address information. A complication is actually being breezed over in this description: a router actually uses a directory scheme known as the Domain Name System to look up the *hostname* in the address (in this case zoggy.clark.com), which provides a more detailed geographic code known as an IP address (think of it as a zip code) for the routing of the data.

5. Once it arrives at the company's router (genericdata.bbb.net), the data is placed in another Ethernet packet destined for the particular PC that appeared in the address (zoggy). That Ethernet address is obtained by looking up the computer's name in a local directory (it is called an Address Resolution Protocol, or ARP, table).

6. Finally, having reached the computer, zoggy, the e-mail is removed from the Ethernet packet and placed into our friend's e-mail arrival box.

20.2.1 The Internet: Three Addressing Schemes

One of the facts exposed by the above treatment is that the exchange of information on the Internet is directed by three different sets of addresses! This may seem unnecessary at first glance, but there are actually good reasons for using each (some of which were indicated in our mail analogy above).

Recounting, the three address schemes are:

OUI Addresses: These 48-bit addresses uniquely identify every Ethernet (and Token-Ring LAN card) ever made. These are permanently attached to each card at the time of manufacture.

IP Addresses: These 32-bit addresses identify every attachment of a machine to the Internet (this has been carefully worded to be exactly correct as a single computer may be attached in more than one way to the Internet). Groups of these addresses, called subnets, are *geographically co-located*.

DNS Hostnames: These alphanumeric addresses parallel the IP Addresses in identifying individual network connections and subnets, but are further distinguished by a domain hierarchy based on some or all of the following: country code, service code, network name, and/or organization name. Let's examine a concrete example. There is a computer on our campus that is known as *ece.wpi.edu*. This name is actually the DNS hostname for the com-

📖 DNS

puter. It is easy for people to remember this name because it breaks down into natural units:

ece: This is the primary computer in the Electrical and Computer Engineering (ECE) Department.

wpi: The ECE department of which we are speaking is in an institution known as WPI.

edu: WPI is an educational institution.

The DNS system was invented not to route information, but to make it easy for people to remember computer addresses. Why not just remember the IP addresses that the Internet routers themselves will use? The IP address that one obtains on looking up ece.wpi.edu in the DNS directory is: 130.215.16.20. Will you remember this address tomorrow?

Why do routers use the IP address instead of directly using the DNS hostname? This address is broken into parts that can be used to route the data over a long trip without being buried in detail. In the case of our example, the first part of the address, 130.215, is reserved for exclusive use by WPI. Thus, based on this part of the address, e-mail can be routed to WPI from anywhere in the world. Once it gets here, the next segment (16) can be used to route the data to a specific building, while the last (20) is routed to the specific machine.

Finally, when the data gets to the router that will place a packet on the Ethernet LAN for the last leg of the trip, the Ethernet address 08-00-2B-BC-C2-BC can be used to alert the specific machine. Although it is complicated, the protocols used to build the Internet actually arise from common-sense solutions to problems of information engineering that have been encountered before in other forms of human communication.

20.2.2 Tracing a Route

There is a means by which we can have every routing device on the path of a datagram report its name to us. Using this we can discover the path that our Internet traffic will take from one site to another. In Table 20.1 we show the record of such a discovery process, from our campus to the computer named rover.acorn.net, which is in the Akron-Summit County Public Library library in Akron, Ohio.

TABLE 20.1   THE ROUND TRIP TIMES REPORTED FOR INTERNET COMMUNICATIONS TO A SERIES OF ROUTERS. ALL TIME INTERVALS ARE REPORTED IN MILLISECONDS.

```
 1   bbnplanet.WPI.EDU (130.215.24.9)   9.215 ms   15.666 ms   16.532 ms
 2   worcester-cr1.bbnplanet.net (131.192.56.25)   36.596 ms   42.497 ms   63.827 ms
 3   cambridge1-mr3.bbnplanet.net (206.34.110.9)   60.083 ms   76.261 ms   56.262 ms
 4   cambridge1-br2.bbnplanet.net (206.34.78.21)   98.313 ms   74.044 ms   27.291 ms
 5   cambridge2-br2.bbnplanet.net (4.0.2.26)   139.187 ms   446.458 ms   482.561 ms
 6   cambridge2-br1.bbnplanet.net (192.233.33.5)   104.088 ms   76.225 ms   61.284 ms
 7   borderx2-hssi3-0.Boston.mci.net (204.70.179.121)   50.918 ms   167.298 ms   51.315 ms
 8   core2-fddi1-0.Boston.mci.net (204.70.179.65)   240.09 ms   29.653 ms   57.768 ms
 9   core3-hssi-1.WestOrange.mci.net (204.70.1.9)   86.49 ms   79.266 ms   105.992 ms
10   ohio-state-university.Washington.mci.net (166.48.43.250)   64.843 ms   78.222 ms   67.779 ms
11   ohio-state-university.Washington.mci.net (166.48.43.250)   104.159 ms   125.177 ms   124.582 ms
12   sot5-atm4-0.columbus.oar.net (199.18.202.25)   160.183 ms   189.177 ms   301.07 ms
13   oeb8-atm0-0.columbus.oar.net (199.18.202.18)   82.77 ms   70.595 ms   144.468 ms
14   alp-oeb-2.oar.net (199.18.105.182)   157.439 ms   123.238 ms   100.807 ms
15   199.18.101.146 (199.18.101.146)   77.474 ms   146.6 ms   91.233 ms
16   rover.acorn.net (199.218.0.2)   78.937 ms   70.749 ms   92.026 ms
```

Two interesting things can be gleaned from Table 20.1. The first is the number of routers (16) that need to be traversed on this path. This provides a good picture of the complexity that underlies that Internet despite the impression one obtains of the Internet being a single entity.

The second piece of interesting information is related to the three numbers at the end of each of the 16 router identification lines. Each router along the path was actually probed three times. Hence, with 16 routers 48 round-trip probes were completed, and the times were recorded. The three numbers report the round-trip time (in thousandths of a second) from our machine initiating the probe until the response returned. For example, the three probes of router number 12 yielded round-trip times of 160.183, 189.177, and 301.07 milliseconds. Note the wide variation from one probe to the next! In fact, while generally the round-trip response for farther routers took longer than for closer ones, since the probing tests are all separate sometimes all three tests of a closer router (like number 12) happened to take longer than the next three probes of a farther router (number 13). This underscores the fact that the network cables and routing equipment in the Internet are all shared! If the level of communications traffic happened to increase momentarily while we were probing router 12, the round trip time would exceed that of number 13 even though this test passed through 12.

20.3 What Makes up the Backbone of the Internet?

From the previous discussions in this chapter, you are probably beginning to form some picture of the structure of the Internet. In this section we will further clarify this structure. When you drop a piece of mail in a mailbox, the letter carrier who picks it up does not carry it all the way to its destination. Obviously this would involve every letter carrier in the world having to travel all over the world on a continual basis. Instead, the mail system is organized to first move mail from individual boxes to post offices, where it can be sorted into collections that are headed either directly to nearby post offices for delivery, or to larger central offices that tie together more distant post offices. In fact, there is a hierarchy of central offices that move larger collections of mail to neighboring central offices, or to offices representing still larger groups of central offices.

The general scheme is based on the fact that we want to collect all the mail headed from the east coast to the west coast into a single shipment for the sake of speed, ease of handling, and cost of shipment.

This is exactly the case for the Internet as well. The various ISPs are like the letter carriers who pick up and deliver the mail to your door. The ISPs will handle movement of data directly that passes from one customer to another of the same ISP. However, data destined for another ISP in the same region is passed between the ISPs through the services provided by a regional Internet access provider. Data headed outside the region will be passed by the regional provider to a national provider, which in turn may purchase access to a backbone cable from a backbone provider to send large collections of data from coast to coast (or similarly large distances). This breakdown of service providers is shown schematically in Figure 20.2.

At a greater level of detail, the Internet loses the appearance of a simple and well organized hierarchy like that presented above. In Figure 20.3 we see an example of a small piece of the Internet in which some of the transmission technologies have been revealed. Here we see, on the left, three LANs (two based on two types of Ethernet and another on a Token-Ring network) that connect to routers at their

FIGURE 20.2 The Internet comprises a system of hierarchical access providers that move data over short and long distances by using the same scheme that has been used by post offices for centuries.

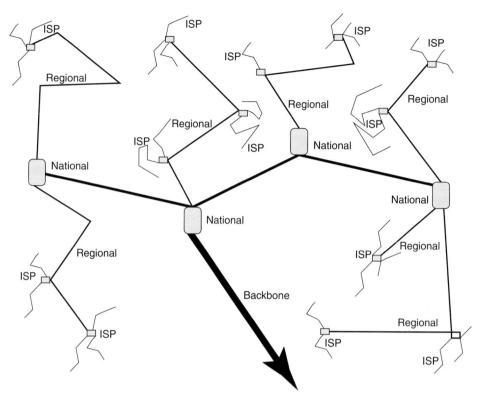

FIGURE 20.3 The Internet is constructed from a wide variety of telecommunication technologies. The use of a common protocol allows us to enjoy the illusion of a single and uniform abstract entity.

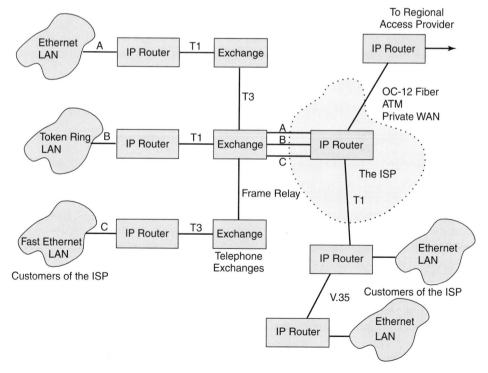

locations in order to connect to an ISP. The ISP will connect them to each other and to the remainder of the Internet. Now, how do these three customers connect to their ISP?

The ISP does not hire a backhoe and dig a trench to lay new wire for this connection. Instead, the ISP leases connections from the local telephone company. Hence, the telephone company provides T1 and T3 lines (described in an earlier chapter of this book) to connect the data from these companies to the telephone exchange switches. Thus, the telephone company's role is to set up virtual circuits from the companies' routers to the ISP's Internet Protocol (IP) router (via lines labeled A, B, and C in the diagram). The telephone company's equipment is actually unaware of the content of the data being moved; its job is simply to be a conduit.

Now, at the ISP, a router examines the Internet addresses in the data packets and makes decisions as to which way to direct the packets. Some are directed (downward in the diagram) via another telephone T1 line directly to other customers of the ISP. The ISP in this case has actually linked two nearby customers via another telephone-company-provided circuit (V.35) so as to not have to run two long high-bandwidth cables to both.

Some data, however, are directed (upward in the diagram) via high-bandwidth connections (in this case an optical-fiber-based Wide Area Network, or WAN) to a regional access provider where it may end up being directed to another ISP or onward toward a national provider.

Summary

In this chapter you have seen that the Internet is a vast piece of information engineering that depends upon the organized cooperation of many organizations. One of the reasons that it was able to grow as quickly as it has, doubling in size (as measured by the number of connected computers) every year and a half, is because of its highly decentralized nature. If a single organization had to plan each and every connection, it would never have happened.

Of course, no one would have been interested in taking their part in constructing the Internet if there were not financial rewards for doing so. In the last five years, the Internet has become a tool of commerce, and that has infused it with the investments needed to fuel further growth. In the next chapter we will examine how commerce is conducted in a system where it appears that no information is private.

Try These Exercises

1. Compare the operation of the Internet to that of the telephone system. Identify specific aspects of each system such as: how a call is set up; how a packet is routed; real-time performance; etc. Compare and contrast these aspects.

2. Choose one from among the Internet connections to which you have access (home, school, or work). Find out the name of the company that provides your ISP service. How large is that company in terms of number of employees, annual revenues, and/or the size of the geographic area served? What is the bit rate of the connection between your system and the ISP? What is the bit rate of the connection that the ISP has for access to their regional or national service provider? You will have to talk to your system administrator, research the ISP on the Web, and perhaps make a call to the ISP itself to get this

information. Members of the class that need to call the same ISP might want to coordinate questions for a single call.

3. Choose one from among the Internet connected computers to which you have access. What is the OUI of that computer's network interface? What is that computer's IP address? What is that computer's DNS host name? What is that computer's domain name? You will need either to talk to your computer's administrator, or obtain help from someone who knows how to query your computer for that information.

4. The use of the Internet for telephone communications (Voice on IP or VoIP) is under active development, and some experts predict that the conventional circuit-switched telephone network will soon disappear. Summarize the advantages and disadvantages of VoIP versus conventional telephony. Address the particular features of packet-oriented and connection-oriented networks with respect to telephone communications.

5. Asynchronous Transfer Mode (ATM) combines some particular features of both packet-oriented and connection-oriented networks. Explain these features, and why this combination may be valuable. You may wish to explore this topic in additional reference works.

6. This chapter describes the characteristics of "Wide Area Networks" (WANs) as opposed to Local Area Networks (LANs) which may be implemented with technology such as Ethernet. Describe the similarities and differences in these two types of data networks.

7. Explain why there is a need for several different types of addresses for use with the Internet. Specifically, explain the use for OUI and IP addresses, and for DNS names.

21 Electronic Commerce and Information Security

Objectives

Much of the excitement of the communications revolution is being generated because of the many fundamentally new services and capabilities which can be provided. The World Wide Web is the primary example that has been presented to this point in this book. In this chapter we look at the broad area of electronic commerce, and its necessary component, data security. Major topics include:

▲ the four fundamentally different threats to data security;

▲ the six basic types of security services which may be provided;

▲ basic principles of cryptography (creating secure codes) and cryptanalysis (the attempt to break the codes);

▲ some examples of classic encryption/decryption schemes;

▲ means of determining the relative level of security of a given coding system;

▲ the concept of a "key," and public and private key crypto systems; and

▲ concepts of digital signatures, digital cash, and other necessary components of electronic commerce.

21.1 Introduction

Since its introduction, the number of users connected to the Internet has grown at an exponential rate, nearly doubling every year! By the middle of 1999 the number of computers connected to the Internet exceeded 50 million.

It is no wonder then that today, in almost every traditional advertisement, a WWW address is provided for immediate access to additional information and services. The market for advertising on the Web itself is so great that some of the earliest commercial Web company success stories include those companies offering Internet search services. Internet search engines can dynamically customize advertisements based on search inquiry topic, dramatically increasing the effectiveness of an advertisement.

In addition to simply advertising over the Internet, many companies have established electronic storefronts permitting electronic commerce over the Internet. For example, in 1999, Amazon.com, Inc. claimed to be the world's largest bookstore, offering over 4.7 million book titles in addition to music CDs and videos, all accessible over the Internet.

Amazon.com provides an excellent example to illustrate the rate at which electronic commerce over the Internet is growing. For the 1996 fiscal year, Amazon.com reported 15.7 million dollars in net sales. In 1997, net sales increased by

838% to 147.8 million dollars. In 1998 those sales climbed again, to 1 billion dollars. By the end of 1999 its sales had reached 1.64 billion dollars.

Cisco Systems, Inc. is a computer networking giant that has also observed increased profits due to conducting business over the Internet, reporting sales of $4.1 billion in 1996, $6.4 billion in 1997, and $8.5 billion in 1998. In the case of Cisco, however, the growth is driven by the effect of the successes of companies like Amazon.com in driving people onto the Internet because of the services that can be offered through digital commerce. Thus these sales increases reflect the growth in numbers of people joining the Internet.

As a result of electronic commerce, many companies have reported reductions in transaction processing time and customer service costs, further contributing to the success of a business. The list of successful Internet-based business ventures is rapidly expanding, and accordingly, technologies supporting the electronic commerce infrastructure are rapidly emerging.

In this chapter we will examine the information engineering technology that makes the use of the Internet for commerce possible. As we saw in the previous chapter, data on the Internet conforms to certain absolute protocol rules. And in many cases, there are many machines handling or capable of listening to transmissions from other machines. How does one conduct private and sensitive financial transactions on such a system without betraying enough information to become susceptible to theft and fraud? The key is the use of information security protocols; that is, secret codes.

21.2 Threats to Information Security

As today's information technology and data networks are used for a broader range of applications, security plays an increasingly important role. To design and operate a secure system, one must first identify the potential security *threats*. Four basic categories of threats commonly recognized by information engineers are:

- Data disclosure;
- Fraud;
- Data insertion, removal, and modification; and
- Denial of service.

Probably the most obvious threat to the security of a system is that posed by data disclosure. By data disclosure we mean the threat of someone being able to read and comprehend our data. For example, if we are transmitting our credit card number over the Internet, we would hope that no one could see it because they could then use it to make purchases in our name. Eavesdropping is an example of an *attack* resulting in data disclosure. As has been stated before, eavesdropping is quite readily accomplished on the Internet. Secret codes provide one remedy for this attack because our credit card number does not become disclosed by someone seeing the coded message.

A second threat increasingly apparent in Internet commerce is the ability to misrepresent identities, referred to as fraud. In order for a consumer to feel comfortable providing an electronic storefront with information such as credit card numbers, the consumer must be able to positively authenticate the identity of the commercial enterprise at the other end of the connection. Likewise, the commercial enterprise will not want to commit a transaction unless the consumer can be identified.

A third threat to the security of a system is data insertion, removal, and/or modification. To illustrate this threat, consider an electronic banking system. If it is possible to modify the data during transit, then it is possible to alter the financial transactions. The attacker need not even be able to understand the data to cause havoc in this situation.

For example, imagine that young hackers, simply seeking the thrill of doing damage on a global scale, were to switch a few bits in a financial data transmission which has been coded with a secret code. While the hackers have no detailed idea about the change in the transaction that will be caused when the corrupted message is decoded, they can be sure that some accounts have been affected.

The fourth threat to the security of a system is denial of service. A denial-of-service attack involves preventing you from accessing data or service by confusing or overloading the computers or networking equipment involved in your transaction.

One mechanism to accomplish such an attack is to consume so much of a shared resource that the resource is not available to other users. For an example that is not Internet related, consider the fact that if someone repeatedly called the 911 emergency phone number without cause and without pause, they would prevent callers in actual distress from finding help.

An example of how denial of service is committed on the Internet is related to a widely publicized means of attack on the Transmission Control Protocol (TCP), known as the SYN flooding attack. TCP is a communication protocol commonly used on the Internet for many kinds of communication. In fact, when you are using your WWW browser, you are actually using TCP to connect and exchange information with WWW servers.

Prior to establishing a TCP connection, synchronization messages are exchanged between the two communicating computers. With the TCP SYN flooding attack, a malicious user attempts to open so many TCP connections with a server that additional incoming connections will be denied because all server resources used to store and track these connections have been used up.

The TCP SYN flooding attack was used to bring down an ISP in New York City on September 6, 1996.[1] Further complicating matters, interactive Web technologies such as Java, JavaScript, and ActiveX increase the difficulty of preventing denial-of-service attacks. With these technologies, a denial-of-service attack can be easily embedded in programs, widely distributed, and executed on computers that were being used to simply "browse the Web."

21.3 Security Services

Just as it is instructive and constructive to list categories of security threats, it is also helpful to list the remedies that we can apply to bypass or reduce the severity of these threats. Several security services have been categorized that we can apply alone or in combination to protect against the threats identified above, including:

- *Privacy*: preventing others from being able to comprehend our data.
- *Authentication*: positively identifying an object or identity.
- *Access Control*: restricting access to data or a service to privileged identities only.
- *Integrity*: ensuring that the data has not been altered since its creation.
- *Nonrepudiation*: ensuring that the originator cannot deny being the source of the data, and that the recipient cannot deny that the data was received.

---

[1] Simon Garfinkel and Gene Spafford, *Web Security and Commerce*, O'Reilly and Associates, Inc., Cambridge, MA; 1997.

- *Replay Prevention*: ensures that data previously deemed valid cannot be resent by an attacker and mistakenly validated by a system a second time.

A privacy service is one that allows us to hide information in plain sight. Secret codes are routinely used on the Internet to do exactly this. In fact, the commercial success of the Internet would not have been possible without major advances in the theory and practice of secret coding technology.

Authentication is used to prove that each end of a transaction is who it claims to be. As you will see in the next section, secret codes play an important role in this too, but ultimately some party, somewhere, must be trusted in order to build a chain of trust down to the end parties. In ordinary transactions, for example, there is often an agreement to trust the Motor Vehicle Bureau to issue drivers' licenses only to the correct people—hence, our check is only accepted if we have our license to present. Companies have appeared on the Internet (known as Certificate Authorities) that provide that trusted-party role for digital transactions.

Access control can be enforced in as simple a fashion as locking the door to a computer with important information and only giving a key to trusted individuals. Access control for computers connected to the Internet is often provided through the use of special equipment or sofware that is called a "Firewall" or "Proxy Server."

Let's examine the operation of a Proxy Server. Suppose you wish to prevent outsiders from having any opportunity to connect to a group of computers in your company; this would prevent someone from finding some vulnerability of your computer (like a weak password checking system) which might lead to a break-in by the attacker and loss of important data. Yet, you also wish to allow all of your computers to be able to contact the World Wide Web so that you can conduct business through online access to other companies. To accomplish this we can connect just one computer, the Proxy Server, to the Internet and place no confidential data on it. This computer then executes proxy server software that allows your other computers to ask it for information from the Internet. Thus, the computers inside "the firewall" have access to the outside thanks to the handling of those requests by the Proxy Server, but only the Proxy Server is threatened by the outside world.

Access control can also involve using transmission cables that cannot be *tapped*, or requiring authentication prior to allowing a computer to divulge the content of certain data files.

Integrity services provide means to determine whether or not data has been altered regardless of the care and resources of the counterfeiter. This may seem impossible to do, but in the next section you will discover that a special application of secret code technology allows the creation of *digital signatures* that provide exactly that capability.

Nonrepudiation services disallow a different kind of fraud than that considered above. Suppose we purchase an expensive watch and then call the credit card company and report our card as having been stolen just before that purchase. Using techniques for nonrepudiation in an Internet transaction allows the credit card company to prove that it was indeed you that made the purchase.

Replay prevention handles a special kind of integrity service loophole. While an integrity service allows us to guarantee that our data has not been corrupted, imagine the havoc that would be generated when someone simply retransmitted the same data. For example, suppose you withdraw some money from the bank. A malicious person can then record this coded transaction and simply replay it a few thousand times. When they are done, your bank account is empty. Replay prevention requires that the transaction have a time-stamp or similar means to distinguish one use of a message from another even if identical transactions are possible.

In the next section we will examine the role of secret codes in providing not only privacy services but several of the required security services.

21.4 Data Security and Cryptosystems

Cryptology is composed of two fundamental fields: cryptography and cryptanalysis. The primary objective of cryptography is to allow two or more users to communicate securely over an insecure medium, such as the Internet. The information to be transmitted, referred to as the plaintext, is encrypted using a predetermined key to generate the ciphertext. The ciphertext is transmitted over the insecure medium to the receiver, who recovers the plaintext using a cryptographic key and algorithm. That is, cryptography is the science of applying secret codes.

Cryptanalysis is the process of recovering the encryption key from the ciphertext; that is, breaking the code. Cryptanalysis teams work hand in hand with cryptography teams because we cannot be sure how good the cryptanalysis practiced by attackers will be. Our only hope for secure transactions is to vigorously attempt to break our own coding systems.

The strength of a cryptosystem (a specific secret code system) can be categorized into two classes:

- computationally secure, and
- unconditionally secure.

A cryptosystem is said to be computationally secure if the best known attack requires an amount of computational resources that is far too excessive to be a threat in practice. A cryptosystem is said to be unconditionally secure if the cryptosystem is secure against an attack with an infinite amount of resources available.

Obviously, if we had a choice, we would want to always use an unconditionally secure cryptosystem. After all, would we rather bet our bank account on a code that cannot be broken, or one that shouldn't be broken in a reasonable amount of time! Unfortunately, while unconditionally secure codes exist, they cannot be used for most purposes because they are simply too difficult to administer. The difficulty that arises is related to the need to somehow communicate to the desired recipient of the coded message (and no one else) the key needed to undo the code and read the message. We will examine this issue next.

Cryptosystems can further be divided into two categories: symmetric key cryptography and public key cryptography. Symmetric key codes have the same problem as unconditionally secure codes: the key to decode the message must be transported to the desired recipient without a chance of falling into the wrong hands. However, computationally secure codes have one advantage: the key is very small in length and is not a burden to transmit (which is not true of the unconditionally secure code key) if we have some secure means to get it there.

Public key cryptosystems provide a means to move information in a secure fashion without the need to secretly deliver a decoding key. This is a rather amazing capability that we will explain in what follows. It has the disadvantage, however, that it takes a tremendous amount of computing to code and decode a lengthy message.

Working together, symmetric key and public key cryptography systems possess the necessary characteristics to achieve information security for a wide variety of systems, including secure electronic commerce, e-mail and WWW interactivity.

One can use a public key cryptosystem to safely deliver the key for a symmetric code with a reasonable amount of computing effort thanks to the small size of the code key. Then, subsequent transactions of large amounts of data can proceed using the fast symmetric code system. This is the basis for essentially all of today's secure Internet data movements.

21.4.1 An Example of an Unconditionally Secure Code

An example of an unconditionally secure cryptographic algorithm is the *one-time pad* code. Historically, one-time pad cryptosystems have been used by diplomats when exchanging sensitive information. In the original application of this type of system, the code by which information is encrypted is contained on the pages of a pad of paper. Two copies of the pad are then made, one to be used to encrypt the plaintext and the second to be used to decrypt the ciphertext.

The ciphertext is obtained by opening the pad to the next available page, and using the text on that page as a code key to generate the ciphertext. One form that this code key can take is simply a string of numbers. Each number is used to shift the letter in the alphabet of the plain text to obtain the ciphertext. Hence, if the code key begins with 3, 1, 4, ... and the text begins with "The" then the cipher text becomes "Wii." If the shift runs off the end of the alphabet, we simply wrap around and continue from the letter A again.

Table 21.1 provides a means to quickly apply the one-time pad code. The top row indicates the number of spaces in the alphabet that a character in the first column is to be shifted. Below the numerical shifts in the top row are corresponding letters from the one-time pad: a space in the pad determines a shift of zero, an A determines a shift of 1, and so on.

After generating the ciphertext, the page is destroyed, never to be used again. Only the possessor of the second pad can then decrypt the information. If either pad is lost or stolen, the encoded information can be compromised.

When the one-time pad is implemented in computer software or hardware, the ciphertext can be obtained easily by using an even simpler strategy well suited to binary encoded information. In this case our one-time pad code key is simply a random string of zeroes and ones. The transformation of plaintext to ciphertext simply involves lining up the binary string to be coded with the code key, and then flipping every plaintext bit that lines up with a 1 in the code key and not flipping those that line up with a 0. The receiver recovers the plaintext by, once again, exactly repeating that process with its copy of the code key. This process is illustrated in Figure 21.1.

Of course, the key can only be used only once if this code is truly unconditionally secure. This gives rise to a fundamental disadvantage of the one-time pad cryptosystem in that the "key" must be at least as large as the plaintext, and that this key must be distributed via a secure channel. In other words, to be able to securely transmit the contents of a 300 page book with unconditional security, we need to first transmit to our recipient a key that has as many characters as a 300 page book, and do it with unconditional security. This is somewhat a chicken-and-egg problem.

Nevertheless, the one-time pad, as simple as it is and with its associated limitations, has been applied to military and diplomatic applications where unconditional security is of critical importance. That's because for certain special purposes, the code transfer can be done in a fairly reasonable fashion. For example, a diplomatic courier can carry a large code book to an ambassador in a foreign land. Then, radio transmissions can be securely made until the book runs out of code letters.

TABLE 21.1 A TABLE FOR GENERATING CIPHERTEXT FROM PLAINTEXT GIVEN A KEY CONSISTING OF EITHER NUMERICAL SHIFTS OR ENGLISH TEXT.

0	1	2	3	4	5	6	7	8	9	10	11	12	13	14	15	16	17	18	19	20	21	22	23	24	25	26
	A	B	C	D	E	F	G	H	I	J	K	L	M	N	O	P	Q	R	S	T	U	V	W	X	Y	Z
A	A	B	C	D	E	F	G	H	I	J	K	L	M	N	O	P	Q	R	S	T	U	V	W	X	Y	Z
B	B	C	D	E	F	G	H	I	J	K	L	M	N	O	P	Q	R	S	T	U	V	W	X	Y	Z	A
C	C	D	E	F	G	H	I	J	K	L	M	N	O	P	Q	R	S	T	U	V	W	X	Y	Z	A	B
D	D	E	F	G	H	I	J	K	L	M	N	O	P	Q	R	S	T	U	V	W	X	Y	Z	A	B	C
E	E	F	G	H	I	J	K	L	M	N	O	P	Q	R	S	T	U	V	W	X	Y	Z	A	B	C	D
F	F	G	H	I	J	K	L	M	N	O	P	Q	R	S	T	U	V	W	X	Y	Z	A	B	C	D	E
G	G	H	I	J	K	L	M	N	O	P	Q	R	S	T	U	V	W	X	Y	Z	A	B	C	D	E	F
H	H	I	J	K	L	M	N	O	P	Q	R	S	T	U	V	W	X	Y	Z	A	B	C	D	E	F	G
I	I	J	K	L	M	N	O	P	Q	R	S	T	U	V	W	X	Y	Z	A	B	C	D	E	F	G	H
J	J	K	L	M	N	O	P	Q	R	S	T	U	V	W	X	Y	Z	A	B	C	D	E	F	G	H	I
K	K	L	M	N	O	P	Q	R	S	T	U	V	W	X	Y	Z	A	B	C	D	E	F	G	H	I	J
L	L	M	N	O	P	Q	R	S	T	U	V	W	X	Y	Z	A	B	C	D	E	F	G	H	I	J	K
M	M	N	O	P	Q	R	S	T	U	V	W	X	Y	Z	A	B	C	D	E	F	G	H	I	J	K	L
N	N	O	P	Q	R	S	T	U	V	W	X	Y	Z	A	B	C	D	E	F	G	H	I	J	K	L	M
O	O	P	Q	R	S	T	U	V	W	X	Y	Z	A	B	C	D	E	F	G	H	I	J	K	L	M	N
P	P	Q	R	S	T	U	V	W	X	Y	Z	A	B	C	D	E	F	G	H	I	J	K	L	M	N	O
Q	Q	R	S	T	U	V	W	X	Y	Z	A	B	C	D	E	F	G	H	I	J	K	L	M	N	O	P
R	R	S	T	U	V	W	X	Y	Z	A	B	C	D	E	F	G	H	I	J	K	L	M	N	O	P	Q
S	S	T	U	V	W	X	Y	Z	A	B	C	D	E	F	G	H	I	J	K	L	M	N	O	P	Q	R
T	T	U	V	W	X	Y	Z	A	B	C	D	E	F	G	H	I	J	K	L	M	N	O	P	Q	R	S
U	U	V	W	X	Y	Z	A	B	C	D	E	F	G	H	I	J	K	L	M	N	O	P	Q	R	S	T
V	V	W	X	Y	Z	A	B	C	D	E	F	G	H	I	J	K	L	M	N	O	P	Q	R	S	T	U
W	W	X	Y	Z	A	B	C	D	E	F	G	H	I	J	K	L	M	N	O	P	Q	R	S	T	U	V
X	X	Y	Z	A	B	C	D	E	F	G	H	I	J	K	L	M	N	O	P	Q	R	S	T	U	V	W
Y	Y	Z	A	B	C	D	E	F	G	H	I	J	K	L	M	N	O	P	Q	R	S	T	U	V	W	X
Z	Z	A	B	C	D	E	F	G	H	I	J	K	L	M	N	O	P	Q	R	S	T	U	V	W	X	Y
	0	1	2	3	4	5	6	7	8	9	10	11	12	13	14	15	16	17	18	19	20	21	22	23	24	25	26
		A	B	C	D	E	F	G	H	I	J	K	L	M	N	O	P	Q	R	S	T	U	V	W	X	Y	Z

Plaintext
1010011010010101101100011111010010100101010
Pad Key
0101010101100101011011110010010000101110010
Flip any bit in Plaintext which has a 1 under it in the Pad Key
1111001111110000110111101101000010001011000
Ciphertext Result
1111001111110000110111101101000010001011000
Flip any bit in Ciphertext which has a 1 under it in the Pad Key
Pad Key
0101010101100101011011110010010000101110010
1010011010010101101100011111010010100101010
Plaintext Result

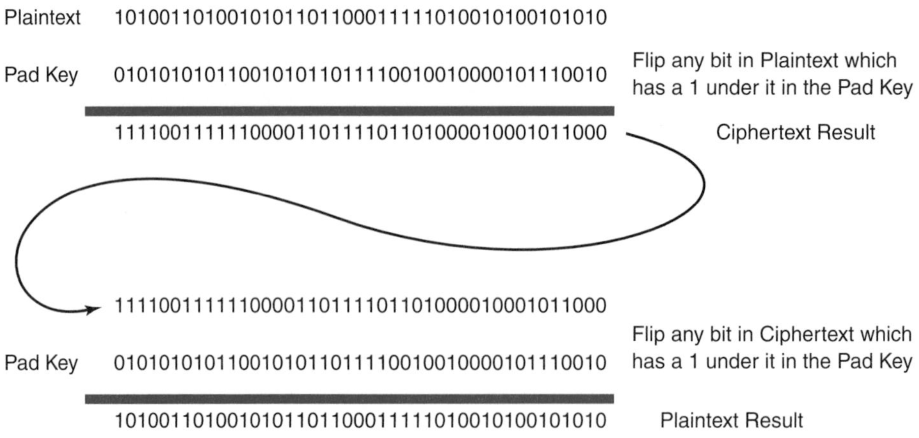

FIGURE 21.1 The operation of a one-time pad cryptosystem.

What should also be clear, however, is that this technique does not extend well to the case of Internet users exchanging Web pages and order information online. While we could wait for a company to send us a one-time pad codebook by paper mail before enacting a secure online transaction, few people would have the patience to work with such a system.

In the next section we introduce the computationally secure code that removes this burden of large codebooks at the cost of unconditional security.

21.5 Computationally Secure Symmetric Key Cryptography

We will now examine a computationally secure code. As mentioned before, computationally secure codes of two types have been devised: symmetric and public key systems. In this section we will discuss private key systems.

In symmetric key (sometimes called private key) cryptography, a single key is used for both encryption and decryption, as illustrated in Figure 21.2. Because symmetric key algorithms are designed to be very fast and easily implemented in hardware, they are often used for data encryption of large files (say, entire textbooks). Symmetric key algorithms can be divided into two categories: block and stream ciphers. A block cipher encrypts a block of data at a time, while a stream cipher encrypts one byte of data at a time. (At the level of this treatment this is not an important distinction.)

An example of a private key cryptosystem is the shift cipher. Figure 21.3 illustrates the shift cipher for the case where each letter is "shifted" by three. For this example, the letter "A" will be represented as "D," "B" will be represented as "E," and so on until the alphabet wraps. Once again we can use Table 21.1 to perform this operation.

So, if one were to use this system to encrypt the word "CRYPTOGRAPHY," one would obtain the ciphertext "FUASWRJUDSKA." By reversing the transformation, the cleartext can easily be obtained from the ciphertext. This special case of the shift cipher, where each letter is offset by some number of characters, was

Plaintext
Symmetric Cipher
Ciphertext
Symmetric Cipher
Plaintext
Symmetric Key

FIGURE 21.2 The operation of a private key cryptosystem.

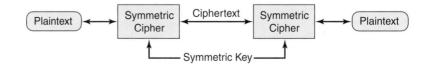

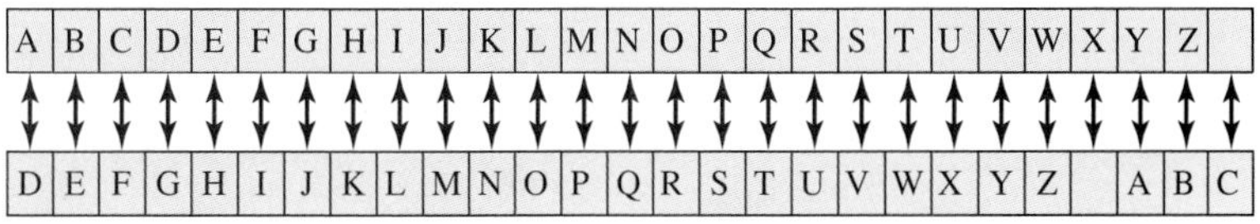

A	B	C	D	E	F	G	H	I	J	K	L	M	N	O	P	Q	R	S	T	U	V	W	X	Y	Z
D	E	F	G	H	I	J	K	L	M	N	O	P	Q	R	S	T	U	V	W	X	Y	Z		A	B	C

FIGURE 21.3 An example of a shift cipher: the letters in the top row are transformed into letters in the bottom row by a shift of all letters by three, and wraparound at the end of the alphabet.

reportedly used by Julius Caesar, and thus is called the "Caesar Cipher." One can easily observe that this system is insecure, as an exhaustive search (where every possible key is tried until meaningful information is revealed) can be completed with minimal effort, requiring at most 25 iterations. Thus the meaning of computation security is well demonstrated to us here. It would take meager computational resources to run through all possible keys and find the deciphered message.

How is this example of a computationally secure coding scheme different than the example we used when illustrating the unconditionally secure one-time pad? While both used an alphabet shifting scheme, in the symmetric code key case there was a simple rule that we had to convey to the other party: shift every letter by three. In the case of the one-time pad, there were as many rules as there were letters to code and no rule that tied them together. Thus, the computationally secure code had both the advantage of a compact code key and the disadvantage of being easy to break, because we could easily try every possible code key (shift by one, shift by two, etc.) until we saw the entire message become readable. We call this kind of attack on the code an *exhaustive search of the key space.*

No such search can work for the one-time pad because *we can get any message from the ciphertext* with some choice of a trial one-time pad key! To prove that to yourself, take the code for "CRYPTOGRAPHY" we stated above with "'FUASWRJUDSKA" as an example. The letters "'FUASWRJUDSKA" decode into the word "BIBLIOGRAPHY" with the one-time pad code word: "DLZGNCCCC-CCC." Now, it should be obvious that there exists a one-time pad code word that could have turned *any* 12 letter word into the ciphertext we have. Thus, we can never know whether we have decoded the word correctly because every result is possible.

21.5.1 Commonly Encountered Symmetric Codes

In 1977, the National Institute of Standards and Technology (NIST; formerly the National Bureau of Standards) published the Data Encryption Standard (DES). The standard requires that NIST review the security of the algorithm every 5 years. DES was last reviewed in 1993 and was approved for unclassified applications until 1998. While DES remains in widespread use, it is no longer secure and must be replaced with a more robust approach. It is expected that the Advanced Encryption Standard (AES) will be approved in the United States in 2001. DES is a block cipher capable of encrypting 64 bits of data at a time using a 56 bit key. The resulting ciphertext is 64 bits in length. The ciphertext can be decrypted to obtain the original bit sequence using the same key used to encrypt the data.

Because the DES key is only 56 bits in length, the security of the algorithm is often questioned, as modern computational resources make the algorithm vulnerable to attacks based on an exhaustive search of the key space. For this reason, various modes of operation believed to strengthen the security of DES have been introduced. The triple-DES algorithm effectively doubles the security of DES by encrypting the data three times with multiple keys. DES and triple-DES are commonly used private key algorithms in both the government and commercial sectors.

TABLE 21.2   COMMON PRIVATE KEY ALGORITHMS

Algorithm	Mode	Block Size (bits)	Key Size (bits)
DES	Block Cipher	64	56
Triple-DES	Block Cipher	64	112
RC2	Block Cipher	64	Variable
RC4	Stream Cipher	Variable	Variable
RC5	Block Cipher	Variable	Variable
IDEA	Block Cipher	64	128

Popular algorithms in use today on the Internet are RC2, RC4, and RC5. Both RC2 and RC5 are block ciphers and RC4 is a stream cipher. All three algorithms were developed by Ronald Rivest of RSA Data Security. RC2 and RC4 are protected as trade secrets of RSA Data Security, and although the algorithms are not patented, trademarks are held on the names of the algorithms. In 1996 the source codes for both the RC2 and RC4 algorithms were anonymously posted on the Internet. All three algorithms use variable length keys. RSA Data Security markets an implementation permitting key sizes between 1 and 2048 bits in length. Because modern computers can readily achieve a brute force attack on a 40 bit key space, 40 bit RC2, RC4, and RC5 are considered relatively insecure and have been approved by the U.S. government for international exportation. For this reason, 40 bit RC2, RC4, and RC5 have found widespread usage in many WWW browsers. When using key lengths greater than 64 bits, the algorithms are believed to be relatively secure for most applications on the Internet today.

Published in 1990 by Dr. X. Lai and Prof. J. Massey and patented by Ascom-Tech AG, the International Data Encryption Algorithm (IDEA) is a symmetric block cipher designed to provide high security while being easily implemented in software and hardware. The IDEA algorithm processes 64 bit blocks of data using a 128 bit key. Although it is generally believed that IDEA provides greater security than DES at much higher data rates, IDEA has yet to see widespread usage as a result of patent issues. Table 21.2 summarizes the characteristics of several common private key algorithms in use today.

21.6 Public Key Cryptography

The concept of public key (also called asymmetric) cryptography was first introduced in a paper published by W. Diffie and M.E. Hellman in 1976.[2] In private key cryptosystems, the same key is used for both encryption and decryption and must be distributed in a secure fashion. With public key cryptography, the algorithm is chosen such that it is computationally infeasible to determine the decryption key given the encryption key and ciphertext. For this reason, the encryption key can be revealed to all interested parties without compromising the security of the system.

Encrypting data using public key cryptography is analogous to dropping an envelope into a slit on a safe, where the envelope can only be obtained by the possessor of the key to the safe. In the same way, the ciphertext can only be decrypted by the possessor of the associated private decryption key. Algorithms that possess

---

[2] W. Diffie and M.E. Hellman, "New directions in cryptography," *IEEE Transactions on Information Theory*, Vol. IT-22, No. 6, Nov. 1976; pp. 644–654.

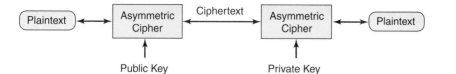

FIGURE 21.4 The operation of a public key cryptosystem.

this quality are said to be "one-way" or "intractable." With an intractable public key algorithm, the private key cannot be easily found even though the attacker has access to both the ciphertext and the public key. Because a search of the entire key space (that is, an exhaustive trial of every possible code key) is always possible with any public key system, public key cryptosystems cannot be unconditionally secure. Figure 21.4 illustrates the encryption and decryption process when using public key cryptography.

An algorithm based on the difficulty associated with factoring large composite numbers into prime numbers is an example of a computationally secure system. What does it mean to factor into prime numbers? If a number can be formed by multiplying two other numbers (77 = 7 × 11) then we say it is composite. If it cannot be formed by multiplying two numbers, we say it is prime (7 or 11). If a number is sufficiently large, say 4229826427947604843480016946490073, then it requires an enormous amount of computer time to determine what numbers must be multiplied to form the composite number. The number in this example took more than 2 minutes to factor on a high-speed workstation, and the amount of time grows rapidly with the number of digits in the number.

On the other hand, the speed of computers grows rapidly with each generation. Every secret code in use today for digital commerce on the Internet is only computationally secure. That is why headlines are made every few months when yet another more powerful computer or cryptanalysis technique succeeds in breaking yet another more powerful code.

Several public key algorithms have been proposed and many are believed to be computationally secure, but none have been mathematically proven to be so. The first public key cryptosystem to be realized was developed by Rivest, Shamir, and Addleman, and is known as RSA. The security of RSA relies on the difficulties associated with factoring large numbers into primes, and to date there are no publicly known attacks capable of efficiently compromising the security of RSA for key sizes greater than 1024 bits. Because computational technology is progressing rapidly, it is not uncommon to find public key cryptosystems using keys with much larger lengths.

Because public key cryptography is often quite complex, the computational cost of encrypting and decrypting data using public key algorithms is usually much greater than that of private key algorithms. As a result, private key algorithms are usually much faster when applied to bulk data transfer. For this reason, public and private key hybrid schemes are often employed. In this type of system, confidentially is achieved by first encrypting the private key of the block or stream cipher (referred to as the symmetric key) using an asymmetric algorithm and the corresponding public key of the recipient. The recipient then obtains the symmetric key by decrypting the corresponding ciphertext using the asymmetric private key. In this fashion, public key cryptography can be used to securely distribute symmetric keys over insecure mediums such as the Internet. This process is usually referred to as key exchange and is illustrated in Figure 21.5.

FIGURE 21.5 The steps involved in symmetric key distribution using public key cryptography.

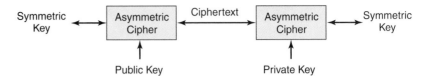

21.6.1 Public Key Standards

Several public key algorithms are in use today. The Diffie–Hellman key exchange algorithm, based on the mathematical properties of the discrete logarithm, is a system for distributing symmetric keys over an untrusted medium in a secure fashion. The RSA algorithm is based on the complexity of factoring large primes and can be used for both creating digital signatures and securely exchanging keys. Similar to RSA, the ElGamal public key algorithm can be used for both key exchange and digital signatures.

21.7 Digital Signatures

In addition to maintaining the confidentiality of information, many public key algorithms can make authentication, nonrepudiation, and data integrity possible. Because public key algorithms are computationally complex and process only a limited number of bits per iteration, a mechanism to obtain a "fingerprint" of the plaintext is desirable. These types of algorithms are known as *message digest* or *hash* functions. A hash function processes an input of arbitrary length and produces a fixed size output.

To understand the motivation for hash functions, consider the following scenario. Suppose we wish to transmit a long contract, which we don't mind if others read as well as the recipient. Although we may not be concerned about confidentiality, we still wish to ensure the integrity of the contract; in other words, we want the recipient to feel sure that they have the original message and not some substitute. We can achieve this by taking the hash of the contract, transmitting the hash to the recipient in a secure fashion (telephone for example), and then sending the contract over an insecure medium (e.g., the Internet). After receiving the contract, the recipient can again take the hash of the contract. If the received hash and the newly computed hash are identical, then the message has not been altered. However, if any bit differs, then the integrity of the message has been compromised.

Secure message digest functions possess three essential mathematical properties:

1. Every input bit influences every output bit.
2. If a single input bit is changed, every output bit has a 50% chance of changing.
3. Given an input and corresponding message digest, it should be computationally infeasible to find another input with the same message digest.

Common message digest functions include MD2, MD4, MD5, SHA, and SHA-1. Developed by Ronald Rivest, MD2, MD4, and MD5 produce 128 bit digests, with MD2 being the most secure and computationally expensive. Some flaws have been found in both MD4 and MD5, and thus collisions (where two input streams result in the same digest) can be calculated. The Secure Hash Algorithm (SHA) was developed by the NSA and produces a 160 bit message digest. Shortly after the publication of SHA, the NSA announced that the algorithm is insecure without

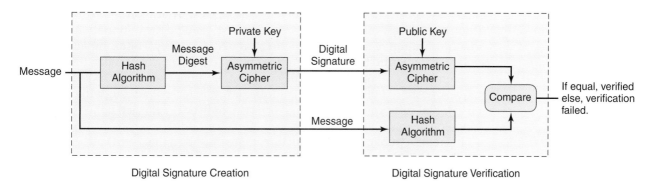

FIGURE 21.6 Process of digital signature creation and verification.

a minor change, and thus revised SHA to create SHA-1. Similar to SHA, SHA-1 accepts a variable length input and produces a 160 message digest. What if we are concerned that both the message and the hash will be compromised? We can form the digital equivalent of a hand-written signature by taking the hash of a message and encrypting the hash using the private key of an asymmetric algorithm, resulting in a digital signature. Because the private key is assumed to be unique, only the corresponding public key can successfully decrypt the encrypted hash. The signature can then be appended to the original message and transmitted to the recipient. The recipient can then verify the signature by taking a hash of the received message and decrypting the signature using the public key of the transmitted message. If the output of the second hash is identical to the decrypted signature, then the digital signature is verified. If any bit between the two differs, the verification fails. Thus, only we can supply the signature that can be decoded into the digest the recipient will calculate. Figure 21.6 illustrates the digital signature creation and verification process.

As with the other codes we have discussed, such techniques are only useful when broadly supported. Developed by the NSA and adopted as a standard by the National Institute for Standards and Technology (NIST), the Digital Signature Standard (DSS) is an example of a commonly used system for digital signatures.

21.8 Digital Certificates

To securely exchange information or verify digital signatures, one must be able to uniquely identify the association of a public key. For example, if a diplomat is trying to encrypt information for the President, how does the diplomat know for certain which is the President's public key? After all, an attack may be in place by advertising the public key, for which the attacker possesses the associated private key, under the President's falsified identity. Digital certificates provide a mechanism to connect an identity (that is, a person or machine) to a public key in a way that can be trusted and verified. With digital certificates, a certain entity (person, company, computer) called a *trusted party* is responsible for verifying a set of credentials according to a predefined policy. If approved, the public key and the credentials are digitally encoded and signed using the trusted parties' private key to form a certificate. The certificate can then be distributed in a public manner, and the identity associated with a public key can be authenticated by verifying the signature on the certificate.

Digital certificates are issued by entities called Certification Authorities (CAs). Prior to issuing a certificate, the CA must first validate the information provided in a certification request according to a predefined policy. For example, one CA's policy may require two forms of photo ID, a social security number, birth certificate, and background check, while another CA's policy may only require that the request possess a unique e-mail address. For this reason, although the signature on a digital certificate may be valid, trust can only be established if the CA's policy is accepted.

To create a public key infrastructure, there must be a root certificate accepted as valid, establishing the chain of trust. In practice, this is often achieved by embedding a root certificate in applications, such as an operating system, Web browser, or security application. A hash of the certificate consisting of a string of characters can then be obtained and displayed to the user. If warranted, this hash can then be verified using an external trusted source of information—for example, the telephone, newspaper, or public directory—to confirm the validity of the certificate.

Through the use of digital certificates and digital signatures, several security services can be realized in practice. Authentication and nonrepudiation are made possible by verification of digital signatures and binding identities to public keys using digital certificates. Successful verification of a digital signature also ensures data integrity, because if a single bit was altered, the verification process would fail. Further, replay prevention can be achieved by embedding a transaction number, synchronized timestamp, or any other type of information that progresses in time in the message, and applying a digital signature to the message itself. Many companies and organizations are getting involved in the CA market and the Public Key Infrastructure (PKI), including Verisign, GTE, Xcert, the U.S. Postal Service, and others. PKI is a term that encapsulates the certification hierarchy and includes various levels of CAs, as shown in Figure 21.7. In this example, a root CA authenticates and issues certificates to subordinate CAs, based on geographical region where certificates are to be issued. Notice, however, this is not the only way a CA's operational domain can be partitioned. For example, instead of organizing the infrastructure in terms of geographic locality, the infrastructure could be partitioned in terms of types of certificates issued, as is done by Verisign, for example.

The root CA certificate must be distributed in a secure fashion, and is often embedded in applications such as the Netscape Communicator or Microsoft Internet Explorer. Using this root certificate, the signatures on subordinate CA certificates can then be verified.

To verify a digitally signed message, one must first obtain the signer's certificate because their private key was used to sign the message and the certificate will supply the public key we need to check the signature. By using the public key embedded in the certificate, one can verify the digital signature, by decoding the

FIGURE 21.7 An example of public key infrastructure.

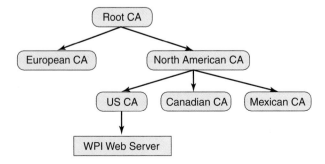

privately coded hash (or message digest), and verify that it is identical to the hash you, the message recipient, code from the message. Therefore the integrity of the message is proven by a match, so long as we believe the authenticity of the signer's certificate.

We can prove the authenticity of the signer's certificate by using the proof supplied by a *trusted* Certificate Authority (CA). The originator of the message can submit their request for a certificate to a CA that we all trust. The CA issues a certificate containing the originator's public key and perhaps other important identifying information, such as their name. The CA signs this certificate with its private key. The CA also often and very publicly publishes its public key so that we all know how to verify messages as having been signed by the CA.

The purpose of publishing very often and publicly is so that we—in particular, the CA—can tell if someone else is trying to fraudulently pose as the CA. One form of publication is for the CA to arrange to have its public key inserted directly into application software, such as Web browsers on distribution by the Web browser development company.

In addition, one can verify the validity of a subordinate certificate by validating the digital signatures on each certificate in the certificate path until reaching a point of trust, such as an embedded root certificate. By verifying the validity of a certificate and thus linking a public key to an identity, we can authenticate the origin of a message because only the corresponding private key could have created the signature.

21.9 Electronic Commerce

Three schemes for accepting credit card payments are commonly employed on the Internet today: offline, online without encryption, and online with encryption. In the offline payment scheme, the credit card number and associated information are provided over an ordinary telephone network. Online credit card payment over the Internet without encryption is vulnerable to data disclosure attacks. However, as various forms of cryptography and payment protocols become increasingly available, payment schemes over the Internet without any form of encryption are becoming relatively rare.

Over the past few years, many payment protocols employing the use of cryptography have been proposed. Of these, a few have survived and are gaining widespread acceptance. Probably the most common form of security used for online electronic commerce over the Internet today makes use of the Secure Sockets Layer (SSL). Developed by Netscape Communications Company, SSL is a standard developed to encrypt data between WWW browsers and servers. When you are using a Netscape Web browser, for instance, the small key symbol on the browser window indicates whether or not your current communications are SSL secure or not (Figure 21.8.)

FIGURE 21.8 The Netscape browser symbolically indicates with a broken key (left) or a full key (right) whether or not a Secure Socket Layer connection is being used at any given time.

Although application of SSL is not limited to electronic commerce, current implementations of SSL can be used to provide various degrees of confidentiality and authentication. Because the technology is well understood and an infrastructure has been established, SSL has become an attractive solution to commercial enterprises entering the online market. Amazon.com is an example of one vendor using SSL to establish consumer accounts consisting of user names, credit cards, and passwords over the Internet while maintaining a moderate degree of security. Alternatively, if a consumer is uncomfortable submitting sensitive information to Amazon.com over the Internet, Amazon.com provides an offline service where credit card and user account information can be submitted over the telephone.

Similar to Amazon.com, Blue Squirrel is an Internet software developer that has established an electronic storefront to market and sell their products online. Using SSL to provide security, Blue Squirrel obtains and verifies credit card information in real time. If approved, Blue Squirrel provides the consumer download access to the software, which is unlocked for operation through a registration process for which you are given a "VIP" password. Once a decision has been made, the consumer can purchase, download, and install the software within minutes. In the near future, adoption of the widely publicized Secure Electronic Transactions (SET) payment protocol is anticipated. SET is an open industry standard for the secure transmission of payment information over communication networks including the Internet. In 1996, MasterCard and Visa jointly endorsed the SET payment protocol for secure electronic commerce. SET employs public and private key cryptography, digital signatures, and digital certificates. Several industry giants are involved with the SET initiative, including MasterCard, Visa, GTE, IBM, RSA Data Security, Terisa, Verifone, and Verisign. Developed by DigiCash from cryptographic patents registered by Dr. David Chaumand, E-Cash is a software based payment system designed to make electronic commerce over communication networks, such as the Internet, possible. With E-Cash, both the consumer and merchant must open an account with a bank that issues E-Cash. Once an account is established, the merchant can create a WWW-based electronic storefront. The E-Cash issuing bank provides the client with special consumer software. Prior to making a purchase, the consumer obtains digital tokens, called digital coins, from an E-Cash issuing bank. E-Cash offers the consumer both unconditional and conditional anonymity. However, the consumer always knows the identity of the merchant.

CyberCash, Inc. developed a payment system that supports both conventional credit card purchases as well as the proprietary CyberCoin micropayment system and the PayNow service. The CyberCoin micropayment system provides a service similar to a debit card, and the PayNow service is intended to provide the benefits of conventional handwritten checks. Prior to using CyberCash technology, the consumer must first obtain the CyberCash wallet software, which is essentially a helper application for the Netscape Navigator or Microsoft Internet Explorer. The CyberCash wallet utilizes public key cryptography to secure transactions with merchant software.

Summary

The goals of this chapter have been twofold: (1) to provide a very broad, high-level overview of the aspects and issues involved in information security; and (2) to give some insight into the means by which these issues are handled. The old, and rather obscure science of cryptology has suddenly been thrust into a central position because modern communications systems (wireless, shared media systems in particular) are by their nature almost completely open to "eavesdropping." Hence the medium itself (unlike even a sealed envelope) provides little or no inherent security. The security must be inherent in the message.

Secure digital systems and Internet communications will certainly become the means of essentially all future financial transactions. The services that can be offered to both consumers and producers through the use of these technologies guarantee that we will see a complete transition to digital cash strategies within our lifetime. The immediate, secure, and verifiable nature of transactions through these technologies will further drive our world into a single economy, single currency model. The little experiment in information technology that we call the Internet will eventually change the face of the entire world.

Try These Exercises

1. Give a specific example of each of the four categories of threats to information security. These examples need not be related to Internet commerce but may be drawn from diplomatic, home, or office situations.
2. Compare the information security issues of the Internet with those of the telephone and postal systems.
3. Give an example of each of the six security services listed in Section 21.3.
4. Make up a specific example of the one-time pad cryptosystem and demonstrate its use on the message: "This is a test."
5. Code a private message using English language text and having at least five common words. Code this message using the Caesar shift code. Now, have another classmate attempt to break it. Compare the difficulty involved in breaking this code with that of a one-time pad code.
6. Using a calculator, how fast can you multiply the following three prime numbers: $7 \times 13 \times 23$. Now, time yourself performing the inverse operation of finding the three prime numbers that form the following number: 20387. Comment on the relevance of this exercise to the operation of computationally secure algorithms.
7. Perform some research on the Web and at your library and determine the current status of micropayment systems and digital cash in the United States.
8. Perform some research on the Web and determine whether or not digital cash systems have been adopted in any European countries.
9. Perform some research on the Web and determine whether any country adopted a personal identification system based on cryptographically secure digital smart cards.
10. Some of the most destructive and widely-publicized Internet security problems have resulted from "denial-of-service" attacks. In one sense these are not security problems at all because no information is compromised. However, the inability to transmit data can be as serious as illegal interception of data. Explain one or more approaches to defending against these denial-of-service attacks. Consider actions taken at routers located on the network as well as at terminals.

22 Voice over IP and the Convergence

Objectives

The final chapter looks ahead only a short distance in time, and presents the specific technology referred to as "Voice over IP" (VoIP) as well as a general look at the convergence of computation with voice and data communications. Major concepts in this chapter include:

▲ the substantial distinctions between human communications, which typically are continuous, synchronous, and of constant bandwidth; and data communications, which are bursty, asynchronous, and of varying bandwidth;

▲ the initial requirement for separate networks in order to accommodate these very different types of traffic, but the growing technical capability of merging them onto one network;

▲ measures of quality, the fact that the importance of each measure differs with the type of information being carried, and that typically an increase in one quality can be traded off against a decrease in another quality;

▲ the specifics of the difficulty of carrying voice with high quality on a packet network using a protocol such as IP;

▲ the concept of Quality of Service (QoS) and the difficulty of assuring a given QoS on an IP network; and

▲ some hybrid networks in which VoIP can be integrated with conventional circuit-based networks.

22.1 Introduction

At the start of the new millennium, it is generally believed by investors and business leaders within the telecommunications industry that soon we will all be using Voice over IP (VoIP) technology. That is, we will be using an Internet connection to make our telephone calls. In fact, while almost all Internet users today use the telephone to connect to an Internet Service Provider (ISP), it has been predicted that in a decade the reverse will be true and that almost all telephone calls will be made through a direct, high speed, Internet connection to an ISP using VoIP technology.

On reading such predictions a number of questions must immediately jump into one's mind: What is VoIP technology? What are the tradeoffs and the incentives connected with the transition to it from traditional phone wiring and services? Is it better, faster or cheaper? If it's such a good idea why didn't the telephone system get built this way in the first place? How will this change my life?

As the reader might have guessed, the IP in VoIP stands for the Internet Protocol. In Chapter 20 we introduced the idea of the Internet Protocol in a rather broad fashion, setting aside the details with which software and information engineers need to deal to perfect systems that operate within the rules of the Internet for a picture of the mail-delivery-like process behind the concept. The Internet Protocol is the set of precise rules used for this packet delivery system. Thus VoIP is based upon a packet-based communications scheme such as described in Chapters 18, 19 and 20 while current telephone technology is based upon circuit–based technology, described in the first part of Chapter 18.

We will have to examine the technical difficulties that arise when a data communications protocol is pressed into service as a voice communications conduit and what will have to happen to the current Internet to make this a viable approach for the transmission of voices. In this chapter we introduce VoIP technology and discuss our transition to it as an example of one of several such dramatic changes in telecommunications technology that are often described as being part of an overall transition called **The Convergence**.

22.2 Circuit-Switched Telephone Systems

The telephone system uses circuit–based connections as discussed in Chapter 18. As will become clear in the following discussion, the operation of a circuit–based connection makes it the natural choice for the implementation of voice communications systems, even when modern digital communications techniques are being employed rather than the original analog signal approach. In fact, it is a natural match for the needs of transmission of any form of continuous and synchronous communications, such as voice, music and video.

What is meant by continuous? During a phone conversation there are no breaks or delays in the progression of sounds between the two ends; that is, the throughput of the connection is continuous. Contrast this continuity with the form of conversation that takes place over a walky-talky or CB radio. In those cases the voice is transmitted when a switch is depressed rather than continuously. You can have a conversation this way, but the continuity is sorely missed.

Synchronism refers to the fact that each tiny element of a voice (the voice samples) must be delivered at the same rate as when they were formed at the other end of the connection. If this does not happen, the voice becomes muddled, distorted and even unintelligible if the lack of synchronism is sufficiently severe.

As a matter of contrast, compare the requirements of continuity and synchronism for typical Web surfing. A Web site delivers spurts of data only in the moments following a mouse click on a hyperlink. Following this high-speed transfer of text, images and sound, there is no movement of data while the page is being read; not until the next click on a hyperlink. Furthermore, during the loading of the Web page information, synchronism is not important. In fact sometimes the text and picture elements come in almost at once, and other times their arrival is slower and intermittent. This lack of synchronism does not, however, impair the readability of the final Web page in any fashion.

The important feature of a circuit–based digital network that makes it the natural choice for voice is that a connection is made which allows each party to pump data representing a voice signal at a given, fixed, rate to the other without flaw and without missing a step: continuous and synchronous data communications.

22.2.1 Sampling and Digitizing Telephone Voices

In Chapters 11, 12 and 13 we described the fact that a voice (any audio for that matter) can be represented as a binary bit stream, a sequence of digital 0 and 1 values. That is, first, a microphone produces a variation in an electrical signal, typically as a time varying voltage, which is the "analog" of the time varying air pressure we directly detect with our ears as sound that we hear. Then, if we sample and digitize, that is, put a number to this voltage's values often enough (at regular moments in time called sample instants) and transmit those numbers, we can reconstruct the voltage (closely enough) and hence also reconstruct the acoustic wave with a speaker (or earphone) at the other end of the connection.

As mentioned in Chapter 13, for telephone quality voice reproduction the number behind the notion of sampling often enough turns out to be 8000 times per second. From the discussion of Chapter 11 we know that sampling at this rate will only preserve information in the voice signal in the range of frequencies from 0 to 4000 Hz. Since the range of human hearing extends to about 20,000 Hz, it comes as no surprise that the quality of telephone connections seems poor in comparison to in-person communications and the quality of high-sample-rate audio communications such as CD audio.

In Chapter 12 we discussed the fact that some information is lost forever when we convert the unrestricted values of the analog voltage representing a sound into the finite number of discrete values during the quantization process. When you call off the distance between two points using the values shown as 1/16 inch tick marks on a ruler, you know that you are throwing away the details about that little bit of distance that separates the true location of the end point and the nearest discrete ruler mark. This lost distance that results from using a ruler is often called round-off error. That same lost information that occurs when digitizing a voltage is called quantization noise. Obviously we want to make this quantization noise small enough that each sample we digitize will be close enough on reconstruction to the true value that it will not interfere with the intelligibility of the phone conversation.

Experiment and experience reveal that each sample is sufficiently accurate if we use a scale of 256 values (tick marks on our voltage ruler) to measure it. From the discussion in Chapter 3 we know that 8 bits of binary data are needed to represent any one of the 256 possible values we obtain after this quantization process.

Putting these numbers together we see that $8000 \times 8 = 64,000$ bits per second result from this process as previously derived in Chapter 13. The important thing to keep in mind about this process, for the purposes of the discussion in this chapter, is that these 64,000 bits per second are generated by this process in a continuous and synchronous fashion. There are no pauses or irregularities of any kind in the creation of this digital data from the analog voice signal, and reproduction of the voice at the far end of the line without any further corruption beyond that incurred during the sampling and digitization requires a continuous and synchronous supply of this information.

22.2.2 Moving Digital Voice in a Circuit-Based Network

We will now undertake construction of a mental model that will greatly assist you in visualizing the movement of data in circuit–based networks and, later in this chapter, packet-based networks.

We saw that during the digitization process a telephone voice is turned into a sequence of numbers, each of which takes one of 256 values. Think of each number as being packaged in a little box. The box contains the 8 bits that represent one sample of our voice signal. Our voice digitizer (often called a coder) makes 8000 of these packages every second, which then have to get moved to the other side of the connection.

These packages cannot be used by the telephone receiver at the other end in just any order. The order of the packages determines the order of the variation of the air pressure that will be created. So, reproduction of the voice depends on keeping the sequence in order. Similarly, the packages must be used to create air pressure variations that are spaced apart exactly as they were when the samples were taken at the transmission end of this conversation. In fact, the only change that we will be able to tolerate is a delay from the time of sampling to the time of reproduction. But that delay must not vary (that would be the same as changing the time interval between the use of the samples) and that delay must not be too large (or the people using the phone will find it very difficult to carry on a natural conversation).

Now, it will turn out that there is more than one way to achieve these requirements within the telephone system that transports the packages from one phone to the other. We will begin by examining the simplest means to do so. By simplest, we mean both to understand, and to construct. The latter simplicity is the reason that this approach was also the choice used for the construction of the existing telephone system.

We will examine a physical system which duplicates the action of a circuit switched digital network. Recall that in Chapter 14 we saw that a conveyor belt with fixed (unchanging) width slots for packages and a fixed speed mimics the action of a fixed bandwidth binary communications system. Thus, such a conveyor, and the digital system that it resembles, provides a simple mechanism for the transportation of a continuous and synchronous sequence of packages from one end to the other end.

So, to transport our digitized voice packages, we need only set up a conveyor system between the two telephones that has a slot width and speed set just right to take up and then deliver an unchanging 8000 packages per second. Thus, packages are picked up exactly at the moments that they are created, and by the simple nature of this system they are dropped off in-order and with the right spacing at the other end to allow reproduction of the voice signal. This action and those described next can be seen in Figure 22.1.

Of course, one conveyor belt does not a telephone system make! We need a way to interconnect different telephones on demand. Recall from Chapter 18 that this is the job of a circuit switch. A circuit switch is a device that we plant at the juncture of many circuits, or conveyor belts in our model. The circuit wires emanating from our homes and businesses converge at central offices of the public switched telephone network that houses these switches. A mechanism in the switch (and there are many ways to do this) picks up the packages from one incoming circuit (conveyor) and drops them onto the right outgoing circuit (conveyor).

Sometimes we need to multiplex many streams of data onto an appropriately faster conveyor for long distance movement of the data. Why? This way, instead of having to build many conveyor belts between central offices, one for each telephone conversation that might leave that office, we need to build only one high speed conveyor to carry a large group at once. Imagine the savings in gears, rollers and conveyor belt material! It's the same reason that one large pipe brings water to your home instead of a separate pipe for every faucet, toilet and bath connection.

Recall from Chapters 13, 15 and 18 our discussions about the T1 line: a single twisted pair of wires that carries 24 conversations rather than one. This is an example of the smallest multiplexed signal in general use and is used extensively

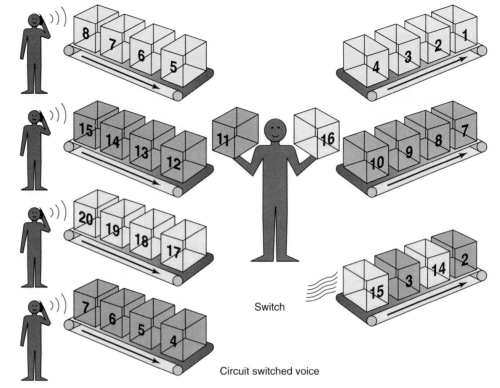

FIGURE 22.1 A conveyor belt analogy for the operation of circuit–based connections, switch and multiplexed line.

for the interconnection of nearby central offices. The benefit of multiplexing becomes ever the more obvious as the number of conversations to be carried over the same route increases. For that reason, it is possible today to buy multiplex systems that can interconnect central offices for the purposes of carrying terrific numbers of conversations over a single fiber-optic cable. For example a so-called OC-192 optical connect can move data at a rate of 10 gigabytes/second over one fiber connection, carrying 129,024 simultaneous conversations.

Figure 22.1 depicts our conveyor–based communication system, the central office switch and the multiplex system. Thanks to the synchronous behavior of all of the conveyor systems, as many data packages are brought to the office each second as can leave by another conveyor. Our humanized switch simply and in an orderly fashion picks up packages from incoming conveyors and places them on the right outgoing conveyors to reach the desired destinations. Circuits that implement this orderly and programmed switching behavior are relatively easy to design and cheap to build.

The job of multiplexing data onto and off high speed conveyors is also simple to picture. The high speed conveyors meant to transport some number, N, of conversations are simply running at a rate N times faster than the single conversation transporting conveyors. The switch need only place the packages onto this high speed belt in a repetitive sequence. The packages will be desequenced at the other end for placement onto single conversation conveyors again.

What happens when someone picks up a phone and dials a number that requests a connection to a conveyor belt that is already taken? Easy: they get a busy signal. What if they wish to connect to a far-away phone to which access is only provided by a high speed multiplex conveyor and, all possible slots are already in use? A special busy signal is issued (an all-circuits-busy signal which beeps more rapidly than the usual one) and the call is not accepted. Thus the circuit switch can never get into trouble by not having enough conveyor slots available because it has the option of simply refusing calls when its capacity to make connections is exceeded.

We will now leave this discussion of an orderly and reasonable scheme for the transportation of continuous and synchronous data and introduce the IP Packet transportation system. This system will appear to be a chaotic and unattractive replacement for what you have just seen. And so it is in many ways.

22.3 The IP Packet Connection

As we said at the beginning of this chapter, the Internet Protocol, or IP, names the set of rules that describe the standard mechanism used by Internet equipment to communicate packets of information. The central notion of this protocol is that there is a scheme for putting standardized addresses on data packets so that routing of each individual data packet can be handled simply from the address attached to it. So, like an envelope in the mail system, if we plucked a packet from anywhere in the Internet, by examining this address we could determine its source and destination. And, if we dropped this packet back into the Internet anywhere else, it would still be routed to the correct destination.

It is probably worth stating at this point, before we dive into the details of Voice over IP, that IP is not the only scheme that was developed to address and send data in packets. It's just the method that has survived a process of natural selection during the early years of data communications growth and is now a de facto standard for internetwork communications. The trend towards Voice over IP that is the focus of this chapter is not a result of any particularly good match between the needs of voice communications and the properties of IP based data networks. Quite to the contrary as you will soon see.

22.3.1 The Drive to IP Networks

Recall from our discussion in Chapter 18 that circuit systems are not well suited for packetized data communications of the type that is generated by Internet services such as Web page retrieval. That is because a circuit–based network is not well suited for exchanges between rapidly changing endpoints. A fundamental limitation of a circuit–based network is that each user can connect to only one endpoint at a time. That is, by arrangement with the central office (by dialing a telephone number) the switch will be programmed to move every package of data you send from your conveyor belt to one other outgoing conveyor belt. There is no mechanism in this situation for individual packages to receive special treatment! If the Internet were constructed from purely circuit–based systems, each click on a hyperlink would involve the dialing-up of a new telephone number and establishment of a new connection.

Now, perhaps this description seems to contrast with the reader's own experience with connecting to the Internet via a computer modem and a dial-up telephone connection. After all, you are connecting via a single circuit–based connection and your modem is certainly not redialing a connection every time you click on a hyperlink. Let's examine what is going on in this instance.

When you connect to the Internet via a telephone connection you are actually making a circuit–based connection to a company known as an Internet Service Provider (ISP). Now, any IP data packets that originate at your computer are simply handled by the telephone switch like those of any telephone conversation: they are all simply and sequentially delivered to the ISP. The ISP takes responsibility for moving these packets into a new system, one which is not circuit–based, in which the addresses on your packets will be recognized and used to route them to the desired final destination. Likewise, the ISP is responsible for capturing all packets addressed to you and placing them all onto the conveyor belt headed to your house via the central office's switch.

Note that while the telephone system has provided a continuous and synchronous connection between your modem and the ISP, we are hardly using it this way! In fact, the only time that useful information is placed on the conveyor from your home to the central office during a Web browsing session is on the widely spaced occasions that you click on a hyperlink. But, the conveyor's speed and slot width and the actions at the central office switch are not tailored to his level of activity. These are still handling 8000 data boxes per second. Thus, our use requires the same amount of bandwidth and effort (electronic though it may be) from the telephone system as does a full voice. That's why we are charged no less money for our low-data-rate Web browsing outgoing interactions than we are for a full telephone conversation.

The situation is actually worse than that just described. While our outgoing data rate (the hyperlink clicks) is very low, we all want fast retrieval of Web pages. When we click on a new link, we want the text, the pictures, the sound, the movie, etc., to be reproduced on our computer immediately. As you have seen in previous chapters, while we can do much to compress each of these information types, the amount of data required to represent audio, pictures and video can be enormous. So, huge data rates would be needed to pander to our impatience for the downloading of Web data in a blink of an eye.

Since the data rate of an ordinary telephone connection will be limited by the 8000 packages per second (64,000 bits/second) rate of the standard conveyor, we will have to buy some better service from the telephone company (or cable company, or satellite service) to our ISP. Since the telephone company uses and offers high-speed digital service lines, we could buy access to one.

Is there anything unappealing about simply buying a higher-speed version of a circuit–based digital service? Yes, we again have the constant-bandwidth and constant cost problem we described above, but worse! While the motivated Internet user could always lease a T1 line from the telephone company for 24 times the bandwidth, they would pay about that many times more for the connection. But the user really doesn't want that bandwidth all the time, only for that small time period that the big graphic at the top of a Web site is being downloaded. Most of the time the user is reading the material that is downloaded. But the cost meter is running the whole time at the same rate, whether the user is actually downloading information or simply reading it.

So, the bottom line is that if someone could provide an on-demand-only high-bandwidth Internet connection which is cost effective by not supplying data handling bandwidth between downloads, most buyers would jump to it. Since the demand for low-cost high-intermittent-bandwidth Internet connectivity is large and growing at immense rates, there is a great deal of market pressure for the creation of new services that would provide this new communications commodity.

It should be obvious by now, however, that we cannot supply this new kind of service given the existing circuits and circuit switches which are tailored to the handling of continuous and synchronous data. Hence new means of connecting to an ISP are needed. These new means involve, in part, getting the high-speed data to and from the central office in a packetized form and, in part, handling this data as intermittent packets once it gets there. For the former, new last mile technologies, as described in Chapter 15, are needed. These include:

- xDSL technology
- Hybrid Fiber Cable distribution and Cable Modem technology
- Direct fiber to the home/business

Of course these could all be used ultimately as high-speed connections to high-cost services that charge for continuous bandwidth as described above. At the central office or where ever the new high-speed last mile connection terminates (for example, cable company office or direct connect ISP office) we also need new switching equipment that works directly with IP addressed packets. This might be easily accommodated through upgrades of existing modern (digital and computer based) telephone switches or may require installation of entirely new IP based packet routing equipment.

22.3.2 To IP or not to IP

So, suppose that the new kind of service described in the previous section matures and becomes readily available and economical. Suppose high-speed access services become universal commodities and each home and business connects to the Internet through one in order to take advantage of the growing commerce and multimedia communications offerings available over the Internet. This change seems not just likely, but actually inevitable in light of the commercial potential of Internet services.

So, it is reasonable to assume that a second artery for information will grow alongside the existing circulatory system that currently supports the telephone system. We have seen in our discussion of the preceding sections of this chapter that this second system is needed because it provides communications services that complement those of the telephone system. The telephone system does an excellent job supplying continuous and synchronous data transfer for a naturally circuit-based networking need but presents an uneconomical means for supporting the intermittent high-speed packetized data requirements of Internet communications.

With the expectation that both arteries will be in place, it is appropriate to ask the question, complementary to the one we have been considering when justifying the need for packet service to the end user, of whether the circuit–based system will be needed anymore.

We will divide this question into two parts. First, we must answer the question of whether or not it is possible to move voice over IP. We can imagine that the answer might be "Yes, but not economically," as we found with the reverse question. Hence, the question bears careful examination. Second, we must ask whether or not there are economic forces at work that will drive us in that direction regardless of any initial costs or lost investment in the past architecture.

22.3.3 Conveying Packets

To facilitate the discussion of problems and solutions associated with moving voice over a packet based network we will describe the operation of an IP network in the same physical terms as we did the circuit network: as a system of conveyor belts (illustrated in Figure 22.2). The backbone (and for that matter, arms

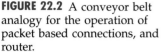

FIGURE 22.2 A conveyor belt analogy for the operation of packet based connections, and router.

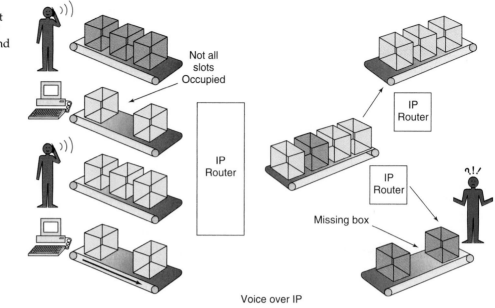

and fingers) of an IP network is constructed from the same digital transmission technology as the telephone system. In fact, most of the Internet is borrowed in concept or directly leased from the telephone companies. Thus, the IP network is again made of fixed speed conveyors as shown in the figure. That is, fixed bandwidth media (wire and fiber cables) are used. In fact, the only thing that really changes is the form of the messages placed on these cables (as described by the Internet protocol) and how this information is interpreted at the junctions of such wires where routers direct the packetized, addressed data to its next way point.

An essential difference in operation is that a user's computer may or or may not put a package into any slot on these fixed speed data conveyor belts. Another less apparent difference is this: since any packet can be addressed to any possible recipient, there is no concept of setting up a connection beforehand. That is, the user launches each packet into the network potentially addressed to a different destination with the expectation that it will be routed there when possible. The user never receives a busy signal. This also means that the network can never deny service to thwart the possibility of insufficient capacity to handle all the packets.

The import of the situation described can only be appreciated by examining the operation of the packet switch, called an IP router, located at the juncture of many cables carrying IP packets. During the construction of the router equipment facilities and cables that interconnect them the information engineer can estimate the expected number of packets that need to be transported between certain way points. But, one never knows how many users will actually try to send information to the same intermediate destination at the same time. For example, a new dot-com company may spring up that receives an enormous amount of attention and has half of the world trying to make a connection for service.

So, what happens if too many packages are trying to get onto the same next-hop conveyor towards their destinations? The router can try delaying the placement of some packages until there is a space. But, it can only juggle so many before they are dropped. Another scenario is one in which there are a sufficient number of outgoing conveyor slots to handle all the incoming data, but, because the router has to inspect the address on each package before it can know where to place it, the router might have to let some packages drop to the floor right off the end of the input conveyors because it just doesn't have the speed to deal with reading and routing so many packages per second.

In Figure 22.2 we see that the data coming from two VoIP telephone users and that from two traditional Internet users have to all pass over one intermediate link on the way to their final destinations. This intermediate link does not have the capacity to handle all this data, however. As a result, one or both of the VoIP users fail to receive a voice carrying data packet on occasion, as illustrated for the lower right-hand-side user.

Why didn't a circuit switch have these same problems? Let's rehash the main points from the last section:

- A circuit-based system makes dedicated circuit connections so that, once established, it is known that an available slot leaves the switch for every package that enters.

- While it can run out of circuit connections for some popular routes, it can issue an all-circuits-busy signal and turn away additional users.

- The handling of the information is so orderly that it takes no interpretation of the data or decisions on the part of the switch to send the data to the correct conveyor once the connection is set up.

Do the problems with the packet switched network adversely affect the operation of most Internet services? In most cases the answer is no. The Internet Protocol provides a numbering scheme for packets so that missing packets can be detected and retransmission can be requested. It is in fact this robustness to all sorts of adversity that in part led to the dominance of the IP protocol for data delivery. When a particular stretch of the Internet becomes overutilized, packets are simply dropped and then retransmitted as capacity allows. The user of this piece of the Internet at such a time as this experiences a slowdown in text and image delivery. Certainly anyone who has used the Internet has upon occasion suffered such a slowdown.

Though annoying, there is also a sense of fairness in this situation. No user is denied service and all users suffer the same slowness. There is a natural balancing of needs and resources at work as well. Those who were simply looking to casually browse the Web are quickly discouraged and leave, opening up more bandwidth for the others. Those who were in substantial need of the data being requested can stay and partition the available bandwidth among themselves.

22.3.4 Moving Voice with Packets

In the preceding sections we saw that packet based delivery, for all its imperfections such as lost packets and variable delay deliveries, does work well for all practical purposes for the retrieval of text-based information and even pictures. But, what does this kind of treatment of data do to voices that have been represented as digital data?

We can break the mistreatment of voice packets into three basic actions (illustrated in Figure 22.3):

Delay All communication systems introduce some delay into the transport of information, even circuit-based systems. Because IP routing involves much more data handling than circuit switching, delays are generally much larger than those encountered with the handling of information in switched cir-

FIGURE 22.3 Transmission of voice data over a packet based network subjects it to three types of corruption: delay, lost packets and variable delay.

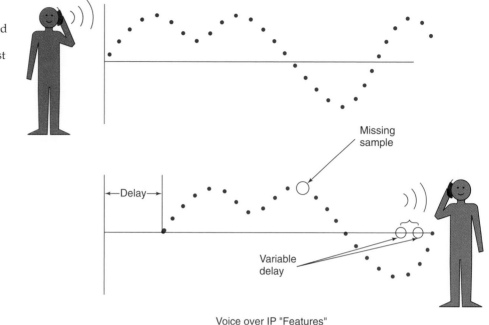

Voice over IP "Features"

cuits. Furthermore, as will be shown below, intentional delays may be added to the ordinary transport delay in a packet switched network in order to hide some of the more immediately corrupting behaviors in the list below. Delay above a certain threshold, however, itself becomes a cause for impaired communications.

Packet loss Packet loss due to temporarily overloaded routers and insufficient cable capacities is not at all unusual in the course of Internet operation. It was stated above that elements of the Internet Protocol can address this by retransmission of missing data. But, if this data arrives too late to be incorporated in the progressive, synchronous reconstruction of the voice waveform, then it is as good as lost.

Variable rate (variable delay) If the transport of data on an Internet connection slows down enough, then again it will not be available for reconstruction of the voice waveform, even though in theory it was not lost and arrived in sequence.

How much delay can you stand? There are two disturbing effects of delay:

• A delay exceeding about 1/6 second between users (1/3 second round-trip) can make a conversation strained and distort the information that is often implied by pauses or lack of pauses. Anyone who has ever had an overseas telephone conversation which was provided though a satellite connection (for reasons described in Chapter 14) is familiar with the awkwardness that such delays introduce.

• If there is any echo from the far side of the connection, an unavoidable feature of the operation of analog telephone sets, a delay exceeding 1/10 second can destroy the concentration of the person who is speaking. While we are discomforted by not hearing our own voice in a telephone earpiece, we are completely confused by hearing our own voice when it is significantly delayed.

The effect of a lost packet is the inability of the receiving digital phone to construct an acoustic pressure value of the right size at the right time. What you would hear if you were listening to a conversation in which packets are lost is a series of clicks if loss is infrequent, or a horrible rasping noise if loss is frequent.

Variable rate transport of IP information occurs when other users of the same intermediate link come and go because the amount of time that the router has to juggle your packages varies. As a result, although not lost, packets of information may arrive too far apart and sometimes too close together to allow playback at a constant rate without introducing gaps or having to drop packets even though they were received! One again the end result is loss of voice fidelity from clicks and rasping reproduction and sometimes altogether skipped intervals of speech that may span one or more words.

The second two problems described in the preceding section can be addressed through what is known as packet buffering or streaming technology, but the trade-off is an increase of the first problem, delay. The idea behind packet buffering is this: the receiver of the packets does not use the packets immediately. The packets are temporarily stored in a buffer, that is, a temporary holding area. What is the advantage? Suppose that there is a momentary slowdown in the delivery of packets from the transmitting side of the connection. Since the receiver is drawing the packets from the buffer at a constant rate, the number of packets in the buffer drops from its average value, while the listener perceives no change since they were drawn from the buffer at the constant rate. When the packet delivery speeds up again, the buffer simply refills itself to its old level as illustrated in Figure 22.4.

In the operation of the packet buffer we see, however, that the cost is the delay from the time at which a packet is inserted into the buffer on arrival from the network till when it is used to reproduce the sound it carries. By making this delay large we place ourselves in the position of a great deal of insensitivity to the vagaries of the operation of the network. Even the effects of packet loss are ame-

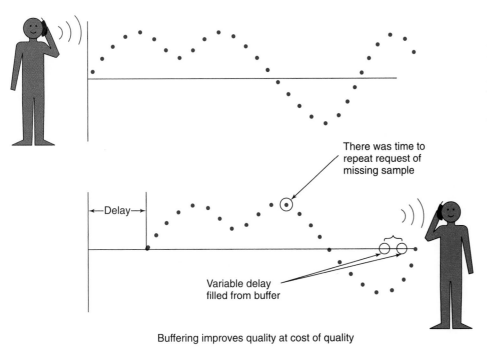

FIGURE 22.4 By temporarily storing some voice samples in a buffer memory we can draw from the store at a continuous rate even though the buffer is filled at a variable rate. However, the quality which is gained is offset by a loss of quality in the form of additional delay.

There was time to repeat request of missing sample

←Delay→

Variable delay filled from buffer

Buffering improves quality at cost of quality

liorated as we insert retransmitted packets at the right place in the buffer if they arrive in time. On the other hand, if we make the buffer too large, we suffer the problems of large delay noted previously.

22.4 How to and Why Move to VoIP?

The reader may come away with the impression from the discussion of the preceding section that VoIP technology doesn't really work, and appropriately so! The experience of the user of VoIP technology today who simply installs VoIP software on their PC and uses an ordinary ISP based connection into the Internet is probably even worse than one would project from the discussion. The connection is generally very noisy, with many drop-outs of the sound and a very long delay—certainly not a quality that one would want to have on a connection when talking to a new business prospect or carrying on a holiday greeting with a family member.

The questions to be answered in this section, then, are two. First, what could be done to improve the infrastructure of the Internet to make this a viable means of transporting voice? Second, given the situation, and the need to make, as it will turn out, wholesale changes in the structure of the Internet, why is it commonly accepted that we will (some say must) convert to this technology in the near future?

22.4.1 How Do You Make VoIP Work?

It was clear from the discussion in the previous section that VoIP suffers from problems that are linked to the lack of guarantees associated with a packet based system for sharing bandwidth. That is, there is no guarantee that sufficient bandwidth will be available to deliver every packet sent in a timely fashion, synchronously and without loss and retransmission.

Unfortunately, it is this very same behavior of a packet system that leads to its versatility and low cost of operation:

- on a moment-to-moment basis, users share the available bandwidth on a cable or within equipment on a fair-split basis, and,

- the Internet service providers don't have to reserve enough bandwidth for all possible continuous data flows, as this is not needed by traditional Internet interactions and would greatly increase the cost of service to the users.

So, again we ask, is VoIP technology really unworkable? The answer is no, it can be made to work well, just not with vanilla Internet connections. We will examine again some of the problems with VoIP and outline how the Internet infrastructure could change to accommodate it.

Reducing Routing Delays

A problem that could not be solved using packet buffering, a problem which in fact is accentuated with packet buffering, is that of packet delay. Because of the need for each router along the route of a packet to open the packet and examine its address, that is to handle the packet in a specialized fashion, there is a handling delay introduced at each juncture of cabling in the Internet. There are two technologies that can be applied to greatly reduce this delay.

Users of personal computers have certainly experienced the effects of the improvement in digital circuit technology that yields a doubling of computing speed approximately every 18 months. Such improvements derive from improvements in basic circuit fabrication technologies fed by funds from the huge market for faster software application speeds. The same kind of market pressure for increased Internet performance is driving the introduction of faster technologies, for example, Application Specific Integrated Circuits (ASICs). Mass production of these technologies, furthermore, leads to the same seemingly paradoxical phenomenon seen with PC computers of dropping costs with higher performance.

The other technology that is being applied and that improves this routing delay is a communications backbone technology called Asynchronous Transfer Mode or ATM, which was described briefly in Chapter 18. ATM is a protocol for the addressing and delivery of data streams like the packet technology of IP. However, it was designed for low-delay routing of relatively few but very high speed multiplexed voice and other high bandwidth data streams. That is, it was not designed to examine packets of data and handle the set of all possible addresses that might result in the routing of a packet to all possible destinations. Instead, it is optimized to route data to one of a few way points from on-the-fly examination of a very small identifier on each of its tiny packetlike data units, called cells.

A good way to contrast IP and ATM is as follows. We saw earlier that IP places each message in an envelope with a full destination address. The handling of IP can be imagined as the action of a mail clerk who reads each envelope and decides which of many mail bags each letter must be placed in on the basis of a reference book that lists the names of all the cities in a state and associates them with one of several outgoing mail bags.

On the other hand, imagine a situation in which the number of possible destinations is very small, say two. Further imagine that we put the data into one of two colors of ping pong ball; either a red or a blue ball. Now, we can fire the balls at high speed across a table and a good player could use his/her paddle to divert the balls either to the right or left without delay or need for in-depth interpretation. If one can imagine many such ping pong tables, side by side, filling a large room, with several colors of balls in play, then one has a picture of an ATM backbone of rapid movement of data cells.

Summarizing the treatment for excess router delays prescribed in the above: if we introduce new equipment, including higher speed routers and ATM backbone technology, we can reduce end-to-end packet delays. That is, if we upgrade much of the equipment that makes up the Internet, we can ameliorate this first problem and be able to carry voice within it with the same quality as the system that we already have and have already paid for. We will certainly have to justify why we would make the above investment and will do so later.

Reducing Effects of Congestion

In addition to routing delay, there were two other problems associated with packet sharing of bandwidth: packet loss and variable delay. Both of these problems were a result of a single cause, congestion. That is, neither problem arises until there are so many packets destined for the same router or the same data link that this congestion of packets makes it impossible to handle them without temporary delay or outright loss.

Once again, there are two solutions that can be and are being applied. These approaches strike to the root of the problem rather than simply burying it with buffering schemes that introduce large scale delays as an unavoidable side-effect. These solutions include upgrades of Internet routing equipment and user software to support Quality of Service (QoS) protocols and the brute force method of simply increasing total available bandwidth on all communication links.

Recall that one of the features of IP packet routing is the equality of treatment of all packets. This provides a service that suffers downgraded performance during busy use periods instead of simply refusing connections in the manner of an overloaded circuit switched system. But as desirable as this behavior is for traditional Internet data exchanges, it makes VoIP unusable in a heavily congested network. Suppose we could reserve some bandwidth? Then VoIP could travel over privileged streams of traffic while the traditional service data was left to contend for the remaining bandwidth. This is indeed the idea of QoS implementations.

If all the Internet routers and end-user software between two points are equipped with QoS implementations, then a VoIP transaction can request an unvarying number of data packages per second across all the cables (conveyor belts) and router (package exchange) junctions. If a particular link or router is already fully subscribed for such high-quality transport data streams, then the request can simply be turned down: in effect, we can recreate the busy signal for Internet data that requests special QoS treatment.

The second approach, that of simply increasing all the bandwidth across the Internet, needs little technical explanation. Obviously with sufficient bandwidth the opportunity for congestion-induced delays becomes improbable. The means to do it are also fairly clear. With ever faster fiber-optic transmission systems becoming available, the cost of additional bandwidth is dropping faster than the prices of new faster personal computers.

But, this approach does need a broad economic justification. One of the reasons that the Internet circulatory system of data paths grew in parallel with the existing telephone system rather than simply being subsumed by it was a matter of economics. By not supporting worst-case levels of bandwidth between all points it could provide intermittent high-speed needs of traditional Internet services at a fraction of the cost of continuous bandwidth as would be supplied by a traditional telephone connection. So, how can we contemplate growing the bandwidth of the Internet when the existing telephone system already provides voice services?

The answer is that we can contemplate this growth because the traditional telephone system already supplies voice services. The structure of the Internet is very flexible, allowing upgrades of individual links on an as desired basis. Thus, it is possible to upgrade a segment of the Internet which is located in a fortuitous position to grab a large piece of long-distance telephone business. The influx of money from that business, of course, defrays the cost of the upgrade. By using the existing telephone system to provide all the end-user services and to conduct the data up to the point where it is picked up and beyond the point where it is dropped off, the Internet provider can skim off a very lucrative part of the telephone business and none of the infrastructure costs that were the result of a hundred years of telephone system investment.

Thus, VoIP services can be built upon a hybrid of an Internet packet based system and the existing system. The existing telephone system can thus be hollowed out from inside, with the hollow growing as interest in special services that only VoIP can provide fuels further development. We will discuss some of those new special services in the next section.

22.4.2 How VoIP Is Already Being Applied

To date there are very few routes in the Internet that support fully ATM-based backbone transmission, fast routers, QoS services and/or uncongested bandwidth resources. Yet VoIP is already being used. We saw in the preceding section that VoIP can be viewed as an opportunistic parasite on the existing telephone system. This view will be further borne out as we examine other opportunities that have been seized by VoIP vendors.

Software Only VoIP

The first application opportunity for VoIP is for providing telephone services from computer to computer anywhere on the Internet simply with the installation of some VoIP application software. This use of VoIP, without the benefit of an up-graded Internet, suffers from all the downsides that we described above. So, why would anyone use such an unreliable and low-performance system? The reason is known as toll bypass. By suffering this low-performance voice link, the user avoids all long distance charges for the call. While certainly not a good choice for a business or most family uses, it does provide a low-cost means to keep in touch with friends who are adventurous enough and frugal enough to get up in the middle of the night when Internet usage falls.

VoIP Gateways and Intranets

There are, however, applications of VoIP within the business community where high performance and dependability are required. One such application makes use of the fact that some large companies have such high data transmission requirements that they have invested in private high-speed data communication connections between their companies' main sites.

Suppose a company has purchased or leases a very high speed fiber connection between two of its campuses. Now the company is positioned to use this link to bypass its long-distance (toll) changes. Equipment can be purchased from several suppliers today that captures the telephone data from a company's PBX telephone switch which was destined for a particular site, converts it to an Internet data stream, and pipes it over the company's so-called Intranet to the other location where it is delivered to a PBX for delivery to an end-user's phone. This interconnection is shown in Figure 22.5. This configuration represents, in miniature, the trend towards hollowing out of the existing telephone system which is predicted above.

The equipment which captures and reroutes telephone conversations over an Intranet in this way is typically called a VoIP gateway. This equipment also typically has means of supplying QoS during busy data periods by not accepting the VoIP rerouting and instead letting the PBX use the usual PSTN connection to handle the traffic. Thus the use of VoIP for toll bypass for companies with a high speed Intranet is a low risk endeavor, as the traditional system, which is losing money from bypassed calls, is still available as a safety net. This is a good example of the opportunistic, parasitic behavior of VoIP.

VoIP in the LAN

Rather than using VoIP gateway technology to bypass the PSTN at the PBX, the PBX itself can be bypassed inside the company. The opportunity to do so arises from the fact that high speed Local Area Networks are an essential business commodity today, thanks to the importance of personal computers, data bases, Web commerce, email and the like in most business activities. But LANs that transport high-speed data throughout the company can do double duty and support VoIP within the confines of the business.

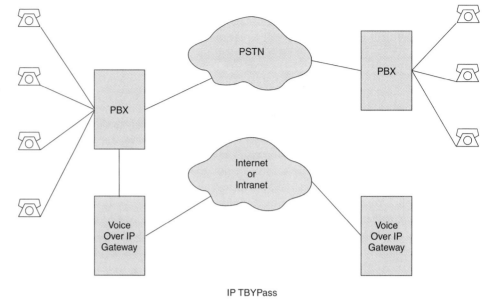

FIGURE 22.5 VoIP gateway
equipment can be used to
create a toll bypass for business calls when the company
has high speed Intranet connections to its other campuses.

The very high bandwidth of new LANs makes this possible at a lower cost than
that of supporting parallel PBX wiring. Furthermore, the use of the PC as a telephone and the LAN as a surrogate PBX eliminates telephone equipment charges
and upkeep and allows use of software that supplies additional services along
with the voice call, such as the ability to share the view of a document during a
conversation.

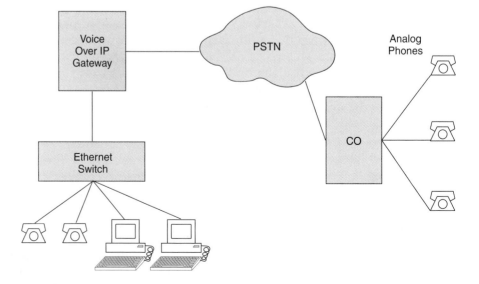

FIGURE 22.6 PCs and VoIP
handsets can be intercon-
nected via a high-speed LAN
while a VoIP gateway funnels
conversations leaving the business through the PSTN.

22.4.3 The Driving Force behind VoIP

In the preceding sections of this chapter we have shown that while VoIP is not an attractive technology with today's Internet, an upgraded Internet can make it feasible. While the upgrade of the Internet will be expensive, the dropping cost of high-bandwidth connections and high-speed equipment will help, and some of the funding will come from the hollowing out of the existing PSTN through opportunistic placement of VoIP spurs. But we return again to the question: why take this path when the PSTN works just fine? Certainly toll bypass can't be the only reason. In fact, if it were, we would expect traditional phone companies to dig in their heels and request regulatory protection from governments. Instead in many cases we see traditional equipment and service sales companies engaging in fast-track efforts to support VoIP. What is happening?

What is happening is the growth of an e-commerce economy around new communication services. In 1999 about 5% of the US economy's transactions took place via the Internet. This is a significant fraction when one considers that the technology is still quite crude and impersonal compared to storefronts and that only a fraction of consumers have access to the Internet yet.

It is believed by most that the drive to e-commerce will be accelerated by the appearance of new efficiencies and personal treatment that will be made possible by next-generation Internet services. A key service in this group is VoIP as a part of Voice/Web integration. We now will examine the promise of the Voice/Web e-commerce frontier.

Imagine that you are looking at a product in a catalog and have a question about it. Today you might write an email inquiry to some general user support contact (if you can find one) and then wait and wait for a reply. If you get a timely answer you next have to find the catalog again. But, in many cases the company will simply lose the sale, since timely responses are rare. This is true because handling of email support questions is an inefficient operation, since questions must be routed to knowledgeable personnel who attempt to interpret questions from sometimes scant descriptions.

Now imagine instead that you click a phone button and are connected to a product-specific support person. Suppose further that this person is automatically presented with the Web page you are looking at and talks to you over your PC. In fact, they may direct you to a product that better fulfills your requirements by taking control of your Web browser momentarily and changing the page that is being displayed. This is an example of Voice/Web integration.

Voice/Web integration will affect the conduct of all businesses. Your insurance agent will be able to show you options on Web pages while talking to you. You will ask your car salesman for a tour of a new-model-year selection of cars on-line while haggling option prices without leaving your home. You will call the grandparents and show them the latest video of junior while talking them through all the funny moments.

Furthermore, the voice at the other end doesn't have to be a real person. Sure, today we can have Web forms that make explanations and instructions available on-line in the form of recorded voice messages. But, who wants to wait for a half minute for a sound clip to download just to get a hint as to how to fill out one line on the form? But, if telephone conversations can be supplied at essentially no delay, then so can all kinds of prerecorded voice assistance as well. The elimination of delay is going to make voice-aided forms and voice-active hyperlink buttons routine. The Internet is going to get very friendly, very fast.

This merging of telephone with computer and network is one example of a trend that has been called **the convergence**. This term has been used so much in media lately, that it has almost lost its meaning. The concept of the convergence is that communications and computing equipment have so much in common that both will someday share the same equipment and the same network, and that the forms of communications will become mixed and inseparable. Sometime soon we will not distinguish a Web interaction from a phone conversation; each communication session with a friend will become a montage of voice, video, data and virtual reality whether the connection is wired, wireless, or over the cable TV, computer, cell phone or pocket computer.

Try These Exercises

1. In this chapter the telephone is used as the example for comparison of connection-based and packet-based communications systems. A similar comparison may be made with television. There are obviously many differences between these two services; there are also some similarities from the point of view of this chapter. Summarize the similarities and differences of telephone and television service, primarily with respect to the two communications standards. Next, summarize the means by which television is distributed at present, and how (if feasible) video service may be provided over a packet-oriented network. Discuss the provision of both standard television as we now know it and other types of video services such as short "instant replays" of portions of sporting events, news clips, educational lectures, and so on.

2. Table 20.1 in Chapter 20 gives some actual roundtrip delay times for test data between a computer located at a university in Worcester and the listed locations, ranging from the Internet gateway computer on that campus to the destination computer in Ohio. What percentage of those 48 delays would represent acceptable performance for VoIP? Explain your answer. Also, comment on the variability of the delay over a given connection for this actual data and the impact on voice quality.

3. Many people now have three or four or even five different communication paths into their homes: wired telephone, cable television, cellular telephone, direct-broadcast satellite television, pager. These all developed and have become successful in the marketplace because of the particular combination of features and services that they provide, compared to their costs. Summarize the major features of each, and explain how the computation-communication convergence may affect them in the future. Are any of these services likely to disappear or merge? Relate your answer in particular to the topics of this chapter.

APPENDIX

A

ASCII Character Codes

Dec	Hex	Binary	Char		Dec	Hex	Binary	Char	
0	00	0000000	NUL	'\0'	64	40	1000000	@	
1	01	0000001	SOH		65	41	1000001	A	
2	02	0000010	STX		66	42	1000010	B	
3	03	0000011	ETX		67	43	1000011	C	
4	04	0000100	EOT		68	44	1000100	D	
5	05	0000101	ENQ		69	45	1000101	E	
6	06	0000110	ACK		70	46	1000110	F	
7	07	0000111	BEL	'\a'	71	47	1000111	G	
8	08	0001000	BS	'\b'	72	48	1001000	H	
9	09	0001001	HT	'\t'	73	49	1001001	I	
10	0A	0001010	LF	'\n'	74	4A	1001010	J	
11	0B	0001011	VT	'\v'	75	4B	1001011	K	
12	0C	0001100	FF	'\f'	76	4C	1001100	L	
13	0D	0001101	CR	'\r'	77	4D	1001101	M	
14	0E	0001110	SO		78	4E	1001110	N	
15	0F	0001111	SI		79	4F	1001111	O	
16	10	0010000	DLE		80	50	1010000	P	
17	11	0010001	DC1		81	51	1010001	Q	
18	12	0010010	DC2		82	52	1010010	R	
19	13	0010011	DC3		83	53	1010011	S	
20	14	0010100	DC4		84	54	1010100	T	
21	15	0010101	NAK		85	55	1010101	U	
22	16	0010110	SYN		86	56	1010110	V	
23	17	0010111	ETB		87	57	1010111	W	
24	18	0011000	CAN		88	58	1011000	X	
25	19	0011001	EM		89	59	1011001	Y	
26	1A	0011010	SUB		90	5A	1011010	Z	
27	1B	0011011	ESC		91	5B	1011011	[	
28	1C	0011100	FS		92	5C	1011100	\	'\\'
29	1D	0011101	GS		93	5D	1011101	]	
30	1E	0011110	RS		94	5E	1011110	^	
31	1F	0011111	US		95	5F	1011111	_	
32	20	0100000	SPACE		96	60	1100000	`	
33	21	0100001	!		97	61	1100001	a	
34	22	0100010	"		98	62	1100010	b	
35	23	0100011	#		99	63	1100011	c	
36	24	0100100	$		100	64	1100100	d	
37	25	0100101	%		101	65	1100101	e	
38	26	0100110	&		102	66	1100110	f	
39	27	0100111	'		103	67	1100111	g	
40	28	0101000	(		104	68	1101000	h	

41	29	0101001	)	105	69	1101001	i
42	2A	0101010	*	106	6A	1101010	j
43	2B	0101011	+	107	6B	1101011	k
44	2C	0101100	,	108	6C	1101100	l
45	2D	0101101	-	109	6D	1101101	m
46	2E	0101110	.	110	6E	1101110	n
47	2F	0101111	/	111	6F	1101111	o
48	30	0110000	0	112	70	1110000	p
49	31	0110001	1	113	71	1110001	q
50	32	0110010	2	114	72	1110010	r
51	33	0110011	3	115	73	1110011	s
52	34	0110100	4	116	74	1110100	t
53	35	0110101	5	117	75	1110101	u
54	36	0110110	6	118	76	1110110	v
55	37	0110111	7	119	77	1110111	w
56	38	0111000	8	120	78	1111000	x
57	39	0111001	9	121	79	1111001	y
58	3A	0111010	:	122	7A	1111010	z
59	3B	0111011	;	123	7B	1111011	{
60	3C	0111100	<	124	7C	1111100		
61	3D	0111101	=	125	7D	1111101	}
62	3E	0111110	>	126	7E	1111110	~
63	3F	0111111	?	127	7F	1111111	DEL

Related Organizations

Below is a list of information-engineering–related organizations.

1. ACM: The Association for Computing Machinery

   - SIGACT (Algorithms and Computability Theory)
   - SIGBIO (Biomedical Computing)
   - SIGCAS (Computers and Society)
   - SIGCOMM (Data Communications)
   - SIGCUE (Computer Uses in Education)
   - SIGDOC (Documentation)
   - SIGGRAPH (Computer Graphics)
   - SIGIR (Information Retrieval)
   - SIGLINK (Hypertext/Hypermedia)
   - SIGMIS (Management Information Systems)
   - SIGMOBILE (Mobile Computing and Communications)
   - SIGMOD (Management of Data)
   - SIGMM (Multimedia)
   - SIGNUM (Numerical Mathematics)
   - SIGSAC (Security, Audit and Control)
   - SIGSIM (Simulation)
   - SIGSOFT (Software Engineering)
   - SIGSOUND (Sound and Computation)

2. AES: Audio Engineering Society
3. AMPS: The Association of Motion Picture Sound
4. ANSI: American National Standards Institute
5. ARPA: Advanced Research Projects Agency
6. APRS: Association of Professional Recording Services
7. ASA: The Acoustical Society of America
8. CCITT: International Telegraph and Telephone Consultative Committee
9. CEC: Canadian Electroacoustic Community
10. EFF: The Electronic Frontier Foundation
11. ETSI: European Telecommunication Standards Institute
12. FIPS: Federal Information Processing Standards
13. IAB: Internet Architecture Board
14. IANA: Internet Assigned Numbers Authority
15. IBS: The Institute of Broadcast Sound

16. ICIA: International Communications Industries Association
17. IEE: Institution of Electrical Engineers

   - Computing and Control Division
   - Science, Education, and Technology Division

18. IEEE: Institute of Electrical & Electronics Engineers

   - IEEE Communications Society
   - IEEE Computer Society
   - IEEE Education Society
   - IEEE Engineering in Medicine and Biology Society
   - IEEE Information Theory Society
   - IEEE Lasers & Electro-Optics Society
   - IEEE Microwave Theory and Techniques Society
   - IEEE Professional Communication Society
   - IEEE Signal Processing
   - IEEE Social Implications of Technology

19. IETF: Internet Engineering Task Force
20. IMTC: International Multimedia Teleconferencing Consortium
21. IRTF: Internet Research Task Force
22. ISO: International Organization for Standardization
23. ISOC: Internet Society
24. ITS: The International Teleproduction Society
25. ITU: International Telecommunication Union
26. NAB: The National Association of Broadcasters
27. NAS: National Academy of Sciences
28. NASA: National Aeronautics and Space Administration
29. NSF: The National Science Foundation
30. NIST: National Institute of Standards and Technology
31. OSA: Optical Society of America
32. SBE: Society of Broadcast Engineers
33. SIAM: Society for Industrial and Applied Mathematics
34. SMPTE: Society of Motion Picture & TV Engineers
35. SPARS: Society of Professional Audio Recording Services
36. SPIE: The International Society for Optical Engineering
37. W3C: World Wide Web Consortium

C

Example Projects

The following sections contain examples of three projects that can be conducted by students who desire to pursue a more in-depth treatment of technical material.

C.1 Project 1: Introduction to the World Wide Web

C.1.1 Introduction

The World Wide Web (WWW, or the Web) is an excellent example of a modern communication system. Most people use the Web primarily to find information; a growing number of people also use it to organize and convey information, like any other means of publication. While the Web is certainly a popular means of achieving these goals, it is not expected that everyone has the same level of knowledge or experience using it. The object of this experiment is to introduce the Web, show you how to find information using the Web, and detail one way to construct Web pages of your own. Please read Chapter 2 of the textbook before performing this experiment.

For this experiment you will need a computer with Web access, a browser (preferably Netscape Communicator), and a CD-ROM drive for the CD that accompanies the text. Note that your browser will be able to access the Web pages on the CD-ROM at all times, but other parts of this project require online Internet access (provided to you via an ISP such as AOL).

C.1.2 Accessing the Web

Accessing the Web can be as simple as starting your favorite WWW browser. This project assumes the availability of Netscape Communicator. While other browsers can be used, the explanations pertain directly to this version of the Netscape browser. With Netscape Communicator, you have all the tools necessary to view Web content from all over the globe and to create your own Web content.

To get to the starting page, put the accompanying CD in the CD-ROM drive of your computer and double click the CD-ROM icon. Next, open the projects directory, and double click the Welcome.html icon, which may simply be marked Welcome.

In the upper part of the browser window, you should see a text box labeled "location." The location box contains the Universal Resource Locator (URL) address for the Web page you are currently viewing. Encoded in the URL is the information transfer protocol (more details on this are provided in Chapter 2), the name of the file that contains that information, and the location of the computer on which that file is stored. You can change the URL by clicking in the text box and editing the

URL by backspacing over it and typing in a new one. (This version of Communicator has the often annoying feature of anticipating your URL from a partial URL. You can click on the end of the URL to un-highlight the text and backspace-remove a portion that is unwanted.)

Most documents contain text or images that when clicked, load a new Web page into the browser. These objects, called hyperlinks (or simply links), allow the user to "connect" his or her Web page to other people's pages across the globe. At the end of the project, you will construct a Web page that links to a few informational pages and a few Web utilities.

We will assume here that you already have a basic working knowledge of the use of a Web browser, rather than dwell on usage that may be quite old-hat to you. Instead we will point out a few features of the Web browser that some less Web-oriented users may not have encountered.

If you click on a Web page with the rightmost mouse button instead of the usual left button, a drop-down menu will appear with some new options. Clicking on the *View Info* selection will reveal several pieces of useful information about the structure, nature, and age of the page that you are viewing. Clicking on the *View Source* selection will cause a new window to be displayed that shows the actual HTML content of the Web page that was displayed. Using this option one can troubleshoot their own work as well as seeing how others have achieved effects that you are enjoying on their pages.

If you similarly right-click on image content in a page, you will be presented with the option: *View Image* (with the name of this image file shown in parentheses). Choosing this option, that image alone will be displayed in your browser window. Right-click on the image in the page referred to above. Write down the URL being displayed at this time in your browser window, as you will need it later.

Another option is the *Save Image as:* selection, which permits you to save a copy of the actual image file to your computer in a directory that you can select by navigation in the style of Microsoft Windows.

C.1.3 Finding Information on the Web

Today, one of the more difficult tasks is finding the *right* information. Because using the Web and creating new content are relatively simple tasks, the amount of information on any given subject is usually quite large. To simplify this process, search engines have been created.

A search engine is a program that contains information from billions of Web pages around the world, and organizes them according to subject or keyword. These search engines provide a friendly user interface in which to type the subjects for which you wish to search, compile a list of possible matches to those criteria, and display a list of hyperlinks to those pages.

While it may at first seem simple to find information on the Web, it can actually be quite difficult. Let's consider the following situation: you are responsible for a report on the recent history of computing in the United States. While the early years are detailed in any number of books, the most recent advances are yet to be published.

The WWW is ideal for finding the most current information since it can take only a few minutes to print, publish, and distribute! So, let's begin by using a popular search engine called WebCrawler (`http://www.webcrawler.com`) to find some references. Searching on the subject `"history computing"` (do not include the quotes when typing this string) results in over 180,000 matches (also called hits). While the items in the list are sorted according to how well they match your criteria, these are just too many sources to read in any reasonable amount of time.

One of the problems is that this search engine is not assuming that you want all of the pages about the *history of computing*, it is simply returning all of the pages that include the words *history* or *computing*. We can restrict the search by using "history AND computing" as our criteria, which returns pages only with both words (in any order and with any separation). The resulting list is only 6,000 entries long. Not too bad an improvement for the addition of a three-letter word.

We can restrict the search even further by using "history AND computing AND 'united states'" (the single quotes should be typed into the search text box—they indicate that the phrase "united states" should be matched as a two-word phrase and not as two separate words), which results in a list of 1,000 entries. You may want to restrict your search even further, but this illustrates the point quite clearly—your search criteria must be specific enough to limit the number of hits.

Note that for every WWW search engine, the syntax for the search criteria can be different. When using any search engine for the first time, find the help option and read about how to construct the search phrases.

Spend a few moments now to learn more about your search options with this particular search engine. Click the WebCrawler help button on the top right of the central page. Explore the basic and advanced search options. You will need to know this to perform a good job on the project exercises that follow.

C.1.4 Procedure and Report

Prepare a report with the following contents. If you have access to a word processor with Web page generation (HTML) capabilities, prepare this report as a Web page.

- Include the HTML text that creates the Welcome.html Web page that you accessed at the beginning of this project (viewable with the "View Source" or similar function of your browser). Explain the functions of the format commands that you find in the html text.
- Include a list of hyperlinks to at least three different search engines, together with a paragraph for each link, describing the major features or unique aspects of each search service.
- Include a list of hyperlinks to at least three different html tutorials. Include a brief summary comparing and evaluating the qualities of each tutorial.
- Finally, write a several-paragraph-long history about the WWW that provides more detail than given in our textbook. Include hyperlinks to all the sources you found on the Web that provided the information. *Be sure to not plagiarize and to obey copyright rules. If you quote someone, give them credit.* Feel free to focus on one part of the history of the Web, such as the pre-Mosaic, Mosaic, and Netscape periods.

C.2 Project 2: Visual Acuity

C.2.1 Introduction and Preparation

This project will explore the fundamentals of visual acuity by having you measure your own acuity with respect to spatial and color information. Please read Chapters 5 and 6 of the textbook before performing this experiment. You will need a ruler (or tape measure) to measure the distance from the computer screen to your eyes. You will also need a partner for the color acuity portion.

C.2.2 Procedure

Human Spatial Acuity

In this experiment you will determine your own visual spatial acuity. As we described in the text, the human eye is capable of resolving approximately 120 pixels per subtended degree. Of course, this depends in part upon the combined correctness of your eye's lens and any corrective lenses. Hence, we would expect your actual spatial acuity to be bounded by this value and typically less. You will now conduct an experiment to determine your own acuity by measuring the distance at which a checkerboard image degrades to the point where it cannot be differentiated from a constant-intensity image.

To perform this experiment, again put the CD in the CD-ROM drive and double click the CD-ROM icon (if you have not done so already). Again go to the projects directory, and double click the acuity.html icon. This Web page causes a Javascript routine to be launched that presents a window into which you can type a number. Enter the value 120. Now press the **display** button. This will generate a new browser window with two gray squares.

The square on the left is a checkerboard (100×100) of white and black squares. The square on the right is a constant-intensity gray area. The number that you typed in the first window set the gray level value of this second box.

If you step sufficiently far away from the screen, the checkerboard will appear to be a constant gray area. Your first task is to try new values for the gray level of the right-hand box until it matches the checkerboard as seen from a large distance. Having this box with a matching intensity will assist you in carefully finding the distance at which the checkerboard pattern first disappears.

When you have identified a good value for the gray level, you are ready for the next part of the experiment.

Carefully measure the distance from the screen to your eyes at the point where the checkerboard nature of the checkerboard *just* disappears. Now measure the size of the checkerboard on your screen.

Now we are ready to compute your personal acuity in pixels/degree given the distances and sizes you have measured. This calculation will be explained in reference to Figure 5.2 in Chapter 5. The angle in degrees of the arc labeled "angle" in Figure 5.2 is given by

$$\theta = 2 \tan^{-1} \left(\frac{(\text{viewing area})/2}{\text{viewing distance}} \right)$$

An example will make this more clear. Consider the act of holding a common piece of paper one foot in front of your face with the longer direction held horizontally. Such a piece of paper has a size of 8-1/2 inches by 11 inches. We can apply a little trigonometry and determine the subtended angle in both directions.

This horizontal angle is given by

$$\theta_{\text{horiz}} = 2 \tan^{-1} \left(\frac{(11 \text{ in})/2}{12 \text{ in}} \right) = 49.25°$$

while the vertical angle is given by

$$\theta_{\text{vert}} = 2 \tan^{-1} \left(\frac{(8.5 \text{ in})/2}{12 \text{ in}} \right) = 39°.$$

Now perform these calculations with your distances, and considering the fact that the checkerboard consists of a display of 100×100 squares (to be precise, the checkerboard consists of 50×50 black squares as well as 50×50 white squares).

Human Color Acuity

In this experiment you will determine a partner's visual color acuity. As we saw in the homework and class discussions, the human eye is capable of resolving approximately 2^{19} different colors. Of course, this depends in part upon your eye's freedom from a variety of well-known visual defects as well as factors such as illumination and recent exposure to bright lights.

Hence, we would expect your actual color acuity to be bounded by this value and to typically be less. You will now conduct an experiment to determine another person's acuity by measuring the smallest change of color that he or she can detect.

To perform this experiment, again put the CD in the CD-ROM drive and double click the CD-ROM icon (if you have not done so already). Again go to the projects directory, and double click the discrim.html icon.

This Web page causes a Javascript routine to be launched that presents a window into which you can type two sets of three digits (from 0 to 255) representing the red, green, and blue components of a color. Once you have typed values into these windows, and click on the display button, a window will pop up with two square areas displayed with the respective colors. Note that if this new window does not appear, it may be behind your browser window.

Now, enter the following RGB values: 128, 0, 0, for the first image and the second image. Have your partner look at the two images and accommodate him or herself with these identical color blocks. Now, have your partner close his or her eyes. While your partner's eyes are closed, change the color in the second of the blocks, say to 135. Make sure that the color selector window is hidden and ask your partner whether the colors in the two blocks are now the same or different. Repeat this several times, slightly modifying the content of all three colors and returning occasionally to identical colors. Keep a record of all the colors you tried and your partner's answer as to whether the colors were the same or not. Derive from these results your conclusion as to the smallest difference your partner can detect when the first block is always 128, 0, 0. Is the person's acuity the same or different when the change is in the red, green and blue directions from the original values? Note that a change in the red values represents a change in intensity, whereas changes in the blue and green directions represent changes in hue (color).

Repeat this test with starting values of 0, 128, 0 (green) and 0, 0, 128 (blue).

C.2.3 Report

For your report, create an HTML file that reports your procedure and results, and answers all of the questions posed throughout this project. Separate your answers into sections just as this project has been written in sections.

C.3 Project 3: The Virtual Reality Modeling Language

C.3.1 Introduction and Preparation

In this project you will first explore some of the basic capabilities of the Virtual Reality Modeling Language (VRML) by manually generating and viewing VRML scenes. Read the textbook chapters on VRML and Data Compression and Image Compression. If your Web browser does not have the COSMO VRML viewer, it may be downloaded from the Netscape Website.

C.3.2 Procedure

Creating and Viewing VRML files

In this project you will use any ASCII text editor (we will assume the use of the Notepad Editor in Windows) to create and save VRML scenes to a text file. Please note that the VRML file must be saved as "ASCII" and not in some other word processor format. All word processors have this capability, but sometimes considerable searching is required! The Cosmo VRML viewer plug-in for Netscape will be used to display the VRML scenes.

As was explained in the reading, a VRML scene is nothing more than an ASCII text file that contains VRML commands that instruct a VRML viewer on how to render a scene. Recall that a VRML scene consists of a hierarchy of nodes (scene graphs) that describe its overall content and appearance. In text, a VRML node has the following structure:

```
TAG { <node content> }
```

The word TAG identifies the type of node, while the left and right braces designate its content. The content of a node is entirely dependent on its type. For example, separator nodes may contain geometry nodes, property nodes, and other separator nodes. Shape nodes, on the other hand, may only contain information that describes the geometry of an object (i.e., shape nodes cannot contain other nodes). The allowable content of every possible type of VRML node is described in the VRML 1.0 and 2.0 specifications. The content of the node types used in this project will be given as part of the examples.

Start the project by launching a single copy of Notepad and a single copy of Netscape Navigator. Enter the following text in Notepad:

```
#VRML V1.0 ascii

Separator {
    Cube {
        width      1.0
        height     1.0
        depth      1.0
    }
}
```

The first line of this text identifies the version of the VRML language being used (in this case Version 1.0). In VRML, any line starting with a pound character (#) is treated as a comment and is consequently ignored by VRML viewer programs. The only exception to this rule is the identification string appearing on the first line of the text. This line must be present in every VRML file.

The scene graph described by the text consists of a single separator node containing a cube with all sides set to one unit in length. Save this text in a file named "vrml_scene.wrl." To view the VRML file in Netscape Navigator, select **File** and then **Open Page ...** from Navigator's main menu bar. Enter the location where you saved the file (e.g., c:temp\grey_ball.wrl) in the text input line of the dialog box that appears. Press the **Open** button when you are done. A VRML model of a cube should appear in Navigator's main window. If the VRML viewer appears but no model is present, make sure you have entered the text exactly as it appears in the example above. If you have to make corrections, the entire model can be reloaded by pressing the Reload button on Netscape's main menu bar.

Experiment with the controls of the VRML viewer located at the bottom of the Web browser. Position the mouse cursor near the center of the screen. Press and hold the left mouse button while moving the cursor toward the top of the browser. As you move the mouse cursor further away from the point at which you pressed the left button, you will see a line extending from that point to the current position of the cursor. You should also see the cube moving closer to your current viewpoint (or your viewpoint moving closer to the cube—everything is relative). Notice that the longer you make the line the faster you move toward the cube. Conversely, the shorter you make the line the slower your velocity. To move away from the cube simply move the mouse cursor toward the bottom of the browser.

The CosmoPlayer plugin for Netscape is capable of operating in two modes; "Movement Mode" and "Examination Mode." "Movement Mode," described in the preceding paragraph, is the default mode of the viewer (i.e., the viewer will appear in this mode each time a VRML file is loaded). To switch to the "Examination Mode" use the mouse cursor to move the lever on the left side of the control panel to an upward position. "Examination Mode" is used to rotate your viewpoint around an object so that it may be viewed from different angles. To rotate your viewpoint press and hold the left mouse button and move the mouse cursor. Practice viewing the cube from different angles. Can you figure out how to make the cube spin by itself?

Adding Color to VRML Objects

In the previous example the color of the cube was never specified. By default, VRML geometries that are not assigned color information are displayed in flat gray. In this section of the project you will learn how to add color to objects.

The Material node is used to specify the color of an object. In VRML, simple color information is expressed as an RGB triplet (i.e., three decimal numbers). The first number indicates the intensity of red, the second the intensity of green, and the third the intensity of blue. Add a Material node to the VRML scene graph created in the previous section. The resulting text should look similar to that given below. Save these changes to the VRML file (vrml_scene.wrl) and press the reload button in Netscape Navigator. Once the VRML scene has reloaded, you will notice that the color of the cube has changed from gray to green. Can you change the color of the cube to red? How about blue? Try experimenting with different colors.

```
#VRML V1.0 ascii

Separator {
    Material {
        diffuseColor    0.0 1.0 0.0
    }
    Cube {
        width           1.0
        height          1.0
        depth           1.0
    }
}
```

Just as important as the presence of a Material node for supplying color information is the position of the node in the scene graph. Recall that a property node only modifies geometry nodes that come after it in the scene graph. For example, if the Material node in the example given above was positioned after the geometry node (Cube) then the cube would be colored gray instead of green (i.e., no color). Verify that this is true by positioning the Material node after the Cube. View the resulting VRML scene in Netscape. *Note:* You should be able to move the node using a simple cut-and-paste operation.

Translation Nodes

Translation nodes are used to specify the position of objects in a VRML scene. By default all objects are placed at coordinates $(0, 0, 0)$. If translation nodes are not used to assign locations to objects, all objects in the scene graph will be stacked on top of each other at the origin. To see that this is true, save the following text to your VRML file and view the file in Netscape.

```
#VRML V1.0 ascii

Separator {
    Sphere {
        radius          1.0
    }
    Cube {
        width           1.5
        height          1.5
        depth           1.5
    }
}
```

Notice that the cube and sphere are both positioned at the origin. In some instances this may be a desirable effect; however, in most cases it is not. Transform nodes can be used to specify a unique location for every object in a scene graph. The following VRML text contains a Transform node that moves the cube two units in the positive direction along the x-axis (to the right). Save this text in your VRML file and view the resulting scene graph using Netscape.

```
#VRML V1.0 ascii

Separator {
    Sphere {
        radius          1.0
    }
    Transform {
        translation     2.0 0.0 0.0
    }
    Cube {
        width           1.5
        height          1.5
        depth           1.5
    }
}
```

Try translating the cube in different directions (both positive and negative) along x, y, and z. With respect to the computer screen, in which direction is the positive z-axis pointing (toward or away from the viewer)? Now make the Transform node the first node in the Separator node. How does this affect the location of the sphere and the cube? What does this tell you about the significance of the placement of Transform nodes? *Hint:* Recall the effect of moving a Material node on the color of objects.

Text Primitives

In addition to providing primitive building blocks such as cubes, spheres, and cones, VRML also provides a special node type named AsciiText for adding text characters to VRML scenes. Creating an ASCII character is just as easy as creating

any other primitive VRML type. The following text illustrates the VRML code
needed to display the letter "Q."

```
#VRML V1.0 ascii

Separator {
    AsciiText {
        string          "Q"
    }
}
```

Unlike the other 3D VRML primitives such as cubes, cones and spheres, VRML
text is planar in nature (i.e., VRML text has width and height but no depth). Thus,
when viewed from the side VRML text may seem to disappear.

Note: The AsciiText node can be used to specify entire strings of text; however, doing so requires considerable effort in terms of configuration (i.e., font selection, font spacing, justification, width, etc.) and is beyond the scope of this project.
For more information on this topic consult the VRML 1.0 specification.

Because text characters are no different from other kinds of primitive VRML
objects, they can be colored and translated using the same techniques outlined
earlier in the project. As an exercise, change the color of the "Q" given in the text
above to red.

Before moving on to the last section of the project, save the VRML text given
above in a file and load it into Netscape for viewing. Make sure you have successfully completed each section of the project before moving on to the last.

Putting It All Together

In this part of the project you will demonstrate your newly acquired VRML model-
building skills. The goal of this section is to construct a VRML scene graph consisting of the letters of your first name. All of the letters should be spaced so that your
name can be read easily and each letter should be a different color. In addition,
at least one letter should be red, one blue, and one green (assuming you have at
least three letters in you first name). Beyond that the coloring is up to you. You
should also place a cube at the beginning of your name and a sphere at the end.
If you have a really long first name (10+ letters) then only construct the first 10.
Conversely, if you have only a few characters in your first name then construct
both your first and last name or just do your first name twice. Figure C.1 shows an
example of a VRML scene generated for the name *Mike*.

FIGURE C.1 Example of VRML
name and primitive objects.

C.3.3 Report

For your report, create an html file that briefly describes your Procedures, answers all of the questions posed throughout this project and includes any Web pages or images that are generated. Separate your answers into sections just as this project has been written in sections.

C.4 Project 4: Exploring the Internet

C.4.1 Introduction and Prelab

Read Chapter 20 in this textbook. The availability and exact names of the commands used in this Project vary from one computer's operating system to another's operating system, and even within versions of the given operating system. UNIX (and Linux) have the most consistent set of commands, and the various Windows operating systems have considerable variety in the commands that are implemented. Hence, this project is recommended for those who are either quite computer literate, or quite adventuresome! Your computer will need Internet access. Also, please note that the example computers used here may have changed. You can often correctly guess the name of a host computer by appending the name of an institution to the correct domain name, such as `.edu`.

C.4.2 Internet Utilities

We will use some Internet utilities to explore the organization of the Internet. To execute these utilities from Windows, you must start a `Command Prompt` window. To do this, click the `Start` button, select `Programs`, and click `MS Dos Prompt`. At the prompt, you can initiate the Internet utilities described below by typing the appropriate command, for example `tracert ece.wpi.edu`, and pressing `Return`.

PING: Is Anybody Out There?

In general, Internet messages are not bound to a particular path. Instead, they can meander their way through many intermediate devices, sometimes making different turns based upon the set of currently operational devices. No requests are made by the intermediate devices to later devices when sending the data, however. It is just sent.

   To find out if a machine resides somewhere on the Internet, we can use `ping`. This program attempts to send a special message to the host we are trying to contact, causing it (or one of the routing devices along the way that fails to find a currently working path) to return with a message indicating success or failure. In addition to determining whether or not the host exists, `ping` returns the round-trip travel time (in milliseconds) to the host. To ping a host, issue the command `ping <hostname>`. The ping implementation on the NT system will send four packets and report on the results for each.

   The machine `internet.wpi.edu` is in Massachusetts, `ljouwert.et.tudelft.nl` is located in the Netherlands, and `dcc.uchile.cl` is in the South American country of Chile. Use the ping command to determine the round-trip travel time to these sites and record the results in your report.

TRACEROUTE: Follow the Path

We can find out whether or not a host is currently reachable on the Internet with ping, but can we find out what path is (actually might be) taken by data bound to that machine? The answer is yes, by using a utility called *traceroute*. This program is based on `ping` (it actually uses the same message with different parameters set) and determines the path taken by data when bound to a specific host at any given time. *Traceroute* organizes this data and displays a table of intermediate host names (both name and IP address) and the round-trip time to reach that device for three successive trials. Note that this command is spelled `tracert` on most Windows machines, and `traceroute` on most UNIX machines.

After issuing the command `tracert wide.ad.jp` (wide is a machine at the University of Tokyo) from the computer named `curley`, the following output was generated:

```
>tracert wide.ad.jp

Tracing route to wide.ad.jp [203.178.136.63]
over a maximum of 30 hops:

  1   <10 ms     10 ms   <10 ms   internet.WPI.EDU [130.215.24.9]
  2    20 ms    <10 ms    10 ms   border3-serial3-7.Boston.mci.net [204.70.22.69]
  3    10 ms     10 ms    30 ms   core-fddi-0.Boston.mci.net [204.70.2.33]
  4     *       411 ms   391 ms   core1.SanFrancisco.mci.net [204.70.4.169]
  5    70 ms     80 ms    90 ms   border1-fddi-0.SanFrancisco.mci.net [204.70.2.162]
  6   100 ms     90 ms    81 ms   keio-wide-japan.SanFrancisco.mci.net [204.70.32.14]
  7   220 ms    271 ms   230 ms   jp-entry.wide.ad.jp [203.178.136.65]
  8   220 ms    241 ms   220 ms   ns.wide.ad.jp [203.178.136.63]

Trace complete.
```

What happens is that *traceroute* launches many data packets onto the net bound for `wide.ad.jp`. The packets can be given a special parameter that causes a router, a specified number of jumps away, to give up and send back a report. For each step in the sequence of transmissions, the intermediate devices return their IP address (which is converted to a hostname and displayed). When the initial host, in this case `curley`, receives this information, it displays the device name and the *round-trip* time (the time to and from that device) for each packet. Note that the entire process, for this particular path, takes between 245 and 274 milliseconds (about a quarter of a second).

Now use traceroute to obtain and document the path and the three round-trip times to each of the three machines used in the last example.

NSLOOKUP: What's in a Name?

An Internet *fully qualified hostname*, like `ece.wpi.edu`, identifies a specific machine (host)name (`ece`) and the Internet Protocol (IP) domain in which that machine resides (`wpi.edu`). Knowledge of this address allows messages to be sent to and from this host computer over the Internet without the possibility of incorrect delivery.

While this Domain Name System (DNS) form is easily identified and interpreted by humans, the intermediate machines that handle the message packet do not operate on the basis of the DNS name (like `ece.wpi.edu`). Instead, the DNS name is translated to a so-called *Internet Protocol (IP) address*. To obtain the IP address associated with any hostname, we can issue the command `nslookup <hostname>` in the command prompt window. Obviously, an application program has more direct means for querying the operating system for this translation of a DNS name into an IP address.

For the hostname mentioned above (`ece.wpi.edu`) we receive the following output,

```
> nslookup ece.wpi.edu
Server:   ece.WPI.EDU
Address:  130.215.16.20

Name:     ece.wpi.edu
Address:  130.215.16.20
```

indicating that the IP address of `ece.wpi.edu` is `130.215.16.20` (the first name and machine listed is always that of the computer supplying the answer, the so-called name server, while the second is the IP address in which the user is interested). Note that the periods in the IP address above are inserted for convenience only and are not part of the IP address. This "dotted decimal notation" is used to represent the 32-bit (binary) IP address in a more readable form in which each number in the range from 0 to 255 represents an 8 bit byte.

Use nslookup to determine the IP addresses of `ece.wpi.edu`, `ljouwert.et.tudelft.nl` and `dcc.uchile.cl`. Record the IP addresses in your project report.

C.4.3 Report

For your report, record the results you obtain in repeating the examples given above in the Project description. Locate some other machines and report the results. Explain your findings.

Glossary

A/D Analog to digital conversion

ADSL Asymmetric digital subscriber line

ARP Address Resolution Protocol

AM Amplitude Modulation, a means to transmit information via radio

AMPS Analog Mobile Phone Service, the first-generation cellular telephone system

Analog A representation of information which can take on an infinitely-fine range of values, such as the temperature in a room. It also exists for every instant of time

Applet A small program, generally written in the Java programming language, which may be run from within a Web browser

ASCII American Standard Code for Information Interchange, the most common means for representing the letters of the alphabet and special characters by integer or binary numbers

ATM Asynchronous Transfer Mode, a connection-oriented data communications protocol

B Byte, 8 bits

b Bit

Bandwidth For signals, a measure of the amount of information contained in the signal (higher bandwidth corresponds to the capacity for more information content); for a transmission channel, a measure of the amount of information which it can transmit

Binary A number system containing only two numbers, zero and one

Bit A binary digit, zero or one

BRI Basic Rate Interface (for ISDN)

Byte Eight bits

C A popular programming language among professional programmers, widely used in such applications as computer operating systems

C++ The "object oriented" version of C

CAD Computer Aided Design

CATV Cable Television

CCITT International Consultative Committee for Telecommunications, an international body which coordinates international communications regarding frequency assignments, etc.

CD Compact Disk

CGI Common Gateway Interface, often used to communicate between user and server via Web pages

CRT Cathode Ray Tube, the glass display device in conventional televisions and computer monitors

D/A Digital to analog conversion

dB Decibel, a measure of relative power, expressed on a logarithmic scale

DES Data Encryption Standard

Digital A representation of information which can take on only a specific set of values, and whose values exist only at specific time instants

DNS Domain Name System, a hierarchical system of names representing computer addresses

DS1 The T1 rate, 1.544 Mbits/sec

DSL Digital subscriber line, the name given to a system to provide medium- to high-speed digital transmission on existing wire "loops"

DVD Originally, Digital Video Disk, now Digital Versatile Disk

Ethernet A common communications standard for Local Area Networking

FAX Facsimile

FCC Federal Communications Commission

FDM Frequency Division Multiplexing

FDMA Frequency Division Multiple Access

FM Frequency Modulation, a means to transmit information via radio

Frame A fixed or variable number of bits into which transmitted data is organized, and which is identifiable by the receiver

Gbit 1,073,741,824 bits

GB 1,073,741,824 bytes

Gbyte 1,073,741,824 bytes

GPS Global Positioning System, a system of satellites by which location anywhere on or above the earth may be determined

GSM Groupe Systeme Mobile (the name, in French, of the committee which established the European digital cellphone standard); has come to mean Global System for Mobile Communications

Hand-off The act of passing communication with a given cellphone user from one cell site to another during a call

HDLC High-Level Data Link Control, a protocol organizing data into frames

HDTV High Definition Television

Holography An optical system by which three-dimensional image information about an object is stored (often photographically), permitting 3-D image reconstruction

HTML Hypertext Mark-up Language, the means by which Web documents are represented

IDEA International Data Encryption Algorithm

IEEE Institute of Electrical and Electronics Engineers

INMARSAT Originally, International Maritime Satellite Organization; now just a name for a company which supplies global satellite communications services

ISDN Integrated Services Digital Network

IP Internet Protocol

ISO International Standards Organization

ISP Internet Service Provider

Java A programming language that is unique in that is intended to be used for programs to be run on a wide variety of different computers, without requiring software changes

JPEG Joint Photographic Experts Group

Key A binary number by which data may be encrypted and decrypted

Kbit 1024 bits

KB 1024 bytes

Kbyte 1024 bytes

LAN Local Area Network

Laser Light Amplification by Stimulated Emission of Radiation

Latency The time required for information transmission, during which the information is not available

LCD Liquid Crystal Display

Loop The name given to the physical wires which run from a telephone central office to the customer's telephone

Mbit 1,048,576 bits (this number arises because it is equal to 2 raised to the twentieth power)

MB 1,048,576 bytes

Mbyte 1,048,576 bytes

MIME Multi-Purpose Internet Mail Extensions, a protocol which allows various forms of attachments to be included with email, which was developed purely for ordinary text

Modem Modulator-demodulator, for converting digital data for transmission by analog means (as on the conventional telephone system) and converting analog data back to digital

MPEG Motion Picture Experts Group

MPEG-2 A standard developed by the MPEG for compression of video data (also MPEG-3)

Nyquist Rate See *Sampling frequency*

NTSC National Television Standards Committee, which developed the original US color television standards

OUI Organizationally-Unique Identifier, for use in data network protocols to identify the sender and recipient

Pixel Picture Element

PostScript A programming language for printed output of text and graphics

Quantization The process by which analog values are represented by integers

RAM Random Access Memory

ROM Read-Only Memory

Router A data communications device which accepts incoming packet data and determines the output port to which it is sent based on the address information and data network protocol in use

Sampling Frequency The rate at which an analog signal is sampled to convert it to digital. The Nyquist principle states that for accurate representation, the sampling frequency must be at least twice the highest frequency contained in the signal to be sampled.

Sampling rate   See *Sampling frequency*

SNR   Signal to noise ratio, a measure of the amount of noise on a channel, compared to the amount of signal

SONET   Synchronous optical network

Spectrum   The representation of the frequency content of a signal

T1   A data transmission rate (1.544 Mbits/sec) and the name of a hardware system which implements that rate

TDMA   Time Division Multiple Access

Trunk   The name given to the connection (physical or logical) between two telephone central offices

URL   Universal Resource Locator

VRML   Virtual Reality Modeling Language

XDSL   Digital Subscriber Line of various types, including ADSL, HDSL, etc.

Index

Prentice Hall

YOU SHOULD CAREFULLY READ THE FOLLOWING TERMS AND CONDITIONS BEFORE OPENING THIS CD PACKAGE. OPENING THIS CD PACKAGE INDICATES YOUR ACCEPTANCE OF THESE TERMS AND CONDITIONS. IF YOU DO NOT AGREE WITH THEM, YOU SHOULD PROMPTLY RETURN THE PACKAGE UNOPENED, AND YOUR MONEY WILL BE REFUNDED.

IT IS A VIOLATION OF COPYRIGHT LAWS TO MAKE A COPY OF THE ACCOMPANYING SOFTWARE EXCEPT FOR BACKUP PURPOSES TO GUARD AGAINST ACCIDENTAL LOSS OR DAMAGE.

Prentice-Hall, Inc. provides this program and licenses its use. You assume responsibility for the selection of the program to achieve your intended results, and for the installation, use, and results obtained from the program. This license extends only to use of the program in the United States or countries in which the program is marketed by duly authorized distributors.

LICENSE

You may:

a.   use the program;
b.   copy the program into any machine-
      readable form without limit;
c.   modify the program and/or merge it into
      another program in support of your use of
      the program.

LIMITED WARRANTY

THE PROGRAM IS PROVIDED "AS IS" WITHOUT WARRANTY OF ANY KIND, EITHER EXPRESSED OR IMPLIED, INCLUDING, BUT NOT LIMITED TO, THE IMPLIED WARRANTIES OF MERCHANTABILITY AND FITNESS FOR A PARTICULAR PURPOSE. THE ENTIRE RISK AS TO THE QUALITY AND PERFORMANCE OF THE PROGRAM IS WITH YOU. SHOULD THE PROGRAM PROVE DEFECTIVE, YOU (AND NOT PRENTICE-HALL, INC. OR ANY AUTHORIZED DISTRIBUTOR) ASSUME THE ENTIRE COST OF ALL NECESSARY SERVICING, REPAIR, OR CORRECTION.

SOME STATES DO NOT ALLOW THE EXCLUSION OF IMPLIED WARRANTIES, SO THE ABOVE EXCLUSION MAY NOT APPLY TO YOU. THIS WARRANTY GIVES YOU SPECIFIC LEGAL RIGHTS AND YOU MAY ALSO HAVE OTHER RIGHTS THAT VARY FROM STATE TO STATE.

Prentice-Hall, Inc. does not warrant that the functions contained in the program will meet your requirements or that the operation of the program will be uninterrupted or error free.

However, Prentice-Hall, Inc., warrants the cd(s) on which the program is furnished to be free from defects in materials and workmanship under normal use for a period of ninety (90) days from the date of delivery to you as evidenced by a copy of your receipt.

LIMITATIONS OF REMEDIES

Prentice-Hall's entire liability and your exclusive remedy shall be:

1.   the replacement of any cd not
      meeting Prentice-Hall's "Limited
      Warranty" and that is returned to Prentice-
      Hall with a copy of your purchase order, or

2.   if Prentice-Hall is unable to deliver a
      replacement diskette or cassette that is free
      of defects in materials or workmanship,
      you may terminate this Agreement by
      returning the program, and your money
      will be refunded.

IN NO EVENT WILL PRENTICE-HALL BE LIABLE TO YOU FOR ANY DAMAGES, INCLUDING ANY LOST PROFITS, LOST SAVINGS, OR OTHER INCIDENTAL OR CONSEQUENTIAL DAMAGES ARISING OUT OF THE USE OR INABILITY TO USE SUCH PROGRAM EVEN IF PRENTICE-HALL, OR AN AUTHORIZED DISTRIBUTOR HAS BEEN ADVISED OF THE POSSIBILITY OF SUCH DAMAGES, OR FOR ANY CLAIM BY ANY OTHER PARTY.

SOME STATES DO NOT ALLOW THE LIMITATION OR EXCLUSION OF LIABILITY FOR INCIDENTAL OR CONSEQUENTIAL DAMAGES, SO THE ABOVE LIMITATION OR EXCLUSION MAY NOT APPLY TO YOU.

GENERAL

You may not sublicense, assign, or transfer the license or the program except as expressly provided in this Agreement. Any attempt otherwise to sublicense, assign, or transfer any of the rights, duties, or obligations hereunder is void.

This Agreement will be governed by the laws of the State of New York.

Should you have any questions concerning this Agreement, you may contact Prentice-Hall, Inc., by writing to:

> Prentice Hall
> College Division
> Upper Saddle River, NJ 07458

YOU ACKNOWLEDGE THAT YOU HAVE READ THIS AGREEMENT, UNDERSTAND IT, AND AGREE TO BE BOUND BY ITS TERMS AND CONDITIONS. YOU FURTHER AGREE THAT IT IS THE COMPLETE AND EXCLUSIVE STATEMENT OF THE AGREEMENT BETWEEN US THAT SUPERSEDES ANY PROPOSAL OR PRIOR AGREEMENT, ORAL OR WRITTEN, AND ANY OTHER COMMUNICATIONS BETWEEN US RELATING TO THE SUBJECT MATTER OF THIS AGREEMENT.

ISBN:0-13-011496-0